Bloom's Modern Critical Views

African American Poets: Wheatley–Tolson
African American Poets: Hayden–Dove
Edward Albee
Dante Alighieri
American and Canadian Women Poets, 1930–present
American Women Poets, 1650–1950
Maya Angelou
Asian-American Writers
Margaret Atwood
Jane Austen
Paul Auster
James Baldwin
Honoré de Balzac
Samuel Beckett
Saul Bellow
The Bible
William Blake
Jorge Luis Borges
Ray Bradbury
The Brontës
Gwendolyn Brooks
Elizabeth Barrett Browning
Robert Browning
Italo Calvino
Albert Camus
Truman Capote
Lewis Carroll
Willa Cather
Cervantes
Geoffrey Chaucer
Anton Chekhov
Kate Chopin
Agatha Christie
Samuel Taylor Coleridge
Joseph Conrad
Contemporary Poets
Stephen Crane
Daniel Defoe
Don DeLillo
Charles Dickens
Emily Dickinson
John Donne and the 17th-Century Poets
Fyodor Dostoevsky
W.E.B. DuBois
George Eliot
T.S. Eliot
Ralph Ellison
Ralph Waldo Emerson
William Faulkner
F. Scott Fitzgerald
Sigmund Freud
Robert Frost
William Gaddis
Johann Wolfgang von Goethe
George Gordon, Lord Byron
Graham Greene
Thomas Hardy
Nathaniel Hawthorne
Ernest Hemingway
Hermann Hesse
Hispanic-American Writers
Homer
Langston Hughes
Zora Neale Hurston
Aldous Huxley
Henrik Ibsen
John Irving
Henry James
James Joyce
Franz Kafka
John Keats
Jamaica Kincaid
Stephen King
Rudyard Kipling
Milan Kundera
D.H. Lawrence
Doris Lessing
Ursula K. Le Guin
Sinclair Lewis
Norman Mailer
Bernard Malamud
David Mamet
Christopher Marlowe
Gabriel García Márquez
Cormac McCarthy
Carson McCullers
Herman Melville
Arthur Miller
John Milton
Molière
Toni Morrison
Native-American Writers
Joyce Carol Oates
Flannery O'Connor
Eugene O'Neill
George Orwell
Octavio Paz
Sylvia Plath
Edgar Allan Poe
Katherine Anne Porter
Marcel Proust
Thomas Pynchon
Philip Roth
Salman Rushdie
J. D. Salinger
Jean-Paul Sartre
William Shakespeare
George Bernard Shaw
Mary Wollstonecraft Shelley
Percy Bysshe Shelley

Bloom's Modern Critical Views

Alexander
Solzhenitsyn
Sophocles
John Steinbeck
Tom Stoppard
Jonathan Swift
Amy Tan
Alfred, Lord Tennyson
Henry David Thoreau
J.R.R. Tolkien
Leo Tolstoy
Ivan Turgenev
Mark Twain
John Updike
Kurt Vonnegut
Derek Walcott
Alice Walker
Robert Penn Warren
Eudora Welty
Edith Wharton
Walt Whitman
Oscar Wilde
Tennessee Williams
Thomas Wolfe
Tom Wolfe
Virginia Woolf
William Wordsworth
Jay Wright
Richard Wright
William Butler Yeats
Émile Zola

Bloom's Modern Critical Views

WILLIAM GADDIS

Edited and with an introduction by
Harold Bloom
Sterling Professor of the Humanities
Yale University

Philadelphia

Property of Library
Cape Fear Community College
Wilmington, NC

©2004 by Chelsea House Publishers, a subsidiary of
Haights Cross Communications.

A Haights Cross Communications Company

Introduction © 2004 by Harold Bloom.

All rights reserved. No part of this publication may be
reproduced or transmitted in any form or by any means
without the written permission of the publisher.

Printed and bound in the United States of America.

10 9 8 7 6 5 4 3 2 1

Library of Congress Cataloging-in-Publication Data

William Gaddis / edited and with an introduction by Harold Bloom.
    p. cm. -- (Bloom's modern critical views)
Includes bibliographical references and index.
   ISBN: 0-7910-7664-4 (Hardcover)
   1. Gaddis, William, 1922---Criticism and interpretation. I. Bloom,
Harold. II. Series.
   PS3557.A28Z924 2003
   813'54--dc21
                                    2003011237

Chelsea House Publishers
1974 Sproul Road, Suite 400
Broomall, PA 19008-0914

http://www.chelseahouse.com

Contributing Editor: Aaron Tillman

Cover designed by Terry Mallon

Cover photo © Marion Ettlinger

Layout by EJB Publishing Services

Contents

Editor's Note vii

Introduction 1
   Harold Bloom

To Soar in Atonement: Art as Expiation
   in Gaddis's *The Recognitions* 3
   Joseph S. Salemi

"For a Very Small Audience": The Fiction
   of William Gaddis 17
   Susan Strehle Klemtner

No More Sea Changes: Hawkes, Pynchon,
   Gaddis, and Barth 31
   John Z. Guzlowski

"*il miglior fabbro*": Gaddis' Debt to T.S. Eliot 43
   Miriam Fuchs

Love and Strife in William Gaddis' *JR* 57
   Stephen H. Matanle

Ironic Allusiveness and Satire
   in William Gaddis's *The Recognitions* 71
   Elaine B. Safer

Carpenter's Gothic; or, The Ambiguities 101
   Steven Moore

Toward Postmodern Fiction 127
   John Johnston

At Home in Babel   163
   Jonathan Raban

A Frolic of His Own: Whose Law? Whose Justice?   173
   Christopher J. Knight

The Importance of Being Negligible   219
   Peter Wolfe

Chronology   257

Contributors   259

Bibliography   261

Acknowledgments   265

Index   267

Editor's Note

My Introduction seeks to mediate between the major influences upon *The Recognitions* and the subsequent influence of Gaddis's masterwork upon Pynchon and other writers.

Joseph S. Salemi, in regard to *The Recognitions*, concludes that true art, for Gaddis, offered a secular redemption, while Susan Strehle Klemtner emphasizes common obsessions in *JR* and *The Recognitions*.

John Hawkes, Pynchon, and John Barth are linked with Gaddis by John Z. Guzlowski, after which Miriam Fuchs traces Gaddis's relationship to T. S. Eliot.

JR's glance into chaos is analyzed by Stephen H. Matanle in terms that evoke the Pre-Socratic shaman, Empedocles, while Elaine B. Safer returns us to the satiric allusiveness of *The Recognitions*, which she relates to Gogol's *Dead Souls*, a novel that Gaddis rightly and greatly admired.

Carpenter's Gothic, for Steven Moore, is an ambiguous apocalypse, the Revelation of William Gaddis, akin to Nathanael West's *The Day of the Locust*, after which John Johnston persuasively locates in *The Recognitions* a crucial origin for the Postmodern novel, including Gaddis's own later work.

Jonathan Raban shrewdly gives us Gaddis as a belated Victorian novelist, almost in the mode of Trollope and praises the comic vivacity manifested by *A Frolic of His Own*. Rather differently, Christopher J. Knight compares Gaddis's fourth novel to John Rawls's theory of justice, while Peter Wolfe concludes this volume with an admiring psychological reading that sees Gaddis as a highly conscious Wagnerite.

HAROLD BLOOM

Introduction

My one personal memory of William Gaddis goes back to a meeting of the American Academy of Arts and Letters, sometime in the later 1990's. We had been introduced perhaps a year before, and he approached me, expressing gratification that I had included *The Recognitions* in a canonical catalog published in 1994. Not knowing him, yet apprehending that his grave and courteous manner did not seem ironic, I stammered that I had admired the novel since 1955, when it was first published, and had reread it several times since, always with a sense of gratitude. Gaddis graciously nodded his head, and walked away. Returning to New Haven that night, I rather weirdly found a copy of the Penguin paperback of *The Recognitions* in my briefcase, where I had not placed it.

This oddity (and I still do not know how the book got there) reflects for me the uncanniness of *The Recognitions*, where the inexplicable is marvelously omnipresent, in an almost Dickensian way. Jonathan Raban sensibly notes that Gaddis, the first so-called Post-Modernist of the American novel, actually is Victorian in sensibility, and might well have pleased Trollope. I wish I could share Raban's admiration for *A Frolic of His Own*, or my close friend the novelist Walter Abish's high regard for *JR*, but alas I don't. *Carpenter's Gothic* also continues to evade me, though it has a legitimate place in a tradition that moves from Brockden Brown through Hawthorne on to Faulkner, Flannery O'Connor, and Cormac McCarthy.

The Recognitions is so rich a work that Gaddis could have rested on his oars forever. It has an authentic literary lineage that begins with the Third Century *Clementine Recognitions*, an early Christian romance. Simon Magus, supposed by some to be the inventor of Gnosticism, is the villain of this curious tale, and this Simon of Samaria, known as the Magus, is the first manifestation of Faustus, the Favored one. Gaddis also draws upon St. Augustine and St. John of the Cross, but is closer in spirit to Melville's *Moby-*

Dick, to Goethe's *Faust*, and very overtly to T. S. Eliot, whose "The Love Song of J. Alfred Prufrock," *The Waste Land* and *Four Quartets* are echoed throughout. In a rather disturbing way, *The Recognitions* parodies Joyce's *Ulysses*, which Gaddis insisted he never had read.

The influence of *The Recognitions* upon novelists from Thomas Pynchon to Jonathan Franzen's *The Corrections* is palpable, and not always fortunate, but Gaddis's outrageous first fiction bridges the long morass in the American novel from Faulkner's major phase to the full maturing of Philip Roth, Don DeLillo, and Cormac McCarthy, and to Pynchon's triumphant resurrection in *Mason and Dixon*. Doubtless the death of Nathanael West, in a car crash, removed an extraordinary imagination far too early, and yet it cleared a visionary space for Gaddis, who was thirty-three, the Chistological age, when *The Recognitions* appeared.

Like Joyce's *Ulysses*, Gaddis's masterwork is less a narrative fiction than it is an epic of consciousness. But *whose* consciousness? Hamlet has his own consciousness, different from what we may infer was Shakespeare's, yet we are not persuaded that Wyatt Gwyon has a mind all his own. Willie the writer (see pp. 272–3 and 478 of *The Recognitions*) is the endless consciousness of his book, and the implicit protagonist of its quest for transcendence.

The Recognitions goes on for fifty-six pages after we behold the last of Wyatt on page 900:

> He had left his windows opened, and the bird was sitting on one of the framed pictures when he came in, and closed the door behind him. But he had already paused to make his notation, "What mean?" before he saw it, when it fluttered across the room to the other picture, and though he tried frantically to chase it toward the front, toward the windows and out, it fluttered the more frantically from one picture to the other, and back across the room and back, as he passed the mirror himself in both directions, where he might have glimpsed the face of a man having, or about to have, or at the very least valiantly fighting off, a religious experience.

The religious experience, conveyed by gentle irony, is the descent of the dove, the Pentecost of the Paraclete, Christ-as-comforter. Here Gaddis affects the ambiguous undulations of the end of Pynchon's *The Crying of Lot 49*, and the more overt intimations of a possible transcendence that culminate Don DeLillo's major works, from *White Noise* through *Underworld*. The sequence of Gaddis, Pynchon, and DeLillo constitutes an ambivalent opening to glory in ongoing American fiction.

JOSEPH S. SALEMI

To Soar in Atonement: Art As Expiation in Gaddis's The Recognitions

Despite the intricacies of structure and design that have gone into the making of *The Recognitions*, there is apparent in the work, as in the flamenco music so loved by Wyatt, "the tremendous tension of violence all enclosed in a framework." Much of what strikes the casual reader as "excessive" in the book—its length, the virulence of its satire, the wide and esoteric range of its allusiveness, the improbability of certain incidents—suggests the extreme lengths to which William Gaddis was prepared to go to create an art commensurate with all reality rather than some limited aspect of it. As with *Moby Dick*, the novel's implications move in wider and wider circles from the bobbing coffin of Queequeg, or the catastrophic final harmony at Fenestrula.

The Recognitions is an obsessive book, in that both author and characters seem driven to extremities of experience, perception, and thought. Individual figures such as Reverend Gwyon, Stanley, and Anselm are obsessed with the ultimate validity of reality, though their obsessions take different forms: arcane theology and philosophy, Catholicism and baroque music, absurdity and religious despair. Recktall Brown is driven by avarice, Otto by prideful self-esteem, Basil Valentine by his personal variety of embittered fastidiousness. These obsessions jar each other in contrapuntal relationships: Valentine and Brown, Stanley and Anselm, Gwyon and Aunt May, and the quasi-protagonist Wyatt in individual relation to each of them. Indeed, it is through the focal character of Wyatt that *The Recognitions* carries on a continual and insistent debate. That debate, which might be termed the obsession of the novel as a whole, revolves around the following double question: *What is the nature of, and what are the conditions for, genuine art?*

That in *The Recognitions* "reality" and "art" are interchangeable metaphors for each other is, I think, clear to every thoughtful reader. The cheap tourist art of Montmartre, the upside-down painting of Max, the distorted portrait of Recktall Brown—each symbolizes and epitomizes the context of life that surrounds it. For Gaddis, art is the touchstone by which the genuineness of life is judged, and the purity of human motives measured. Wyatt is not only an individual artist, but an Everyman whose concerns are universal; his art—and art in general—is no mere adornment or addition to life, but life itself in the deepest and truest sense. This is part of the achievement of the novel: it succeeds in turning the simple analogy of art and life into a baffling and frightening identity. In *The Recognitions* questions that ostensibly deal with aesthetics actually are questions that probe to the very core of the human condition.

The Recognitions is remarkably self-reflective, in that the novel abounds in authorial comments about itself, its style, its difficulties—even its probable reception by critics. Part of the parody of the book is directed at itself, as if Gaddis were holding up a mirror to his work as it progressed. The comparison is an apt one, I think, for Wyatt uses mirrors in his work to obtain deliberate effects, and a sense of "the obscure reveries of the inward gaze" is sustained throughout the novel. This kind of conscious self-scrutiny, which unlike a conventional prologue or epilogue is intrinsic to the work itself, indicates that Gaddis's own art as a novelist, as well as Wyatt's as a painter, is a thematic and structural concern. *The Recognitions* is a first novel, and as such displays more than its share of self-consciousness, but the author's insistent scrutiny of his protagonist's aesthetic[1] may well have served as a personal exorcism of similar demons troubling his own art.

It will be useful, in this regard, to consider the kind of artist Wyatt is, and the kind of art he recognizes as genuine. His aesthetic is one of precise and severe laws that aim at the creation of such genuine art. I have used the word genuine here deliberately. It must be carefully distinguished from original, which in the lexical context of *The Recognitions* has a slightly pejorative connotation. The quest for originality is denigrated in the novel more than once as a misunderstanding of the artistic task. Wyatt quotes his teacher, Herr Koppel, on the subject:

That romantic disease, originality, all around we see originality of incompetent idiots, they could draw nothing, paint nothing, just so the mess they make is original ... Even two hundred years ago who wanted to be original, to be original was to admit that you could not do a thing the right way, so you could only do it your own way.[2]

These sentiments are recalled in the comments of Stanley, who, as I hope to demonstrate, works successfully within the laws of Wyatt's aesthetic. In a discussion of modern painters, Stanley says:

Some of them have set out to kill art ***—And some of them are so excited about discovering new mediums and new forms *** that they never have time to work in one that's already established. (p. 186)

Genuine art, on the other hand, respects the achievements of the past and consciously builds upon them. It is concerned not with the vagaries of period style, but with transfigured reality, with that captured moment of luminous significance that Wyatt calls *recognition*.[3] Such art is only secondarily original in the Romantic sense, but primarily seeks out, as Stanley puts it, "the origins of design," the archetypes of formal perfection which art can only reproduce in a reflected image.

Wyatt's chosen mode of expression is that of the fifteenth-century masters, in particular the Flemish primitives. Even before his forgeries we see him working in hand-made tempera, a medium suited to carefully defined forms and precise detail, and one which demands painstaking discipline and subtlety of the artist who employs it. It is singularly appropriate that Wyatt should choose as his artistic archetypes the works of van der Weyden, Bouts, David, van der Goes, and Memling, all of whom, despite differences, share a peculiar sensitivity and vision. This vision includes themes of pious, almost quietistic devotion, meticulous attention to small objects and fine lines, and above all a consciously architectonic composition, with figures poised in a hieratic manner that suggests to Wyatt "that sense of movement in stillness."[4] All these things comprise more than a mere technique for Wyatt; they are signs of a special religious awareness in an artist that mark his work with *recognition*. We may apply to Wyatt what one critic has said of one of the Flemish primitives: he "paints not so much a visage as a certain disposition of the soul."[5] Throughout *The Recognitions*

Wyatt defines his aesthetic in these terms, and when they are finally mocked and denied he is driven to murder.

Curiously enough, it is in some comments on flamenco music that Wyatt most fully and lucidly expounds the artistic impulse that animates him:

> That's what it is, this arrogance, in this flamenco music this same arrogance of suffering, listen. The strength of it's what's so overpowering, the self-sufficiency that's so delicate and tender without an instant of sentimentality. With infinite pity but refusing pity, it's a precision of suffering ***—the tremendous tension of violence all enclosed in a framework, ... in a pattern that doesn't pretend to any other level but its own, do you know what I mean? ***—It's the privacy, the exquisite sense of privacy about it ***—it's the sense of privacy that most popular expressions of suffering don't have, don't dare have, that's what makes it arrogant. (pp. 111–112)

This aesthetic of disciplined agony is continued when Otto parrots these opinions in a talk with Wyatt's wife Esther:

> This kind of stringency of suffering, this severe self-continence of suffering that looks almost peaceful, almost indifferent. But in a way it's the same thing, this severe quality of line, this severe delicacy and tenderness. (p. 123)

It is easy to see the reality that such art suggests, and which Wyatt desires to make his own. It is a reality marked by breadth of vision, chaste dignity, and controlled intelligence. Wyatt's aesthetic is typically that of a certain kind of "melancholic" artist, if we might use that term in its full traditional significance as a humor. It is an aesthetic which is extremely conscious of technique and manner, often to the extent of forcing creativity into a Procrustean bed of preconceived forms. It sees itself as supremely serious, tending to a rejection of frivolity and play as inappropriate or unworthy of the truly artistic. It cherishes a personal piety (whether religious or secular) that invests reality with numinous, even mystical significance. It is an art of distillation rather than the wide swath, of the delicate jewel rather than the rough-hewn stone. Moreover, it tends to exalt suffering as the origin and subject matter of all truly great creation, choosing themes and *motifs* reminiscent of Virgil's *Sunt lacrimae rerum, mentem et mortalia tangunt.*

At its worst, this art lapses into stiltedness and preciosity; at its best, it is subtle, refined, and capable of piercing discernment and sensitivity. By way of illustration, let me suggest that Wyatt's art is in a position analogous to that of Pound at the time of *Hugh Selwyn Mauberley*. It is an art which has developed a high degree of technical proficiency in small, limited forms ("medallions" or fine work in "porcelain," as Pound puts it). The drawback to perfection in small, limited forms (the "separate objects" that so intrigue Wyatt) is the danger of stagnancy and hyper-refinement, just as the danger in wide "epic" vision is banality and inflation. A healthy tension between the two modes is ideally desirable, although individual artists and periods lean to one or the other. In *The Recognitions* Gaddis is acutely conscious of the simultaneous polarity and complementarity of these two modes, and it might be a useful point of departure for structural criticism to consider the novel as a continuing counterpoint between them. Gaddis shows his love for (and skill with) fine detail and suggestion in the finely woven texture of his description and the labyrinth of his allusions; he reveals an impulse to epic scope in his effort to tie a welter of plots, characters, places, and conflicting and parallel levels of meaning into a coherent symphony.

What concerns us here, however, is the manner in which Wyatt's work has shaped his actions and attitudes in ways that isolate him from other persons. The tense rigidity of his art is mirrored in uncongenial withdrawal, even from his wife, who complains that "this restraint, this pose, this control you've cultivated, Wyatt, it becomes inhuman ..." (p. 97). Like a human simulacrum of Flemish saints and Madonnas, he maintains a silent privacy, becoming more and more sparing of words, refusing to "make explicit things that should be implicit" (p. 121). In spite of her deep love for Wyatt, Esther sees—and suffers from—the indifference and arrogance of her husband's almost hierophantic solitude.

Wyatt, not very much at ease with others by nature, grows intolerant of the bland stupidity of those he meets. It is often difficult to tell where a satiric authorial voice chastising the foibles of the literary-artistic world ends, and where a misanthropic Wyatt begins:

> It's suffocating. Right this minute, she's talking. They're down there right this minute and that woman with the granulated eyelids is talking *** the instant you look at them they begin to talk, automatically, they take it for granted you understand them, that you recognize them, that they have something to say to you, and you have to wait, you have to pretend to listen, pretend you don't know what's coming next while they go right on talking

with no idea what they're talking about *** Who are they, to presume such intimacy, to ... go right on talking. And they really believe that they're talking to me! (pp. 107–108).

The woman in question represents the world of shallow art and intellectual falsity which throughout *The Recognitions* is parodied and attacked, mostly through the devastating technique of quoting its representatives *verbatim*. Cliques of dishonest critics, backbiting literati, the entire rout of cocktail party intellectuals and pen-pushers—all are mercilessly exposed. In its form and structure *The Recognitions* is thoroughly modern, but in its cumulative judgment of these representatives of modernity, it is profoundly anti-modern. Like Pound's *Cantos* or Eliot's *Waste Land*, the novel betrays bitterness over a world gone rotten with oversimplification, facile moral relativism, glib, hucksterized psychology, latitudinarian religion, and amorphous, undisciplined art. This is a world where the equally pompous dogmas of Establishment and Anti-Establishment are indifferent or hostile to the labor of genuine creation, and where *Invidia*, *Ira*, and *Avaritia* are as virulent as ever. Above all it is a world of cliches, publicity, pretentious faddism in thought, and fatuous posturings by both the great and the small.

What this world lacks most, from the vantage point of Wyatt's art, is dignity. The self-possessed privacy of genuine *recognition*, the chastened and awed silence in the face of a significance deeper than the merely human, is absent, and the absence renders characters trivial and clownish. What makes Otto so ridiculous, for example, is the lack of such inner dignity and self-possession. His art, like his life, is a wretched patchwork of fraudulent play-acting and stilted monologues. Otto senses something of what the genuine artist must be in Wyatt, but he remains enamoured of the surface appearances of profundity, sophistication, and posturing masculinity. His lust for the social approbation that the honorific title of "artist" carries is more fatal to his art than the prodigious lack of talent he displays.

In a real sense, Wyatt's forgeries are more genuine than the products of Romantic originality. When Basil Valentine accuses him of calumniating the old masters with counterfeits, Wyatt refutes the charge vigorously:

Do you think I do these the way all other forging has been done? *** No, it's ... the recognitions go much deeper, much further back *** the experts with their photomicrography and ... macrophotography, do you think that's all there is to it? Some of them aren't fools, they don't just look for a hat or a beard, or a style they can recognize, they look with memories that ... go beyond themselves, that go back to ... where mine goes. (p. 250)

Where that memory goes is back to the fifteenth century, not only in regard to the technique but also the spirit of the craft of that time. Wyatt is, literally, a dedicated artisan of Bruges or Ghent:

> —And ... any knock at the door may be the gold inspectors, come to see if I'm using bad materials down there, I ... I'm a master painter in the Guild, in Flanders *** I've taken the Guild oath, not for the critics, the experts, the ... you, you have no more to do with me than if you are my descendants, nothing to do with me *** the Guild oath, to use pure materials, to work in the sight of God ... (p. 250)

But wherein does the genuineness of a work of art consist, according to Gaddis? I suggest that these three criteria are involved in the judgment of a work of art in *The Recognitions*:

a) Does the work in question adhere to the "origins of design"?
b) Is it a faithful reflection of the artist's "recognition" of this design?
c) Does it refuse to serve any motive beyond these two?

Wyatt's forgeries perhaps fulfill the first two criteria, but they violate the third. Their value is vitiated by the intrusion of avarice and pride; indeed, it is the greed of Recktall Brown and the self-centered isolation of Wyatt that have called them into being. Despite Wyatt's rationalizations, deceit and falsity have riddled his art; his playing at medieval craftsman only serves to cover the continuing and deliberate fraud that he must perpetrate to satisfy his employer. A man of consummate technical proficiency, Wyatt dedicates himself solely to the reduplication of medieval techniques, hoping that through the perfection of such skills alone he will recapture the mysterious *Innigkeit* that gives art its life. Thus Wyatt calls himself a "craftsman," but the very stridency with which he insists upon this self-definition hints at the serious doubts entertained (unconsciously by Wyatt, consciously by Gaddis) concerning the usefulness of deriving the *elan* of art from craftsmanship alone.

And yet it is by means of such self-definition that Gaddis sets Wyatt— and one other character, I believe—apart from all other figures in the novel. Wyatt is the sensitive and profound soul, living in but not of the world around him. Like his father, who serves in the novel as a kind of emblematic prologue to Wyatt's life and troubles, he is a brooding, complex, self-sequestered person, obsessed with plumbing the depths of an occult truth. Wyatt's designing of bridges relates him, metaphorically, to his father. Each is a *pontifex* ("bridge-builder") or high priest: Reverend Gwyon in terms of divine ceremonies, Wyatt in terms of human art. It will be remembered that Esther complains bitterly of Wyatt's self-contained, priestly solitude, and even calls him a priest. Such juxtaposition reinforces the novel's insistence on the intimate connection between art and religion, or more properly, between the secular and sacred attempts to interpret reality, to bridge the gulf between what we see and what we imagine.

It is through the unwitting agency of his father, moreover, that Wyatt has his first chance at forgery. Reverend Gwyon's purchase of the Bosch table-top painting of the *Seven Deadly Sins* introduces a tangible symbol that appears and is alluded to over and over again in the novel. The metaphoric importance of this table in *The Recognitions* cannot be stressed enough. One is never certain as to the authenticity of the painting; Gaddis carefully confuses the issue. Is it the original Bosch? Is it the copy ordered by the Conte di Brescia? Is it Wyatt's copy? But the real question to be asked and answered is this: To what extent are we oblivious of our enslavement by the sins allegorized on the table, the sins of pride, avarice, envy, and lust that drive us to trickery and deceit? This larger moral question goes beyond the minor issue of the painting's genuineness. Whatever its provenance, the table serves as a stunning emblem throughout the novel of the *unconscious* fraud and falsity of human motives. Gaddis is masterful in his use of the table to bring into high relief the venality of characters who are not even aware of their place and judgment in a wider cosmic framework. Consider this cameo of Recktall Brown, almost medieval in its moral caricature:

> We've wasted half the God damn afternoon as it is, waiting for you. He turned to Basil Valentine, raising the left hand, with the diamonds, and the cigar which dropped its ash on Gula, gluttony, before him. (p. 241)

Wyatt is a divided self, whose two warring halves are externalized in other characters. Basil Valentine represents the demands of Wyatt's aesthetic carried to a poisonous, suicidal extreme. Valentine is the waspish, sterile intellect—it is no accident that there are homosexual overtones to his character—cut loose from all human fellowship. Although his appreciation of art is informed and intelligent, he is merely a connoisseur without sympathy or love for the objects he appraises. As a spoiled Jesuit, he is a mirror image of Wyatt's deepest psychological conflicts, and his role as a secret traitor highlights the furtive, repressed nature of that image in relation to Wyatt. The cryptic Gypsy words on his gold cigarette case ("Much I ponder why you ask me questions, and why you should come thither") suggest a mysterious, riddling quality about Basil Valentine that is often associated with a psychological "shadow" in the Jungian sense. In confrontation with Valentine, Wyatt faces certain dark truths about his own life and art.

Wyatt's other self is revealed in Stanley, who labors exactly as Wyatt does, and according to the same laws. Like Wyatt, he is set apart from others in the novel—and indeed, his death from falling stones in the book's climax is in reality a death by proxy of Wyatt (re-christened Stephen after the first Christian martyr, who died by stoning). That Stanley's aesthetic accords with Wyatt's can be seen in his attitude towards the music he is writing:

> How could Bach have accomplished all that he did? and Palestrina? the Gabrielis? and what of the organ concerti of Corelli? Those were the men whose work he admired beyond all else in his life, for they had touched the origins of design with recognition. And how? with music written for the Church. Not written with obsessions of copyright foremost; not written to be plated by men in worn dinner jackets, sung by girls in sequins, involved in wage disputes and radio rights, recording rights, union rights; not written to be issued through a skull-sized plastic box plugged into the wall as background for seductions and the funnypapers *** It [the work] must be finished to a thorough perfection, as much as he humbly could perceive that, every note and every bar, every transition and movement in the pattern over and against itself and within itself proof against time: the movement in the Divine Comedy; the pattern in a Requiem Mass; prepared against time as old masters prepared their canvases and their pigments, so that when they were called to appear the work would still hold the perfection they had embraced there. (pp. 322–323)

I have quoted at length because the passage illuminates not only the art of Stanley and Wyatt, but also the art of *The Recognitions*. The statement goes to the heart of Gaddis's aesthetic intentions in a rather long and difficult novel, and one whichh many readers react to with baffled impatience. If one does not appreciate the art of a symphony, with its variations on a theme, improvisations, reminiscences and recapitulations, then the novel will be tedious in the extreme. But If one is willing to put into the study of a work of art an effort commensurate with the effort that went into its creation, then the rewards can be great. And it Is well to remember that all genuine art demands this kind of attention, for art is meant to be more than an ephemeral amusement, as the length and difficulty of the *Aeneid*, the *Divine Comedy*, the *Faerie Queene*, and *Paradise Lost* indicate.

In Stanley we see the same striving for perfection, the same disdain for the popular, the same sense of *recognition* that motivates Wyatt. Stanley's and Waytt's shared preference for the controlled "Classical" over the chaotic "Romantic" lends support to my suggested analogy to Pound, and both exhibit a melancholic piety which makes them solitary figures, qualitatively different from those around them. But what differentiates the composer from the painter is his genuine religious faith. Stanley gladly believes what Wyatt (along with his father) cannot accept: that he is the man for whom Christ died. It is the lack of such faith which drives Reverend Gwyon to a sterile insanity, which makes Anselm raging, Lear-like figure, and which is the real source of the loveless incommunicability of Wyatt's character. The "privacy of suffering" that is so Important to Wyatt betrays a stiff-necked pride that will not stoop to share its feelings with fellow-sufferers, a pride which is almost Satanic in its haughty Isolation. Esther instinctively senses the cruelty of such pride:

> —Preclusion of suffering .... privacy of suffering ... if that's what it is, suffering, then you ... share it. (p. 116)

Consider, for example, Wyatt's revulsion at the "vulgarizing" of the Passion. He rejects the sentimentality of cheapened public emotion:

> Has there ever been anything in history so exquisitely private as the Virgin mourning over Her Son? (p. 127)

The irony of such a thought is that the Passion of Christ is specifically directed to all the world—its very *raison d'être* is "public" in the widest possible sense. The aloof privacy that Wyatt cherishes is esoteric, while the religious significance of Christ's sufferings is of its very nature exoteric in its appeal to all men. Wyatt's awareness does not go beyond the beauty of a religious *motif* to its universal human meaning. Faith for Wyatt—as for his father—is a self-contained niggardliness of the spirit that rejects the one reality that unites the human and the divine: communion.

It is Basil Valentine who shakes the foundations of Wyatt's private aesthetic-religion. Over the corpse of Brown he excoriates Wyatt for a fraud more sinister than forgery:

> —Vulgarity, cupidity, and power. Is that what frightens you? Is that all you see around you, and you think it was different then? Flanders in the fifteenth century, do you think it was all like the Adoration of the Mystic Lamb? ***—Yes, I remember your little talk, your insane upside-down apology for these pictures, every figure and every object with its own presence, its own consciousness because it was being looked at by God! Do you know what it was? What it really was? that everything was so afraid, so uncertain God saw it; that it insisted its vanity on His eyes? *** Because maybe God isn't watching. Maybe he doesn't see *** everything in its own vain shell, everything separate, withdrawn from everything else. Being looked at by God! Is there separation in God? (pp. 689–690)

Basil Valentine has put his finger on the question that Wyatt cannot answer without hesitation: how much of his aesthetic is traceable not to a rarefied "medieval" sensibility, but rather to a loveless and tormented childhood? Every tenet in Wyatt's aesthetic can be viewed, psychologically, as a rationalization of early conflicts and guilt. The disparagement of originality finds its roots in the terror of original sin instilled in Wyatt by his aunt when he first began to draw. The love of privacy and "violence all enclosed in a framework" are merely adult versions of the secretive repression and fear of his childhood. And, most symbolically of all, the loving God who solicitously looks at every detail is simply a palatable counterfeit of the stern Christ of the Bosch table-top, who with the warning *Cave, cave, Dominus videt* ("Beware, beware, the Lord sees") stares out in judgment from amidst a host of sins.

I certainly do not mean to write off Wyatt and his aesthetic in a psychologically reductionist manner. This would be to fall into one variety of simplistic narrowness that Gaddis attacks in the modern world. It is crucial to an understanding of *The Recognitions* to realize that Gaddis uses this *particular* falsity in Wyatt's life as an image of the spurious core of human life *as a whole*. It would be a mistake to look upon Wyatt as an individual troubled by idiosyncratic mental habits, all the result of a curious upbringing. He, like most of the other characters in the novel, is in many ways more of an archetype in a moral drama than a person in a realistic story. Yet he is also unmistakably human, and it is a mark of Gaddis's artistry that he is able to create characters who are clearly part of the world, and at the same time implicated in a metaphysical scheme of things transcending their own lives. The force of Wyatt's past is as vividly present to the reader as it is insistently at work in Wyatt's life, but rather than allow Wyatt to be conveniently pigeonholed as a clinical "case history," the art of *The Recognitions* forces upon the reader the question which modern psychology cannot bear to listen to, much less answer: Even if it is so that a man's ideas and actions stem from sordid or unhappy incidents in his childhood, why should those ideas and actions not be judged solely on their own merits *as* ideas and actions? The question is not explicit in *The Recognitions*, but the cumulative force of Gaddis's art raises it, and with it the specter of those traditional realities of free will, faith, sin, and grace.

Here indeed is the aesthetic which lies at the core of *The Recognitions*, both as a work of art and as a statement *about* art. The words of Stanley that "the Devil is the father of false art" take on an ethical, even metaphysical meaning in this light. The creation of art is an act of atonement, in that it constellates true significance in the midst of falsity, redeeming that falsity just as the cross redeems sin. In point of fact, Gaddis's position seems to be that genuine art atones not only for false art, but for false life as well. Stanley's work expiates the falsity of Waytt's and that same work is the instrument of his martyrdom. This martyrdom, as I have mentioned, is actually that of Stephen-Wyatt, for Gaddis has deliberately created a "mystical participation" between these two characters, corresponding to the relationship of Redeemer and Redeemed. Art is the ultimate expiation for through it not only suffering, but the falsehood which lies at the core of existence is transfigured beyond the pettiness and sordidness of its context and origins. Thus, as Stanley's music "soared in atonement," the shaky edifice of falsehood trembles and falls, and this final counterpoint of upward release and triumph and downward collapse and fatality is art's perfect image of both man's implication in falsehood, and his capacity for redemption.

NOTES

1. I use the term *aesthetic* as a noun to indicate the peculiar vision of beauty that a given artist enjoys. One's *aesthetic* would include not only specific preferences of form (proportion, composition, line, color) but also a less definable sense of psychic satisfaction that is experienced in one work rather than another.

2. William Gaddis, *The Recognitions* (New York: Harcourt, Brace & world, 1955), p. 39. All citations are from this edition. NOTE that Gaddis frequently uses

ellipses in his prose. To distinguish Gaddis's ellipses from those that reflect a portion of his text excluded by Prof. Salemi, the latter shall be indicated by three asterisks (***).

3. Cf. Wyatt's reaction to a Picasso: " ... it was one of those moments of reality, of near-recognition of reality ... When I saw it all of a sudden everything was freed into one recognition, really freed into reality that we never see, you never see it" (pp. 91–92).

4. *The Recognitions*, p. 96. Here Wyatt is speaking of the arch, but it applies equally, as other quotations show, to the Flemish school.

5. Germain Bazin, *Memling* (New York: French Library of Fine Arts, 1939), p. 17.

SUSAN STREHLE KLEMTNER

"For a Very Small Audience": The Fiction of William Gaddis

While the fictional achievement of William Gaddis is massive, both in importance and in sheer volume, the critical reception of his two novels has been skimpy and uncertain. *The Recognitions* (1955) met with mixed reviews; *Time* and *Newsweek* praised the ambitiousness but condemned the confusion and opacity of this thousand-page work; *The New Yorker* objected that "Gaddis appears to know every last thing about his characters except how to make them touch our hearts."[1] Published after a twenty-year silence, *JR* (1975) fared no better, it was termed "an unreadable text,"[2] and while another reviewer acknowledged that "William Gaddis is an extraordinarily gifted, obsessive novelist," he read *JR* "with stupefaction that a man could write a novel, of almost 800 pages about people who are just so many comic strips."[3] As an index of the scant scholarly attention paid to Gaddis, only one article on *The Recognitions* was published before 1971, which argued a comprehensive debt to Ulysses and *Finnegans Wake*.[4] Though the parallels to Joyce are convincing, Gaddis ironically asserts, "I have never read Joyce's *Ulysses*."[5]

The uncertain reception of Gaddis's novels is understandable; the reviews indicate common problems in both for a casual reader: complexity of event and structure, unusual treatment of character, a difficult narrative surface. Gaddis self-consciously anticipates his lack of an audience in both

From *Critique: Studies in Modern Fiction* XIX, no. 3, (1978). © 1978 by Heldref Publications.

works. A character in the first novel comments about somebody writing a novel called *The Recognitions*: "My, your friend is writing for a rather small audience, isn't he."6 In *JR* one artist tells another whose important novel has gone unrecognized, "you must have known when you were writing it, you must have known you were writing it for a very small audience."7 If Gaddis's novels have achieved only a very small audience because of their difficulties, they deserve a much larger one because of their importance. In particular, *JR* is an extraordinary achievement—richly funny and powerfully accurate; it is more successful in several ways than *The Recognitions*. We shall here characterize both works, with an emphasis on their differences, and then explore the themes of *JR* in detail. With its more limited ambitions and sustained black-humor vision, *JR* should assure William Gaddis a long overdue recognition and a prominent place in contemporary fiction.

The Recognitions portrays an artist, Wyatt Gwyon, who assumes heroic stature from the outset. When he is a child, his Aunt May tells him, "A hero is someone who serves something higher than himself with undying devotion" (R 38); Wyatt's higher principle turns out to be a spiritually infused art. He rejects the notion of originality to become a dedicated forger of the Flemish Old Masters: "Because they found God everywhere. There was nothing God did not watch over, nothing, and so this ... and so in the painting every detail reflects ... God's concern" (R 270). Though Wyatt's works are sold at great profit and his abilities exploited, he successfully resists and refuses those who would possess him. Early on, he leaves his father and a New England family tradition of Calvinist ministry; later, he leaves his wife, Esther. He is exploited by the corrupt businessman, Recktall Brown, but remains uncorrupted and eventually rejects Brown by attempting to claim his own forgeries. When Brown dies, the art critic, Basil Valentine, tries to adopt Wyatt; Wyatt stabs him and leaves for Europe. There, the counterfeiter, Sinisterra, tries to enlist him in his scheme of mummy making, but Wyatt, renamed Stephen, flees to a Spanish monastery to "restore" old paintings by removing the paint. In our last glimpse of him, Wyatt/Stephen sets off alone, rejecting entanglements and other people's schemes for deliberation and simplicity: "Now at last, to live deliberately [....] There's no more you and I [....] The work will know its own reason [....] Yes, we'll simplify. Hear?" (R 960).

One of the most extraordinary qualities of *The Recognitions* is its ambitiousness. It is vast in scope, covering a span of some thirty years and ranging from New York to Europe. It is encyclopedic in knowledge; the literary sources and references include not only Joyce but Augustine, Saint John of the Cross, Thoreau, Melville, T. S. Eliot, and dozens more. In tracing its religious themes, the book explores Catholicism, Calvinism, various forms of mysticism, and Mithraism, the worship of the sun. The scientific lore contained in the novel ranges from counterfeit mummy-making to counterfeit money-making to the method for analyzing the date of a painting. Several levels of discourse are included: from graffiti to sermons, from inebriated party chitchat to serious debates of aesthetic principles.[8] The novel left several reviewers with the uncomfortable sensation that Gaddis had poured everything he knew into it; his character Stanley could speak for the author when he says: "And now it's impossible to accomplish a body of work without a continuous sense of time, so instead you try to get all the parts together into one work that will stand by itself and serve the same thing a lifetime of separate works does" (R 658).

One reason for the heavy literary allusiveness of the novel is its presentation of artistic creation as an act of atonement; art has metaphysical significance in *The Recognitions*.[9] Several characters experience artistic creation as a kind of transcendental perception of truth. The recognitions evoked in the title are revelations of religious certainty, when the fragmentation and chaos of modern culture are stripped away to reveal simplicity, necessity, and love. The poetess, Esme, struggles for epiphany: "It was through this imposed accumulation of chaos that she struggled to move now: beyond it lay simplicity, unmeasurable, residence of perfection, where nothing was created, where originality did not exist: because it was origin" (R 321). In Wyatt's paintings, "the recognitions go much deeper, much further back" than in most forgeries, because when he paints "I've taken the Guild oath, not for the critics, the experts [....] the Guild oath, to use pure materials, to work in the sight of God" (R 269). Like them, the composer Stanley finds "a moment when love and necessity become the same thing" in his creation of music which "soared in atonement" at the novel's end. Art, as the fragments of past creations, the creations of the characters, or Gaddis's novel itself, has redemptive power in *The Recognitions*.

Gaddis's first novel is a profoundly serious exploration of aesthetics and religion, with some moments of comic relief. As recognitions are treated with earnest respect in the novel, failures of recognition become ridiculous. In one very funny incident, Otto arranges to meet his father for the first time in a large hotel; because he is unable to achieve any sort of recognition, he mistakes Mr. Sinisterra for his father and accepts counterfeit money as a genuine gift. Another blackly humorous episode involves a grotesque failure of recognition; during a large party, a little girl appears several times to ask for sleeping pills for her mother downstairs. None of the guests who give her pills understands the situation. Some two-hundred pages and several weeks later, the little girl stands guard over the decaying corpse, which she does not recognize for what it is, with a fly swatter: "She's still asleep, and I'm keeping the flies off her" (R 801). Yet another humorous failure of recognition occurs when the monks at a Spanish monastery mistake the Reverend Gwyon's ashes for wheat germ and bake them into loaves of bread. Rich in humor as it is, the novel is primarily concerned with an earnest exploration of aesthetic recognition, and the comic failures form a minor counterpoint to the dominant theme.

While *JR* shares a similar preoccupation with art, it is a very different novel in several respects. Its protagonist, Edward Bast, is not as heroic as Wyatt Gwyon; while he shares Wyatt's innocence, he is successfully manipulated throughout the novel. He has been hired as a composer in residence at a Long Island elementary school, but he is fired when he injects too much grim reality into a televised lesson on the "fairy tale life of Mozart." He is then taken up and used by JR Vansant, apathetically driven eleven-year-old with a runny nose, torn sweater and sneakers, and the cold ambition of Flem Snopes. Bast becomes "Edward Bast, Business Representative" for JR, whose business dealings are no more sophisticated than his spelling. Though Bast tries repeatedly to withdraw, his lack of money to pay a debt to JR and his innate courteous timidity make him continue. He works doggedly on his music in a disastrous apartment on East Ninety-sixth Street where hot water constantly gushes from a broken faucet. As the novel ends, Bast finally achieves the heroism Wyatt had assumed from the beginning and, like him, rejects entanglements in other people's schemes: "no, no I've failed enough at other people's things I've done enough other people's damage from now on I'm just going to do my own, from now on I'm just going to fail at my own" (JR 718).

JR is far more limited in scope than *The Recognitions*. The time covered in the narrative is only three or four months; it is set in the fall, at some point during the Nixon presidency.[10] The novel opens as the leaves have begun to turn and closes before Christmas; the seasonal decline with no Nativity reflects the sterility of the natural and civilized world in the book. Similarly, it is much more restricted in space than its predecessor; the settings alternate between New York City and an unnamed Long Island community, with a few stops in Astoria along the way. While the book has no narrative divisions at all, a regular structural alternation is established between the city and the island, as characters scurry back and forth on the trains. Moreover, *JR* makes sparing and subtle use of allusions; for example, JR says "hurry up hey, it's time" (JR 171), but the allusion fits his character—especially in the substitution of "hey" for "please"—without seeming ostentatious. Relatively few such allusions, however, are used; while aesthetic fragments could redeem the damaged world of *The Recognitions*, the world of *JR* is ruined past redemption.

The creation of art appears in *JR* as a worthy action, with no ability to save or redeem the world. Like *The Recognitions*, the novel includes a great many plagiarists and failed artists: the teacher, Jack Gibbs, began a work on mechanization and the arts sixteen years ago and will never complete it; Mr. Schramm succeeded in writing a movie Western but commits suicide before finishing his novel; Mr. Gall has written a Western novel lifted directly from Schramm's movie; and Thomas Eigen has been working for years on a play which also turns out to be plagiarized from Schramm. Unlike *The Recognitions*, however, *JR* includes no truly successful artists: Bast is forced by his need for money to abandon project after project; the only composition he completes is a score for a stockbroker's movie about hunting big game. The score does not "soar in atonement"; rather, it is sold to a maker of pornographic films. The painter, Schepperman, completes several works which are described as powerful, but they are owned and locked in a vault by the wealthy Zona Selk.

Art fails to redeem in the novel because its audience is incapable of exaltation—or even appreciation. Bast plays a recording of a Bach cantata for JR "to show you there's such a thing as as, as intangible assets," but all JR hears is "this here lady starts singing up yours up yours so then this man starts singing up mine." Bast rages at his inability to respond:

> There's nothing you can't destroy even, even music a glorious piece of music I thought it could rise above anything even your, even you I thought maybe you'd hear something there some speck just a speck in you somewhere might wake up might be exalted for an instant you hear me? Even an instant! (JR 658)

Because American culture as it is presented in the novel is incapable of awakening or exaltation, the artist's problem becomes one of motivation: if his creation is considered worthless by his audience, can it have any worth? In *JR* art has no culturally redemptive power, but it can achieve worth "for a very small audience."

JR is far more concerned with failures of recognition than with moments of religious or aesthetic perception; thus the novel assumes a tone of sustained black humor. Where Gaddis's first novel suggested solutions to the problem of despair in the perception of simplicity, necessity, and love, his second novel admits, in a tone of desperate glee, that the problem cannot be resolved. One source of humorous despair in the novel is the empty absurdity of the business world and the uselessness of its products. When a young man appears at the door selling greeting cards for all occasions, Jack Gibbs points out their inadequacy for all truly important occasions:

> —Got a friend jumped out a window, got a card for that?
> —Well gee I, maybe get well ...
> —Can't get well went home and hung himself got a card for that?
> —Well gee I, I don't think so but maybe you could ...
> —Got a woman on alimony sleeping with a book salesman hell of an occasion, got a card for that?
> —Well gee I, like here's sympathy. (JR 405)

People, especially the wealthy and the busy, also prove humorously inadequate in their response to death. For the Mexican prostitute hired by General Motors to service Mr. Grynszpan, death offers another kinkier, possibility for business: "—I ave a busy schedule. Wen e's ere?—Look he's not here he's gone he's dead but come in, I ... —E's dead? That's not nice no, I don do that. Goodbye" (JR 722).

The inadequacy of sympathetic characters to take any useful action to relieve human suffering provides other rich instances of black humor. Bast, who is profoundly sympathetic but powerless and destitute, receives a poignant letter from a Mrs. Srskic: "Our famili is quite ruined. My husband is very sick, death sick, without hope of guerishing. I beg you to send for him some cloth and underwear, pijame, all very very used." Bast's friend, Rhoda, reads him the letter and suggests that he could send the woman some of the absurdly useless gifts that have poured in the JR Corp, which are literally all Bast owns:

> —I mean like why don't you send them those deluxe barbeque tools and this fucking computer for broiling steaks man [....] I mean her husband's sitting there in no underwear without hope of guerishing man like you could send him that electric heated towel stand that came yesterday to hang his pijame on while his neckties rotate and Mrs. Zrk is running around with the deluxe barbeque tools waiting for this solid state computer to broil their steaks and chops to perf ...
> —Look damn it what am I supp ... (JR 557–58)

Gaddis jokes about the destruction of language and ideals, about human inadequacy and death, about the cosmic absurdity of his characters' quest for order and beauty in a world of squalor and chaos. His jokes suggest that he finds neither a solution nor a fully adequate response to despair.

While both of Gaddis's fictional worlds are characterized by a "sense of disappointment, of something irretrievably lost" (R 131), Gaddis radically shifts the way he defines the problem. The source of loss and despair in *The Recognitions* appears as the fragmentation and separation of a once-unified world; in *JR* these symptoms are traced to the entropic decline of a chaotic and random world. While fragments can be collected and ordered, to reverse the enervating process described in the second law of thermodynamics is impossible: Stanley manages "to get all the parts together into one work," but Bast cannot turn off the flow of hot water that represents a pointless loss of energy. At the Long Island school, another falsely optimistic televised lesson insists that "the total amount of energy in the world today is the same as it was at the beginning of time," but Jack Gibbs turns the lesson off to tell his class about entropy: "Order is simply a thin, perilous condition we try to impose on the basic reality of chaos" (JR 20). Gibbs is preoccupied with entropy throughout the novel; he describes the autumn as "life draining out of the sky out of the world" and explains his own inability to write as "problem just no God damned energy" (JR 119, 585). Gibbs marvels that Bast can compose in the Ninety-sixth Street apartment, where entropy defies any ordering process: "—Problem Bast there's too God damned much leakage around here, can't compose anything with all this energy spilling you've got entropy going everywhere. Radio leaking under there hot water pouring out so God damned much entropy going on think you can hold all those notes together know what it sounds like?" (JR 287). As the loss of energy, the decline toward inertness, and the increase of disorder, entropy dominates the world of *JR*.

One important manifestation of the entropic process, as it appears in the fiction of both Gaddis and Thomas Pynchon, is the loss of communication. *JR* is made up almost entirely of spoken words, with very little narrative description or authorial comment, yet for all the speaking that occurs, little communicating is accomplished. Most of the dialogues in the novel become monologues because one character dominates and cuts the other off; *JR* is full of interruptions and sentence fragments. But even when both characters manage to complete their sentences, misunderstandings proliferate. Again, Jack Gibbs explains:

> read Wiener on communication, more complicated the message more God damned chance for errors, take a few years of marriage such a God damned complex of messages going both ways can't

get a God damned thing across, God damned much entropy going on say good morning she's got a God damned headache thinks you don't give a God damn how she feels, ask her how she feels she thinks you just want to get laid, try that she says it's the only God damn thing you take seriously about her. (JR 403)

As Gibbs's examples indicate, the marriages in the novel provide clear demonstrations of communication loss; with so "God damned much entropy going on," no couple can achieve understanding. Gibbs's wife has divorced him, Thomas Eigen's wife leaves him, Amy Joubert's husband leaves her, and the Stampers and Bartletts are among other minor couples who split up. But the marriages form only one among many examples; communications are also lost between friends, lovers, business partners, lawyers and clients, bosses and secretaries.

As human communication is lost and energy declines, inert things come to dominate the settings of *JR*. Two of the most important locales in the novel, the Long Island school and the Ninety-sixth Street apartment, literally fill up with objects so that people can no longer move about. At the school, unused testing equipment and appliances for a home ec center move the retarded children and the kindergarten "out of business," as principal Whiteback explains to Major Hyde:

—Whiteback had to set the little retreads up in business over in east seven Vern ...
—No well in fact we had to put them into ahm, out of business that is to say Major [....] of course since kindergarten had been held in ahm, where first grade was scheduled before we ran into problems spacewise with ahm, schedulewise that is. (JR 453–54)

At the apartment, which is crammed to the ceiling in some places with cartons of books and papers, film cans, old newspapers, and used paper bags, each day's delivery of mail for the JR Corp threatens imminent catastrophe. Books, brochures, gifts—like the electric letter-opener and the rotating necktie-rack—fill the apartment to the point where each trip to the door becomes increasingly dangerous.

Several recurring motifs reinforce the notion of entropic decline and also unify the novel. Among these, the most significant is a repeated pattern of spilling, falling, and scattering; these actions increase randomness and disorder. On the first page, the first narrative description in the book states, "Sunlight, pocketed in a cloud, spilled suddenly broken across floor through the leaves of the trees outside" (JR 3). The natural world in which sunlight can break and spill is a precariously fragile one; solar energy does not warm or light but dissipates in JR. Within the first scene of the novel, attorney Coen spills papers and drops his glasses; in the second scene, Amy Joubert drops a sack of coins which spill and scatter through the grass, against a background of "the rhumba now spilling from the bank" (JR 19). In the principal's office Miss Flesch spills her coffee, Dan di Cephalis spills the pages of a script, and Jack Gibbs spills a pailful of "what was stopping up the plumbing in the junior high" (JR 50). In the apartment, a box of slides is spilled, Gibbs's notes are scattered, a can of "enchilavies" is dropped on Bast's musical score, and a whole pile of cartons comes crashing down.

A one-man entropic agent in his own right, JR begins by causing a catastrophe which brings "the pile of chairs cascading to the stage and scattered the Rhinemaidens in disheveled pursuit" (JR 36). Throughout the novel, JR carries a battered portfolio which never quite succeeds in containing his schoolwork, mail, free offers, newspapers, and corporate documents; he spills the whole load in the post office, on the train, outside the principal's office, and in several other places. While JR's actions accelerate entropy, a few characters make futile attempts to oppose it: Bast picks up the coins Amy Joubert has spilled in his first appearance in the novel, and Dan di Cephalis mops up Miss Flesch's coffee, picks up her script, and saves energy by turning off lights. These efforts prove essentially useless, however, because the falling and dropping proceed too quickly in too many places. All of the spilling and scattering underscores Gaddis's more explicit suggestion that order is imposed perilously "on the basic reality of chaos."

People are similarly afflicted by the manifestations of chaotic randomness in another recurring motif: injuries and accidents are prevalent throughout *JR*. Among the more dramatic instances, Miss Flesch and a book salesman are injured in one car crash, Dan di Cephalis and Major Hyde are wounded in another, artist Schepperman accidentally cuts off an ear, Schramm throws a pencil at the wall and it bounces back into his eye, and a retarded boy with a cap pistol is shot to death by a narcotics agent. Coach Vogel, himself badly scarred by several years in the New York City schools, summarizes the situation: "Why, it's like the morning after Blenheim Mister Gibbs, walking wounded everywhere" (JR 341). These "walking wounded" reinforce the accidental quality of experience in an advanced entropic state.

Because they live in a chaotic world without a sense of history or culture, most of the characters respond by seeking the ordering power of money. Money lifts one above the entropic process; it gives one the power to control inert objects, to manipulate other people, and to create constellations of order around one's own central importance. "—Money ... ?" is the first word and primary question of *JR*. Money dominates most conversations at the school and in the corporations; it preoccupies the artists as well as the politicians. The directors of the school rarely mention education but spend hours discussing the budget: "—And there's this twelve thousand dollars item for books.—That's supposed to be twelve hundred, the twelve thousand should be for paper towels" (JR 25). John Cates, president of Typhon International, explains that "the only damn time you spend money's to make money," and Major Hyde asserts that "if you don't spend you don't get" (JR 109, 23). Congressman Pecci is repeatedly called to the phone to discuss bills for his services, and even Bast makes statements like "It's not that it's the money, it's the money" (JR 37). The few described settings also reflect the importance of money; the drapes in a corporate board room are a "tasteful gold-on-blue arrangement of denarii, ducats, shekels, and similar bright testaments to long submerged mercantile struggles" (JR 92).

JR himself is at once the chief symbol and the most pathetic victim of the drive for money and power. In an early appearance, he is aptly cast as the dwarf who renounces love and steals the mythic Rhinegold in Wagner's opera; he accomplishes the theft of real coins in a rehearsal. He goes on to build a corporate empire based on avarice; rather than pay the debts of the companies he acquires, he simply takes over the creditors. He ruins one entire town because he does not care about the people: "this isn't any popularity contest hey." Bast repeatedly urges compassion for people, and JR as regularly insists on the superior importance of money: "No but holy shit Bast this is serious, I mean like I'm sorry about your friend and all but holy shit this is like five million dollars" (JR 299). JR looks at the world and sees only money: "everything you see someplace there's this millionaire for it"; he looks at people and sees expendability: "these here stuffed Eskimos that shows how they live" (JR 473–75). Noticing JR's face in a class picture, another character remarks, "ever see so much greed confined in one small face?" (JR 461).

But for all his undeniable greed, JR is also a touchingly helpless product of the world around him. Amy Joubert remarks that "there's something quite desolate, like hunger" about him. Jack Gibbs gives him a used, dusty handkerchief to replace the "indescribable wad of, of cloth" that he has used, and JR thanks him, saying, "No but, but I mean people don't usually give me things" (JR 338). Near the end, JR sniffles as his pathetic hopes are exploded; he tells Bast "I just, always, I mean I always thought this is what it will be like you and, and me riding in this here big limousine down, down this, this here big street" (JR 636). In all his corporate exploits, he has simply been trying to find a purpose, "trying to find out what I'm suppose to do," and he has quite naturally looked to the adults around him and imitated them. At several points he has even quoted from John Cates, Whiteback, Hyde, and others in justifying his actions. While we never learn what his initials actually stand for, they clearly suggest "Junior," as his character clearly suggests a junior reflection of his elders. If this eleven-year-old's obsession with money is ominous, it is also typical of every one of his peers: Donny di Cephalis plays a money-eating machine, and David Eigen responds, when his mother asks how much he loves her, "Some money" (JR 267).

The concern of JR with money is exceeded only by its concern with worth; the two themes are intertwined from the first page of the novel. Julia and Anne Bast, Edward's aunts, recall their first reaction to paper money:

—Money ... ? in a voice that rustled.
—Paper, yes.
—And we'd never seen it. Paper money.
—We never saw paper money till we came east.
—It looked so strange the first time we saw it. Lifeless.
—You couldn't believe it was worth a thing. (JR 3)

The rest of the novel is anticipated in this conversation; JR's empire is constructed of paper, and while he becomes a millionaire on paper he never appears one in reality. He never uses his paper money, not even to replace the torn sneakers or sweater. By the novel's end, money is clearly not only lifeless but an agent of lifelessness; its worth is called into question at the beginning, and its worthlessness firmly established by the end.

The search for some form of worthy activity preoccupies most of the sympathetic characters in the novel; like Wyatt Gwyon in *The Recognitions*, they realize that "looking around us today, there doesn't seem to be much that's worth doing" (R 628). John Cates remarks that for most people, "Only damn reason they think something's worth doing's they get paid to do it," but his niece, Amy Joubert, teaches even though she does not need money, because she wants to do something worthwhile. Similarly, Norman Angel tries to retain control of the company he has helped build in order "to keep it doing something that's, that's worth doing" (JR 359). The artists have special problems in defining the worth of their creations; while Schepperman sells his blood for money to buy paint "because he thinks one painting's worth more than his own" blood or life (JR 48), Schramm commits suicide because he is not sure his art is worthy. He could not create a work of art that would redeem the accidental quality of his experience:

> It was whether what he was trying to do was worth doing even if he couldn't do it? whether anything was worth writing even if he couldn't write it? Hopping around with that God damned limp trying to turn it all into something more than one more stupid tank battle one more stupid God damned general, trying to redeem the whole God damned thing by ... (JR 621)

For Schramm, Eigen, and Gibbs, worthy art must redeem the insignificance of the artist and the illiteracy of the audience; their efforts are doomed to failure. For Bast and for Gaddis, art may be worthy without being able to redeem anything; *JR* creates its worth out of the tacit admission that experience cannot be turned "into something more than one more stupid tank battle."

Edward Bast arrives at a definition of artistic and human worth late in the novel, with the help of a Mister Duncan who shares his hospital room. Duncan insists that winning is not what it is all about, but rather failing with a sense of dignity and self-respect. As Duncan dies, Bast achieves one of the few limited revelations in the novel: "I've been thinking of things you've said as though just, just doing what's there to be done as though it's worth doing or you never would have done anything you wouldn't be anybody" (JR 687). What Bast realizes is that worth is limited and relative; it does not adhere to things, nor even to accomplished actions, but to people. The dignity of the actor creates the worth of the action, as he stumblingly tries to explain: "nothing's worth doing till you've done it and then it was worth doing even if it wasn't because that's all you ..." (JR 715).

For Bast, as perhaps for Gaddis, his art was and continues to be worth creating, whatever the condition of his audience. He does not expect to win fame or money, as he does not expect others to recognize the worth of his creations. In a conversation with Eigen as the novel ends, Bast says of his new composition, "I mean until a performer hears what I hear and can make other people hear what he hears it's just trash isn't it Mister Eigen, it's just trash like everything in this place" (JR 725). Bast's heavily ironic statement can also be taken as a final comment on *JR*; the audience of both works may be small, but neither creation is "just trash." Both works stand on their own, with or without recognition, proving the worth of the art and the artist. William Gaddis has, by now, surely earned recognition with the excellence achieved in his fiction. In their accuracy of vision, their rich humor, and their enduring artistry, Gaddis's novels merit a very large audience.

NOTES

1. The *Time* and *Newsweek* reviews appeared in the issues of 14 March 1955; *The New Yorker* note appeared on 9 April 1955, p. 117.

2. George Steiner, rev. of *JR* by William Gaddis, *The New Yorker*, 26 January 1976, p. 108.

3. Alfred Kazin, rev. of *JR* by William Gaddis, *New Republic*, 6 December 1975, p. 18.

4. Bernard Benstock, "On William Gaddis: In Recognition of James Joyce," *Wisconsin Studies in Contemporary Literature*, 6 (1965), 177–89.

5. William Gaddis, quoted in Bob Miner, rev. of *JR* by William Gaddis, *Village Voice*, 13 October 1975, p. 53.

6. William Gaddis, *The Recognitions* (1955; rpt. New York: Bard, 1974), p. 398. Subsequent references are to this edition, cited as R. Because Gaddis makes frequent use of ellipses, editorial ellipses are in brackets.

7. William Gaddis, *JR* (New York: Knopf, 1975), p. 417. Subsequent references are to this edition, cited as JR.

8. For a fuller discussion of the novel's encyclopedic range, see David Madden, "On William Gaddis's *The Recognitions*," in *Rediscoveries*, ed. David Madden (New York: Crown, 1971), pp. 292–304.

9. Joseph S. Salemi, "To Soar in Atonement: Art as Expiation in Gaddis's *The Recognitions*," *Novel*, 10, No. 2 (Winter 1977), 127–36.

10. References to the end of the Vietnam war suggest the Nixon presidency; at the very end of the novel, JR has apparently received a letter from Nixon encouraging him to enter politics.

JOHN Z. GUZLOWSKI

No More Sea Changes: Hawkes, Pynchon, Gaddis, and Barth

Traditionally, the sea has held a strong attraction for man. In the opening paragraphs of *Moby Dick*. Ishmael, perhaps one of the most articulate interpreters of the sea, speaks of this attraction. We are all "water-gazers," he declares, drawn to the sea as if it were a magnet, drawn as if by some "magic."[1] This magnetic magic has also attracted writers. For centuries, they have spoken of the sea as a realm of psychological rebirth and the sea journey as a voyage into the unconscious from which the traveler, previously alienated from his inner realms, returns whole, restored, at peace. As Auden argued, the sea is a "symbol of primitive potential power," a symbol of inner "essences," and the sea journey is a symbol of "the exploration of the self."[2] Hamlet, Ishmael, Hemingway's Santiago, and others—all have gone down to the sea, and there experienced a transformation, a rebirth, a sea change. However, this traditional attitude toward the sea and the unconscious that it often represents is being challenged by a number of recent American novelists, such as John Hawkes, Thomas Pynchon, William Gaddis, and John Barth. These writers have created characters who are estranged from the sea and the unconscious inner sea that it often suggests: Allert in Hawkes's *Death, Sleep & the Traveler* and Oedipa in Pynchon's *The Crying of Lot 49* fear the sea and struggle to isolate themselves further from it: Wyatt Gwyon in Gaddis' *The Recognitions* seeks the inner sea but cannot discover it:

From *Critique: Studies in Modern Fiction* XXIII, no. 2, (Winter 1981-82) © 1981 by Heldref Publications.

and Todd Andrews in Barth's *The Floating Opera* parodies the concept of the sea change.

Allert, the protagonist-narrator of *Death, Sleep & the Traveler*, dreads both the sea that he sails on and the inner sea of the unconscious. The two are, in his eyes, one. Offering his reaction to the sea at the end of the voyage with which a good part of the novel is occupied, Allert writes, "I plan never again to look at the rough sea though I am filled with it, like a sewn-up skin with salt."[3] Peter, Allert's psychiatrist and friend, further clarifies the analogy by describing a treatment he observed for curing the insane. Under the supervision of the staff of an asylum, a patient was subjected to a series of induced comas, each of which drove him deeper into himself. As Peter states,

> The patient was traveling inside himself and in a kind of sexual agony was sinking into the depths of psychic darkness, drowning into the sea of the self, submerging into the long slow chaos of the dreamer on the edge of extinction. The closer such a patient came to death the greater his cure. The whiter and wetter he became in his grave of rubber sheets ... and the deeper his breathing, the slower his pulse, the more he felt himself consumed as in liquid lead, the greater the agony with which he approached oblivion, then the greater and more profound and more joyous his recovery, his rebirth. (143)

Such death, such sleep, and such travel, however, are not for Allert. He reacts to Peter's description first with silence and then with the statement, "There are certain days when I do not enjoy your company" (144). Allert obviously wants no sea changes.

He responds as he does because he fears both literal drowning and the metaphorical drowning Peter speaks of. Writing of the cruise he took on a pleasure ship, Allert repeatedly reflects on and displays his fear of the sea upon which he once sailed. Identifying himself with the ocean liner, he writes of the terror he experienced as he imagined a "torpedo speeding through the, black night" toward the vulnerable ship (7–8), a torpedo which threatened to force him into the sea. Later, after diving to the bottom of the ship's pool, he tried to remain there as long as possible to propitiate "the god of all those in fear of drowning at sea."[4]

What he fears in the actual sea is what he fears within himself: the puzzling, killing creatures of his heart of darkness, and the equally frightening prospect that these creatures do not exist.[5] While aboard the ship, he felt threatened by "the rising and diving monsters of the deep" (28).

These find their counterpart in his inner depths. He feels that a "man-sized bat-like shadow" crouches there, ready to attack. Both seas, he believes, also conceal death. Beneath the surface of the sea lie the "bones and shells of the earth's cemetery" (159); beneath the surface of his external self lie "dark and spongy land mines" (72). His fear of what awaits him beneath both surfaces is compounded by his inability to understand the things that exist beneath these surfaces. As he states, he dreads the "incomprehensible" quality of the deep (7) and the "inexplicable" quality of his inner sea (90). Finally, Allert fears that despite his fears nothing exists beneath either the surface of the sea or the surface of his personality. Once, when the ship stopped moving, the calmness of the sea, with its suggestion that there was "nothing" under its waves, caused in him a fear he "had never known" (7). That fear reappears later in his dream of the tent of "dry and hairless animal skins," a dream of his inner self. Within the tent of skins, beneath their surface, he finds only "desolation" and "nothing at all" (74).

Faced with the inexplicable, with death, and with the possibility that what he fears does not exist within him, Allert seeks sanctuary on the surface of his self. He turns away from his inner sea, his inner self, and fabricates a mask, the crafting of which shields him from a confrontation with his "psychic sores" and transforms the "surface of the bright ocean" within him into an opaque "sea of lead" (164). The mask he crafts is that of an unexceptional, candid man in love with his inner self who is simultaneously exceptional, deceptive, and separated from his inner sea. The tensions inherent in such a paradoxical facade create a "dead surface" (124) that cannot be pierced to discover the reality beneath that surface. Crafting his mask, Allert hopes to prevent himself from drowning in his inner sea.

A small but significant detail in Allert's narrative serves as a clue to his method of self-masking. His initial description, occurring on the first page of his wife's appearance as she leaves him does not coincide with his second description, occurring at the end, of her appearance in the same scene. While in the first he says she is wearing a "gray suit," a "silk dress," and a "black blouse" and is carrying a "straw suitcase in either hand" (1), in the second he notes that she is wearing "white slacks" and a "red knitted top" and is carrying a small suitcase of lambskin and a handbag.[6] These conflicting descriptions of surfaces, like the contradictory aspects of Allert's mask, create a third surface, an impregnable surface which foils any attempt to discover the truth beneath it.

Displaying this method of self-masking, of surfacing, Allert boasts of his unexceptionalness: "During all this time" (the eight or nine years covered in his narrative) "I have thought of myself as moderate, slow-paced, sensible, overly large, aging. But ordinary, always ordinary" (135). Against this aspect of his mask, he juxtaposes, with apparent eagerness, repeated references to his extraordinary sexual proclivities. He tells the reader and reveals to other characters that he collects pornographic pictures, practices voyeurism, participates in a *menage a trois* with his wife and his friend Peter, and has a kinky shipboard romance with a young girl, whom he may or may not have killed at the end of his voyage. The other aspects of his mask—his candor and his deceptiveness, his love of psychic slime and his fear of it—are developed in the same way and serve the same purpose. The tensions between these contradictory elements of his mask are ultimately irreconcilable. Existing side by side, they create a "dead surface" for Allert's others, his reader, and himself, a surface which Allert hopes can never be pierced. Crafting a mask and concerning himself with its surface, Allert hopes to escape a confrontation with the inner depths, the inner sea he dreads.

The sea as an emblem of the unconscious is also central to Pynchon's *The Crying of Lot 49*. As its narrator suggests, the novel's protagonist, Oedipa Maas, like Allert, senses that the ocean possesses "something tidal" and "primal" that corresponds to something deep within man.[7] The ocean sends "feelers past eyes and eardrums, perhaps to arouse fractions of brain current your most gossamer microelectrode is yet too gross for finding" (37). Again like Allert, Oedipa fears the sea without and the sea within. She continually, to use the narrator's phrase, stops short of the physical sea, the Pacific, and the psychic sea, the deep "sink" of primal, "redemptive" emotions within man (122, 37). She cuts herself off from her inner sea of emotions and from those persons who could cause her to respond emotionally.

Oedipa's estrangement from her inner sea and from others and her desire to further the estrangement are forcefully rendered in a key scene in which she meets the pathetic sailor. Searching for clues in San Francisco to the Trystero conspiracy, she comes upon an old, broken and forlorn salt, "huddled, shaking with grief" (92) and delirium tremens in a doorway. Gripped by the poignancy of his condition, she responds initially with her emotional inner sea: "Overcome all at once by a need to touch him" (93), she comforts him in her arms and feels his tears against her breast as he begins to cry. After she takes his hand in hers and helps him to his room, however, she becomes so "lost in the fantasy" of helping him—of buying him a new suit, of complaining to the landlord about the condition of the room the sailor lives in (94)—that she neither feels his hand withdrawing from hers nor hears his cries turn to sighs. Shortly, deciding that "nothing she knew of would preserve ... him" (96), she leaves the sailor—and the inner emotional seas he might have guided her to—and continues on her quest for the meaning of the Trystero.

Oedipa's failure to respond to the cries of the sailor and others in the novel arises from her alienation from and fear of her inner life, the depths of the primal sea within her. Such cries demand that she go into herself, the narrator states, "further down perhaps than she could reach" (3). Faced with such demands, she reacts with "near panic," with the feeling that she is "about to lose control" (4). Oedipa avoids such panic and retains control by creating a seawall between her self and her private experience and a corresponding "buffer" (6) between herself and others. Her tendency is suggested in the scene in which she plays Strip Botticelli with Metzger the lawyer. While they watch a confusing movie which—significantly—describes the drowning of the crew of a submerged submarine, Oedipa agrees to remove a piece of clothing for each wrong guess she makes about the film. Although she repeatedly guesses incorrectly, "the progressive removal of her clothing" brings her "no nearer nudity" (26). Her body remains unrevealed and unrevealable because, in preparation for the game, she dressed in multiple layers of panties, nylons, slacks, blouses, and other garments.

This tactic, like Allert's self-masking, is symptomatic of Oedipa's response to situations that might require her to reveal herself to others or reveal her inner sea to herself. Her reaction to the pathetic sailor, cloaking him in a fantasy and thus separating herself from him and from any further emotional response to him, is only one instance of this tendency. A more pervasive example is Oedipa's obsessive commitment to the quest for the Trystero: a mysterious, underground organization, which may or may not exist, dedicated to "serving as a channel of communication" (80) for the disinherited and the isolated. First coming upon hints of its existence in her role as the executor of Pierce Inverarity's will, she uses the conspiracy as a buffer between herself and others, and between herself and the depths of her private experience. When she stops in her quest for Trystero to reflect on the men who have had the most intimate contact with her and who now are separated from her, she does not view their loss from the perspective of her emotional inner sea but rather from the perspective of her obsession with the Trystero. She feels that the conspiracy is somehow responsible for her husband's addiction to LSD, her psychiatrist's madness, and Metzger's relationship with a depraved young girl. Likewise, the suicide of Dribblet, her "best guide to the Trystero" (114), briefly penetrates "to the sanctuary of her heart" but then becomes lost in the quagmire of her speculations concerning the conspiracy. She prays to his corpse to release its memories so that she will know if his suicide "had anything to do with Tristero" (121).

At the end of the novel, standing between two steel rails on a track bed miles from the sea, Oedipa has a vision of the meaning of the Trystero, a vision of communication, of people responding to people. The tracks she stands on, she imagines, lead to other tracks, whole webs of tracks, which lead to "squatters" who are "in touch with others, through the Tristero." Along these same rails are linemen's tents in which "nameless" people, using the linemen's equipment, live in "the very copper rigging and secular miracle of communication" (135). The vision, although attractive to her, is ironic. Oedipa has used the Trystero not as a means of achieving communication with others and with herself, but rather as a way of forestalling communication. She has allowed herself to "plunge" through the complexities of a conspiracy layered as dense as her "own streetclothes in that game with Metzger" (36) in order to avoid a similar plunge through the layers of seawalls and buffers which shield her from her inner sea and from others. The cry she hears at the end of the novel, therefore, is not "the cry that might abolish the night" (87); it is neither her own inner cry nor that of someone like the sailor, a cry that might open a bridge to her inner sea. Instead, the cry she hears at the end is merely an auctioneer's announcement that Lot 49, one of Inverarity's stamp collections and a further clue to the Trystero, is to be auctioned. At the end, Oedipa is sill landlocked, still deaf to those other cries, still constructing layers between herself and others, still constructing seawalls between herself and her inner sea.

While Allert and Oedipa fear the sea and what the sea emblematizes, Wyatt Gwyon in Gaddis' *The Recognitions* seeks the inner sea but cannot discover it. Speaking of the sea upon which Wyatt once sails, the narrator suggests its meaning for Wyatt: "Boundlessly neither yes or no, good nor evil, hope nor fear, pretending to all these things in the eyes that first beheld it, but unchanged since then, still its own color, heaving with the indifferent hunger of all actuality."[8] "Whole," undifferentiated, and flowing, the sea in Gaddis' novel is an emblem for unconscious reality, the reality that exists beneath all surfaces, the surfaces of the actual world and the surfaces of the individual. Gaddis argues in his novel that man is isolated from unconscious reality. For man, unconsciousness and consciousness are discrete realms.

The nature of such discreteness and the attempt to overcome it are fleshed out in those sections of the novel dealing with Wyatt. As a boy, he suffered an intense fever in which he glimpsed the fundamental nature of this fragmentation. Everything, he sensed, is divided into two distinct realms: a surface called consciousness, and a subsurface, sea-like one called unconsciousness. As the narrator states, consciousness is "a succession of separate particles, being carried along on the surface of the deep and steady unconscious flow of life." Normally, man lives in consciousness, lives on the surface. He sees everything, including his own being, as being composed of discrete particles, and he is completely unaware of the single sea-like "deeper flow" that undulates beneath the surface reality of the universe, nature, society, and the self. During his fever, however, Wyatt's repeated faintings plunged him into this flow where nothing is separate. He experienced it both within his being and within reality. Inside of him, "Deliria embraced in his memory, and refused to discriminate from one another, from what had happened and what might have happened" (58). Outside of him, he saw "the throbbing flow of night," a landscape of "intimacy" in which "particles" were not "separated into tangible identities" (60–61). Although his fever abated, Wyatt's memory of the undifferentiated states of unconscious existence never faded. His life becomes a search for such moments of ontological and epistemological recognition. He seeks to re-experience the flowing inner sea that lies both beneath his surface and the surfaces in the world outside him.

Wyatt turns to art as a means of recapturing this recognition. He feels that painting provides him with the means of approaching the state of recognition he seeks. After viewing a work of art (significantly Picasso's *Night Fishing in Antibes*), he tells his wife, Esther, that a great painting allows one to achieve moments of "near-recognition of reality" in which "all of a sudden everything is freed into one recognition," freed into a bunion of all things that, living in consciousness, normally "we never see" (102). Such moments in which the unconscious is revealed are, however, brief and infrequent. If one looks at a painting for too long, Wyatt adds, it becomes "familiar," and then, instead of experiencing a recognition, the viewer sees merely the painting. Furthermore, these recognitions are rare; Wyatt believes they occur "Maybe seven times in a life" (102). Finally, such recognitions are somehow incomplete. They are, as Wyatt says, near-recognitions, and, although he does not explain to Esther what he means, the implication is clear. Art allows one, to use a word Wyatt uses throughout the discussion, to "see" everything as non-discrete, to "see" the unconscious sea beneath surfaces, but art does not allow the viewer to plunge into non-discreteness, to plunge into the unconscious flow. In his best moments, man can approach a state of recognition, but he cannot fully enter it. To some degree, he is always cut off from the sea within himself and the flowing reality beneath the surfaces of the external world.

In part, the novel chronicles Wyatt's efforts to achieve recognition, to see not only the unconscious flow in the art of another but to plunge into this flow. As a painter himself, he tries a number of strategies for uncovering and entering unconsciousness. While still a child, he starts several original drawings but never completes them.[9] Unfinished, they are vague: forms are only half-seen, unfixed: "The original works left off at the moment where the pattern is conceived but not executed, the forms known to the author but their place daunted; still unfound in the dignity, of the design" (60). The narrator also stresses the flowing quality of Wyatt's unfinished portrait of his mother: it leaves "its lines of completion to the eye of the beholder" (64). Describing the reaction of Wyatt's father to this work, the narrator states, "Once he'd seen it he was constantly curious, and would stand looking away from it, and back completing it in his mind and then looking again as though, in the momentary absence of his stare and the force of his own plastic imagination, it might have completed itself. Still each time he returned to it, it was slightly different than he remembered intractably thwarting the completion he had managed himself" (64). With emphasis on the vagueness of these unfinished works, the descriptions stress the similarity between the works and Wyatt's vision of the unconscious sea with its "throbbing flow" and freedom from "conceits of separation" (60–61). Through the unfinished works, Wyatt is attempting to recapture the sense of recognition he experienced during his fever.

But these attempts fail. As he grows older, Wyatt forsakes his unfinished original works—perhaps because the process has "become familiar" and, therefore, the recognitions too infrequent—and turns to copying the works of the masters. Defending the copies, the forgeries, to the art critic, Basil Valentine, Wyatt argues that they are not simply fakes which reproduce the surfaces of the works they imitate. Rather, he says, his copies are founded on recognitions that "go much deeper, much further back" (269). While doing them, he momentarily transcends all discreteness. Using the materials and techniques of the Dutch masters, he becomes one with the artists who created the original works. His "whole consciousness" is again "consumed" as it was in childhood (51). He tells Valentine that, painting these forgeries, "I'm a master painter in the Guild, in Flanders, do you see? And if they come in and find that I'm using the ... gold, they destroy the bad materials I'm using and fine me" (269; ellipsis in original). Such consumption of his consciousness, however, is not complete. As with the unfinished originals, Wyatt eventually abandons this strategy for attaining recognition and turns to another.

When he is last seen in the novel, living in a monastery in Spain, Wyatt is still searching for his recognitions and has become a "restorer" of great paintings. Instead of working to preserve them, however, he is scraping away their layers of varnish and paint with the intention of returning these works to their original, bare canvases. By turning to such strategy, in a sense the opposite of Allert's and Oedipa's, Wyatt hopes to enter again into that state of unconsciousness he seeks. Like his earlier unfinished works and his forgeries, however, the strategy provides him only with near-recognition, not with the ultimate sense of recognition. His failure is first suggested by the means he takes to reach the sea of unconsciousness. By scraping away the "layers and layers of colors and oils and varnish" (932), he is contributing, although unknowingly, to fragmentation rather than eliminating it. Each layer he removes is one separated from the preceding and succeeding layers. Furthermore, Wyatt himself seems to be aware that his acts of restoration are not the final solution to the problem of a world and a self that are both given to discreteness. The janitor of the monastery, a murderer who has spiritually become one with the girl he killed and who thus apparently has attained some sort of recognition, tells Wyatt that he must leave the monastery to continue his quest for recognition: "He sent me on," Wyatt states, "to find what ... what he has here" (955; ellipsis in the original). Aware of the existence of the unconsciousness but separated from it, Wyatt is still seeking the means of opening himself to his inner sea and to the flowing reality that exists beneath all surfaces when he disappears from the novel.[10]

In *The Floating Opera*, Barth administers the coup de grace to the belief that man can find psychological rebirth through experiencing the sea. While Hawkes, Pynchon, and Gaddis describe the tragedy of isolation from inner and outer seas, Barth parodies the concept of the sea change. Initially, the reader expects the novel to chronicle a traditional retelling of a sea journey and its concomitant sea change. The protagonist, Todd Andrews, states that he has always desired to build a boat and escape to the sea. For Todd, constructing a boat is a "deed almost holy in its utter desirability," and the sea possesses—as it did for Ishmael—an "attractiveness" that adds "intensity" to his longing.[11]

What the sea is for Todd is similar to what the sea is for Wyatt: a boundless realm in which there is no discreteness. Such meaning is suggested by Todd's statement that he wishes to build a boat and "to slip quietly" from his moorings, "to run down to the river, sparkling in the sun, out into the broad reaches of the Bay and down to the endless oceans" (57). The holy deed that Todd desires to accomplish is a movement from "finite boundaries" to the "unbound infinite." While the former is suggested by Todd's use of the imagery of moorings and of rivers and bays with their shores, the latter is suggested by his use of the phrase "endless oceans."[12] Furthermore, as the novel argues as well, such movement is also a journey from rationality—with its power to isolate one from others, to create an island of oneself—to emotionality, with its power to unite one with others, to create an endless ocean of persons.

But Todd never completes his boat. Concomitant with his desire for unbound infinities is an equally strong, or perhaps stronger, desire for finite boundaries, for clearly drawn distinctions and separations, for moorings and shores. When he finally reaches the water, the encounter is significant because it occurs on a docked showboat, "The Floating Opera." Testing the water, so to speak, in this way, Todd experiences a sea change that is a parody of sea changes: it is a sea change that is, in effect, no great change at all.

In the novel's first sentence, Todd states what appears to be the motive for his writing: "The explanation of a day in 1937 when I changed my mind" (1), the explanation of why he decided not to commit suicide on that particular day. After a myriad of digressions regarding his various other writings and his past, Todd comes to the description of the moment when he decided not to take his life. He had planned to blow up himself, "The Floating Opera," and the 699 people who had gathered for a performance aboard the vessel. When the planned explosion fails to go off, Todd experiences a sea change.

He decides not to commit suicide (apparently a significant decision), but the significance of the change is undercut by Todd in three ways. First, the language that accompanies the change is mundane in the extreme. When, following the abortive explosion, he asks himself why he does not attempt to commit suicide again, he does not rhapsodize about the effect the sea has had upon him. Instead, he answers his question laconically with another question. "Why bother?" (242). Second, he later cloaks the change in the language of rationality and logic, a language of "premises," "reasonings," and "conclusions" that has nothing of unbounded infinities about it, a language that denies the power of the endlessness of oceans. And third, Todd undercuts the significance of his sea change by suggesting that the change he experienced aboard "The Floating Opera" is no different from the other three "major mind-changes" that he had experienced in his life.

Each of these changes teaches him the same lesson: the need for rationality, a rationality that separates him from himself and from others, a rationality that rejects the importance of what the sea emblematizes. His early sexual encounter with a young girl ends with his realization of the ludicrousness of his emotions and "animality" (121). Later, his foxhole meeting with the German ends with Todd bayoneting the soldier and becoming convinced that he himself could not expect much from either himself or his "fellow animals" and that he, therefore, must cultivate the "technique of thinking clearly" (67). Lastly, Todd's collegiate period of debauchery teaches him the need for "reasoned ... hard control" over his passions and animalistic weakness (134). Todd does experience a sea change, but it is one that denies the importance and power of sea changes. He is as moored to his rationality and its finite boundaries at the end of the novel as he was at the beginning.

The rejection by Hawkes, Pynchon, Gaddis, and Barth of the possibility of a sea change stems from their sense of man's altered nature. The traditional concept of the sea change is premised on the belief that man can experience his inner self, his inner sea. However, as various critics argue, the modern age with its emphasis on the surface of life has decimated the inner self.[13] One of the most extensive analyses of the modern loss or diminution of man's inner self appears in the works of R. D. Laing. He senses that "something Dreadful" has happened to man. "We are bemused and crazed creatures," he writes, isolated from one another, from the material world, and from the "authentic possibilities" of the inner world. A stranger to his inner self, the ordinary person is merely a "shriveled, desiccated fragment of what a person can be."[14] His actions no longer stem from his inner self. Instead, they stem from his "egoic self" (137), a mask that he has been led to believe is his true self but which bears as little resemblance to it as a Polaroid snapshot of the Grand Canyon bears to the Canyon itself. Furthermore, this "something Dreadful" that has happened is not only man's estrangement from his true self; the "Dreadful" is also the belief by many that this estrangement is "normal" and that the inner self neither exists nor needs to exist (54). To such an age with such an understanding of the inner self, the sea change is as foreign as the masted ships that once sailed the seas. The magnetic magic that Ishmael once spoke of as being in the sea now either repulses man or is so weak that it cannot be fully felt.

NOTES

1. Herman Melville, *Moby Dick* (New York: Modern Library. 1950). pp. 1–2.

2. W. H. Auden, *The Enchafed Flood, or The Romantic Iconography of the Sea* (New York: Random House, 1950), pp. 20, 122.

3. John Hawkes, *Death, Sleep & the Traveler* (New York: New Directions, 1974), p. 16. Subsequent references are to this edition,

4. Hawkes, p. 33, Donald J. Greiner, *Comic Terror: The Novels of John Hawkes* (Memphis: Memphis State Univ. Press, 1978), p. 259, believes that Allert loves his inner world, that he is "eager to probe the darkness of his unconscious being." Although attractive in the light of Hawker's repeated statements of his own eagerness to explore the unconscious, such a reading of the novel ignores Allert's own statements concerning his fear of the sea and the self, the extensive self-masking that he does and the repeated references to surfaces that draw the reader's attention to these masks and surfaces, and the imagery of enclosed water. If Allert is eager to explore his unconscious inner sea, his eagerness extends only to the amount of probing that he can do in a pool, a bucket, or a glass of psychic water.

5. Frederick Busch, "Icebergs, Islands, Ships beneath the Sea," in *A John Hawkes Symposium: Design and Debris* (New York: New Directions, 1978), pp. 50–63, argues

that the ship in this novel and elsewhere in Hawkes is an image of the psyche, of the inner world. At least in regards to *Death, Sleep & the Traveler*, this interpretation is suspect when seen in the light of the substantial number of sea/inner-self equations made throughout the novel. The ship is not the psyche but a means of avoiding it.

6. I am indebted to Greiner, p. 250, for his sharp detective work in discovering this detail concerning Ursula's appearance.

7. Thomas Pynchon, *The Crying of Lot 49* (New York: Bantam, 1966), p. 37. Subsequent references are to this edition.

8. William Gaddis. *The Recognitions* (New York: Avon, 1974), p. 902. Subsequent references are to this edition.

9. Tony Tanner, *City of Words* (New York: Harper & Row, 1971), pp. 393–400, suggests that Wyatt's failure to complete his originals stems from his Puritan background, one that regards originality as the province solely of God and brands those who invade this province sinners. While undeniably correct in part, this interpretation does not fully explain Wyatt's abandonment of his originals before they are completed. Wyatt's act of beginning an original work, regardless of whether he finishes it or not, is clearly as much a sin as completing such a work. He is no less sinful, as he admits, for merely starting an original work than he would be if he were to complete it (Gaddis, pp. 41, 956).

10. Susan Strehle Klemtner, "'For a Very Small Audience': The Fiction of William Gaddis," *Critique*, 19, No. 3 (1918), 61–73, argues that art in *The Recognitions* is redemptive. To support her contention, she refers to the epiphanies Wyatt and two other artists, Esme and Stanley, achieve. Like Wyatt, however, these artists also fail to achieve complete recognitions. While Esme's inward voyage ends in terror (Gaddis, p. 322), Stanley's glimpse of his death leads to a confusion filled with "conflicts he did not yet understand" and "questions he could never answer" (Gaddis, p. 1015). Both characters, like Wyatt, remain separated from their private experience. Art does not redeem them from consciousness.

11. John Barth, *The Floating Opera* (New York: Bantam, 1972), p. 57. Subsequent references are to this edition.

12. The terms "finite boundaries" and "unbound infinite" as well as much of my own understanding of how the sea is used in this novel come from Charles B. Harris, "Todd Andrews, Ontological Insecurity, and *The Floating Opera*," *Critique*, 18, No. 2 (1976), 34–50.

13. The depthlessness of modern man is discussed by various writers, among them: Saul Bellow, "Some Notes on Recent American Fiction," in *The Novel Today*, ed. Malcolm Bradbury (Totowa, N.J.: Rowman and Littlefield, 1977), pp. 54–69; Wylie Sypher. *The Loss of the Self in Modern Literature and Art* (New York: Vintage, 1961): and William Barrett, *Irrational Man: A Study in Existential Philosophy* (Garden City: Doubleday Anchor, 1961).

14. R.D. Laing. *Politics of Experience* (New York: Pantheon, 1969), p. 26. Subsequent references are to this edition.

MIRIAM FUCHS

"il miglior fabbro"
Gaddis' Debt to T.S. Eliot

If *The Recognitions* seems complicated and often obscure, one aspect of it remains clear, and that is the profound impact of T.S. Eliot. Perhaps only a discerning reader will realize the formal impact of the poetry—the shifting points of view, the juxtaposition of past and present, and the spatialization or organization of events according to location rather than chronology. Even a casual reader, however, will sense the thematic impact of Eliot's poetry—arid landscapes, mourning women, questers, imposters, fertility figures, chapels, bells, burials, and resurrections. Although the majority of shared motifs comes from *The Waste Land* and *The Four Quartets*, echoes can be heard from many of Eliot's poems.

Something as specific as "Twit twit twit" from *The Waste Land* (l. 203)[1] becomes the title of a book that Max or one of his friends brings to a Greenwich Village bar. Prufrock's fear that his female companion would rebuke him with "'That is not what I meant at all. / That is not it, at all'" is muttered by Otto Pivner when Esme seems less than enamored with him. Otto insists: "Oh, look, that isn't what I meant. [...] That isn't what I meant at all."[2] Guests leave a party saying, "Yes, well ghood night, eh? Ghood night ... goo night, goo night, goo night ..." (680), just as friends leave the London pub in *The Waste Land*: "Goonight Bill. Goonight Lou. Goonight May. Goonight. / Ta ta. Goonight. Goonight" (ll. 170–71). Someone asks Stanley,

---

From *In Recognition of William Gaddis*, eds. John Kuehl and Steven Moore (1984). © 1984 by Syracuse University Press.

"Is it 'Ils vont prende le train de sept heures' or 'de huit heures'" (182), and the answer may be found in Eliot's "Lune de Miel": "Ils vont prendre le train de huit heures." Stanley quotes, "It's 'birth and copulation and death'" (193) from "Fragments of an Agon" in *Sweeney Agonistes*, while a literary critic disdains "claims of time past and time future, both contained in this limicolous present" (626), varying the opening of *The Four Quartets*: "Time present and time past / Are both perhaps present in time future, / And time future contained in time past." The "Murmur of maternal lamentation" heard in *The Waste Land* (l. 368) metamorphoses into Mount Lamentation, which Wyatt sees from his window while he grows up in his father's New England parsonage. The most frequent echo derives from J. Alfred Prufrock, who reassures himself that "there will be time" to face all that he fears. When Otto asks Esme if she loves him, she answers, "If there were time" (484), and as Mr. Pivner waits day after day for Otto to call, "And still, even in sleep, he knew there would be time" (293). After his wife's death, Gwyon imagines her protestations right up to Purgatory: "If there had only been time. [...] If only there were time. [...] if you'll only tell me what I should do ..." (15). Gwyon knows there is a lesson in Camilla's death, but believes "There would be time" (ibid.) to discover it, and thirty years later he is still muttering the same refrain (419). Stanley also worries about being summoned to Purgatory without enough preparation. Unlike Mrs. Porter and her daughter in *The Waste Land*, he rarely washes, since the "overwhelming question" is: "Would he have time to wash himself to perfect newness, dress in un-worn, uncreased garments?" (321).

These examples should not give the impression that Gaddis borrows liberally and randomly from Eliot; the paraphrases and quotations are part of the form and substance of *The Recognitions*. It is as though characters and conflicts of *The Waste Land* are placed in a midtwentieth-century sound chamber so that their monologues, dialogues, inflections, and gossip are remarkably familiar. The chamber reverberates with other sounds as well, but Eliot's are an essential component. Voices rise out, fleeting but unmistakable, as testimony of underlying beauty, calm, and harmony, of (as Basil Valentine tells Wyatt) the only secret worth knowing. The secret of *The Recognitions* is the secret behind the cacophony of *The Waste Land* and the knowledge revealed through the harmonies of *The Four Quartets*. There are many perspectives through which Gaddis' dense, difficult, and brilliant novel may be understood, and Eliot's poetry is one of the most important.

Gaddis believes with Eliot that "inexplicable splendour" lies under the grime of our "unreal" cities, and, like Eliot, he darts from one location to another to reveal the extent of that grime. Also like Eliot, Gaddis creates a spatial construct in which voices at various locations seem to vibrate simultaneously in pretentious hypocrisy. The "splendour" is hard to detect.

For example, in part 1, chapter 1, the third-person point of view cuts across Paris like a camera, creating a montage from a single evening in August. As it scans the Right Bank, the Terrace of the Dôme, the Pont d'Auteuil, the Bourse, Montmartre, and the Montrouge Cemetery, part of one conversation is juxtaposed to another. The same procedure is used in New York, where Wyatt, his acquaintances, and countless anonymous citizens board buses and subways to locations in Greenwich Village and Central Park, or walk up and down the avenues. J. Alfred Prufrock hopes he will have enough time "To prepare a face to meet the faces that you meet," and the third-person voice of *The Recognitions* expands on his words: "It broke up and spread itself, in couples and threes and figures of stumbling loneliness, into the streets, into doorways, they all went into the dark repeating themselves and preparing to meet one another, to reassemble, rehearse their interchangeable disasters ..." (315). The lives of these people are, by necessity, an ongoing charade because they have renounced or lost track of their beginnings. Without this knowledge, they have no future and no opportunities for authentic growth.

Eliot's work emphasizes the need to recognize the past as a point of origin—personal, ancestral, religious, historical, and cultural. To serve as negative examples, he shows one wastelander after another enacting rituals that none of them understands, thereby debasing the fundamental meaning. In "East Coker" of *The Four Quartets*, Eliot insists that "In my beginning is my end," and without acknowledging an origin there is only fragmentation. Many characters in *The Recognitions* who are severed from their origins remain hopelessly isolated from their community and from those who care about them. Wyatt conceals part of his past from his wife Esther, and, as in *The Waste Land*, their sexual encounters become automatic and loveless, a series of isolated gestures. With masculine aggressiveness, Esther mirrors the male pursuers of *The Waste Land* who settle for impersonal responses, since lovemaking is an impersonal ritual. Their staccato dialogue could very well belong to the clerk typist and the carbuncular young man: "Wyatt? What. How are you? Fine. I mean how do you feel? Empty" (100).

Wyatt's trade as a forger of old Flemish masters elevates the execution of line above the origins of conception. Since his goal is perfection, success is ensured by reproducing what has already been produced and refined. Only years later does Wyatt realize that his respect for the perfect forgery has forestalled his own growth, something that "East Coker" warns against: "The knowledge imposes a pattern, and falsifies, / For the pattern is new in every moment / And every moment is a new and shocking / Valuation of all we have been." His knowledge is false because in using another artist's masterpiece, Wyatt accepts a pattern but rejects possibilities of newness. The pattern contains nothing that is his own and is there-fore too limited a beginning to be authentic. Gaddis puns on someone else who also sacrificed an essential part of himself for a supposedly higher goal, "Origen, that most extraordinary Father of the Church, whose third-century enthusiasm led him to castrate himself so that he might repeat the *hoc est corpus meum, Dominus*, without the distracting interference of the rearing shadow of the flesh" (103). Those who distort or abjure their personal origins, in effect, castrate their own maturation. Wyatt similarly ignores Esme's authenticity by seeing only those parts of her he can use to forge Madonnas. In contrast, Esme understands her origins and her basic nature—her free sexuality, even her addiction to drugs. Despite the disorder of her personal life, she possesses a transcendent and "inexplicable splendour" that draws other people, except Wyatt, to her.

Gaddis continues to unearth endless varieties of contemporary grime— fraud, forgery, plagiarism, counterfeiting, fear, neglect, deceit, and corruption. He also recreates the tensions between burial and resurrection, between winter and spring. Part 1 of *The Waste Land* is entitled "The Burial of the Dead," and part 1, chapter 1, of *The Recognitions* is about just that. Gwyon and his wife Camilla cross the Atlantic by ship, and she is stricken with appendicitis. The surgeon on board is forced to operate, but Frank Sinisterra, impersonating a doctor, is fleeing the American authorities who want to arrest him for counterfeiting. Like Madame Sosostris, Sinisterra's talent is limited; he cannot redeem Camilla's future, nor can "the wisest woman in Europe" (l. 45) see as much of the future as she should. After Camilla dies on the operating table, Gwyon does not allow her to be buried at sea (like Phlebas the Phoenician), and she is interred on the rise behind a Spanish village that possesses wasteland qualities. In the poem there is "Rock and no water and the sandy road / The road winding above among the mountains / Which are mountains of rock without water" (ll. 332–34). San Zwingli is similarly "built of rocks against rock, streets pouring down between houses like beds of unused rivers" (16). The prophet of *The Waste Land* insists that life can be resurrected, and Camilla, true to the symbolism of her name, becomes the flowering corpse, the dying and reviving goddess of *The Recognitions*. Those who gradually sense Camilla as part of their own origins, and those who perceive her eternal spirit as integral to their own temporal selves are moving out of the disintegration of *The Waste Land* toward the integration of *The Four Quartets*.

Wyatt is luckier than his mother. He is almost, but not quite killed by his doctors, and it seems to be Camilla's spirit that redeems him. Gaddis echoes both "Gerontion" and *The Waste Land* to emphasize the corruption of the physicians who are baffled by Wyatt's illness:

> Winter thawed into sodden spring, cruel April and depraved May reared and fell behind, and the doctors realized that this subject was nearing exhaustion, might, in fact, betray them by escaping to the dissection table. [...] With serious regret, the doctors drew their sport to a close, by agreeing on a name for it: *arathema grave*. After this crowning accomplishment, they completed the ritual by shaking hands, exchanging words of professional magic, mutual congratulation and reciprocal respect, and sent the boy home to die. (42–43)

As in *The Waste Land*, April is cruel for not bringing relief to Wyatt, who has been dying all winter. Although spring arrives, it reaches depravity before effecting renewal. "Depraved May" is taken directly from "Gerontion":

> In the juvescence of the year
> Came Christ the tiger
>
> In depraved May, dogwood and chestnut, flowering judas,
> To be eaten, to be divided, to be drunk
> Among whispers; by Mr. Silvero
> With caressing hands, at Limoges
> Who walked all night in the next room;

Wyatt parodies Eliot's Christ, appearing in spring but falling into the hands of imposters who divide and mutilate their victim. The doctors' sham rituals around Wyatt's emaciated body echo the actions of Mr. Silvero, Hakagawa, and Madame de Tornquist, who all fail to resurrect the body of Christ. In the "juvescence" of his twelfth year, Wyatt is sent home to die. It is no wonder, then, that an anonymous voice later reminisces about an earlier time of youthful innocence: "In Istanbul in the summer, [...] it was Istanbul, wasn't it? We used to take long rides in the cistern, in the summer ... " (74). Even though the rides occurred in the summer, the gentleness and nostalgia bring to mind Marie's recollection of sledding in *The Waste Land*: "And when we were children, staying at the archduke's, / My cousin's, he took me out on a sled, / And I was frightened. He said, Marie, / Marie, hold on tight. And down we went" (ll. 13–16).

Wyatt's father quietly puts his ailing son in touch with eternal spirits. Gwyon understands the ineffable relationship between Camilla's spirit and the Barbary ape he brought home from Spain. The whole family silently understands this connection, especially after the animal uproots Aunt May's beloved hawthorn tree, an action that quickly leads to the death of Wyatt's fanatic Calvinist aunt. No one mourns. Gwyon brings the ape to Wyatt's bedside and murders it in ritual sacrifice. Wyatt screams in pain, imagining that nails are being driven through his feet. Sacrifice of the animal, in which Camilla seems reincarnated, leads to Wyatt's recovery.

In contrast to characters such as Wyatt, who eventually struggle to "unweave, unwind, unravel / And piece together the past and the future" ("The Dry Salvages"), are the hordes of humanity who ignore the past and debase their origins. Otto Pivner connects "Nothing with nothing" like the masses in *The Waste Land* (l. 302) despite his attempts to connect everything to himself. His origins belong to other people because he steals aesthetic vocabulary from Wyatt, romantic phrases from Esme, mannerisms from observing his reflection in mirrors. He counterfeits his past (Did he, in fact, graduate from Yale?), and so he has no future. He immediately transforms his experiences into the play he is writing so that he hardly has any present. The moment he thinks something significant has occurred to him, Otto imagines his protagonist, Gordon, one step further in the play. Symbolically, Otto is writing himself out of existence. When Dr. Fell calls him by the name of Gordon, Otto answers.

Agnes Deigh's husband relinquished his last name when he married. Giving up his original identity contributes to the sterility of their marriage. Agnes and her husband live apart, do not make love, meet occasionally for breakfast. Agnes' sexuality suffers further when she cannot convince guests at a party that she is really a woman, not a man in drag. Dozens of other characters similarly show the disastrous results of denying origins and debasing traditional rituals. Obfuscated by ignorance or greed, the quest for renewal becomes a travesty. Tony Tanner summarizes the congestion of wastelander activity in *The Recognitions*: "Life becomes a sort of ongoing carnival of clutter, filling up with stuff at the same time as it seems to be coming apart and falling to bits."[3]

The antipode to the confusion, barrenness, and rootlessness is the "inexplicable splendour," apprehensible to only a few. Concealed but immutable, it is the fulfillment that derives from knowing one's beginnings. It is the recognition of the eternal and the sacred in the midst of the temporal and the profane. Those in *The Waste Land* who understand the challenge of such splendor are most often the first-person personae. These include the subjective voices of the German aristocrat, the speaker who addresses Stetson, the Thames poet, the Old Testament poet, Ferdinand from *The Tempest*, Tiresias, the Fisher King, Buddha, and Saint Augustine. Their lines rise above the discontinuous twits and jugs of the poem to blend into a single, coherent, but fluid consciousness.

Robert Langbaum explains these personae, who usually speak very briefly, as comprising a single protagonist but not in the usual sense. The "I" is the total of each voice from each epoch; it "acquires delineation or identity not through individuation but through making connection with ancient archetypes."[4] Each voice—the saint, the poet, the king, whoever—is a tribute to the order of the past and a lament over the chaos of the present. For instance, as the woman in the burnished bedroom reproaches her companion for knowing nothing, seeing nothing, and remembering nothing, the voice of Ariel from *The Tempest* breaks through: "I remember / Those are pearls that were his eyes" (ll. 125–26). This line nostalgically recalls a beauty to which the woman is oblivious. Other lines of first-person personae similarly recall harmony and lyricism: "By the waters of Leman I sat down and wept ..." (l. 183); "Sweet Thames, run softly, for I speak not loud or long" (l. 184); "O Lord Thou pluckest me out" (l. 309); "We who were living are now dying" (l. 329); "Shall I at least set my lands in order?" (l. 426). These and other lines lament that the past has been severed from the present, and "East Coker" urges the same need to recover the past: "There is only the fight to recover what has been lost / And found and lost again and again." A similar fight takes place in *The Recognitions*. Evidence of authenticity may be found beneath a forgery, expressed by a murderer, conveyed by a drug addict, or obscured by insipid and incessant talk; but it exists, enduring and everlasting.

An ever-present consciousness, represented by the "I," finds its way into *The Recognitions*. The meaning of the first-person voice is contrasted to the meaning behind the third-person voice. For instance, when Esme realizes that Wyatt will never love her, will use her only as a starting point for his forged Madonnas, she tries to discard what he "stole" by referring to herself in third person. Otto asks if she has been modeling, and Esme replies: "Sometimes she did" (482) and "She does not see him anymore" (483). "You'll be all right alone? Now she will" (484). One afternoon Agnes Deigh writes to a dentist, asking for the meaning behind his middle initial, which just happens to be "I." Stanley's translation of a Michelangelo poem laments the theft of the "I":

O God, O God, O God,
Who has taken me from myself

>   from me myself
> Who was closest (closer) to me
> And could do more than I
>   most about me
>   What can I do? (322)

Basil Valentine, the art dealer who sells Wyatt's forgeries, expresses the fragility of the authentic "I": "There's as much difference between us and ourselves as between ourselves and others?" (553). When Wyatt, in despair, declares that "*No one knows who I am*" (439), he is right, and only painfully and gradually does he learn the expansive implications of the "I," Recognition of his inviolable self will lead him to a profound unity, a unity understood by each "I" of *The Waste Land*.

The fleeting first-person voices of *The Waste Land* emerge unpredictably, and together they establish a subtle but unmistakable presence. Camilla's spirit also manifests itself in unlikely places and through unlikely characters, and it unifies the living and the dead, Catholicism and Protestantism, Spain and America. Wyatt perceives it at the moment of Camilla's death even though he cannot know she has died. Her spirit emanates through the Barbary ape Gwyon brings home from San Zwingli as though metempsychosis has taken place. In addition, Camilla's body is mistaken for the little girl next to whom she is buried. Instead of exhuming the remains of the Roman Catholic rape victim, the Spanish authorities send Camilla's Protestant bones to Rome, where they are canonized and worshiped by thousands of Catholic pilgrims.

Although he does not know it, Wyatt is inextricably linked to Esme through Camilla. Esme becomes the next incarnation of her eternal spirit. As Wyatt's warehouse goes up in flames, Esme discovers a set of earrings. She runs into another room and pierces holes through her ears: "When she came out, wearing the Byzantine earrings, there was blood on them and on her shoulders, running down in singular unpaired lines over her bared breasts" (469–70). Esme cannot realize that she performs an action Camilla performed forty years earlier. A guest had brought the same set of earrings as a gift for the young bride. Without even waiting for him to depart, Camilla had dashed into another room, pushed the needles through her lobes, and "burst in again with wild luster in her eyes, wearing the gold earrings, blood all over them" (14). Doing what she feels she must, Esme naturally partakes in cyclical time and ritual, achieving a deep communion with Camilla.

The instant Camilla's spirit manifests itself, Esme seems transformed, suddenly enriched with the knowledge of the ages. She composes a letter to

Wyatt to protest his treatment of her. Her earlier efforts to write amounted to nothing but ludicrous imitations of *carpe diem* poetry. Now her prose is muddled, but sophisticated and abstruse. She writes about the nature of painting, reality, and death, transcending her limitations of self-expression just as her beauty has always transcended her own awareness.

This transformation is important because it represents a successful unity that other characters in the novel strive for. The difficulty of achieving it is stated in "Burnt Norton":

> Words strain,
> Crack and sometimes break, under the burden,
> Under the tension, slip, slide, perish,
> Decay with imprecision, will not stay in place,
> Will not stay still.

Gaddis chooses specific words from this passage to convey Esme's struggle to write before she finds Camilla's earrings:

> The words which the tradition of her art offered her were by now in chaos, coerced through the contexts of a million inanities, [...] and when they reached her hands they were brittle, straining and cracking, sometimes they broke under the burden which her tense will imposed, and she found herself clutching their fragments, attempting again with this shabby equipment her raid on the inarticulate. (299)

Both authors place writing in a tactile context where words are rigid, easily cracked, having been corrupted by "Shrieking voices / Scolding, mocking, or merely chattering, / Always assail[ing] those who try to purify them ("Burnt Norton").

Camilla's presence infuses not just Esme, but also Wyatt, though he must first journey back to Spain. His experience seems right out of "The Dry Salvages":

> But to apprehend
> The point of intersection of the timeless
> With time, is an occupation for the saint—
> No occupation either, but something given
> And taken, in a lifetime's death in love,
> Ardour and selflessness and self-surrender.

Wyatt is the quester, embedded in linear time, finally meeting the buried corpse, now part of sacred time, on consecrated ground, where heaven and earth intersect. Camilla, of course, is soon to become a saint through error, and Wyatt learns from her that love and necessity become, at some point, synonymous. Self-surrender does not mean obliterating one's self and origins for a work of art; it does mean, however, that one surrenders the notion of perfection (and thereby surrenders forgery) in order to accept the imperfections of a life that must be lived through.

Unassailable knowledge emerges not just through the omnipresent "I," but also through a second device—spatialization. Resembling the straight cut in film editing as opposed to the dissolve, spatialization rests on the assumption that physical location is as effective as chronology in unifying material. An author is therefore free to jump from one city to the next as Eliot does in *The Waste Land*. *The Four Quartets* is similarly built upon a spatial foundation, for history is perceived according to geography, not linearity. "Burnt Norton" refers to a house in Gloucestershire and "East Coker" to Somersetshire, England; "The Dry Salvages" to rocks near the Massachusetts coastline; and "Little Gidding" to an Anglican village in seventeenth-century England. Although time shifts back and forth and scenes constantly change, the geography provides a clearly discernible structure that cuts across the boundaries of time.

Sharon Spencer describes this technique as a device by which "every location in space, every *lieu*, is infused with its own time, or simultaneity of times."[5] Since each chronological period is subsumed by the location, a spatialized work lacks sharp divisions between past, present, and future. Gaddis often achieves this blurring of time. Neither the third-person narrative nor the characters are particularly precise about time, and voices drone on for too many pages at a time, from too many separate conversations, for chronology to remain clear. But location is crucial. For instance, the motif of barren terrain heightens the reflexive quality of *The Recognitions* and provides unity. Whenever a tourist approaches San Zwingli, nearly identical words describe it. It is first mentioned as close to a "rock-strewn plain" (7). Next comes an expanded version:

> San Zwingli appeared suddenly, at a curve in the railway, a town built of rocks against rock, streets pouring down between houses like beds of unused rivers, with the houses littered like boulders carelessly against each other along a mountain stream. Swallows dove and swept with appalling certainty at the tower of the church. (16)

More than an abundance of rocks suggests that Gaddis was thinking of "What the Thunder Said." The mountains need water, a chapel is present, and Eliot's hermit thrush is now swallows, reminiscent of the line, "*Quando fiam uti chelidon*—O swallow swallow" (l. 429). This same passage is repeated almost word for word in part 3, chapter 3, when Sinisterra approaches the village just as Gwyon did: "San Zwingli appeared suddenly, at a curve in the railway" (776). There are only slight differences. Gwyon had climbed "to the pines behind the tower," and Sinisterra climbs "the hill toward the town." Gwyon had "paused to breathe the freshness of manure," and Sinisterra pauses to sniff the surrounding pines before noticing "the delicious freshness of cow manure." Both voyagers rediscover "senses long forgotten under the abuse of cities."

When Wyatt goes to the monastery where Gwyon recuperated after Camilla's death, he finds the old man who tolls the bells of a secluded chapel (which appear in both *The Waste Land* and *The Four Quartets*). The old man turns out to be the murderer of the little girl next to whom Camilla was buried. Rather than being sent to prison, he was allowed to live close to the location of his sin, where he daily recalls the action by tolling the bells. The old man possesses the only secret worth knowing and attempts to teach it to the younger penitent. But one morning Wyatt finds the entrance to the monastery locked. Suddenly he realizes that the murderer's penance has taught him something about the enduring nature of sin, but that he himself must complete the lesson. *The Four Quartets* could be used to describe Wyatt's progress. "The Dry Salvages" suggests that such "moments of agony ... are likewise permanent" and that "We appreciate this better / In the agony of others, nearly experienced / Involving ourselves, than in our own." The old man's agony has involved Wyatt, but now he must see himself as the sole source of his sins and the sole origin of his future. Each moment lived and each selfish act reverberate endlessly; what might have been in his life and what actually took place "Point to one end, which is always present" ("Burnt Norton").

Wyatt cannot reverse time in order to redeem the past. Gaddis and Eliot both believe that the most fulfilling and authentic way to perceive life is spatially and eternally, absorbing chronology into larger dimensions and harmonies. Wyatt decides that living in the present means he will "marry someone else's mistake, to atone for one of your own somewhere else, dull and dead the day it begins" (898). One person's beginning must intersect with another person's middle, which may intersect with a third person's end, and so on. This is the means by which contraries are resolved: "And right action is freedom / From past and future also" and "Time the destroyer becomes time the preserver" ("The Dry Salvages"). Wyatt makes his decision:

> —And how do you atone? By locking yourself up in remorse for what you might have done? Or by living it through. [...] Or by going back and living it through. [...] If it was sin from the start, and possible all the time, to know it's possible and avoid it? Or by living it through. (896)

He can't return to Esther or Esme, and he can no longer live in a rarefied atmosphere of perfection, which is merely a sham. Living, giving, and allowing himself to receive from others is the only secret worth searching for and worth knowing.

Wyatt's lesson takes place approximately nine hundred pages through the novel. It is a dramatic climax to the coherent narrative thread of his life. Knowing that the plot will motivate a reader to push forward through hundreds of pages of spatialized conversations, Gaddis withholds the climax as long as possible. *The Recognitions*, though, is about both missed and successful discoveries. The reader who concentrates on a linear pattern will probably miss the central message of the novel that first appears hundreds of pages earlier. The reader who thinks spatially, looking for recurrent patterns, settings, and dialogues, can discover the theme when it first occurs. Gaddis shares with Eliot the insistence that sacred knowledge is everywhere, and so he inserts it in earlier chapters, as Eliot inserts it in the "I" personae of *The Waste Land*. The knowledge is described in *The Four Quartets*, but it is placed in each section so that it will harmonize with the next.

Characters who express timeless knowledge are themselves unaware of what they know—another missed recognition. For example, Agnes Deigh writes to the dentist, Dr. Weisgall. She apologizes for having informed the police that she saw him through a window beating a young woman. Told by police that this was his own daughter, she writes: "'Dear Doctor Weisgall. Perhaps it is not until late in life that we realize that we do not, ever, pay for our own mistakes. We pay for the mistakes of others, and they ... '" (556). Her words nearly match Wyatt's final recognition: "To run back looking for every one of them [mistakes]? every one of them, no, it's too easy. [...] the sin is only boring and dead the moment it happens, it's only the living it through that redeems it" (898). The meaning is the same: although knowledge may come late, each person is not punished directly for his mistakes and cannot atone directly for them; he is punished for someone else's and atones for someone else's, just as that person does for him. Agnes' letter seems unimportant only because the reader is probably concentrating on Wyatt, not on the content of a letter written by a character who has nothing to do with the linear tale.

Mrs. Deigh is not the only person to express the central idea of the novel. Frank Sinisterra also learns that he has not been punished directly for killing Camilla on his operating table. When he meets Wyatt in Spain and learns that Wyatt is Camilla's son, he knows it is time to atone. Time past and time future are contained in time present, and Sinisterra's words echo Agnes Deigh's letter: "No, you can't You can't ... not to them, but you ... if you've like sinned against one person, then you make it up to another, that's all you can do, you never know when you ... until the time comes when you can make it up to another. Like I once ... this woman, I ..."(814).

Perhaps even more ironic than these lost lessons is the fact that Wyatt himself expresses the problem of seeing behind a familiar form. Describing a revelation from Picasso's *Fishing at Antibes*, he explains:

> —When I saw it all of a sudden everything was freed into one recognition, really freed into reality that we never see, you never see it. You don't see it in paintings because most of the time you can't see beyond a painting. Most paintings, the instant you see them they become familiar, and then it's too late. (92)

Wyatt forgets his own words about looking past the predictable in order to reach what is meaningful, and his warning applies also to the reader of *The Recognitions*. The conventions of a particular form may cause a reader to apprehend less than what is there. Like the fixed and mechanical lives of wastelanders that forestall individual development, an automatic and conventional response to *The Recognitions* will delay an understanding of Gaddis' themes.

Another way to discover the central idea of this novel is to go beyond its dizzying surface to the work of T.S. Eliot. Wyatt's development can be viewed in the context of *The Four Quartets*, while the civilization that crumbles around him can be viewed in the context of *The Waste Land*. This comparison in no way diminishes the individual accomplishment of William Gaddis. In fact, it was Eliot who said that skilled writers will always benefit by being looked at in relation to the great writers of the past, while the derivative writers will be exposed: "It is a judgment, a comparison, in which two things are measured by each other."[6] Understanding Eliot as the echo in the garden, the voice behind the waterfall, the pattern behind the prose is essential. First, it provides a literary background for this difficult novel, and second, it reveals *The Recognitions* as among the most sophisticated and rewarding literary works of the twentieth century.

Notes

1. All quotations from Eliot's poetry have been taken from *Collected Poems: 1909–1962* (New York: Harcourt, Brace & World, 1963).

2. William Gaddis, *The Recognitions* (New York: Harcourt, Brace & World, 1955), 447. Subsequent references to this work will be cited parenthetically in the text.

3. Tony Tanner, review of *The Recognitions*, *New York Times Book Review*, 14 July, 1974, 27.

4. Robert Langbaum, "New Modes of Characterization in *The Waste Land*," in *Eliot in His Time: Essays on the Occasion of the Fiftieth Anniversary of "The Waste Land,"* ed. A. Walton Litz (Princeton: Princeton University Press, 1973), 100.

5. Sharon Spencer, *Space, Time and Structure in the Modern Novel* (New York: New York University Press, 1971), xx.

6. T.S. Eliot, "Tradition and the Individual Talent," in *Selected Prose of T.S. Eliot*, ed. Frank Kermode (New York: Harcourt Brace Jovanovich, 1975), 39.

STEPHEN H. MATANLE

*Love and Strife
in William Gaddis'* JR

The Problem of Chaos

William Gaddis' *JR* is a novel without conventional narrative divisions. And yet this apparently seamless novel is about things coming apart at the seams. In this sense, *JR* continues the investigation of a problem that Gaddis identified in his notes for *The Recognitions* as "the separating of things today without love."[1] Characters in *JR* find themselves separated from each other, and from themselves, in a variety of ways. The human body is fragmented, reduced to separate parts, and physical contact among characters is often hazardous. This situation is compounded by a kind of ocular chaos, a fragmentation of the visual field, for which eyeglasses are a metonymy. Most important, human communication, reduced to disembodied speech, frequently generates misunderstanding and disorder.

Jack Gibbs, a science teacher and failed writer, is the novel's preeminent authority on disorder. In fact, his first speech in the novel is an impromptu lecture on precisely this subject. Interrupting a studio lesson, Gibbs makes a futile effort to enlighten his students by challenging their assumptions about order:

—Before we go any further here, has it ever occurred to any of you that all this is simply one grand misunderstanding? Since

---

From *In Recognition of William Gaddis*, eds. John Kuehl and Steven Moore (1984). © 1984 by Syracuse University Press.

> you're not here to learn anything, but to be taught so you can pass these tests, knowledge has to be organized so it can be taught, and it has to be reduced to information so it can be organized do you follow that? In other words this leads you to assume that organization is an inherent property of the knowledge itself, and that disorder and chaos are simply irrelevant forces that threaten it from outside. In fact it's exactly the opposite. Order is simply a thin, perilous condition we try to impose on the basic reality of chaos ... ²

Although Gibbs is talking specifically about the reduction of knowledge to information, the significance of his remarks transcends this immediate context, for in the world that he inhabits, chaos is inherent in virtually every aspect of human life.

Gibbs is concerned throughout *JR* with the difficulty of imposing order on "the basic reality of chaos ..." This notion clearly informs the book he has been trying to write, as well as his attitude toward it. He describes it to Amy Joubert as "a book about order and disorder more of a, sort of a social history of mechanization and the arts" (244). Order is both the subject and the strategy of the book. A history of organization, it represents Gibbs' effort to organize imaginatively the past. However, the book exists only as a fragment. Begun over ten years ago, it remains unfinished. When Gibbs finally tries to resume work on the book, he can barely "get going on it" (583). Victimized by various distractions and by a lack of energy, he spends most of his time reading aloud from the first part of the book, losing his place, making a few minor changes, and searching for his notes. However, when he accidentally finds the notes in one of the cardboard boxes crammed into the Ninety-sixth-Street apartment, he is appalled by the evidence of his own ambition: "'God hundreds of them' ... finally coming to rest on H–O with the torn carton drawn close 'started with eighteen seventy-six have to get them all back in, Christ how did I, look at that what did I think I was doing!'" (586). By "getting a fresh start" (565) on the book, Gibbs had hoped to restore some order to his life and to demonstrate to Amy his strength of purpose. Yet his work is repeatedly interrupted by telephone calls, a nice irony, since the notes for his book "started with eighteen seventy-six" (586), the year the telephone was invented. His energy dissipated and his concentration fragmented, Gibbs finally abandons the book. In a sense, his "social history" is a victim of what it diagnoses, as it succumbs to the very conditions it describes.

Gibbs' preoccupation with order and chaos also informs his frequently allusive speech. For example, when he accosts Edward Bast and Amy Joubert in a New York cafeteria, he weaves allusions to T.S. Eliot's "Hysteria" into his speech: "Get those breasts to stop shaking we may be able to collect some fragments of the afternoon I'll concentrate on that" (120). Like the speaker in Eliot's prose poem, Gibbs embarks on a project to combat distraction. Trying to convince Edward Bast that Amy is "out on her feet," Gibbs claims that "in spite of its appetizing symmetry woman's body's an absolute God damned chaos" (ibid.). In *JR*, however, it is not merely the female body that is a chaos, but the human body. Furthermore, this notion is reinforced by Gibbs' several allusions to Empedocles.

The Rule of Strife

In an early scene in *JR* a character named Gall, who has been hired by a foundation to write a book on its "in-school television support program" (39), visits the school on Long Island where much of the novel's action takes place. Stopping to copy down the motto inscribed above the main entrance, he explains to Mr. Ford, the program specialist: "it might make a good epigraph for this book when I find out what it means" (20). A little later in the novel, during a conversation in the school principal's office, Gall asks Jack Gibbs about the motto: "That line over the main entrance here? in Greek? I thought, is it Plato? or ... " (45). Gibbs suggests that he "try Empedocles," and while Gall tries to spell it, Gibbs continues: "I think it's a fragment from the second generation of his cosmogony, maybe even the first ... " (ibid.). In any case, it represents a stage in the life of the world "when limbs and parts of bodies were wandering around everywhere separately ... " (ibid.). A few pages later Major Hyde, a member of the school board, complains: "I'm trying to have a serious discussion with these Foundation people on closed-circuit broadcast and you butt in with arms and legs flying around somebody's eyes looking for their forehead what was all that supposed to be!" (48). Gibbs replies: "He was asking about one of the pre-Socratics, Major, the rule of love and the rule of strife in the cosmic cycle of Emp ... " (ibid.). Like some of Gibbs' other allusions, such as the one to Eliot, this allusion to Empedocles is partly a characterization of his immediate environment and partly a reflection of his ideas about order and chaos.

Gibbs' advice to Gall, that he "try Empedocles," is curious in a couple of respects, not the least of which is that the inscription over the main entrance does not come from Empedocles. Furthermore, Gibbs knows this. As Whiteback, the school principal, explains: "It was his idea to make it look like a quotation from Herkahm, yes from the classics that is to say simply by adding curlicues to the letters in that motto his friend Schepperman gave us which sounded ahm, sounded all right at the time of course until we found out it was communist" (456). In fact, the motto is a familiar quotation from Marx's *Critique of the Gotha Program*: "From each according to his ability, to each according to his needs." Thus, without the curlicues, the motto reads: "FROM EACH ACCORD ... " (20). However, once this mystery is solved, it still remains unclear why Gibbs attributes the quotation to Empedocles. The answer, I think, is that Gibbs is being ironical. Far from embodying Marx's ideal, the school's teachers and administrators are almost uniformly incompetent, and the children's needs are routinely ignored. This discrepancy is further emphasized by the implicit contrast between Marx's vision of harmony and Empedocles' "rule of strife." More important, Gibbs' allusion is, at least in part, a response to what is going on around him. In the wake of Edward Bast's unorthodox presentation on Mozart, the principal's office is in chaos. Hurrying to switch off the television set, Major Hyde trips over somebody's foot. A control knob comes off in Congressman Pecci's hand. Bodies are cropped arbitrarily by the television camera. Meanwhile, Bast relates the "fairy tale life" (40) of Mozart, interspersed with scatological excerpts from Mozart's letter of 28 February 1778 to his cousin Maria Anna Thekla. This scene of disorder, then, inspires Gibbs' allusion to Empedocles.

Empedocles' world is ruled by two forces, Love and Strife. The function of Love is to unite, to make one out of many, and incidentally to cause rest. The function of Strife is to separate, to disperse things without apparent design, and incidentally to cause movement. These two forces rule in periodic alternation. Love combines and binds the elements into the Sphere, a single, homogeneous whole. However, at a certain time, "fixed ... by a broad oath,"[3] the power of Strife begins to increase until it finally destroys the perfect balance of the Sphere and "scatters the elements randomly, so that they enter into haphazard combinations with one another."[4] According to Denis O'Brien, "Strife's share is essentially a process, a battle, a time of change and conflict, a time of increase and decline, where there is no place for victory and so for peace and permanence."[5] Now if this is the nature of Strife's influence, it seems reasonable to assume that the world of *JR* may be represented as being ruled by Strife. Much of the novel's action happens in a "town where all allusion to permanence had disappeared or was being slain" (18). Moreover, one of the novel's major concerns is the separation of a common language into different modes of discourse. As O'Brien suggests, "our own world falls in the period of movement when the power of Strife is on the increase."[6] Furthermore, "as time goes on, the power of Strife in the world becomes even greater, the different parts of our bodies will no longer be, able to hold together."⁷ This is precisely the situation dramatized by *JR*. The body is incoherent, fragmented into a variety of parts, deprived of stability and balance.

The possibility that *JR* represents a world that is ruled by Love is easily dismissed. The separating power of Strife clearly holds sway over most of the human relationships in the novel. Love is either absent or deformed by selfishness. Edward Bast suffers from a hopelessly romantic obsession with his cousin Stella, underscored by his trying to set to music Tennyson's "Locksley Hall." Stella in turn uses Edward's desire in order to retain control of a family business. When Miriam Eigen asks her son how much he loves her, he replies: "Some money ... ?" (267). And Jack Gibbs, the only character in the novel who says "I love you" (501), waits for Amy Joubert to return from Switzerland and then, according to Thomas Eigen, avoids her: "When she finally called he wouldn't speak to her, heard her voice he pretended he was an old black retainer" (725). Most of the marriages in the novel end in divorce, and families are consequently divided and dispersed. There is not even any guarantee that members of one's family are blood relations. "Dad" diCephalis turns out to be "An elderly drifter" (685) who eats dog food and plays the saxophone. His true identity is unknown, as both Dan and Ann diCephalis have assumed that he is the other's father. In these and other instances, human relationships fail to exhibit the cohesion that characterizes the rule of Love.

In his poem *On Nature*, Empedocles emphasizes the effects of Love and Strife on the development of mortal creatures. Furthermore, he sometimes conceives of the Sphere, produced by the increasing power of Love, in anatomical terms. For example, in fragment 29 Empedocles defines the Sphere negatively. It consists in the absence of protrusions: "For there do not start two branches from his back; [he has] no feet, no swift knees, no organs of reproduction; but he was a Sphere, and in all directions equal to himself." By contrast, fragment 57 describes a world no longer whole but divided into a variety of parts: "many foreheads without necks sprang forth, and arms wandered unattached, bereft of shoulders, and eyes strayed about alone, needing brows." This is the fragment which Gibbs refers to in his conversation with Gall. In that same conversation, Gibbs summarizes fragments 59–61, a description of the stage in which "parts are joining up by chance, form creatures with countless hands, faces looking in different directions ... " (45). These same images reappear later in the novel as Gibbs is jostled in Penn Station: "elbows found ribs and shoulders backs 'place is like the dawn of the world here, this way' ... countless hands and unattached eyes, faces looking in different directions" (161). The narrative description here corroborates Gibbs' analogy between the subway passengers and Empedocles' "creatures" by employing images taken directly from Empedocles. Yet the reduction of the body to its parts is not confined to the passengers on the subway.

Throughout *JR* characters are consistently presented in terms of their hands, feet, elbows, knees, eyes, backs, shoulders. And these separate parts accidentally come into contact with others. In the second scene of *JR*, one of the novel's many bodily collisions occurs:

> Bast's elbow caught Mrs Joubert a reeling blow in the breast, she dropped the sack of coins and he stood for an instant poised with raised hand in pursuit of that injury before the flush that spread from her face to his sent him stooping to recover the sack by the top, spilling the coins from its burst bottom into the unmown strip of grass, and left him kneeling down where the wind moved her skirt. (19)

A moment later, as Bast tries to recover the spilled coins, Amy Joubert steps on his hand. Jack Gibbs, wherever he goes, creates a disturbance when he tries to arrange his limbs. For example, sitting beside Amy on the train, he finally manages to get "one knee wedged over the other looking deliberately slumped, a foot dangling in the aisle" (244). On a similar occasion, Amy complains: "Your knee can you move your knee, Jack can't you just sit ... " (476). JR, a sixth-grader and the title character of the novel, is as restless as Gibbs. Sitting next to Edward Bast on the train, JR tries to arrange himself:

> He wedged a sneaker more tightly into the seat ahead bringing the heap higher with his knees, sinking slowly until a nostril came in reach of his thumb, finally—I just wondered, I mean can you make much doing that? writing this here music I mean? he paused, his elbow grinding against the arm hung limp beside him. (127)

The human body in *JR* is an awkward assemblage of limbs. Moreover, characters tend to move clumsily and abruptly. This tendency is emphasized only when their movements accidentally resemble dance steps. For example, Whiteback, as he moves toward his car, is described as having "retired in the box step of the rhumba" (19), and Jack Gibbs, in a New York cafeteria, makes "an abrupt turn that the right bar of music just then might have claimed for a moment from a tango" (115). One might expect the body to behave more gracefully in erotic contexts, but this is not the case. In fact, during the sexual act, limbs often seem to have been "caught in some random climax of catastrophe" (137). This is, in Empedocles' terms, simply one more instance of the dominance of Strife over Love.

In the only idyllic scene in the novel, Jack Gibbs and Amy Joubert spend a weekend together, during which they frequently make love. However, it is sometimes difficult to know precisely what they are doing. Even the simplest descriptions of their bodies seem fragmented: "The weight of her leg warm over his gone rigid for his twist away leaving only his back to her where she kissed his shoulder in the darkness and clung as though for warmth until, as of its own weight, it eased away" (483). In this passage, the merely contiguous relations among separate parts of the body suggest a certain tension between Love and Strife. Indeed, Gibbs has just experienced the frustration of impotence induced by alcohol and eagerness. Yet even when the descriptions concern sexual acts, the lovers' bodies are never represented as whole, but rather as constellations of fingers, shoulders, knees, elbows, and orifices:

> ... where his lips moved she suddenly fell wide, hand drawing closer stripping vein and color as his knee rose over her and jarred the telephone, still holding closed as though against a sudden plunge, or sudden loss, when the telephone rang, her arms came free, came up, her shoulders' struggle against his knee come down and legs drawn tight in a twist away as the telephone box went to the floor and she got the receiver wrong end round. (493)

This passage is not unlike those describing the faction of limbs on the train. The fragmentation of the body makes it difficult to visualize the action. Moreover, this is characteristic of the entire novel. The reader cannot always easily "see" what is going on. Instead, he must rely on what he "hears." Yet discourse too is ruled by Strife, whose influence may be observed in the plurality of voices, the separation of words from the things they name, and the disembodiment of speech.

THE PLURALITY OF DISCOURSE

JR consists almost entirely of dialogue, of "voices meeting and parting" (155). Perhaps the most prominent characteristic of verbal discourse in *JR* is its heterogeneity. The novel is traversed by all kinds of discourse: social, economic, legal, political, scientific, literary. As these modes of discourse intersect, compete, and absorb one another, it becomes increasingly clear that no one of them is privileged. Each authorizes itself.

The extent to which these various modes of discourse succeed in asserting their authority depends largely on their instrumental value. Early in the novel, Jack Gibbs asks the school principal about the source of his nearly incomprehensible jargon: "Speak of tangibilitating unplanlessness, where'd you pick up that language, Whiteback?" Whiteback defends his jargon by relying on an implicitly instrumentalist view of language: "You, you have to speak it when you talk to them" (50). In a world of duplicity, you use double-talk. There is no true word, no inevitable correspondence between sign and referent. Thus, when Edward Bast accuses JR of using a word without knowing what it means, JR replies, "so why should I have to know exactly what it means?" (296). After all, he is paying a lawyer to know what words mean.

Yet lawyers, in *JR* at least, are not always the most reliable arbiters of disputes about the meaning of a word. In a conversation with Anne and Julia Bast, a lawyer named Coen offends and confuses the two elderly sisters by using words like "bastard," "lunatic," and "emancipated" in their special legal sense. Mr. Beaton, of the law firm Beaton, Broos and Black, must explain to Amy Joubert that he is using the word *charity* "in its tax law connotation" (212). Words such as *charity* are especially susceptible to being degraded in *JR*, presumably because they do not refer to anything tangible. One of the clearest examples of what an instrumentalist view of language can do to words is JR's definition of "goodwill." Near the end of the novel, Bast complains about JR's attempt to "find out how much all that goodwill is worth" (654), and JR replies, "No wait hey I mean holy shit I don't mean where everybody's crazy about us and all, see goodwill that means the excess of the purchase price over the value of these net tangible assets." Bast, of course, violently protests: "That's not what it means!" (655). However, Bast is wrong insofar as he fails to recognize the extent to which meaning is contextual.

Several of the novel's characters, including Bast, resist the dissociation of signs from their referents. Amy Joubert, for example, clings sentimentally to a reference theory of language. When she sees the words "ethical product" used to describe a prescription drug, she is appalled. On another occasion, Mr. Davidoff, a public-relations man, addresses her social studies class in front of the Treasury steps. After listening to him talk about "standing here in the cradle of American history" (82), Amy wonders "who ever stood in a cradle" (118). Amy Joubert shares with Esme, a character in Gaddis' first novel, *The Recognitions*, a sense that words have been hopelessly debased, that language is "in chaos, coerced through the contexts of a million inanities."[8] But whereas Esme tries to recover that moment when words were indistinguishable from the things they named, Amy merely laments its passing. In *The Order of Things*, Michel Foucault describes this rupture by invoking the story of Babel:

> In its original form, when it was given to men by God himself, language was an absolutely certain and transparent sign for things, because it resembled them .... This transparency was destroyed at Babel as a punishment for men. Languages became separated and incompatible with one another only insofar as they had previously lost this original resemblance to the things that had been the prime reason for the existence of language. And the languages known to us are now spoken only against the background of this lost similitude, and in the space that it left vacant.[9]

The story of Babel, then, dramatizes the fall of the word from its original harmony with the world. Language is henceforth dispersed, and the space "left vacant" by "this lost similitude" is filled with a proliferation of words, a multitude of voices, a plurality of discourse.

One of the most distinctive voices in *JR* belongs to Whiteback. In a conversation with Vern, the district superintendent, his speech is characteristically hesitant and diffuse: "Yes well of course we ahm, community-relationswise that is to say Vern you don't get popular support without the ahm, how did that Flesch woman put it yes without the support of the community of course she had a gift for expressing ideas and my job is ahm ... " (220). Whiteback in fact has two jobs. He is both the school principal and president of the bank. As such he exemplifies the confusion and disorder generated by competing modes of discourse. When Gibbs asks whether he has considered giving up either the bank or the school, Whiteback replies: "Yes well of course the ahm, when I know which one of them is going to survive" (340–41). Near the end of the novel, the question is effectively settled when the school is purchased by the JR Corp and operated by a Mr. Stye, "which he's like this branch manager" (649). By that time, however, Whiteback has been given a job with the FCC.

The irony of Whiteback's new career is impossible to miss, since his own powers of communication are so feeble. Intimidated by the very language he insists on using, Whiteback often finds himself hopelessly entangled in tautologies and circular arguments. On one such occasion, he tries to explain that he has had to turn down Dan diCephalis' application to refinance the mortgage on his house because of an irregularity in its construction. It is perhaps worth quoting a substantial portion of this speech, as it typifies Whiteback's use of language:

> —Yes no nobody's blaming you Dan, we know you didn't build it yourself it was, of course it was the builder who ahm, who built it of course but the, since the term of a mortgage is related to, dictated by the number of years the house is reasonably expected to stand depending on its, directly related to the way it's built, constructed you might say, the wall studs having a direct bearing on the part of the structure so that of course the farther apart they are in a given space the fewer there are of them because the fewer there are of them the farther apart they have to be placed. (226–27)

In cases such as this, one might say that Whiteback's language is speaking him, dragging him along behind it. Yet in spite of its redundancy and circumlocution, this instance of Whiteback's speech seems quite lucid compared to his telephone conversations. In the course of the novel, he has a telephone line to his bank installed in the principal's office. As a result, bank business and school business furiously compete for his attention, the two telephones sometimes "ranting at each other" (180), as they are elsewhere in the novel left lying "on desks, hung from cords, berating one another" (52).

For some of the characters in *JR*, the telephone is no longer a convenience. During his romantic weekend with Amy, Jack Gibbs complains that he is "always afraid the damned telephone's going to go off the minute we ... " (499). Indeed, the telephone does "go off" in the passage quoted earlier. For Gibbs, the telephone is like a bomb or a loaded gun, capable of reducing him to "dead weight" (504) with its ring. Similarly, the Bast sisters are constantly irritated by wrong numbers and offers of free dance lessons. Since the telephone seems only to disrupt their privacy, they feel that selling their telephone stock would be "like selling some poor soul shares in a plague ... " (229). Instead of improving communication, the telephone increases frustration and misunderstanding.

The telephone effectively eliminates any possibility of checking language, since it reduces the available channels of communication to one, the human voice. Now while this feature of the telephone promotes confusion, it also offers certain advantages to JR, whose financial manipulations affect nearly every other character in the novel. When the Hyde kid suggests that JR, because of his age, is going to get into trouble borrowing money from a Nevada bank to buy thousands of surplus navy picnic forks, JR dismisses the warning:

> —I mean these funny hours my mother's always working how do I know when she's going to walk in, like I mean this here bond and stock stuff you don't see anybody you don't know anybody only in the mail and the telephone because that's how they do it nobody has to see anybody, you can be this here funny lookingest person that lives in a toilet someplace how do they know, I mean all those guys at the Stock Exchange where they're selling all this stock to each other? They don't give a shit whose it is they're just selling it back and forth for some voice that told them on the phone why should they give a shit if you're a hundred and fifty all they ... (172)

JR uses the telephone to conduct business because it transmits only his voice, which he is able to disguise by stuffing his filthy handkerchief into the mouthpiece. JR's success, then, depends on his being absent to others, on his using the telephone to disguise the fact that he is a scruffy urchin in a torn sweater and sneakers, "frayed, knotted, and unshorn in other details" (57).

Since voices in *JR* are frequently "boxed," it is not always possible to appeal to gestures or facial expressions to check the meaning and intention of speech. This is to some extent a problem both for the characters and for the reader. For example, *JR* begins in the middle of a conversation, whose participants are not immediately identified or described. The reader is cast adrift on a stream of dialogue, cut loose from the conventional moorings of attribution and exposition. As most of the dialogue in *JR* is unaccompanied by descriptions of mental processes, feelings, motives, or facial expressions, we have no way to verify precisely the intended meaning of what we "hear." Refusing to allow his language to articulate subjective experience, Gaddis eschews interior monologue or other techniques for exploring consciousness from the inside. Our only sense of the characters' thoughts, intentions, and desires must be derived from what they say to one another. Similarly, the characters themselves draw inferences from each other's audible speech and observable behavior.

Yet visible perception in *JR* tends to be unreliable. On those occasions when a character responds to visual cues, he is likely to misinterpret them, as

Edward Bast does when he "sees" Amy Joubert holding a cigarette which is really a cracker: "she'd turned the profile of her raised chin and, one finger delicately cocked, her hand risen with a white cracker to her parted lips where Bast abruptly thrust a lighted match" (117). Depending on visual signals for information about the world, one risks not only embarrassment but also injury. Thus, Mr. Skinner, a textbook salesman, is involved in one of the novel's several automobile accidents when the school janitor directs him into traffic. As Whiteback explains, "he says Leroy signaled him right out that blind corner in front of a truck, one of those big asphalt trucks ... " (46). Perhaps the most revealing instance of the unreliability of visual perception occurs when Amy Joubert tries to make JR see the moon. JR has just suggested that "everything you see someplace there's this millionaire for it?" (473), and Amy is horrified at the idea:

—And over there look, look. The moon coming up, don't you see it? Doesn't it make ...
—What over there? He ducked away as though for a better view, —No but that's, Mrs. Joubert? that's just, wait ... (474)

Amy fails to convince JR that there are objects in the world whose worth is intangible, but Edward Bast, near the end of the novel, renews her effort:

—But she's can't you see what she, why did you duck away! can't you see what she was trying to tell you she ...
—What tell her it's this top of this here Carvel icecream cone stand? tell her does she want to bet her ass if there's a millionaire for that? (661)

Both JR and Amy are apparently looking at the same object, yet each sees something different. Furthermore, there is no way to know which of them is right. Since the narrator confirms neither perception, we are faced with an unresolved conflict between Amy's romanticism and JR's instrumentalism.

While Amy and JR practice incompatible ways of seeing the world, other characters have difficulty seeing it at all. One such character is Whiteback, whose glasses metonymically reduce him to a cipher. Near the beginning of the novel, for instance, Whiteback is momentarily blinded by the sun, which "caught him flat across the lenses, erasing any life behind them in a flash of inner vacancy" (18). On another occasion, "catching light from nowhere, his lenses went blank" (175). However, Whiteback is once again merely an extreme example of a general phenomenon, a kind of ocular chaos in *JR*. Few of the novel's characters look directly at one another. Instead, their gazes are deflected, and lines of vision fail to intersect. Such is the case in this description of Amy, her uncle, and her father:

> Mrs Joubert sitting knees clenched reading through tortoise shell glasses, looking up just then elsewhere to ask—must I read all this now? elsewhere the weather side of Cates hunched, back to door, reading papers with a look pinched through gold rims that rose abruptly and glanced off hers to cross the desk lusterless with— just the cobalt? where Moncrieff's glance over heavy black half frames and the huddled permanent of a secretary had already passed them both and returned. (94)

These glances do not connect the characters. Instead, they reinforce the separation already suggested by the metonymic reduction of the characters to different styles of eyeglasses.

The world of *JR*, then, is characterized by disorder and instability. In Empedocles' terms, it is ruled by Strife, whose function is to separate. Thus, we discover that the human body in JR is fragmented, separated into parts, deprived of unity and equilibrium. Language is separated into different forms of discourse, and signs are separated from their referents. Finally, voices are "boxed," disembodied. In fact, *JR* ends with just such a voice: "So I mean listen I got this neat idea hey, you listening? Hey? You listening ... ?" (726). It is, of course, JR talking on the telephone, and there is an ominous note of excitement in his voice.

NOTES

1. William Gaddis, notes for *The Recognitions, 1945–51*, as quoted in Peter W. Koenig, "Recognizing Gaddis' *Recognitions*," *Contemporary Literature* 16, no. 1 (1975): 67.

2. William Gaddis, *JR* (New York: Alfred A. Knopf, 1975), 20. Subsequent references to this work will be cited parenthetically in the text.

3. Empedocles, fragment 30, trans. Kathleen Freeman, in *Ancilla to the Pre-Socratic Philosophers* (Oxford: Basil Blackwell, 1956), 56. All further references to Empedocles' fragments will be cited parenthetically in the text.

4. Helle Lambridis, *Empedocles: A Philosophical Investigation* (University, Alabama: University of Alabama Press, 1976), 59.

5. Denis O'Brien, *Empedocles' Cosmic Cycle: A Reconstruction From the Fragments and Secondary Sources* (Cambridge: Cambridge University Press, 1969), 101.

6. Ibid., 2.

7. Ibid.

8. William Gaddis, *The Recognitions* (New York: Harcourt, Brace & World, 1955), 299.

9. Michel Foucault, *The Order of Things*, a translation of *Les mots et les choses* (New York: Vintage, 1973), 36.

ELAINE B. SAFER

Ironic Allusiveness and Satire in William Gaddis's The Recognitions

William Gaddis's satire may be considered even more passionate than Pynchon's, his sense of mission more obvious. In "The Rush for Second Place," Gaddis satirizes the materialism of twentieth-century American society, which has exchanged "the remnants of the things worth being for those presumably worth having."[1] Gaddis uses farce and incongruity to criticize a society in which a good appearance, being liked, and influencing people enable a man to get ahead. He lampoons a society whose members are constantly on the move without meaningful direction, aimlessly drifting along what Nikolai Gogol has termed "tortuous, blind, impassable, devious paths," never able to find "eternal truth."[2]

In public lectures, Gaddis often praises Gogol's *Dead Souls*.[3] In fact, Gaddis in many respects is a twentieth-century Gogol. Certainly, they have expressed similar intentions. Referring to *The Recognitions*, Gaddis relates: "I thought that I was the first one to discover that the world was filled with false values and I was going to tell them. So I elaborated the 900 and some pages. It was a sense of mission." Making reference to *JR* (1975), he explains: "Twenty years later I did the same thing. I had to tell them that the stock market and this whole myth about free enterprise was just high comedy."[4] Gaddis's most recent novel, *Carpenter's Gothic* (1985), satirizes the power residing in society's religious, political, and business institutions. Gaddis's

---

From *The Contemporary American Comic Epic: The Novels of Barth, Pynchon, Gaddis, and Kesey* (1989). © 1989 by Wayne State University Press.

intent recalls Gogol's: "Who's going to tell the truth if not the writer?" Gogol points out that because of his humor, the reader may praise him for being "a cheerful sort of fellow," but this is not enough. Gogol desires that readers see and criticize themselves in his characters.[5]

Gaddis's distress over the materialism in twentieth-century America echoes Gogol's concern, a century ago, over the greed and corruption of Russia, its loss of spiritual goals. Both desire to expose counterfeits in their society. In *Dead Souls*, Gogol depicts counterfeits through his character Chichikov and those with whom the man comes in contact. The epic novel focuses on the development of a comic incongruity: dead serfs are treated as though they are alive for the purpose of the census. Through irony, the author emphasizes that the landowners not only exploit their living serfs but they also wish to profit from selling the dead. Gogol accentuates the comic aspect of this exploitation by having the protagonist, Chichikov, offer landowners the opportunity to sell him dead serfs, or dead souls, whose names are on the old census and for whom the landlords still have to pay a tax. The price of the dead serfs is subject to haggling, as is evident in the conversation between Chichikov and the landowner Sobakevich:

> "God damn it," Chichikov thought, "this one's talking of selling before I've even mentioned the idea!" And he said aloud: "And what price would you have in mind? Although it's really rather strange to use the word price in speaking of such merchandise." "Well, since I don't wish to charge you a kopek above the proper price, it'll be one hundred rubles apiece," Sobakevich said. "A hundred!" Chichikov cried .... "I, for my part, would suggest ... eighty kopeks per soul." ... "But it's not bast sandals I'm selling," [responded Sobakevich].[6]

The similarity between Gaddis and Gogol goes beyond mission. Both authors use black humor and the comic-grotesque as a means to develop their satiric epics. To criticize the materialistic orientation of society, Gaddis, instead of naming his characters, often represents them in terms of their possessions. A large diamond ring tells us Recktall Brown is present; a Mickey Mouse watch points to Agnes Deigh. This develops a "gloomy but also grotesquely comic"[7] vision reminiscent of that of Gogol, who ridicules Russia's businessmen and petty officials by reducing them to objects they sell and garments they wear: in looking at a store window, people appear unable to differentiate between the red-faced vendor and the samovar that he markets except for the fact that "one of them had a pitch-black beard";[8] in a government office Chichikov observes "an ordinary light gray jacket ... *its* head twisted to one side ... as, with zest and flourish, *it* wrote out some court decision" (italics added).9

In "The Rush for Second Place," Gaddis criticizes twentieth-century society for making appearances and material success all important, for carrying out the advice of Willy Loman in *Death of a Salesman*, to aim to be liked,10 advice similar to that which Gogol mocks when he relates Chichikov's father's parting counsel to his son: "Always try to please your teachers and your superiors." This, he explains, is the way to "get ahead." If Chichikov is to have friends, he is instructed to "pick the richer ones .... Money will do everything for you."11

IRONIC ALLUSIVENESS

Gaddis's major means of ridiculing the shallow, materialistic bent of society is through ironic allusiveness. Like Pynchon and other postmodern epic writers, he uses this method extensively to develop satiric comedy. While traditional writers like John Milton and Cotton Mather use allusions to strengthen the connection between the themes and values in their works and similar ones in earlier epics, Gaddis alludes to earlier literature in order to show an ironic contrast with the precepts of his era. He returns to literary depictions of traditional beliefs and behavior from earlier centuries to show—by contrast—the superficialities of twentieth-century America.

By allowing the reader to enjoy the disparity between twentieth-century concerns and traditional values evident in the original sources, Gaddis laughingly exposes the counterfeits.12 He depends on what Umberto Eco calls the "'encyclopedia' of the spectator,"13 the literary knowledge of the reader, which can be called upon to develop ironic contrasts between an earlier work and the present one. In *JR* Gaddis alludes to his own *The Recognitions* and calls attention to the comic incongruity between the book itself and the banal and arrogant comments of some twentieth-century book reviewers. He cites reviews of seven novels, all anagrams for *The Recognitions*.14 Comments include: "a narrow and jaundiced view, a projection of private discontent"; "so ostentatiously aimed at writing a masterpiece"; "nowhere in this whole disgusting book is there a trace of kindness or sincerity or simple decency" (*JR* 515).15

In order to mock the false assertions masquerading as the truth in twentieth-century American society, Gaddis tries to strip the contemporary scene of its apparent normality. By defamiliarizing the present reality for readers, he calls attention to the need for an inner reality that has traditional meaning and basic truths. Gaddis's method is spelled out in *The Recognitions* by Wyatt Gwyon as he speaks of seeing Picasso's *Night Fishing in Antibes*: "When I saw it all of a sudden everything was freed into one recognition. [...][16] You don't see it in paintings because [....] the instant you see them they become familiar, and then it's too late" (92).

Recognizing includes "the action or fact of perceiving ... a thing as having a certain character or belonging to a certain class" (that is, in terms of others of its type). It also includes the experience of being able "to know again," of being capable of viewing an object as being "identical with something previously known."[17] When the present perception is contrary to expectations (that have been set by what had been known), readers laugh at the contemporary scene and appreciate its inadequacies.

In order to ridicule the present, Gaddis encourages readers to draw upon an encyclopedic range of earlier writings: transcendental works, alchemical tracts, Flemish paintings, the third-century *Clementine Recognitions*, Goethe's *Faust*, and T.S. Eliot's *The Wasteland* and *Four Quartets*. He focuses on these lofty works of the past, steeped in religious and philosophical significance, to satirize the "materialistic, grab-all-you-can" twentieth-century American society.[18]

Transcendental References

Gaddis often develops ironic references to transcendental themes and to great transcendentalist thinkers like Ralph Waldo Emerson. He begins one of his party scenes in *The Recognitions* with an epigraph from Emerson's essay "Old Age": "America is a country of young men" (169) who, Emerson writes, are "too full of work hitherto for leisure and tranquillity."[19] Emerson's notion of the energetic and productive work of young men and the wise balancing of solitude and sociability in old age makes ironic and comic the futile activity in the novel's contemporary American gatherings "full of people who spen[d] their lives in rooms" (176): the young people, alienated from each other and from the natural environment; the poet, myopic and unable to see beyond the printed page instead of having an eye that "can see far," an eye that "seems to demand a horizon";[20] the poet capable only of viewing "simply a series of vague images [... to be] faced with lowered eyes as though seeking a book at hand to explain it all" (*Recognitions* 179). With sharp humor, the narrator ridicules different types of shallow behavior of contemporary party-goers. Some engage in incommunicative dialogue: "—*Him* Byronic? Miss

Stein demanded.—I said *moronic*, said Mr. Schmuck's assistant" (656). Others mask their identities: Ed Feasley meets a girl whom he finds attractive. After the party, he exclaims to a friend: "Chrahst, I found her, the girl in the purple dress. Standing right beside me at the next urinal" (315). Others appear to be arguing philosophically over such inane points as whether a death should be classified as a suicide or an accident because the man, who had attempted to hang himself, fell to his death when the rope broke (180).

To see clearly the lack of meaning in twentieth-century society's social gatherings, Gaddis suggests that one think about where America had been and where it is. His description of contemporary parties directly contrasts with those more meaningful gatherings in American history of the "Transcendental Club" in which Emerson, Alcott, Frothingham, Fuller, and others exchanged ideas on such subjects as "American genius—the causes which hinder its growth," "the actuality of intuition," and "the immanence of God."[21] Such significant issues are never topics of conversation at the parties Gaddis describes.

The author sounds like a comic prophet, a modern Jeremiah, listing the transgressions of his contemporaries, whose thoughts center on trivialities. Such people deflate religion by telling banal jokes about how it is "all right to kiss a nun [....] as long as you don't get into the habit" (103); others treat lightly an author's endeavors, as does the critic who, when asked "You reading that [book]?" responds: "No. I'm just reviewing it. [...] All I need is the jacket blurb to write the review." That the omniscient author describes the book as *The Recognitions* compounds the cynicism: "It was in fact quite a thick book," whose dust jacket has bold lettering that stands forth "in stark configurations of red and black" (936). In such a society, the author cynically prophesies that nothing is holy.[22] In such a society, materialism has supplanted transcendentalism and science has replaced religion. The narrator, with wry humor, explains:

> Science assures us that it is getting nearer to the solution of life, what life *is*, ... ("the ultimate mystery"), and offers anonymously promulgated submicroscopic chemistry in eager substantiation. But no one has even begun to explain what happened at the dirt track in Langhorne, Pennsylvania about twenty-five years ago, when Jimmy Concannon's car threw a wheel, and in a crowd of eleven thousand it killed his mother. (566)

Flemish Art

Gaddis creates much of his ironic dialogue with the past by developing allusions to fifteenth-century Flemish art. He evokes a desire for a lost age that produced painters whose art "would bring tears to the eyes of the devout."[23] In *The Recognitions* the protagonist yearns for the piety and devotion he believes were part of the context of fifteenth-century Netherlandish painters—Roger van der Weyden, Hubert and Jan van Eyck, Dirc Bouts, and Hans Memling. Wyatt wishes to be part of an age when painters displayed an exquisite sense of piety, such as van der Weyden and Bouts conveyed in their Madonnas and their Descents from the Cross. Copying these fifteenth-century Flemish masters, Wyatt mixes tempera to approximate their paint and attempts a psychic affinity with their philosophical and emotional states of mind. He paints masterpieces that connoisseurs judge to be the work of the original Netherlandish painters. He seems to transport himself to their golden age and virtually presents his gift to the guild as an artist in Flanders. He thinks of the guild oath, "to use pure materials, to work in the sight of God" (*Recognitions* 250).

Gaddis develops the ironic allusive mode by caustically contrasting Wyatt Gwyon's nostalgia for painterly beauty with the present world, where randomness and disconnections abound. For a time, the transforming power of Wyatt's imagination creates a sense of meaning and beauty for readers. But the shift of focus from the sacred and serious to the profane and the ludicrous jars readers. The black humor tone that emerges from the depiction of these incongruities mixes components of pain with humor, horror with farce.

The title of Gaddis's postmodern comic epic novel indeed derives from the third-century *Clementine Recognitions*, in which Clement, seeking salvation, journeys to Palestine and becomes a follower of Saint Peter. Basil Valentine, a central character in Gaddis's *Recognitions*, holds the same name as the Renaissance author of the alchemical treatise *The Triumphant Chariot of Antimony*.[24] The novel also can be considered a "bop version" (661) of Goethe's *Faust*, which centers on the issue of redemption. Such references call to mind a physical journey in Palestine and the quest for a new Jerusalem, the redemption of matter and the redemption of the soul, man's desires and the justification of God's ways. These are the major sources that are called upon and contradicted in the novel. As the expectations created by these are frustrated, the reader appreciates the "ironic ploy" and, with a combination of pleasure and pain, enjoys the grim joke that comes from the incongruity.[25]

ALLUSIONS TO THE *CLEMENTINE RECOGNITIONS*

From early childhood, Gaddis's twentieth-century protagonist, Wyatt Gwyon, is fascinated by the story of Saint Clement, who was martyred by being tied to an anchor and thrown into the Black Sea (44). According to theological tracts, Clement had argued for apostolic succession against Gnosticism and other heretical beliefs. Legend relates that when Clement was thrown overboard, the waters parted and a tomb appeared at the bottom of the sea, signifying the beatification of Clement.

Wyatt connects the story of Saint Clement and a legend his father had told him about a celestial being who came down a rope into the atmosphere of this world and drowned (44). Wyatt continually ponders the possibility that human beings are fished for by celestial beings who watch their actions: "Can't you imagine that we're fished for? Walking on the bottom of a great celestial sea, do you remember the man who came down the rope to undo the anchor caught on the tombstone?" (115) he asks his wife years later. Wyatt wants to be fished for; he yearns for salvation, for signs of God's grace in a fallen world.

References to the legend of Saint Clement point out ironic connections between the hero of the *Clementine Recognitions* and Wyatt Gwyon, hero of the absurd. The *Clementine Recognitions*, a long, episodic work, describes the young adulthood of Saint Clement of Rome (first century A.D.). The treatise affirms orthodox Christian doctrine by emphasizing the traditional connection between this world and a new Jerusalem, between the protagonist Clement and every man seeking eternal salvation.

In the twentieth-century *Recognitions*, however, the character Basil Valentine explains to an acquaintance:

> Tell your [writer] friend *Willie* that salvation is hardly the practical study it was then. What? ... Why, simply because in the Middle Ages they were convinced that they had souls to save. Yes. The what? The *Recognitions*? No, it's Clement of *Rome*. Mostly talk, talk, talk. The young man's deepest concern is for the immortality of his soul, he goes to Egypt to find the magicians and learn their secrets. It's been referred to as the first Christian novel. (372–73; first italics added)

Basil Valentine's comment on the *Clementine Recognitions* reveals the comic-ironic contrast between the sacred and the profane, between religion and

Mammonism. In addition, his comment has a significant error. He says that Clement goes to Egypt to find the magicians and learn their secrets. In the original, though Clement wishes to consult with magicians about immortality, he quickly turns from such actions because "transactions of this sort are hateful to the Divinity" (*Clem. R.* 78). Instead of traveling to Egypt, land of magic and the occult, Clement sails to Palestine, where he meets Saint Peter, who teaches him how to progress toward salvation. Accompanying Peter on his missionary journeys to various cities, Clement sees Peter heal the sick and give peace to those in turmoil (*Clem. R.* 136). As he hears Peter discourse on the consistency of Christ's teaching and listens to him debate with Simon Magus, he appreciates how goodness and logical argumentation can convince people to believe the teacher of truth and abhor Satan and his followers. United with his lost father, mother, and brothers, Clement watches his father repent for having been seduced by Simon Magus, and he hears Peter explain: "As God has restored your sons to you, their father, so also your sons restore their father to God" (*Clem. R.* 210). The journey with Peter through Palestine enables Clement to appreciate the ultimate significance of things, the "Alpha and Omega, the beginning and the end, the first and the last" (Rev. 22:13).

The progression of the hero in the *Clementine Recognitions* provides a framework by which to compare Wyatt Gwyon's ironic quest for salvation in Gaddis's twentieth-century novel. Wyatt is estranged from his father, Reverend Gwyon; he has no guide like Saint Peter to reconcile him with father or God. When he finds a souvenir from the basilica of Saint Clement in Rome, Wyatt appeals to his father for information about the martyred saint. Reverend Gwyon gives the boy no Christian counsel; instead, he is engrossed in the fact that under the basilica geologists found a pagan temple for worshipers of the Persian god, Mithras. The "subterranean sanctuary [...] afloat with vapors from two thousand years before" (44) is more vital to him than Wyatt's concern about salvation. Reverend Gwyon's comments suggest that his pilgrimages to Rome and Spain are an ironic reversal of the voyages of early Christian pilgrims. Instead of pilgrimages heightening his connection to the Church, they alienate him from Christianity, his congregation, and his son.

The pattern of father–son estrangement is evident throughout Gaddis's *Recognitions*. As a young boy, Wyatt accidentally kills a wren and goes to his father's study to confess. Instead of atoning and receiving guidance, Wyatt stands waiting outside his father's forbidding study door, while the minister remains silently facing him from inside the room. As an adult, Wyatt again wants to repent his actions. He travels home to the New England parsonage but again is unable to communicate with his father.

In the carriage barn of the New England parsonage, amid peals of thunder and lightning, Wyatt finally blurts out: "Father ... *Am I the man for whom Christ died?*" "Louder than laughter," the narrator relates, "the crash raised and sundered them in a blinding agony of light in which nothing existed until it was done." The narrator continues, "Then it seemed full minutes before the cry, pursuing them with its lashing end, flailed through darkness and stung them to earth. Water fell between them, from a hole in the roof. The smell of smoke reached them in the dark" (440). In the traditional allusive mode, lightning and thunder would signify a prophetic moment full of God's presence; water would imply Baptism and regeneration. This scene, however, comically frustrates all expectation for Baptism, reducing to nothing the reader's vision of the grand image of John the Baptist and Christ. Contrary to expectation, the scene deflates all prophetic symbolism to the gross details of a metal washtub whose water is wasted. The lightning drives a hole in the washtub and the water gushes out. Unlike the Baptism of Christ, which brings the Father and the Son together, this gush of water physically enforces the separation of the father and son. There is no sign of God's presence or of salvation in this black humor scene. There is no link that will connect Wyatt to his God or to his father. There is only the ironic "denseness and that strangeness of the world [which] is the absurd."[26]

Wyatt's eventual communication with the Reverend Gwyon takes on a sharper tone of black humor. At the age of thirty-three (Christ's age at the Crucifixion),[27] Wyatt's Puritan guilt leads him to a penitential act. He goes to the town of San Zwingli, near Madrid, and visits the grave of his mother, Camilla, who died when he was three.[28] Then he travels south to the Spanish monastery in Estremadura, where his father had stayed after Camilla's death. In these surroundings, Wyatt, now known as Stephen (name of the first Christian martyr), unwittingly eats his father's ashes baked in the bread that the monks have served. The monks have mistaken the ashes (mailed to them in an oatmeal box) for wheat germ.

The monks use the ingredients in the cereal box to bake bread, which is served to Wyatt: "The bread crumbled because of its fine gray texture. He [Wyatt] crammed half of it into his mouth [...] As he chewed, a thoughtful expression came to his face for the first time." "His eyes," we are told, were fixed upon a painting but were "focused far beyond it. He chewed on" (870–71). By eating the ashes, Wyatt inadvertently carries out the form as well as the spirit of his penitential act. Wyatt's eating this bread made from the ashes parodies the ceremonial action of the Eucharist: the Sacrament that conveys to the believer the Body as well as the Blood of Christ; the

Sacrament that signifies Christ's gift of eternal life to mankind through His death and resurrection. That Wyatt eats the bread made from his father's ashes is Gaddis's satiric response to the ultimate question of faith. In this bizarre way Wyatt becomes one with the Father/father.[29]

Adding to the distress and comedy of the situation is the outrageous punning on the protagonist's newly acquired name, Stephan Asche: the name on the forged passport that Mr. Yák has prepared for him (795). Black humor intensifies as apparently random happenings begin to coalesce. We recall that Stephen was Reverend Gwyon and his wife Camilla's original choice of the name for their son (27). Now, thirty-three years later, the counterfeiter Mr. Sinisterra (known as Mr. Yák) restores Stephen's name by giving him a forged passport.[30] Mr. Sinisterra was responsible for Camilla Gwyon's death thirty years before, when he posed as a ship's surgeon and accidentally killed her during an operation for appendicitis. Recollection of these happenings increases the dual tone of seriousness and humor that accompanies the bizarre communion of father and son.

The absurdities surrounding Wyatt's quest for communion with his father and its parodic connections with the Eucharist help develop the broader ironic contrast between Wyatt and the hero of the third century *Recognitions* who affirms his belief in God and is united with his father as well. The ironic contrast also is developed by means of Wyatt's futile quest for Camilla, as opposed to Clement's successful meeting with his mother after years of separation. Wyatt's longing for his mother also connects to his implicit desire for help from Mary, the Blessed Virgin.

The Virgin Mary's divine motherhood, the belief that Mary intercedes on behalf of man and dispenses God's grace with a mother's love, provides a range of associations that connect to Wyatt's sense of the mystical presence of his mother, who died when he was three. As a child, he believes he has a vision of his dead mother. As an adult, he notices that his paintings of the Madonna resemble Camilla. Wyatt seems to pursue intimations of Camilla as he would suggestions of divine motherhood. He seems to be appealing to Mary's intercessory power, higher than all other saints. The mystique around Camilla, envisioned by Wyatt, is ironically fulfilled when the Church mistakes her body for that of the eleven-year-old Spanish girl whom it has declared a saint and accidentally canonizes Camilla in her place (791–92).

An absurdist vision and a black humor tone emerge as we recall the description of the violent killing of the little Spanish girl and the odd reaction that greets the announcement of her canonization years later. The girl is assaulted on her way home from her first Communion by a man who believes intercourse with a virgin will cure his disease (16), a rationale evidently used by others in history. The narrator explains that New Yorkers, like Mr. Pivner, avidly read newspaper accounts of the Spanish girl's beatification, not because she will be a saint but because they are anxious to gather information about her rape and murder (291).

Incongruities between the sacred and the profane reach farcical proportions in the cemetery near Camilla's grave, as Wyatt, seeker of salvation, accidentally meets and befriends Mr. Yák, who becomes virtually a guide and a father surrogate for him. Mr. Yák's actions as guide are in direct contrast to those of Clement's guide, Saint Peter; Mr. Yák does not explicate the Law but evades the law. In San Zwingli, Spain, as in New York City, he is in disguise. In false mustache and toupee, he gestures rigidly and automatically like a mechanical slapstick actor: he keeps "tugging at his mustache [...] and then pressing it anxiously back in place" and, we are told, he "might have worn a hat, but for fear his hair [might] come off with it when it was removed" (777–78). The counterfeiter, Mr. Yák, is a Bergsonian caricature of "something mechanical encrusted on the living,"[31] a comic buffoon, the object of laughter.

Laughter, essentially, is a reaction to perceived contradictions or incongruities, and these reach an extreme in the interchanges between Wyatt and Mr. Yák. Wyatt, the idealist, feels burdened by the sinful accumulation in the fallen world, while Mr. Yák, the materialist, has always easily accommodated himself to sin, as when, after accidentally killing Camilla, he crosses himself and murmurs, "*The first turn of the screw pays all debts*" (5), or when, sought for counterfeiting charges, he leaves New York for Spain, thinking of himself as a pilgrim on a voyage to the "Eternal City, in a Holy Year, [...] like those early pilgrims to the Holy Land" (496), or when, thirty years after killing Camilla, he justifies his counterfeiting activities to Wyatt: "I'm not a bum. [...] I'm a craftsman, an artist like, see? ... and they got jealous of my work" (785). Mr. Yák is a caricature of the twentieth-century decadent, in contrast to the devout young artist who yearns for salvation. Brought together, these dissimilar figures generate laughter, but the laughter wavers when we comprehend that Wyatt, who searches for communion with father and mother, is virtually adopted by the degenerate Mr. Yák.

Mr. Yák shows paternal interest in Wyatt, who, in contrast to Yák's own son, Chaby Sinisterra, is intelligent and industrious. A comic-ironic tone develops as this degenerate surrogate father keeps telling the sensitive aesthetician, the deeply religious Wyatt: "I knew you weren't a bum" (786). It is equally strange that the surrogate father, essentially a father of lies, continually insists, "I'm an artist," when in reality he is a counterfeiter. Wyatt's accidental meeting with his surrogate father, Mr. Yák, and the incongruities that ensue contribute to a frenzied tone of black humor, as memories of death and distress mingle with details of farce. Irony seems to be implied by the surroundings themselves, particularly the fact that villagers of San Zwingli seem unaware that their Catholic town is named after Huldreich Zwingli, the Swiss Protestant reformer whose treatises argued against the major tenets of Catholicism.

An ironic allusiveness emerges as events in Wyatt's twentieth-century world are recognized as being in stark opposition to those in the third-century *Clementine Recognitions*. This emphasizes the difference between people in early Church history, who looked to Scripture for guidance, and those in the twentieth century, like Mr. Pivner, who lack spiritual inclination and turn to newspapers as a guide for a meaningful life. Intertextuality emphasizes the comic incongruity between the early Christians who affirmed their faith when told of miracles, like the appearance of a tomb at the beatification of Saint Clement, and those twentieth-century readers who are feverishly drawn to the story of the little Spanish girl's canonization for its sensational details.

The intertextual focus also emphasizes the contradiction between the early Christian treatises, which handle the story of Saint Clement with reverence, and Gaddis's black humor novel, which uses the subject of saints as material for comedy. The little Spanish girl, whose body is left behind in the graveyard, is a comic counterpart to Saint Clement. Her body remains in the graveyard while Camilla's is mistakenly taken in her place to be canonized in Rome: "When they took her out of the graveyard here to put her somewhere else when she was beatified they thought she looks [*sic*] kind of big for an eleven-year-old girl, but the way the body was preserved after forty years almost, so that made them sure it's a saint" (791).

The incident is extended to ludicrous proportions as Mr. Yák/Sinisterra carries out his intention of using the "left behind" corpse as a basis for a mummy that he wishes to sell. Mr. Yák exclaims, with glittering eyes and trembling hands, "This is just what we want" (793). Once in his room, in a nearby pension, Mr. Yák sets up his materials for mummy making. He pours colorless liquid from one test tube to another, changing it to red and then back to colorless. Parodying religious ritual, he chants: "Water into wine, wine into water. [...] Water into blood, blood into a solid. Remember the miracle at Bolsena? Watch." He then quickly drops from the sacred to the material details of science: "A little aluminum sulphate dissolved, a few drops of phenolphthalein" (794).

Yák is a cartoon figure: he grabs for his hairpiece, putting it on backward; he uses clichés repeatedly, such as "You're safe as a nut"; and he sounds like a poor imitation of a middle-class businessman as he promotes the fraudulent enterprise of making a mummy: "There's work to do. [...] You don't want to do nothing? That's the way you get into mischief. You get into mischief, doing nothing" (795–96).

This farce ends with Yák and Wyatt walking the mummy to the railway station: "Be careful. We pretend it's an old woman, see? Only when we get on the train she's real stiff in the joints, see?" In the train's compartment, Yák, a caricature of a counterfeit man, "patted down the shock of black hair, pressed the mustache, and cleared his throat with satisfaction." The narrator comments on all three of them "looking in what light there was through the smoke like a weary and not quite respectable family. The conductor, at any rate, showed no rude curiosity when he tapped at the glass panel, slid the door open, and took three tickets from Mr. Yák, who had bounded to his feet to meet him" (811–12). When the shawl partially falls off the mummy, a woman gasps, grabs her husband, and they politely leave the compartment: "—And my God! ... did you see her face?—Syphilis, her husband said" (815).

In Gaddis's black humor novel, chance occurrences seem to coalesce in a bizarre design that is an ironic reversal of the meaning found in literature depicting traditional heroes, such as Saint Clement, in the *Clementine Recognitions*. With Peter as guide, Clement learns about God's goodness, affirms his faith, and is reunited with his parents. In direct opposition, Wyatt Gwyon seems to fulfill the ludicrous role of absurdist hero that Basil Valentine had, by chance, predicted for him: "I suppose you ... well, let's say you eat your father, canonize your mother, and ... what happens to people in novels? I don't read them" (262).

Allusions to Alchemy

Gaddis's second major inversion of the allusive mode to develop absurdist comedy is based on medieval alchemy: the traditional pursuit of the redemption of matter and the redemption of the soul.[32] The narrator in *The Recognitions* refers to famous masters such as Raymond Lully—"a poet, a missionary, a mystic" (77)—figures who spoke in religious terms and believed they could bring mankind back to the golden age before the Fall. Such men "had seen in gold the image of the sun, spun in the earth by its countless revolutions, then, when the sun might yet be taken for the image of God" (131–32). The incongruity between the spiritual nature of the traditional alchemical pursuit of gold, on the one hand, and on the other, the material focus in the world of the twentieth-century novel is a source of comic irony.

The narrator's crude language underlines the reduction: "once chemistry had established itself as true and legitimate son and heir, alchemy was turned out like a drunken parent." The child, continues the narrator, "had found what the old fool and his cronies were after all the time"; they had found gold in all its varieties. The narrator deflates the present status of gold by ironically juxtaposing it with that of the past: "a cube capable, at the flick of a thumb, of producing a flame, not, perhaps, the *ignis noster* of the alchemists, but a flame quite competent to light a cigarette" (132–33). Contemporary man is satirically portrayed as placing material possessions over spiritual concerns. For the alchemist, on the other hand, "being and having the stone were the same thing."[33]

One of the central figures in *The Recognitions*, Basil Valentine, is obviously linked to the medieval alchemist Basilius Valentinus, who called himself a Benedictine monk. The early alchemist's ostensible concern was with the soul; Basilius admonishes, "You must truly repent you of all your sins, confessing the same, and firmly resolve to lead a good and holy life ... by opening your hand and your heart to the needy."[34] In contrast, Gaddis's Valentine is purely concerned with matter, with accumulating gold artifacts: a signet ring, cuff links, a cigarette case, a bull figurine.

Gaddis, however, like Pynchon, develops a comic-ironic perspective that relates not only to the present but also to the past. The alchemist Basilius Valentinus, as was mentioned earlier, was a shadowy figure whose background was suspect. He signed his treatises as a Benedictine monk, yet his name never appeared in records of the order.[35] He prefaced his works, including *The Triumphal Chariot of Antimony*, with the admonition that people repent of their sins and lead a virtuous life, yet, according to legend, he may have poisoned monks by giving them an alchemical elixir derived from antimony.

Gaddis's Valentine is a comic variation on Valentinus. He is a Jesuit-educated art critic, a mysterious man who gives the acquisition of wealth top priority in all his dealings. He has a contractual agreement with the dealer Recktall Brown and, for a fee, praises as originals the forgeries (including Wyatt's) that Brown places for sale.

The scheme Valentine and Brown work out goes something like this: Valentine arrives at the showing, engages in discussion with other art critics, who have access to the latest scientific methods of detecting art forgery (for example, X-ray pictures, infrared and ultraviolet rays, different types of microscopes; 250). Valentine states that he is satisfied that the paintings are original; his comments convince others; the forgeries command high prices from patrons of the arts looking for originals. And Valentine shares in the profit with Recktall Brown, whose descriptive name denotes his coarse behavior.

In this satiric novel, Wyatt also enters into an agreement with Recktall Brown, creating paintings that the latter sells as originals. The comic ploy that Gaddis uses is that, despite his desire for salvation through art, Wyatt still agrees to a sinful contract for money with the Devil. When Valentine inquires of Wyatt, "Tell me, does Brown pay you well?" Wyatt responds, "Pay me? I suppose. The money piles up there." When Valentine asks about the money, Wyatt answers: "The money? you ... can't spend love" (261–62).

Painting, for Wyatt, is a religious act of devotion, an act of purification. By preparing his artist's medium and his study as an alchemist would prepare his complex materials and laboratory, Wyatt sets up an alchemical paradigm that acts as a touchstone for the redemption of his soul.[36] In Wyatt's study, pots of paint are always boiling and changing color; eggs are used to make tempera; and the oil of lavender, used in the base for Wyatt's paints, emits a mysterious "odor of sanc-tity" (270), akin to the fragrance of the holy water used by Egyptian alchemists in processing their color theory of alchemy (248).[37] Black humor develops, however, because despite his intelligence and expertise, Wyatt naively agrees to a contract with Brown without appreciating its deleterious effect.

Wyatt is engaged in a refining process. He employs an alchemical paradigm to pursue spiritual purification, a means of virtually leaving behind the sinful accumulations of a fallen world as he uses his imagination to create the world anew in art.[38] His practice of preparing tempera by hand and of creating colors that approximate those of the fifteenth-century artists parallels the experimentation of alchemists, whose series of changes and renewals of matter were aimed at deriving a universal solvent, an "elixir" that would refine matter and cause it and the alchemist to regain a prelapsarian state: achieving heaven's gold and the perfection of Adam and Eve.[39] Like the traditional alchemists, Wyatt is driven by a vision of perfection. However, though Wyatt works feverishly and sleeps little, he increasingly becomes dismayed by the barren existence of an absurd world.

At the end of the book, Wyatt seems psychologically shattered by personal disasters: the loss of his paintings, his separation from Esme (the model who shares his yearnings), and his inability to be reconciled with his father or with God. He lives in the Spanish monastery in Estremadura. There he occupies himself by scraping off paint from original masterpieces (for example, a Valdes Leal and an El Greco) in an attempt to free the paintings of the accumulations of time that damage color and obscure beauty. Ironically, Wyatt goes so far in his restoration as to razor blade the paintings themselves and return the canvases to their original emptiness (870–75). Accentuating the grotesquely comic nature of the act, so incongruous with what one believes to be Wyatt's sensitive, artistic nature, is the exclamation of the fat man in a brown suit: "Boy, that big picture was some mess wasn't it, the Rubins" [*sic*] (879).

Now, it would be comforting to believe that Wyatt (Stephen) "is pushing on to a more comprehensive idea of restoration—namely, the restoring of reality to itself," that he is "making a gesture of 'recalling' the 'falsifications' of even the greatest artists."[40] However, the absurdist novel, like Camus's *The Myth of Sisyphus*, withdraws such soothing answers. The recognition here is that when one divests the world of all accumulations, one reaches only an empty purification, signifying nothing. To illuminate the comic absurdity of the endeavor, Gaddis has the character Ludy caution: "But you can't [...] take that painting and ... and do what you're doing" (872).

It is ironic that Wyatt, who forever yearns to "soar in atonement," never meets the devout Stanley, the musician who appears to be his soul mate in the novel. Like Wyatt, Stanley dwells on the past, and, like him, he wishes to reach God through his artistic creation—a Requiem Mass to be played on an organ in the ancient Italian cathedral Fenestrula. Stanley finally completes the work and plays the concerto in the church, without paying attention to the warning of the Italian priest: "*Per favore non bassi ... e non strane combinazioni di note, capisce*" [Please, no bass ... and no strange combination of notes, understand] (956). The resounding music causes the structure to collapse: "Everything moved, and even falling, soared in atonement" (956).[41] That the "gigantic" organ in the small church was the "gift" of a well-meaning American adds to the tragicomic character of the scene.

The grotesque, cartoon quality of the cathedral scene is underscored by our recollection of an earlier episode (in France) in which the reader—with a Hobbesian sense of eminency—observes another edifice destroyed by an American's inability to understand a foreign language: Arny, in trying to eliminate smoke from his hotel room, rushes to open the window without reading the sign on it: "*On est prié de n'ouvrir pas ce fenêtre parce que le façade de l'hôtel lui compter pour se supporter*" [It is requested that the window not be opened because the front of the hotel counts on it for support] (942). The narrator explains that "with some effort he opened the window, smoke billowed out, and the facade of Henry's Hotel collapsed" (942). Gaddis further deflates the significance of Stanley's act of atonement by informing the reader that the concerto was recovered and "is still spoken of, when it is noted, with high regard, though *seldom played*" (956; italics added).

We react to Stanley's death as we do to that of his mother, who believes in meeting God for the Last Judgment in as whole a body as possible. Doctors have removed her leg, her appendix, and her tonsils. Finally, after watching her dentures dissolve in a solution a nurse has administered incorrectly, she leaps to her death from the hospital window: "It was too much. She must get where she was going while there was still time" (561).[42]

The quest of Stanley's mother for salvation is a parody of all absurd quests in the novel, ranging from Wyatt's desire to achieve salvation through art and the author Willie's desire to write about salvation in a novel that looks back to the *Clementine Recognitions* and Goethe's *Faust*. Calling attention to his own artifice, the postmodernist Gaddis has Basil Valentine warn that the writer Willie would be ill advised to use the *Clementine Recognitions* and Goethe's *Faust* as sources for his novel because their subject, salvation, is no longer a "practical study." *The Recognitions*, like Stanley's Requiem Mass, will be written for "a rather small audience" (373), one, the novel satirically implies, that will not be influenced by its position in the marketplace.

GOETHE'S *FAUST* AND *THE RECOGNITIONS*

Gaddis's third major inversion of the allusive mode, for satiric purposes, is to Goethe's *Faust*, an epic that celebrates the growth of its hero in this world and his eventual redemption in heaven. Gaddis calls attention to his ironic-comic stratagem by having a character say: "We're shooting *Faust* now, a sort of bop version, we've changed him to this refugee artist" (661). The importance of this farcical intertextual dialogue with *Faust* is stressed at the opening of the novel by means of an epigraph from the "Laboratory" scene where Wagner is making Homunculus.[43]

> MEPHISTOPHELES (*leiser*): Was gibt es denn? [(whispering) What is it, then?]
> WAGNER (*leiser*): Es wird ein Mensch gemacht. [(whispering) A man is being made.] (*Recognitions* 3)

Other details that echo Goethe's work include the black poodle Wyatt encounters on the street (135), the intimation that Brown, like Mephistopheles, has "cloven feet" (676), Brown's "contract" with Wyatt, and the allusion, in the first line of Gaddis's novel, to the "Carnival Masque" scene in *Faust* (227–58 [II.i.5065–5986]).

"Even Camilla [Wyatt's mother] had enjoyed masquerades" (3), explains the narrator in the opening line of *The Recognitions*. Camilla liked masquerades "of the safe sort where the mask may be dropped at that critical moment it presumes itself as reality" (3). She would shun, the reader infers, the sort of satire evident in the "Carnival Masque" scene in *Faust*, which discloses the crowd's avarice as they push and scramble for the gold and jewels thrown to them by characters in the parade. She would be grieved by the satirist in Goethe's procession who wishes "to sing, and utter, / That which no one wants to hear" (235 [II.i.5297–98]). This reference cautions us that Gaddis, like Goethe's satirist, will mock the characters as they parade before us.

Many details in Camilla's procession in the Spanish town of San Zwingli echo those in Goethe's "Carnival Masque" scene. The maidens in Goethe's great Roman Masquerade are away from home, in the German court, inhabited by Catholics. The American Camilla is in a *Catholic* ritual march in Spain. The maidens from Florence, however, are beautifully dressed and sell their wares to prospective suitors (232 [II.5198ff.]); Gaddis's grand "*Spanish affair*" in San Zwingli contradicts such promise, for it carries Camilla not to a prenuptial masquerade but to her grave, to be buried (as Protestant Aunt May exclaims) "with a lot of dead Catholics" (3). The contradiction of such meaning develops derisive humor in *The Recognitions*.

Gaddis plays off his piece against *Faust* in order to exhibit the comic futility of Wyatt's yearning for salvation in a world in which vanity and hypocrisy are the norm, and in which God no longer seems to exist. This method develops an intertextual dialogue with the earlier text.[44] Such a conversation is fraught with comic irony.

The early scenes in Faust clearly establish that God is watching man's activities, that He will reward good and punish evil. The "Prologue in Heaven" contrasts the following: God's goodness and the Devil's evil; God's creativity and Mephistopheles's urge toward destruction; God's assertion of man's sufficiency to stand firm against dark inclinations, his ability to advance toward the "true way" (14 [I.329]), and the Devil's wish to tempt Faust to damnation. These early passages in the drama emphasize the importance of man's activity in this world as preparation for eternity. The Lord explains to Mephistopheles: "While Man's desires and aspirations stir, / He cannot choose but err" (13 [I.317]). A "good man" (14 [I.328]) has the ability to advance toward the light of salvation. This idea is reiterated by the angelic choral as it tells Faust: "Thus is the Master near,— / Thus is He here! (34 [I.806–7]). The affirmation culminates in the final angelic celebration of Faust: "Whoe'er aspires unweariedly / Is not beyond redeeming" (500

[II.v.11936–37]). These lines stress celestial love and grace as angels bear Faust's immortal essence to heaven.

Faust, in Part I, vacillates between romantic hopes of heavenly ascent and pessimism and despair over the straitened circumstances of life (62 [I.1545]). Dissatisfied with the natural world while at the same time mocking man's delusion about higher things, he spurns man's belief in God: "Cursed, also, Hope!—cursed Faith, the spectre! / And cursed be Patience most of all!" (64 [I.1605–6]). The chorus cries out that Faust has destroyed "the beautiful world" (64 [I.1609]). As the epic progresses, however, the hero learns patience and turns from self-absorption to concern for his fellowmen and for God.

Before signing the contract with Mephistopheles, Faust makes the following stipulation: "When on an idler's bed I stretch myself in quiet, / There let, at once, my record end! / ... Canst thou with rich enjoyment fool me, / Let that day be the last for me!" (66–67 [I.1692–97]). It is to this that Faust signs his name in blood. As a result of his pact with Mephistopheles, Faust travels and partakes of a range of pleasures: carousing in taverns, participating in festivals at the imperial court, wooing the innocent Gretchen, and meeting and wedding the beautiful Helen of Troy. Yet, throughout, whether with Gretchen or later with Helen, Faust is never satisfied with this world. He continually aspires and thus never loses to the Devil. This need to be ever aspiring brings him close to God and, eventually, wins him salvation.

Goethe, in a conversation with Eckermann, explains the religious significance of Faust's actions. He indicates that the continual striving, the refusal to be satisfied with the offerings of a fallen world, shows a divine spark in Faust and makes him worthy of redemption: the striving "becomes constantly higher and purer ... and from above there is eternal love coming to his aid."[45] For Goethe, this conforms to the religious belief that divine grace is needed to assist man to heavenly bliss. Goethe acclaims the heroic potential in man and God's "eternal love."[46]

Wyatt also makes a pact with the Devil. Recktall Brown finds Wyatt in his apartment, despondent and despairing. He offers him a "contract" in the form of a business agreement. He proposes that Wyatt shall create his own art works. Recktall Brown, the art dealer, will sell these as newly discovered originals, and Wyatt will share in the profits.

The incongruity between Recktall Brown's materialistic perspective and Wyatt's spiritual orientation gives a comic-grotesque edge to the contractual episode. This is evident in the incommunicative dialogue in which Brown and Wyatt engage as they use the term "significance." Brown informs Wyatt: "We're talking business. [...] Money gives significance to anything." Wyatt, missing the point, tries to explain: "A work of art redeems time." Brown responds, "And buying it redeems money" (144).

Wyatt's involvement with the art dealer is as serious for him as is Faust's with Mephistopheles. Gaddis parallels the important actions of Wyatt with the farcical behavior of the minor character Otto, just as Goethe burlesques Faust's actions with those of his comic counterpart Wagner.[47] Otto is a caricature of Wyatt in almost all respects. Wyatt is a sincere artist; Otto, a pretentious plagiarist whose work sounds unusually familiar to all who hear it. Wyatt travels to Spain because he wishes to become spiritually close to the journey of his father and mother; Otto goes off to a banana plantation in South America so that he can look glamorous when he returns to New York. Wyatt is loved by the model Esme; Otto, after what he believes was a night of memorable lovemaking, finds that Esme does not even remember who he is (207). Otto also makes a travesty of the search for the father motif, so important for Wyatt. Otto and his father, Mr. Pivner, hope to recognize each other by their green scarves. However, when Otto, in the lavatory, sees Pivner looking intently at him (actually "staring [...] down at the bit of wool protruding from the coat's pocket") he fears the man intends to accost him sexually and thus looks at him with contempt. This frightens the father: "After a shrugged fluster and buttoning beside him, he [Otto] was alone" (566–67).

Comic parallels to Wyatt's conduct also are created by the contract between Recktall Brown and his servant, Fuller. Brown, who first meets Fuller while on a Caribbean cruise, buys the ignorant Fuller with a "set of gold teeth, and a promise of magic" (223). Their contract is that Fuller will work for him, submit to his punishments, and Brown, in turn, will turn his servant's skin white. Fuller's belief in the magical ability of Brown and of his black poodle provides comic relief for the evil power of Brown over Wyatt like that of Goethe's Mephistopheles over Faust (Mephistopheles, of course, transforms himself into a poodle before the "Pact Scene" in *Faust*). Fuller believes that the "poodle and their master communicated" (223). He asks the poodle: "You goin to write it down in your report. [...] Some day I goin to discover where you keep it and destroy every page" (345).

In Wyatt's first and last meetings with Recktall Brown, the scenes overflow with Faustian echoes that relate Brown to Mephistopheles and Wyatt to Faust. A brittle humor develops, in spite of the danger to Wyatt, because of the exaggerated details that make the characters appear to be cartoon figures of the Faustian originals. When Brown first knocks at Wyatt's study door, something ominous causes Wyatt to draw "back as though threatened" (140). Then, as a parody of the Devil, Brown complains that people say bad things about him: "You'd think I was wicked as hell, even if what I do for them turns out good" (141). In addition, a strange thing happens to Brown's face as he confirms the contract with Wyatt: "His eyes, which had all this time seemed to swim without focus behind the heavy lenses, shrank to sharp points of black, and like weapons suddenly unsheathed they penetrated instantly wherever he turned them" (146). This calls attention to Mephistopheles and his spirit dog, which had "fiery eyes" and was "terrible to see" (51 [I.1255]).

In Goethe's drama, Faust, alone in his study, picks up the Bible and labors to translate the opening verse in the Gospel of Saint John (50 [I.1224]). Wyatt contradicts this religious tone, when, in a parallel situation, he chants: "*Dog! Dog! Dog!*" The narrator observes that "no sound contested his challenge [...] for spelling the Name of God backwards, no response to God, if not the Name, reversed three times" (139).[48] The black poodle in the study scene and the "contract" with Brown foreshadow the later allusions to Mephistopheles during the Christmas party, the locale where expectation of Wyatt's possible atonement is—in a comic-grotesque manner—reduced to nothing.

The deflation of the sacred at the Christmas party sets the tone for Wyatt's mock heroism and his ironic quest for redemption. At the party Brown (seeming to have the fearful concern of the Devil) swerves as he passes the low Bosch tabletop of the Seven Deadly Sins near the fireplace (663). Valentine, as though reacting to the allusion, asks: "What the devil's the matter with you." The dark humor increases as Brown replies: "Not a God damn thing the matter with me." Brown's laughter, calling to mind hell fires, rises "in an eructation of smoke" (663–64). When he pulls on his prized suit of armor over his legs, one guest states that he might be "wearing false calves" like Mephistopheles in "that ponderous thing by Goethe [...] to cover his cloven feet" (676).

In this context, surrounded by party-goers whose banality is transparent, such as Mr. and Mrs. Schmuck, Wyatt tries to redeem himself by revealing that the valued paintings Brown is selling are forgeries, and that he, Wyatt, is the forger. The scene develops more cartoon qualities as the distressed Wyatt, eyes aglitter, wearing one suit on top of another, tries to inform the people that the paintings are frauds. The incongruity between the seeker of salvation and the crass, moneyed people causes bitter laughter. For these people, the sensitive artist is a "lunatic come back again," a person ready to "go up in flames." Wyatt's attempted atonement is the object of ridicule: "Won't do, won't do at all ... can't hev this sort of thing, invading a private gathering, eh? A man's home is his mphht what d'you-call-it, don't you know," observes one man, unable to complete the literary allusion. The man then turns to a fellow guest: "I say, my dear fellow do be a bit more careful, you're spilling your drink all over me" (676–77). The seeking of atonement at this sacrilegious Christmas party is ludicrous. Some people "turn their attention, and some their backs, on this diverting visitor who stood looking feverishly round, holding up a handful of charred wood, whispering—Where is he? [....] Brown!" (677).

Wyatt and Brown—Faust and Mephistopheles—face each other. The scene evokes echoes of Goethe's *Faust*, when Mephistopheles tries to prevent the saved Faust from being carried off to heaven. In *The Recognitions*, however, all becomes slapstick. Mephistopheles is deterred from evil action not because angels carry the hero away but because the devil himself, who has just managed to put on a suit of armor, crashes from his perch on the balcony to the room below and lands not far from the Bosch tabletop of the Seven Deadly Sins, near the rising flames of the fireplace (677).

There is an important difference between the ridicule in *Faust* and that in *The Recognitions*. Goethe balances indignation at man's greedy activities with a vision of man's possible goodness and creativity in this world, and his eventual redemption in heaven. *The Recognitions*, on the other hand, emphasizes man's futile efforts in a meaningless world. The major difference between Faust and Wyatt is that Faust achieves redemption while Wyatt does not.

Some critics believe that Wyatt, at the close, does progress toward hope and renewal. They point to his remarks to the popular religious novelist Ludy—"Love, and do what you want. [...] Now at last, to live deliberately. [...] Yes, we'll simplify" (899–900).[49] They point to the time Wyatt spends with the Spanish woman Pastora, finally living for the moment, instead of always thinking of the past. However, an intertextual reading of *The Recognitions* and Goethe's *Faust* clarifies that Wyatt's situation is a comic deflation of Faust's.

Faust's pact with Mephistopheles to remain ever aspiring speaks obliquely to Wyatt's activities after he leaves New York City for Spain. Wyatt's new philosophy to "love, and do what you want" (899), to luxuriate with Pastora, emphasizes taking joy in the "moment" and abandoning his former aspirations. In response to Mr. Yák's warning—"You don't want to let yourself go to hell like this, do you hear me?"—Wyatt says, "No, [...] It's just the other way" (803). He believes that he and Pastora are in love.

At first glance, this change in Wyatt seems to be healthy. He has shifted from being a withdrawn recluse, engaged solely in his art, to being an active lover. He even insists that giving love to Pastora can atone for withholding it from another woman in the past, thus expiating his guilt for the mistreatment of Esme (guilt similar to Faust's because of his neglect of Gretchen). On the other hand, however, Wyatt, in thinking only of being with Pastora, shows the contentment with the moment that Faust withstands.

Wyatt's aim to live deliberately burlesques his former yearning for the ideal past. In addition, according to the Faustian pact, to be caught up entirely in life is damning. It shows no yearning for eternal love or divine grace. The allusions to *Faust* thus ironically comment on Wyatt's final "affirmation." The reader recalls Faust's caution to Euphorion—"touch but with thy toe the surface, / Like the son of Earth, Antaeus" (406 [II.9610–11])—which locates Faust in relation to both the physical and spiritual, this world and the next. Faust grows to appreciate the importance of the two. Wyatt, on the other hand, never does.

The tragicomic absurdity of Wyatt's situation is also underlined by the comparison he makes between himself and the great epic hero Odysseus. When with Pastora, he thinks of himself as Odysseus, but with a significant twist. In contrast to Odysseus's slaying the suitors whom Penelope has kept in abeyance, Wyatt connects himself to the suitors and wishes "to supersede where they [lovers of the prostitute Pastora] failed, lie down where they left." He intends to live the moments through "where they happened," insisting, "It's only the living it [sin] through that redeems it" (898).[50]

Wyatt's activities in the last stages of his quest parody the meaningful close of Faust's life on earth when he is welcomed to heaven by the angelic choir. There is a sharp irony in Gaddis's novel through contrast with the last vision of Faust amid the melodious strains of the angelic chorus:[51]

> All things transitory
> But as symbols are sent:
> Earth's insufficiency
> Here grows to Event:
> The Indescribable,
> Here it is done:
> The Woman-Soul leadeth us
> Upward and on! (506 [II.v.12104–11])

The last glimpse we have of Wyatt is at the Spanish monastery where he, intent on "restoring" paintings, razor blades them into fragments. His reach for the spiritual through the restoration of art, like his earlier quest for connection with the Reverend Gwyon, culminates in bizarre action. In the earlier scene at the monastery, he becomes one with the father/Father in a parody of the Eucharist. In this later effort at spiritual satisfaction, he cuts away at the creative work of great artists, literally denuding the canvas of Rubens's nudes. He destroys rather than restores. The fact that Wyatt meticulously razors the paintings, despite the warnings of Ludy and the exclamations of the man in the brown suit, shows how rigid and mechanical this Bergsonian figure has become. Wyatt's actions confuse the reader, causing him not to know whether to laugh or cry at the humor emerging in the artist's absurd quest for meaning.

Wyatt, throughout his life, looked at the Bosch tabletop of the Seven Deadly Sins (owned first by Reverend Gwyon and later by Recktall Brown). He always trembled while observing the eye of Christ in the center of the tabletop, and reading the inscription: "*Cave, Cave, D^s videt*" [Take care, take care, God is watching] (25). Now, at the end of the book, Wyatt no longer believes in God's presence. Not only does he feel that God is not watching him, but he also concludes that the masters of the golden age of Flemish art created paintings that seemed to show a vain effort in handling the "fear there was no God" (875).

For Wyatt, the world seems analogous to a hellish sea in which celestial people would be doomed to drown, just as Saint Clement drowned in the Black Sea with an anchor around his neck. But in Wyatt's twentieth-century world there is no miraculous sepulcher, no salvation. Instead, there are only continual parties and chance meetings; people often seem to be all afloat in the dusky ambiance of a Stygian flood. The narrator relates: "Like undersea flora, figures stood weaving, rooted to the floor, here and there one drifting as though caught in a cold current, sensing [...] what one expressed as—Something submarine, as he paddled the air before him, and went on" (656–57). People glide past one another like variously colored fish, blinded by self-preoccupation.

In this setting, the hero's journey has been reduced to the movement from one party to the next. His company includes crass members of society: Crémer, the art critic who requires a percentage of a painter's sale price for a good review; Radcliffe graduates who misspell words and perversely place a *t* in *genial*; and a husband and wife who separate when each publishes a novel with the other as protagonist.

The Recognitions presents a world in which the artist Wyatt continually searches for meaning, a glimpse of a lost paradise, a sign that God is watching. Instead he finds only randomness. People are recognized by surface details of trivia (a green scarf, a fedora hat, a gold signet ring, a large diamond ring) and by their cartoon behavior (repeating an unusual pronunciation such as "Chr-ah-st" or showing a propensity to make counterfeit twenty-dollar bills). Such a flattening of human beings deflates the dignity of man.

The Recognitions is a book about false resurrections, such as the mistaken canonization of Camilla Gwyon in place of the young girl chosen by the Church. It is a book about counterfeiters who parody God's creation. It is a book about the ironic desire to soar in atonement in a world in which God is not watching, a world in which God may never have been watching.

The Recognitions is a comic epic about a world in which people are guided by a Bible of commercialism whose readers range from the monks in the Spanish monastery in Estremadura to the inhabitants of crowded tenements in New York City. In Estremadura, a monk enthusiastically peruses the books of a visiting religious novelist with the hope of finding a copy of *Como Ganar Amigos y Vencer Todos los Otros* [How To Win Friends and Influence People] (859). In Manhattan, Mr. Pivner avidly reads Dale Carnegie's explanation about "a new way of life," an alchemical "elixir" (the narrator sarcastically interjects) that exchanges "the things worth being for the things worth having." Continuing the ironic reversal of the sacred to the material, Carnegie emphasizes: "You owe it to yourself, to your happiness, to your future, and *TO YOUR INCOME!*" (498–500).

In this upside-down world, a minor and rather negative character—Benny—proclaims: "We're comic. We're all comics. We live in a comic time. And the worse it gets the more comic we are" (640).[52] Thus does Gaddis use jest to spend his rage, as he recognizes the absurdist vision that emerges from the contrast between the ideal and its loss.

NOTES

1. William Gaddis, "The Rush for Second Place," *Harper's* (April 1981): 36.
2. Nikolai Gogol, *Dead Souls*, trans. Andrew R. MacAndrew, Foreword by Frank O'Connor (New York: New American Library, 1961), 236. References to *Dead Souls* are to this edition.
3. William Gaddis, "Why I Write," lecture at the University of Delaware, 1 May 1985.
4. Gaddis, University of Delaware, 1 May 1985. Malcolm Bradbury, "The House That Gaddis Built," review of Carpenter's Gothic, by William Gaddis, Washington Post Book World (7 July 1985): 1, has called *The Recognitions* "the starting place for a whole new direction in contemporary American fictional experiment, opening the path for Thomas Pynchon and the modern labyrinthine novel." Cynthia Ozick, "Fakery and Stony Truths," review of *Carpenter's Gothic*, by

William Gaddis, *New York Times Book Review* (7 July 1985): 1, calls William Gaddis "new coinage: an American Original." At the same time, however, she points out that such a claim would "fall into his own comedy," for "originality is exactly what he has made absurd; unrecognizable." Tony Tanner, *City of Words: American Fiction, 1950-1970* (New York: Harper & Row, 1971), 393, praises "this amazing one-thousand-page work" for being "immensely rich and funny" and for ushering in a "new period of American fiction in which the theme of fictions/recognitions has come to occupy the forefront of American writer's consciousness"; Steven Moore, Introduction, *A Reader's Guide to William Gaddis's The Recognitions* "a precursor of what in later years may be considered one of the most creative periods in American literature."

5. Gogol taunts the reader for being unwilling to have the "Christian humility" to ask himself: "Am I not, even slightly, somewhat of a Chichikov" (276).

6. Gogol 115–16.

7. René Wellek, Introduction, *Dead Souls*, Nikolai Gogol, trans. Bernard Guilbert Guerney (New York: Holt, Rinehart, and Winston, 1961) xiii. See also Philip Rahv, *Literature and the Sixth Sense* (Boston: Houghton Mifflin, 1969), 197, who points out that *Dead Souls* moves from "levity to despair."

8. Gogol 14.

9. Gogol 160. See also Donald Fanger's discussion of the novel's paradox: "Living people and dead ones may be clearly distinguished in the action, but the cumulative sense of the text denies this distinction." "*Dead Souls*: The Mirror and the Road," in Nikolai Gogol, *Dead Souls*, ed. George Gibian, trans. George Reavey (New York: Norton, 1985), 471.

10. "Rush" 36.

11. Gogol 253.

12. Lloyd Grove, "Gaddis and the Cosmic Babble: Fiction Rich with the Darkly Funny Voices of America," *Style, The Washington Post* (23 August 1985): B10, observes that Gaddis satirically emphasizes the confrontation between the desire in twentieth century America to reestablish the values of the nation's heritage, on the one hand, and, on the other, the inclination to "grasp at mere counterfeits."

13. See Umberto Eco, "Innovation and Repetition: Between Modern and Post-Modern Aesthetics," *Daedalus* 114, no. 4 (1985): 170.

14. Scramble the letters of *The Recognitions* and you can come up with titles such as "I CHOSE ROTTEN GIN," "OI CHOTTERING ONES," "THE R I COONS IGNITE," "THE ONION CREST G I," "TEN ECHOES RIOTING" (JR 515).

15. See *Book Review Digest* (1955) for excerpts from the original review of *The Recognitions*, which include statements from Milton Rugoff (JR's Milton R. Goth), the *New York Herald Tribune Book Review* (13 March 1955); Granville Hicks (Glandvil Hix); Maxwell Geismar (M Axswill Gummer); and *Kirkus* (Kricket Reviews).

16. Brackets are used to distinguish editorial eclipses from those in *The Recognitions*. Frederick Karl, *American Fictions, 1940/1980* (New York: Harper & Row, 1983), 183 points out that "Gaddis's aim is clearly to defamiliarize the familiar so as to force us to experience it freshly." Thomas LeClair, "William Gaddis, JR, and the Art of Excess," *Modern Fiction Studies* 27 (1981–82): 590, calls this method a "mimetic aesthetic." He emphasizes that "Gaddis was suggesting that art must admit its imitation of other art to free itself from unknowing copying and to restore the full being of its subjects." Gaddis's novels provide "a new vision of contemporary reality";

John Leverence, "Gaddis Anagnorisis," in *In Recognition of William Gaddis*, ed. John Kuehl and Steven Moore (Syracuse, N.Y.: Syracuse University Press, 1984), 39, comments on the novel's "aesthetic theme of recognition, that is, originality is not invention but a sense of recall, a recognition of patterns that are already there."

17. Oxford English Dictionary.

18. Quoted in Cindy Smith, "William Gaddis Rails Against Misrepresentation" [University of Delaware], The Review (30 April 1985): 18.

19. From Ralph Waldo Emerson, "Old Age," Essays of Ralph Waldo Emerson (Garden City, N.Y.: Blue Ribbon Books, 1941), 548.

20. Ralph Waldo Emerson, "Nature," *CW* 1:13.

21. See Odell Shepard, *Pedlar's Progress: The Life of Bronson Alcott* (Boston: Little, Brown, 1937), 246–61; for further discussion of the content of some of the conversations, see Lawrence Buell, *Literary Transcendentalism: Style and Vision in the American Renaissance* (Ithaca, N.Y.: Cornell University Press, 1973), 82–89.

22. Kathleen L. Lathrop, "Comic-Ironic Parallels in William Gaddis's *The Recognitions*," *Review of Contemporary Fictions* 2 (1982): 32, points out that "the author /prophet sounds far more like Milton Berle than Jeremiah."

23. Erwin Panofsky, *Early Netherlandish Painting* (Cambridge, Mass.: Harvard University Press, 1966), 1:2, refers to this alleged remark by Michelangelo.

24. *Recognitions of Clement, The Ante-Nicene Fathers*, ed. Alexander Roberts and James Donaldson (New York: Scribner, 1903), vol. 8, hereafter referred to parenthetically in the text as *Clem. R*. This third century work is actually a pseudo-Clementine tract. Saint Clementine of Rome, the follower of Saint Peter, lived in the first century A.D. For information about the text see the Introductory Notice. Basilius Valentinus, *The Triumphal Chariot of Antimony*, trans. Arthur Edward Waite (London: Vincent Stuart Ltd., 1962); see also Basilius Valentinus, "Practica," in *The Hermetic Museum*, ed. Arthur Edward Waite, (London: John M. Watkins, 1953), vol 1: 311-57; hereafter referred to parenthetically in the text as *HM*.

25. See Eco's analysis of the way such an author invites the reader "to play upon his encyclopedic competence" (171).

26. Albert Camus, *The Myth of Sisyphus and Other Essays*, trans. Justin O'Brien (New York: Vintage, 1955), 11.

27. Wyatt indicates that he is thirty three when he speculates on his life in relation to Christ's: "Why, two thousand years ago, thirty three was old, and time to die" (876).

28. That Camilla Gwyon died thirty years prior to Wyatt's visit to San Zwingli indicates that Wyatt was three at her death. This squares with the fact that "Wyatt was four years old when his father returned from Spain" (18) after traveling for several months following Camilla's death.

29. John Seelye, "Dryad in a Dead Oak Tree: The Incognito in *The Recognitions*" (Kuehl and Moore 79), observes: "The ritual of the Eucharist, as in a Black Mass, becomes an obscenity."

30. In the early part of *The Recognitions*, the protagonist is referred to as "Wyatt." In the middle, he is not referred to by name, and toward the end he is called "Stephen." On a literal level, we realize that the change to Stephen arises from Wyatt's assuming the identity of Stephen Asche, from the Swiss passport that Mr. Sinisterra/Yák forges for him. On a symbolic level, we appreciate that Wyatt finally

has taken on the name of Stephen, first Christian martyr, the name his parents originally designated him (27). Perhaps Gaddis wishes to call attention to the literal and symbolic levels by using the different spellings Stephan/Stephen. Bernard Benstock, "On William Gaddis: In Recognition of James Joyce," *Contemporary Literature* 5 (1965): 181, observes that "Stephen" is" the name Gaddis goes to use for him, returning him full circle to the Stephen he should have been." Frederick Karl, "Gaddis: A Tribune of the Fifties" (Kuehl and Moore, 180), comments on "the paradoxes and ironies" of the name, for after burning his paintings, turning them to ashes, Wyatt assumes the name Stephen Asche: "He is the first Christian martyr, born out of the ashes of his own work." See also Steven Weisenburger, "Paper Currencies: Reading William Gaddis" (Kuehl and Moore 149–50), for a discussion of names in the novel.

31. Henri Bergson, "Laughter," in *Comedy*, ed. Wylie Sypher (Garden City: Doubleday, Anchor, 1956), 84.

32. See John Leverence's discussion of links with alchemy in the novel. "Gaddis" (Kuehl and Moore 42). See also Moore, who discusses the importance of alchemy "in unifying the symbolic elements ... and in providing a spiritual 'plot' to complement (and justify) the narrative of the novel" (*Reader's Guide* 10).

33. Leverence, "Gaddis" (Kuehl and Moore 40).

34. *HM* 1:316.

35. See John Read, *Prelude to Chemistry: An Outline of Alchemy* (1936; reprint, Cambridge, Mass.: M.I.T. Press, 1966), 183. Basilius Valentinus could have been a charlatan alchemist like the one whom Chaucer describes in the "Canon's Yeoman's Tale."

36. A typical alchemical laboratory had furnaces, odorous vapors arising from boiling liquids, various vessels with matter in different stages of change, emitting a variety of color in the process. Usually sulphur, mercury, copper, lead, and occasionally antimony were dissolved, separated, and reunited. They often were combined with organic substances such as eggs, blood, and excrement. Very important in the laboratory was a book of prayers, for the worker would appeal to divine help as he carried out his process. See Wayne Shumaker, "Alchemy," The Occult Sciences in the Renaissance (Berkeley: University of California Press, 1972) 170–75. See also Moore, who observes that the "secularization of salvation ... takes the form of the redemptive power of art" (*Reader's Guide* 18).

37. In regard to color changes, the alchemist Cremer observes: "When the mixture is still black it is called the Black Raven. As it turns white it is named the Virgin's Milk, or the Bone of the Whale. In its red stage, it is the Red Lion. When it is blue, it is called the Blue Lion. When it is all colours, the Sages name it Rainbow" (*HM* 2:77). Basilius Valentinus explained that the alchemist using antimony "can colour it red or yellow, white or black, according to the way he regulates the fire" (*Triumphal Chariot* 48). For a discussion of the "seasons" or "states" of the alchemical process, see also Martinus Rulandus, *A Lexicon of Alchemy* [1612], trans. A.E. Waite (1893; reprint London: John M. Watkins, 1964), 421–22; and Titus Burckhardt, *Alchemy*, trans. William Stoddart (1960; reprint, Baltimore: Penguin, 1974), esp. 182–95.

38. Gaddis states (in his notes): "The process of art is the artist's working out of his own redemption." Peter Koenig, "'Splinters from the Yew Tree': A Critical Study of William Gaddis's *The Recognitions*" (Ph.D. diss., New York University, 1971, 90.

39. The alchemist Raymond Lully explains the process: "In our art, the thing that is unjustly defiled by the one will be absolved, cleansed and delivered from that foulness by another that is contrary to it" (*Recognitions* 222).

40. Tanner, *City of Words*, 398; see also David Madden, "William Gaddis's *The Recognitions*," in Rediscoveries, ed. David Madden (New York: Crown, 1971), 304: "The achievement of the orchestration of Gaddis's technical devices is the creation ... (of a) perhaps spiritual, state of recognition." Grace Eckley, "Exorcising the Demon Forgery, or the Forging of Pure Gold in Gaddis's *Recognitions*," In *Literature and the Occult*, ed. Luanne Frank (Arlington, Tex.: University of Texas Press, 1977), 128, says that the occult serves as the "unifying force" in the novel, developing the anticipatory pattern of details pointing to Wyatt's redemption. For Peter William Koenig, "Recognizing Gaddis's *Recognitions*," *Contemporary Literature* 16 (1975): 71, "the novel offers no final answers to the questions it raises, but ... the very suggestiveness and structure of his questioning constitutes a partial answer."

41. Karl comments that Stanley's death "while his ... work soars in atonement, is a perfect expression of Henry Adam's virgin and dynamo: the machine crushes, the Virgin saves" (*American Fictions* 186); Christopher Knight, "Flemish Art and Wyatt's Quest for Redemption in William Gaddis's *The Recognitions*" (Kuehl and Moore 65–68), writes that Gaddis points out "the failure of not only Wyatt's but also his own quest for redemption through art .... Scraping the paint off the El Greco canvas in the monastery is symbolic of his recognition of this limitation. Truth must finally be sought beyond art's boundaries." On the other hand, Joseph S. Salemi, "To Soar in Atonement: Art as Expiation in Gaddis's *The Recognitions*," Novel 10, no. 2 (1977): 136, argues: "Stanley's work expiates the falsity of Wyatt's and at that same work is the instrument of his martyrdom." For Salemi, "Art is the ultimate expiation, for through it ... falsehood which lies at the core of existence is transfigured beyond the pettiness and sordidness of its context and origins." It is the frustrated desire to affirm this view, I think, that develops the black humor of the absurd in *The Recognitions*.

42. The leg incident becomes the source of farce when it is stolen, carried about town, and finally left in a train where it causes a commotion when "a shabby old man had found something" (340; see also 317, 325–326). This "coincidentally" happens in the same car in which Stanley is riding.

43. Johann Wolfgang Von Goethe, *Faust: A Tragedy*, trans. Bayard Taylor (New York: Macmillan, 1930), II.ii. 6834–35. Further references to *Faust* are listed parenthetically in the text; page numbers are to Taylor's edition, and line numbers have been added in brackets.

44. See Eco 170.

45. Johann Wolfgang Von Goethe, *Conversations of Goethe with Eckermann and Soret*, trans. John Oxenford (London: Smith, Elder, 1850), 2: 400.

46. Emil Staiger, "On the 'Great Lacuna' and the Pact Scene," *Faust: A Tragedy*, trans. Walter Arndt and ed. Cyrus Hamlin (New York: Norton, 1976), 515–16, emphasizes the celebration of "incessant endeavor, striving and accomplishment" in Faust, the "symbol of the German soul." He also, however, thinks that Goethe, though seeing this as "spiritually justifiable behavior," would condemn this "eternal unrest ... as tragic madness."

47. See, e.g., Wagner's imitation of Faust in the "Laboratory" scene in which Wagner is unaware of Mephistophelean magic in the creation of Humunculus (297 [II.ii.6820–7004]).

48. Moore points out that "Wyatt's aside to the dog during the preceding pages parallel those of Faust to the poodle Mephistopheles" (*Reader Guide* 127). But, neither Moore nor anyone else, to the best of my knowledge, has closely examined these connections.

49. Leverence argues that there is an "alchemical parallel" to Wyatt's giving up the world and planning to simplify his life: "Wyatt has found wisdom through simplicity, even as the minor opus finds its completion with the simple purity and symbolic wisdom of silver." "Gaddis" (Kuehl and Moore 42).

50. Many critics see Wyatt's act as more promising than I do and stress his comment, "It's only the living it through that redeems it" (898). Miriam Fuchs, "'il miglior fabbro': Gaddis' Debt to T.S. Eliot" (Kuehl and Moore 103), explains that each person "is punished for someone else's [sin] and atones for someone else's, just as that person does for him." Knight observes: "Gaddis defiantly argues for the reality of sin and, in turn, the possibility, through love, of redemption" (68). David [Peter] Koenig, "The Writing of *The Recognitions*" (Kuehl and Moore 31), writes: "Wyatt still has at least the possibility of finding redemption." However, Koenig does point out that Gaddis "deliberately reduced Wyatt's visible means of salvation" in the novel as compared to Gaddis's plans in the notes.

51. Harold Jantz, *The Form of Faust* (Baltimore: Johns Hopkins University Press, 1978), 83, describes our last vision of Faust as movement from darkness to light, "death and resurrection, an end situation followed by a promise of continuity ... a condemnation followed by vindication." This is the pattern in the drama as a whole. Neil M. Flax, "The Presence of the Sign in Goethe's Faust," *PMLA* 98 (1983): 192, discusses the rainbow at the close as "a symbol provided by a divinely ordered nature"; Stuart Atkins, *Goethe's Faust: A Literary Analysis* (Cambridge, Mass.: Harvard University Press, 1958), 272–74, also stresses the sense of a regularly ordered design in *Faust*.

52. Koenig explains: "The hope that Gaddis extinguished in his plot he rekindled through parody." 'The Writing" (Kuehl and Moore 31).

STEVEN MOORE

Carpenter's Gothic; *or, The Ambiguities*

In the years following the publication of *JR*, Gaddis occasionally taught at Bard College, an experience he described as follows:

> My friend William Burroughs used to say that he didn't teach creative writing, he taught creative reading. That was my idea in the Bard courses I taught, especially "The Theme of Failure in American Literature," where we read everything from Dale Carnegie's *How to Win Friends and Influence People* to William James' *Pragmatism* to *Diary of a Mad Housewife*. What I was trying to do was raise questions for which there are no distinct answers. The problems remain with us because there are no absolutes.[1]

Carpenter's Gothic is likewise a course in creative reading, a novel that raises questions for which there are no distinct answers, and one that counters absolutes with ambiguities. "There's a very fine line between the truth and what really happens" is a dictum that echoes throughout the novel,[2] but while half the characters proclaim the truth and the other half expose what really happens, an ambiguity that neither half wishes to acknowledge prevents the reader from attaining an absolute certainty about many of the

---

From *William Gaddis*. © 1989 by Twayne Publishers.

novel's events and returns him or her to the air of uncertainty that is the chief climate of our ambiguous times.

This much can be deduced: *Carpenter's Gothic* concerns the last month in the life of Elizabeth Booth, "a stunning redhaired former debutante from the exclusive Grosse Point area in Michigan" and "the daughter of late mineral tycoon F R Vorakers" (255). Former head of Vorakers Consolidated Reserve (VCR) in southeast Africa, her father committed suicide eight or nine years before the novel opens when his bribery practices were in danger of being exposed. At his funeral, Paul Booth, a Vietnam veteran and proud Southerner (actually an orphan of uncertain heritage) who "carried the bag" for the briberies, seduced Liz (as he calls her) and took her as his second wife. He quickly ran through much of her money in a number of ill-considered schemes to get rich; the rest of her money is tied up in a trust administered by "Adolph," much to Paul's frustration. Four years before the novel's present Liz survived an airplane crash, and four years later Paul is still pursuing a bogus suit for the loss of his wife's "marital services." Financial difficulties have led the couple to quit New York City for a rented house up the Hudson River—a ninety-year-old house in "Carpenter Gothic" style—whence Paul hopes to make it big as a media consultant. As the novel begins, his most promising client is the Reverend Elton Ude, an evangelical preacher from the rural South who with Paul's help parlays an accidental drowning during a baptism into a providential call for a multimedia crusade against the forces of evil, a.k.a. the powers of darkness (namely communism, teachers of evolution, the "Jew liberal press," and secular humanists everywhere). Using the house simply as a place "to eat and sleep and fuck and answer the telephone" (244), Paul spends most of his time elsewhere. Liz's younger brother Billy pays an occasional disruptive visit, but she spends most of her time fighting off boredom and coping with an unending series of phone calls, many concerning the whereabouts of the house's absentee landlord. Enter mysterious stranger.

A man apparently in his late fifties, McCandless began as a geologist and in fact did the original exploration of the African ore field that is now up for grabs between VCR and the Reverend Ude, who has a mission and radio station there. Disgusted at the increasing CIA involvement with the various movements toward independence in Africa beginning in the 1950s, McCandless drifted for years: he married and fathered a son named Jack (who once attended school with Billy), supported himself by teaching and writing articles for encyclopedias and science magazines, and even wrote a novel about his African experiences with the CIA. The first marriage ending in divorce, McCandless married a younger woman named Irene, but she left him two years before the novel opens. He is presently being hounded by both the IRS and the CIA, the latter in the uncouth person of Lester, a former colleague of his African days who is convinced McCandless retains vital information regarding the ore field under dispute.

McCandless arrives one misty morning to reclaim some papers stored in a locked room. Coming to life at his appearance, Liz transforms McCandless into a wearily romantic "older man" with a mysterious past, and on his second appearance a week later takes him into her bed during one of Paul's many absences. McCandless leaves the next afternoon in the company of Liz's brother Billy, whose conversations with McCandless (there and later that night in New York City) solidify his earlier resolve to go to work for his father's company in Africa. Shortly after their departure, Paul arrives home in tatters (the victim of an attempted mugging) with all his media plans in tatters as well. Paul is $10,000 richer—keeping for himself a bribe Ude intended for Senator Teakell and the FCC—and has paid a black youth $100 to assassinate the minister. That night paid arsonists mistake another house for McCandless's and burn it to the ground.

A week later McCandless returns to find the house ransacked and Liz griefstricken at the news of her brother's death aboard an airplane shot down off the coast of Africa, a strike targetted for Senator Teakell who was ostensibly on a fact-finding mission "defending the mineral resources of the free world" but actually watching out for his own financial investments there. McCandless is preparing to leave the country—he has accepted Lester's offer of $16,000 for his papers—but fails to persuade Liz to go with him. After he leaves Liz receives a brief visit from McCandless's first wife, both mistaking each other for the second wife Irene. Alone in the house after she leaves, Liz suffers a heart attack, symptoms of which were displayed throughout the novel, though dismissed by her doctors as high blood pressure. Because the house is still in disarray after the break-in that morning, the press mistakenly reports her death as the result of attempting to interrupt a robbery in progress. Paul believes this story, and though distraught at her death, he loses no time making sure both her and Billy's money will come to him, and he is last seen on the way to their funeral using the same seductive line on her best friend Edie that he used on Liz many years before.

As is the case with any summary of a Gaddis novel, this one not only fails to do justice to the novel's complex tapestry of events but also subverts the manner in which these events are conveyed. Opening *Carpenter's Gothic* is like opening the lid of a jigsaw puzzle: all the pieces seem to be there, but it is up to the reader to fit those pieces together. Paul's refrain "fit the pieces together you see how all the God damn pieces fit together" (205) doubles as

Gaddis's instructions to the reader. The author doesn't make it easy: the initials VCR are used throughout the book but not spelled out until thirty-three pages before the end; a letter from Thailand arrives on page 48 but its contents not revealed until two pages from the end; names occur in conversations that are not explained until pages later, if ever. Ambiguity is introduced in the very first line of the novel ("The bird, a pigeon was it? or a dove"), and though this particular ambiguity is cleared up at the end of the first chapter ("It was a dove"), the novel is rife with other ambiguities that are never resolved. Even after multiple readings, several events remain ambiguous, sometimes because too little information is given, sometimes because there are two conflicting accounts and no way to confirm either. As Paul complains later, "pieces fit together problem's just too God damn many pieces" (212).

Such narrative strategies are designed not to baffle or frustrate the reader but to dramatize the novel's central philosophic conflict, that between revealed truth versus acquired knowledge. Nothing is "revealed" by a godlike omniscient narrator in this novel; the reader learns "what really happens" only through study, attention, and the application of intelligence. The reader learns that McCandless has married twice, for example, by noting that Mrs. McCandless is old enough to have a twenty-five-year old son (251), but Irene young enough to still use Tampax (150; cf. the handwriting on p. 31) and to have her youthful photograph praised by Lester (132). If several events remain ambiguous after such study, the reader must live with those ambiguities rather than insist on absolute certainty, much as the intellectually mature individual abandons the absolutes of revealed religion for the ambiguities of actual life. In this novel Gaddis plays not God but the philosopher who announced the death of God: "Objections, non-sequiturs, cheerful distrust, joyous mockery—all are signs of health," Nietzsche insists. "Everything absolute belongs in the realm of pathology."

To his credit, Jesus never spoke of absolutes, but his followers in *Carpenter's Gothic* do. The Reverend Ude insists that Christ "built this great edifice of refuge for the weak, for the weary, for the seekers after his absolute truth in their days of adversity and persecution" (80). The same zealous certainty inspires the efforts of "a charming Texas couple who keep an eye out for schoolbooks that undermine patriotism, free enterprise, religion, parental authority, nothing official of course [McCandless explains to Billy], just your good American vigilante spirit hunting down, where is it, books that erode absolute values by asking questions to which they offer no firm answers" (184).[3] The catalog of conservative values here is important: *Carpenter's Gothic* is not simply a satire on fundamentalism but a critique of the ways such absolutist thinking can lead to imperialism, xenophobia, rapacious capitalism, and the kind of paranoid cold war ideology enshrined in a *New York Post* headline at the novel's (and perhaps the world's) end: "PREZ: TIME TO DRAW LINE AGAINST EVIL EMPIRE" (259).

But none of this is new, as McCandless reminds both Billy and Lester in his harangues against Christianity. Just as Marlow in Conrad's *Heart of Darkness* prefaces his tale of European imperialism in Africa with a reminder of Roman excursions into ancient Britain, McCandless several times sketches bloody moments in the history of Christianity (128, 142, 190–91, 236, 243) and locates this militant impulse in the Bible itself: the god of the Old Testament "is a man of war" (243; Ex. 15:3) and the son of god in the New Testament warns his followers "I come not to send peace but a sword" (142; Matt. 10:34). The fundamentalist fervor that McCandless lashes out against is not a topical subject that will date Gaddis's novel, but rather the latest and potentially the most lethal manifestation of a religion that has caused more bloodshed than harmony in its two-thousand-year history. The carpenter of "the profit Isaiah" (80) and the carpenter's son of the gospels together have created a Gothic nightmare of blood, guilt, persecution, righteousness, and intolerance—one meaning of Gaddis's ambiguous title.

"A PATCHWORK OF CONCEITS, BORROWINGS, DECEPTIONS"

A more important meaning of the title comes late in the book. At an awkward moment in his last conversation with Liz, McCandless welcomes the opportunity to discuss a neutral subject—the house's "Carpenter Gothic" architecture:

> —Oh the house yes, the house. It was built that way yes, it was built to be seen from the outside it was, that was the style, he came on, abruptly rescued from uncertainty, raised to the surface—yes, they had style books, these country architects and the carpenters it was all derivative wasn't it, those grand Victorian mansions with their rooms and rooms and towering heights and cupolas and the marvelous intricate ironwork. That whole inspiration of medieval Gothic but these poor fellows didn't have it, the stonework and the wrought iron. All they had were the simple dependable old materials, and the wood and their hammers and saws and their own clumsy ingenuity bringing those grandiose visions the masters had left behind down to a

human scale with their own little inventions, [...] a patchwork of conceits, borrowings, deceptions, the inside's a hodgepodge of good intentions like one last ridiculous effort at something worth doing even on this small a scale [...]. (227–28)

If one discounts the self-deprecating tone—Gaddis is no "country architect" with only "clumsy ingenuity"—this can easily double as a description of *Carpenter's Gothic* itself. Gaddis found his "simple dependable old materials" in what he described to one interviewer as the "staples" of traditional fiction and set himself a task: "That is, the staples of the marriage, which is on the rocks, the obligatory adultery, the locked room, the mysterious stranger, the older man and the younger woman, to try to take these and make them work."[4] In addition to these staples of plot, he depends on the staples of certain generic conventions. Gaddis's "patchwork of conceits, borrowings, deceptions" brings under one roof a number of genres: the Gothic novel, the apocalypse, the romance (in all senses), and the metafictional meditation, along with elements of Greek tragedy, Dickensian social satire, the colonial novel, the political thriller, documentary realism, the contemporary Vietnam veteran's story, and what Roy R. Male calls "cloistral" fiction. Each is a room jammed into Gaddis's Gothic construction, a little invention (only in comparison to his first two novels) of great ingenuity.

As McCandless says, Carpenter Gothic houses were meant to be seen from the outside and hence were designed with an emphasis on outward symmetry, even if it resulted in such deceptions as "twinned windows so close up there they must open from one room but in fact looked out from the near ends of two neither of them really furnished, an empty bookcase and sagging daybed in one and in the other a gutted chaise longue voluted in French pretension trailing gold velvet in the dust undisturbed on the floor since she'd stood there, maybe three or four times since she'd lived in the house" (226–27). (Note how perfectly this captures Paul and Liz's relationship: united under one roof, they are nonetheless divided by a wall of differences, his intellectual bankruptcy and lust caught by the empty bookcase and sagging daybed, her monied background and pretense to culture exposed by the chaise longue, "neither of them really furnished" with culture, taste, or education.) The novel conforms to strict Aristotelian unities: the action occurs in a single setting over a short period of time, which internal references date October–November 1983.[5] A near-perfect symmetry balances the novel's seven chapters: the first takes place at sunset, the last at sunrise; the second and sixth begin with Liz climbing the hill from the river; the end of the third is linked to the beginning of the fifth with verbal repetitions (cf. 94–95 with 151); the central chapter, the fourth, takes place on Halloween and features the long conversation between McCandless and Lester that provides most of the historical background to the present-day events in the rest of the novel—the central heating of Gaddis's Gothic, as it were.

The Gothic novel is of course the most obvious genre Gaddis exploits in *Carpenter's Gothic*, adapting as many of its stage properties as is feasible: the isolated "mansion," the locked room, the endangered "maiden," the mysterious stranger, even the witching time of year that allows for references to Halloween ghosts and a haunted house (148). The "unwavering leer" of the Masai warrior on a magazine cover follows Paul around as spookily as the moving eyes of an old portrait, and Liz has a dream premonition of death during the unholy hours between All Saints' Eve and the Day of the Dead. A parody of older Gothic novels, *Carpenter's Gothic* also incorporates long quotations from *Jane Eyre*, Charlotte Brontë's parody of even older Gothic novels.

The Gothic mode is not a new departure for Gaddis. Those chapters of *The Recognitions* set in New England creak with Gothic machinery: the heretical priest poring over curious volumes of forgotten lore, the deranged servant, supernatural statues, apparitions, the gloomy atmosphere that hangs over the desolate landscape, and the same attraction/repulsion felt by earlier Gothicists for Italianate Catholicism. Nor is the Gothic mode a new departure for American literature; Leslie Fiedler's *Love and Death in the American Novel* goes to great length to demonstrate that Gothic is the most characteristic form of classic American fiction. At the fleeting disappearance of James's and Wharton's ghosts, the genre took two directions in modern American literature: the Southern Gothic of Faulkner, O'Connor, and early Capote; and the supermarket Gothic that Alexander Theroux has wittily described (in his great Gothic romance *Darconville's Cat*) as "the genre of course of Hoodoo, Hackwork, and Hyperesthesia, the popular dust-jacket for which always showed a crumbling old mansion-by-moon-light and a frightened beauty in gossamer standing before it, tresses down, never knowing which way to turn."[6] The New England Gothic tradition of Hawthorne and Melville has had few followers among serious contemporary novelists aside from Djuna Barnes, early Hawkes, some Pynchon, and the occasional anomaly (like Kerouac's *Dr. Sax* or Brautigan's *Hawkline Monster*).

Why would Gaddis revive this outmoded genre in the technological eighties? Partly for the challenge of reclaiming an exhausted genre (as Barth and Sorrentino like to do in general, and as Joyce Carol Oates has done with the Gothic in particular), but largely because the "symbols and meanings" of

Gothic, Fiedler points out, "depend on an awareness of the spiritual isolation of the individual in a society where all communal systems of value have collapsed or have been turned into meaningless clichés."[7] Liz's physical and McCandless's intellectual isolation underscore the extent to which both have lost that connection between themselves and the world that McCandless reads of in V. S. Naipaul's novel (150, quoted at the end of chapter 1). With all of Jane Eyre's restlessness but none of her independence, Liz is the persecuted maiden in a Gothic melodrama: "when you feel like a nail everything looks like a hammer," she confesses to McCandless (223), reversing one of his cracks about fundamentalists. Psychologically immured in her Carpenter Gothic tower, Liz's choice between Paul and McCandless amounts to "being the prisoner of someone else's hopes [... or] being the prisoner of someone else's despair" (244). Liz finally perishes in that prison, subverting the happy ending of most Gothic fiction.

McCandless has much in common with the Gothic hero-villain, a mixture of Faust, Don Juan, and the Wandering Jew—all coming to stand, Fiedler argues, "for the lonely individual (the writer himself!) challenging the mores of bourgeois society, making patent to all men the ill-kept secret that the codes by which they live are archaic survivals without point or power."[8] McCandless feels Christianity is just such an archaic survival, but his attempts to expose its ill-kept secrets of militarism, misogyny, and superstition have met with failure: called upon to testify at a "creationist" trial in Smackover—similar to one held in Arkansas in December 1981—he learned that fundamentalists are not simply ignorant (lacking knowledge) but stupid (hostile to knowledge), heirs to the anti-intellectual tradition in America that Richard Hofstadter has written about. An intellectual hero of sorts, McCandless is also the villain of the piece, however. He hopes to put his house in order (226), like Eliot's speaker at the end of *The Waste Land*, but he succeeds only in spreading disorder and chaos. Not only is he indirectly responsible for Billy's death, but he is as responsible as anyone for the nuclear showdown that looms over the novel's final pages. Possessing the facts about the ore field, he withholds this information, partly because he won't be believed (239), partly because of the Gothic villain's willingness to see his corrupt civilization go up in flames. During her longest and most powerful speech, Liz hurls exactly this accusation at him:

> —And it's why you've done nothing ... She put down the glass, —to see them all go up like that smoke in the furnace all the stupid, ignorant, blown up in the clouds and there's nobody there, there's no rapture no anything just to see them wiped away

for good it's really you, isn't it. That you're the one who wants Apocalypse, Armageddon all the sun going out and the sea turned to blood you can't wait no, you're the one who can't wait! The brimstone and fire and your Rift like the day it really happened because they, because you despise their, not their stupidity no, their hopes because you haven't any, because you haven't any left. (243–44)

The references to apocalypse and Armageddon here toward the end of the novel indicate the Gothic overlaps with another genre, the apocalypse. While the Gothic developed out of Jacobean drama, apocalypse originates in religious writings and mythography, bearing witness to the strange fact that cosmic catastrophe has been a fear and a hope of almost every society—a fear of extinction no matter how richly deserved, and a hope for purgation and another chance to start anew. The literary apocalypse is used by a writer to render judgment on society, a heretical desire to destroy that which God created. God said let there be light; the apocalyptic writer, like Melville at the end of *The Confidence-Man*, puts out the light.

Unlike other modern literatures, American literature has a strong, almost obsessive tradition in apocalyptics. The first "best-seller" in our literature was Michael Wigglesworth's long poem *The Day of Doom* (1662), and since then most of our major novelists have dealt in the apocalyptic: Hawthorne, Melville, Mark Twain, Faulkner, West, O'Connor, and among contemporary novelists, Ellison, Barth, Baldwin, Burroughs, Pynchon, Vonnegut, Coover, Elkin, and DeLillo. It is tempting to divide these into the two traditional camps of apocalypsists—the hopeful and the despairing—but many of these writers display both tempers: *Moby-Dick* is hopeful (Ishmael survives the catastrophe), but *The Confidence-Man* is despairing (nothing follows this masquerade).

Like Melville, Gaddis has written both forms: with Stanley composing a *dies irae* (322) and Willie speaking of "the doctrine of last things" (478), *The Recognitions* is certainly an apocalypse, but because Wyatt survives the cultural collapse that destroys the rest of the novel's characters, it can be called a hopeful one—hence Gaddis's disavowal of apocalyptic intentions in the interview quoted near the end of chapter 1. In *Carpenter's Gothic*, however, both forms of apocalypse are set against each other: Ude and his followers are obviously banking on a hopeful apocalypse when they will be able to enjoy a "space age picnic in the clouds" while the rest of us are frantically consulting our Survival Handbook (135), and consequently they interpret all signs of cultural breakdown in terms of those foretold in the

Book of Revelation. McCandless interprets those same signs in the despairing apocalyptic temper of the Melville of *The Confidence-Man* or the Twain of *The Mysterious Stranger*. And yet, McCandless is himself a mysterious stranger with a nihilistic vision as despairing as Twain's devil's. A Christian reading of *Carpenter's Gothic* would expose McCandless as the antichrist of the novel, spreading despair and disorder everywhere he goes. (The Christian reader might even find correspondences between the novel's seven chapters and the seven seals in Revelation.) While signs and the interpretive context we place them in are themes in the novel, these particular ones are among the "deceptions" of the Carpenter Gothic style, however, and should not be seriously entertained.

Both McCandless and Ude can be held partially responsible for the literal apocalypse that begins at the end of the novel—"10 K 'DEMO' BOMB OFF AFRICA COAST War News, Pics Page 2" (259)—but McCandless's sin is only one of omission; Ude's is the more fatal one of commission. Like Tod Hackett in Nathanael West's *The Day of the Locust* (with which *Carpenter's Gothic* has tonal similarities), Gaddis presents fundamentalists' "fury with respect, appreciating its awful, anarchic power, and aware that they had it in them to destroy civilization."[9] Although fundamentalists themselves may seem incapable of doing much more than breaking schoolbus windows and bombing abortion clinics, they are associated throughout the novel with right-wing politicians whose paranoid style of politics (as Hofstadter named it) can indeed help fundamentalists satisfy their apocalyptic yearnings. Fundamentalism or paranoid politics is not unique to America; as McCandless tells Billy:

> —The greatest source of anger is fear, the greatest source of hatred is anger and the greatest source of all of it is this mindless revealed religion anywhere you look, Sikhs killing Hindus, Hindus killing Moslems, Druse killing Maronites, Jews killing Arabs, Arabs killing Christians and Christians killing each other maybe that's the one hope we've got. You take the self hatred generated by original sin turn it around on your neighbors and maybe you've got enough sects slaughtering each other from Londonderry to Chandigarh to wipe out the whole damned thing, [...]. (185–86)

What the world and the novel need now to counteract this hatred and the polemical tone is love, or at least a romantic subplot. But the possibilities for love in both spheres are limited.

Gaddis's working title for *Carpenter's Gothic* was "That Time of Year: A Romance," and like the "Gothic" in the published title, "romance" here means many things. As a genre, it has much in common with the Gothic; in fact, the latter is largely the romance pushed to extremes. The romance does, however, place greater emphasis on the picturesque, the idyllic, and the more conventional forms of love. (Love in the Gothic tends toward lust or perversion.) Gothic and romance "claim a certain latitude" from such constraints of realistic fiction as verisimilitude and plausibility, as Hawthorne argues in his famous preface to *The House of the Seven Gables*—another novel centering on a Gothic house and a debilitating family heritage—and Gaddis has always claimed this latitude.

Carpenter's Gothic displays the romance's indifference to strict realism: as in *JR*, events move impossibly fast; its countless coincidences strain belief; and there is an overwhelming emphasis on the negative that would be out of place in a more realistic novel. When Paul opens a newspaper "without knocking over the bottle" (203), the narrator draws our attention to this rare event, because elsewhere, no one can reach for anything without upsetting whatever glass is closest at hand; no one can cook anything without burning it; no one can turn on the radio without hearing a distressing item of news; checks are delayed while bills arrive swiftly; cars and trucks are always breaking down, buses caught in traffic jams; clocks, newspapers, even dictionary definitions are unreliable; the novel is tyrannized by Murphy's Law, where anything that can go wrong does so, and usually at the worst possible moment. Hawthorne insists that the romancer "may so manage his atmospheric medium as to bring out or mellow the light and deepen and enrich the shadows of the picture," and Gaddis has pursued the latter option with such a vengeance that *Carpenter's Gothic* joins Selby's *Last Exit to Brooklyn* and Sorrentino's *The Sky Changes* as one of the darkest novels in contemporary American literature. Even its humor is black.

Only the brief affair between McCandless and Liz admits any light into the novel. Here Gaddis turns from the Hawthornian romance to sport with the Harlequin romance, using every cliché in the style book: the bored debutante-housewife, the older man with an exotic background, the obligatory adultery, the revivification of said debutante after one night in the older man's arms, prompting her to sigh with a straight face, "It's an amazing thing to be alive, isn't it ... " (151). There is even the offer to take her away to faraway lands and the dutiful decision to stand by her man for reasons she cannot quite articulate; echoing Stella in Williams's *A Streetcar Named Desire*, Liz can only say, "It's just, I don't know. Something happens ... " (89).

Gaddis redeems these clichés by subjecting them to much more rigorous artistic control than is common, carefully integrating them with the patterns of imagery and literary allusion at work throughout the novel. Each genre Gaddis adapts has a reference point in a classic text: the Gothic in *Jane Eyre*, the apocalypse in the Book of Revelation (the most frequently cited biblical text), and the romance in the Shakespearean sonnet that provided Gaddis's earlier title:

> That time of year thou mayst in me behold
> When yellow leaves, or none, or few, do hang
> Upon those boughs which shake against the cold,
> Bare ruined choirs, where late the sweet birds sang.
> In me thou see'st the twilight of such day
> As after sunset fadeth in the west;
> Which by and by black night doth take away,
> Death's second self, that seals up all in rest.
> In me thou see'st the glowing of such fire,
> That on the ashes of his youth doth lie,
> As the deathbed whereon it must expire,
> Consumed with that which it was nourished by.
> This thou perceiv'st, which makes thy love more strong,
> To love that well which thou must leave ere long.

When Liz echoes the sonnet's concluding couplet by telling McCandless at the end of the novel, "I think I loved you when I knew I'd never see you again" (245), she unconsciously completes a series of references to the sonnet that begins on the novel's first page. In fact, much in the novel is encapsulated in the sonnet: the autumnal and predominantly nocturnal settings, the recurring references to empty boughs and yellow leaves outside and the fire grate inside cold until McCandless arrives to rekindle it—and of course the relationship between the older man and his younger lover. Similarly, the poem generates much of the novel's imagery. On those rare occasions when Gaddis's characters stop talking, the text gives way to luxurious descriptions of the dying landscape, passages as colorful as the vegetation they describe, and imitative in their gnarled syntax of the intertwined vines, branches, and fallen leaves.

The equation of autumn with late middle age in the poem's first quatrain is spelled out with scientific precision by McCandless (who had quoted a few words from the sonnet on p. 167):

> —all those glorious colours the leaves turn when the chlorophyll breaks down in the fall, when the proteins that are tied to the chlorophyll molecules break down into their amino acids that go down into the stems and the roots. That may be what happens to people when they get old too, these proteins breaking down faster than they can be replaced and then, yes well and then of course, since proteins are the essential elements in all living cells the whole system begins to disinteg.... (228–29)

A page later, McCandless picks up the sunset image in the second quatrain of the poem:

> —Finally realize you can't leave things better than you found them the best you can do is try not to leave them any worse but they [the young] won't forgive you, get toward the end of the day like the sun going down in Key West if you've ever seen that? They're all down there for the sunset, watching it drop like a bucket of blood and clapping and cheering the instant it disappears, cheer you out the door and damned glad to see the last of you.
> But the sun she looked up for was already gone, not a trace in the lustreless sky and the unfinished day gone with it, leaving only a chill that trembled the length of her. (230–31)

In this brilliant orchestration of images, Gaddis combines the literal setting of this conversation and the metaphors from sonnet seventy-three with an echo from Revelation, which Liz will pick up later in the same conversation ("Apocalypse, Armageddon all the sun going out and the sea turned to blood" [244; cf. 185])—all leading to a symbolic alignment of organic decay (leaves, light, people) with cultural decay, and suggesting that fundamentalism is a malign but not unnatural cancer in the body politic, accelerating an otherwise inevitable process. As Cynthia Ozick was the first to point out, "It isn't 'theme' Mr. Gaddis deals in (his themes are plain) so much as a theory of organism and disease. In 'Carpenter's Gothic' the world is a poisonous organism, humankind dying of itself."[10] McCandless "doesn't much like getting old," his first wife will later say (250), nor does he much like watching the disintegration of civilization, but apart from raging against the dying of the light, there's little he can do to halt either.

As Shakespeare's sonnet is a seduction poem of sorts, the words "death" and "expire" probably carry their secondary Elizabethan meaning of orgasm.

If so, the trope has its counterpart in *Carpenter's Gothic*, where a description of Liz after lovemaking (163) is used again to describe her position at death (253). Her death, of course, upsets the parallel with the sonnet—as it does with the Gothic—but it does fulfill the expectations of the dove imagery likewise present from the novel's first page. Watching the neighborhood boys bat a dead dove back and forth, "a kind of battered shuttlecock moulting in a flurry at each blow" (1), Liz turns away, catching breath for the first time. Throughout the novel Liz is closely associated with doves and is clearly a kind of battered shuttlecock herself—literally in her relationship with Paul (9, 22), figuratively with Billy and McCandless. Once again braving the dangers of cliché, Gaddis invests Liz with all the symbolic qualities of a dove (peace, innocence, gentleness) and even has her bleat like a dove (163–64). The symbolism is self-explanatory, but again Gaddis manages to make the cliché work: when this "sweet bird" emits "a choked bleat" as she dies, even a reader hardened by the savage ironies of modern literature must feel that peace and innocence have indeed fled from this world for good. The dove of the Holy Ghost is treated no better by the novel's militant Christians, and at the symbolic age of thirty-three Liz even has aspects of Him the fundamentalists profess to worship.

Most of the other genres that have rooms in Gaddis's house of fiction can be treated more briefly. In its use of a single stage setting and small cast, its reliance on messengers (by letter and phone), and its adherence to Aristotelian unities, *Carpenter's Gothic* has the formal design of Greek drama, a subject McCandless once taught (252). Like an adaptation by O'Neill or Eliot, Gaddis's novel includes a dark heritage of paternal guilt, features continual offstage atrocities, and even has its Furies in the neighborhood kids always smirking through Liz's windows. Reviewer Frederick Busch instead found several parallels to Dickens's *Bleak House*, and rightly so.[11] Gaddis's social crusader instincts encourage the parallel, as does his use of Dickensian names for his unsavory manipulators (Sneddiger, Grimes, Stumpp, Cruikshank, Grissom, Lopots). In particular, Gaddis shares Dickens's faith in the novel as an instrument for social improvement and his ability to make family disputes representative of larger social disputes. Gaddis goes so far as to correct von Clausewitz on this point: "it's not that war is politics carried on by other means it's the family carried on by other means" (241). The African episodes reported at secondhand are reminiscent of those novels featuring Anglo-Americans abroad that run from Conrad's *Heart of Darkness* and several books by Forster and Waugh through contemporary novels by Graham Greene, Anthony Burgess, and Paul Theroux—not to mention the multinational political thrillers of more commercial novelists. *Carpenter's*

Gothic is also a textbook example of "cloistral" fiction, a genre centering on a mysterious stranger's visit to a closed community and the moral havoc that results, epitomized by such stories as Melville's "Bartleby the Scrivener" and Mark Twain's "The Man That Corrupted Hadleyburg."[12]

Of more interest is Gaddis's contribution to the growing body of Vietnam War fiction. Paul's Vietnam experiences are referred to only sporadically in the novel, but by piecing together the clues his tour of duty can be reconstructed—though only after separating the "official" truth from what really happened. He somehow managed to win a commission as a second lieutenant, much to the contempt of his adopted father, who reportedly told him "that he was God damn lucky he was going in as an officer because he wasn't good enough to be an enlisted man" (91). A platoon leader in the 25th Infantry, Lightning Division, he quickly alienated himself from his men by insisting on "All this military bullshit with these spades from Cleveland and Detroit in his broken down platoon out there kicking their ass to show them what the southern white officer class is all about" (193). After turning in his crew chief, a black nineteen-year-old named Chigger, for using heroin, Chigger "fragged" him; that is, he rolled a grenade under Paul's bed in the Bachelor Officer Quarters. He was pulled out by Chick, his radiotelephone operator, and the Army covered up the incident by blaming an enemy infiltrator—the story Paul later uses. Paul is discharged at the same grade he entered, an indication of his incompetence, for as McCandless points out elsewhere, officers welcome a war for "the chance to move up a few grades, peace time army they'll sit there for twenty years without making colonel but combat brings that first star so close they can taste it" (238). Paul leaves behind a native mistress, pregnant with his child: "it was a boy" he learns at the end of the novel (260).

Paul parlayed his bogus reputation as "this big wounded hero" into a job with Vorakers Consolidated Reserve, but years later, as the novel opens, he is still plagued by terrible memories of Vietnam: the machinegun fire (8), nearly crashing in a helicopter (83–84), and the aftermath of the fragging incident: "you know how long I laid there? How many weeks I laid there blown right up the gut watching that bottle of plasma run down tubes stuck in me anyplace they could get one in? Couldn't move my legs I didn't know if I had any, God damn medic breaks the needle right off in my arm taped down so it can't move can't reach down, dare reach down and and see if my balls are blown off, my balls Liz! I was twenty two!" (45). When a black nineteen-year-old mugger attacks Paul late in the novel, he sees in the mugger's eyes the same hatred he saw in Chigger's and kills him, for "They never taught us how to fight, they only taught us how to kill" (241).

The difficulty Vietnam veterans have had readjusting to society has already become a literary staple, and Gaddis's vets (Chick and Pearly Gates as well) have as difficult a time as any. But Gaddis once again subverts the cliché by portraying Paul as responsible for his own troubles. Not only did he bring the fragging upon himself, but in a sense he joins the enemy—not the Viet Cong, but Vorakers, Adolph, Grimes, and the other power brokers: "God damn it Billy listen! *These are the same sons of bitches that sent me to Vietnam!*" (242). Yet so strong is his lust for prestige and money that Paul willingly sacrifices his sense of moral outrage to join the very power structure that nearly killed him, thereby sacrificing any sympathy his Vietnam ordeal might otherwise have earned him.

The generic text Gaddis uses here as a reference point, though unacknowledged, is Michael Herr's brilliant *Dispatches* (1977), an impressionistic account of the two years (1967–68) Herr covered the Vietnam war for *Esquire*, and an aesthetic exercise in rescuing "clean" information from official disinformation and the vagaries of memory. Gaddis borrows one anecdote from Herr's book ("never happen sir" [214])[13] and perhaps found a number of his other Vietnamese details there: Tu Do street, Drucker's bag of ears, the raunchy language Paul uses on the phone with Chick, and some of the war jargon (sapper, ville, "the old man," greased, BOQ). More importantly, *Dispatches*, like Gaddis's novel, investigates the gap between the "truth" and what really happens, specifically, the Pentagon's pathological allegiance to an official truth that had no basis in reality. The references to Vietnam in *Carpenter's Gothic* act as a grim reminder that his theme is no abstract problem in epistemology but one that in this case left 130,000 American casualties dead, maimed, and missing.[14]

Finally, it should be noted that another writer Gaddis borrows from in *Carpenter's Gothic* is the author of *The Recognitions* and *JR*. Richard Poirier once described Pynchon's second novel, *The Crying of Lot 49*, as "more accessible only because very much shorter than the first [*V.*], and like some particularly dazzling section left over from it."[15] At first glance, the shorter and more accessible *Carpenter's Gothic* might similarly look like a particularly dazzling section left over from *JR*; in fact, one reviewer went so far as to say "its main plot comes from pages 96–103 of *JR*; substitute Liz Vorakers Booth for Amy Cates Joubert, change the African locale from Gandia to somewhere near South Africa, and there it is. Even the names Ude and Teakell come from *JR*."[16] There are important tonal differences between Gaddis's three novels, of course, but it is possible to hear other echoes from the earlier two: Liz may have actually read *The Recognitions*, for she refers to the passage where Arnie Munk got so drunk he folded up his clothes and put them into the refrigerator (13; *R* 175) and to Rev. Gwyon's remark about "the unswerving punctuality of chance" (223; *R* 9), which also appears on Jack Gibbs's page of quotations (*JR* 486). For his third novel Gaddis returned to some of his source books for the first: to the 14th edition of the *Encyclopaedia Britannica* for the Battle of Crécy (147), the *Pilgrim Hymnal* for two militaristic hymns (142), Cruden's *Concordance* for biblical citations, and Eliot's *Four Quartets* for at least one line ("to recover what had been lost and found and lost again and again" [155], from "East Coker"). Even McCandless's novel has its echoes from *The Recognitions*, especially in his protagonist Frank Kinkead's decision "to live deliberately" (139), the same Thoreauvian vow Stephen makes (*R* 900). From *JR* he borrowed Pythian Mining in addition to the other names enumerated above and hints broadly at a connection between JR and Paul Booth when Adolph dismisses the latter as knowing "as much about finance as some snot nosed sixth grader" (209).

Much of this is little more than the kind of cross-referencing one finds in the novels of Faulkner, Barth, or Sorrentino. *Carpenter's Gothic*'s relationship to its huge predecessors seems to be hinted at in McCandless's description of his own novel: "it's just an afterthought why are you so damned put out by it," he asks Lester. "This novel's just a footnote, a postscript" (139). That "this" can refer to both novels, and the fact this particular line occurs in a real novel about an imaginary novel by an imaginary character who resembles a real author calls attention to the ambiguous status of fiction, blurring that fine line between truth and what really happens by offering fine lines that seem all the more true because they never happened. The ontology of all fictions—literary, religious, patriotic, and personal—emerges as one of Gaddis's principal preoccupations in *Carpenter's Gothic* and makes this novel not merely a footnote, a postscript to his megafictions, but a virtuosic exercise in metafiction.

That's All She Wrote

The nature and production of fictions is a recurring topic in the dialogues that make up the bulk of *Carpenter's Gothic*, ranging from Paul's rather primitive notion of literary fiction (112) to McCandless's more sophisticated attacks on such "fictions" as religion, occult beliefs, and ethnocentrism. Gaddis's use of fiction to explore the status of fiction is characteristic of metafiction, that genre that calls attention to itself as fiction and flaunts the artificiality of art.[17] Though more realistic than such exemplary metafictions as O'Brien's *At Swim-Two-Birds* or Sorrentino's *Mulligan Stew*, *Carpenter's*

Gothic takes full advantage of the resources of this genre to clarify the distinction between (and preferability of) ambiguity over absolutism and to warn against the dangers of mistaking fiction for fact.

The *Webster's New Collegiate Dictionary* (8th ed.) that Gaddis lambastes for inaccuracy each time Liz consults it (94, 248) gives three definitions of "fiction," each amply illustrated in *Carpenter's Gothic*. In fact, so many variations are played on this theme that it might be useful to resort to the sophomoric strategy of arguing directly from this dictionary's definitions, especially since Gaddis may have looked at them.

First Definition

> 1 a: something invented by the imagination or feigned; *specif*: an invented story <distinguish fact from~> b: fictitious literature (as novels or short stories) <a writer of~>.

Gaddis has always shown writers writing: in *The Recognitions*, Otto's struggles to concoct his play and Esme's to write poetry are dramatized, as is Jack Gibbs's work on *Agapē Agape* in *JR*. *Carpenter's Gothic* features two writers of fiction, both of whose works, however, blur the dictionary's distinction between fact and fiction. McCandless's novel is the object of Lester's extended scorn, partly because it follows the facts of the author's African experiences so closely that it doesn't merit the name fiction. The only aspects "invented" by McCandless seem to be slanderous aspersions (129), romantic self-aggrandizement (136–37), and pompous rhetoric (*passim*). Similarly, Liz's work in progress begins as autobiographical wishful thinking (63–64), but after McCandless's appearance begins to resemble a diary, reaching the point where her "fictional" account of an event is indistinguishable from the narrator's (cf. 163 and 257).

To modify Webster's definition, this is fact feigning as fiction, but perhaps a necessary sacrifice of "what really happens" to the "truth," that is, to something closer to how the authors experienced an event than a strict recital of the facts would allow. This is why Liz objects to the fanciful notion of setting up a mirror on Alpha Centauri in order to see through a telescope "what really happened" earlier in her life: "But you'd just see the outside though, wouldn't you" (153). Uninterested in aesthetic distance, Liz feels a writer's subjective sense of an experience is more important than the objective facts of the experience, a point she tries to impress upon McCandless, who prefers technical writing: "I'm talking about you, about what you know that nobody else knows because that's what writing's all about isn't it? I'm not a writer Mrs Booth I mean lots of people can write about all that, about grasshoppers and evolution and fossils I mean the things that only you know that's what I mean" (168). McCandless counters with "Maybe those are the things that you want to get away from," a position similar to Eliot's.[18] He made a better objection to Liz's point when he said earlier that too many writers "think if something happened to them that it's interesting because it happened to them" (158–59).

The aesthetic debate here concerning subjectivity vs. objectivity and the legitimacy of autobiography in fiction began in *The Recognitions*, where Hannah complained of Max's painting, "he has to learn that it isn't just having the experience that counts, it's knowing how to handle the experience" (*R* 184). In his third novel Gaddis enlivens the debate by showing how the autobiographical writer can confuse the invention of fiction with the invention of self, using fiction as an actor uses makeup to create a new persona, even a new life. For Liz, writing fiction offers "some hope of order restored, even that of a past itself in tatters, revised, amended, fabricated in fact from its very outset to reorder its unlikelihoods, what it all might have been" (247). Writing gives Liz access to what Billy calls her "real secret self" (193), the self Wyatt struggles to find in his quest for individuation, and the self Liz lost sight of "twenty, twenty five years away when it was all still, when things were still like you thought they were going to be" (154). Bibbs to her brother, Liz to her husband, Mrs. Booth to McCandless, "the redhead" to Lester, she resists this fragmentation of her identity by these men to insist "my name my name is Elizabeth" (166), the stuttered hesitation underscoring the difficulty she is having recovering the name of her true self from the men in her life.[19] Appropriately, her writing is conducted in secret; hidden in her drawer, her manuscript is a metonymy for her self, itself hidden so far from her husband that he is numbed when he comes across the manuscript after her death, written "in a hand he knew spelling little more than bread, onions, milk, chicken?" (257). Her failure to write parallels her failure to live, both captured in the flip title Gaddis briefly entertained for the novel: "That's All She Wrote."

Although McCandless completed and published his novel, it was published under a pseudonym; that, along with Lester's verdict ("rotten"), suggests his novel lacks the honesty and integrity he strives for in personal conduct. In an impressive apologia, he explains that one's life is a kind of fiction, to be crafted as carefully as a work of art:

—All that mattered was that I'd come through because I'd sworn to remember what really happened, that I'd never look back and let it become something romantic simply because I was young and a fool but I'd done it. I'd done it and I'd come out alive, and that's the way it's been ever since and maybe that's the hardest thing, harder than being sucked up in the clouds and meeting the Lord on judgment day or coming back with the Great Imam because *this fiction's all your own*, because you've spent your entire life at it who you are, and who you were when everything was possible, when you said that everything was still the way it was going to be no matter how badly we twist it around first chance we get and then make up a past to account for it .... (169; my italics)

If McCandless's fiction is indeed rotten, it is because he failed to construct it with the same fierce integrity that he constructed the "fiction" of his self. Like Hemingway's Frederic Henry, McCandless welcomes "facts proof against fine phrases that didn't mean anything" (228), but from Lester's quotations it sounds as though he preferred fine phrases when writing fiction. A better model would be Hemingway's reclusive contemporary Robinson Jeffers, parts of whose poem "Wise Men in Their Bad Hours" McCandless quotes on occasion (127, 161). Jeffers managed to put the same fierce integrity into his life as in his work, a synthesis McCandless apparently aims for but falls short of. If Liz's manuscript is a metonymy for her life, McCandless's study serves as his—a dusty, cobwebbed, smoke-filled room of books and papers that he continually tries to clean up, but where he manages only to create greater confusion and disorder. Alone, apparently friendless, estranged from his son and former wives, he sells out to the CIA for $16,000 and is last seen heading for the tropics, where the only way you know where you are is the disease you get (246). Again, failure in art means failure in life.

Second Definition

2: an assumption of a possibility as a fact irrespective of the question of its truth <a legal–>.

McCandless would argue that religions and metaphysical systems are possibilities (at best) assumed as facts by their followers, whose adherence to these fictions parodies an artist's quest for permanence in art:

—no no no, his voice as calming as the hand along her back, it was all just part of the eternal nonsense, where all the nonsense comes from about resurrection, transmigration, paradise, karma the whole damned lot.—It's all just fear he said,—you think of three quarters of the people in this country actually believing Jesus is alive in heaven? and two thirds of them that he's their ticket to eternal life? [...] just this panic at the idea of not existing so that joining that same Mormon wife and family in another life and you all come back together on judgment day, coming back with the Great Imam, coming back as the Dalai Lama choosing his parents in some Tibetan dung heap, coming back as anything—a dog, a mosquito, better than not coming back at all, the same panic wherever you look, any lunatic fiction to get through the night and the more farfetched the better, any evasion of the one thing in life that's absolutely inevitable [...] desperate fictions like the immortal soul and all these damned babies rushing around demanding to get born, or born again [...]. (157)

McCandless twice uses "fiction" here in the sense of Webster's second definition, as he does elsewhere: "talk about their deep religious convictions and that's what they are, they're convicts locked up in some shabby fiction doing life without parole and they want everybody else in prison with them" (186). The crucial difference is that literary and legal fictions are recognized as fictions; religious fictions are not. Fundamentalists, he implies, are like poor readers who first mistake a work of fiction for fact, then impose their literal-minded misreadings on others—at gunpoint if necessary. Not only are fundamentalists "doing more to degrade it taking every damned word in it literally than any militant atheist could ever hope to," he fumes, but they don't even recognize the contradictions in the Bible any attentive reader would note (134, 136). The status of fiction and the validity of interpretation thus become more than academic matters for literary theorists; if the fundamentalist misreadings of sacred fictions prevail, aided by politicians misreading their constitutions, Armageddon will put an end to all fictions.

All the world's a text, Gaddis implies, and all the men and women merely readers. In *Carpenter's Gothic* leaves from a tree become leaves from a book within half a sentence (197), and bed sheets still damp from Liz and McCandless's lovemaking become in the next paragraph sheets of paper that will become damp with ink to describe the event (198). Gaddis's characters are forced to read the world around them despite the general illegibility of that "text": the clock is untrustworthy, the newspapers unreliable, the dictionary inaccurate, even words misleading: Liz and Madame Socrate founder on the French homonyms *salle* and *sale* (26; cf. the confusion over *sale* and *salé* in *The Recognitions*, 943), the two meanings of "morgue" confuse her (225), and half-listening to the radio's account of "a thrilling rescue operation by the Coast Guard" (116) Liz is puzzled the next day about a "thrilling rescue by postcard" (158). Even single letters cause confusion, leading Paul to think Billy doesn't even know how to spell Buddha (85). Ambiguity haunts the simplest words.

Gaddis's most brilliant dramatization of the vagaries of interpretation recalls the doubloon Melville's Ahab nails to the mainmast of the *Pequod*. Anxious to give a distracted Liz "the big picture" of the various religious and political complications in which he is enmeshed, Paul draws a diagram showing these various groups and the interactions between them. The first to interpret this diagram, after Paul, is the narrator, who offers humorous asides on the shapes that grow beneath Paul's hand (the administration is represented by "something vaguely phallic"), cruel social innuendo ("all his blacks down here ... a smudge unconnected to anything"), and ending with the fanciful observation that Paul's flow-chart arrows "darkened the page like the skies that day over Crécy" (100–1, 107). When McCandless comes across this drawing, he only sees the scribblings of a child (118), as does Lester when he first sees it (124). But looking at it again (147), Lester realizes it does indeed resemble the battle of Cressy (as he pronounces it), though he needs to adjust the figures in the drawing somewhat, much like a critic pounding the square peg of a thesis into the round hole of a text. In addition to foreshadowing the militaristic results of the Teakell-Ude-Grimes cartel—Armageddon promises to be the last use of firepower as the battle of Crécy was the first—and exposing the childishness of it all, this example highlights the dangers of interpretation that surround all the characters, none of whom commands a vantage point from which "the big picture" can be seen, but each of whom believes he or she holds the right interpretation of the text. A fable for critics.

Gaddis's own text has already generated the same kind of contradictory readings; with at least seven types of ambiguity in it, this is not surprising, though a few of the readings are. The novel struck most reviewers as savagely pessimistic, but one felt Gaddis "makes his optimism plain enough on the surface. The book ends with no period, indicating continuation. It hints at reincarnation, if only as a fly."[20] No comment. More than one reviewer accused McCandless of being mad. There are a few teasing innuendos to that effect, but his "madness" is more likely one more of the deceptions inherent in Carpenter Gothic, one made by linking Mrs. McCandless's remark that her former husband spent time in a hospital (250) with Lester's taunting question "you used to say I'd rather have a bottle in front of me than a frontal lobotomy where'd you get that, that's somebody else too isn't it because you've got one" (140). But the clever line is only a gag from a Tom Waits song of the mid-seventies, and Lester's accusation is strictly metaphoric; he goes on to say "the figures on lung cancer right in front of you like the facts staring those primates square in the face out there choking on Genesis and you say it's just a statistical parallel and light another." Gaddis realizes (if McCandless doesn't) that the choice between the truth and what really happens is not as easy to make as McCandless pretends it is, but rather owes more to the instinct to cling to what he later castigates as "any lunatic fiction to get through the night and the more farfetched the better, any evasion of the one thing in life that's absolutely inevitable" (157). Faced with the inevitability of death, McCandless panics as easily as any fundamentalist, but that is hardly a sign of madness; the reader should not be misled by talk of lobotomies and lunacy into thinking McCandless was in that hospital for anything worse than malaria (152). Yet another critic has suggested that Paul and Edie team up to murder Liz![21] Although there is some question who is telephoning as she expires—both Paul and McCandless know the ringing code (246)—there can be no question Liz is alone, hitting her head on the kitchen table as she goes down. Yet see how I resist the ambiguity, insisting on certainty; it's a hard habit to break.

Third Definition

3: the action of feigning or of creating with the imagination

This activity thus emerges as both constructive and destructive in *Carpenter's Gothic*, an action that can be used for self-realization or misused for self-delusion. At one extreme is the "paranoid sentimental fiction" of the American South (224) or the "serviceable fiction" of the African Masai that justifies their stealing cattle from other tribes because of "their ancient belief that all the cattle in the world belong to them" (121). At the other extreme are such fictions as *Heart of Darkness*—which McCandless declares "an excellent thing," even though Liz ascribes it to Faulkner and confuses it with Styron's *Lie Down in Darkness* (158)—and Jeffers's "Wise Men in Their Bad Hours." Gaddis's characters largely misuse fiction and are more often seen feigning than creating anything worthwhile. But Gaddis himself faced and overcame the same problems in writing this novel, one that exemplifies the proper use of fiction and achieves the ideal set in the concluding lines of the Jeffers poem, the lines McCandless never quotes, perhaps because his creator has reserved them for himself:

> Ah, grasshoppers,
> Death's a fierce meadowlark: but to die having made
> Something more equal to the centuries
> Than muscle and bone, is mostly to shed weakness.
> The mountains are dead stone, the people
> Admire or hate their stature, their insolent quietness,
> The mountains are not softened nor troubled
> And a few dead men's thoughts have the same temper.

McCandless's Carpenter Gothic has stood ninety years, he boasts; Gaddis's *Carpenter's Gothic* should stand at least as long.

Notes

1. *Bard College Bulletin*. November 1984. Gaddis originally wrote two additional sentences: "Keeping the question open, as I did at Bard, is a difficult way to teach; it's not like teaching mathematics. This puts a great deal of responsibility directly on the teacher's shoulders."

2. *Carpenter's Gothic* (1985; reprint, New York: Penguin, 1986), 130, 136, 191, 193, 240; hereafter cited in the text. This paperback edition contains a few corrections, adjusts the paragraphing on pp. 1 and 25, and restores a line accidentally dropped from the first edition.

3. McCandless is quoting reporter Dena Kleiman's essay on Mel and Norma Gabler entitled "Influential couple scrutinize books for 'Anti-Americanism," *New York Times*, 14 July 1981, C4.

4. Grove, "Harnessing the Power," B10.

5. The only anachronism in the novel's time scheme is the headline Liz notes on p. 28, which appeared on the front page of the *New York Times*. 25 July 1980.

6. Alexander Theroux, *Darconville's Cat* (Garden City, N.Y.: Doubleday, 1981), 73.

7. Fiedler, *Love and Death*, 131.

8. Ibid., 133.

9. *The Complete Works of Nathanael West* (New York: Farrar, Straus, 1957), 366.

10. Ozick, rev. of Carpenter's Gothic, 18. Cf Robinson Jeffer's use of organic decay to describe America's decline in his poem "Shine, Perishing Republic" (1924), which Gaddis read while working on *Carpenter's Gothic*. He briefly considered using a phrase from this poem, "thickening to empire," as the title for his third novel. (All the alternative titles I mention come from a conversation we had in August 1984.)

11. Frederick Busch, "A Bleak Vision of Gothic America," *Chicago Tribune*, 14 July 1985, "Bookworld," 28.

12. See Roy R. Male's *Enter Mysterious Stranger: American Cloistral Fiction* (Norman: University of Oklahoma Press, 1979).

13. Michael Herr, *Dispatches* (New York: Knopf, 1977), 26.

14. The Statistics are Gaddis's: see "The Rush for Second Place," 37.

15. Richard Poirier, review of *Gravity's Rainbow* by Thomas Pynchon, *Saturday Review of the Arts* 1 (3 March 1973): 59.

16. Al J. Sperone, "Mr. Gaddis Build His Dream House," Village Voice. 13 August 1985, 43.

17. I am indebted to Sara E. Lauzen's witty and informative "Notes on Metafiction: Every Essay Has a Title," in *Postmodern Fiction: A Bio-Bibliographical Guide*, ed. Larry McCafferty (Westport, Conn.: Greenwood Press, 1986), 93–116. See also her essay on Gaddis in the same volume (374–377).

18. In "Tradition and the Individual Talent," Eliot writes, "Poetry is not a turning loose of emotion, but an escape from emotion; it is not the expression of personality, but an escape from emotion; it is not the expression of personality, but an escape from personality. But, of course, only those who have personality and emotions know what it means to want to escape from these things" (*Selected Prose*, 43).

19. James Perrin Warren puts it differently: "The names record the attitude of the namers: Billy needs a sister locked in the childhood he has never escaped; Paul needs a secretary; McCandless needs an adulteress; and Elizabeth needs an Elizabeth" (review of *Carpenter's Gothic*, *Southern Humanities Review* 21 {Spring 1987}: 192).

20. Richard Toney, review of *Carpenter's Gothic*, *San Francisco Review of Books*, Fall / Winter 1985, 8. I should point out that this review and his earlier one in the same journal on *J R* (February 1976, 12–13) are otherwise quite insightful.

21. Johan Thielmans, "Intricacies of Plot: Some Preliminary Remarks to William Gaddis's *Carpenter's Gothic*," in *Studies in Honour of René Derolez*, ed. A. M. Simon-Vandenbergen (Ghent: Seminarie voor Engelse en Oud-Germaanse Taalkunde, 1987), 617.

JOHN JOHNSTON

Toward Postmodern Fiction

> The postmodern would be that which, in the modern, puts forward the unpresentable in the representation itself; that which denies itself the solace of good forms, the consensus of a taste which would make it possible to share collectively the nostalgia for the unattainable; that which searches for new presentations, not in order to enjoy them but in order to impart a stronger sense of the unpresentable. A postmodern artist and writer is in the position of the philosopher: the text he writes, the work he produces are not in principle governed by pre-established rules, and they cannot be judged according to a determining judgment, by applying familiar categories to the text or to the work. Those rules and categories are what the work of art itself is looking for. The artist and the writer, then, are working without rules in order to formulate what *will have been done*.
> —Jean-François Lyotard, *The Postmodern Condition*

Lyotard's definition of the postmodern has the virtue of isolating what is often considered to be most fundamental to postmodern art and literature: its questioning of the limits of representation by focusing attention on what is "unpresentable" in representation. Since notions of the subject and of subjectivity have been tied to particular forms of representation at least since Descartes, it makes sense that as an emerging critical term, "postmodernism" should also designate the questioning and even radical dissolution of the

---

From *Carnival of Repetition: Gaddis's* The Recognitions *and Postmodern Theory*. © 1990 by the University of Pennsylvania Press.

individual subject as it too has been generally represented since the Renaissance. Of course, the term is not always or even often used in this specific sense. Just as concepts like the, "subject" or "representation" are frequently employed in a variety of ways, with their meanings shifting from context to context, so "postmodernism" has also been variously employed to denote the present technological, postindustrial era, the new artistic period style succeeding modernism, and even the contemporary cultural paradigm or *epistēmē*. In the more restricted domain of literary history, the term has been used increasingly to refer to the radically disjunctive, antirealistic and later explicitly "textual" writing that began to appear in the 1950s and early 1960s and which continues to appear to the present day.

In previous chapters, I have indicated how *The Recognitions* participates in this emergent postmodernism by giving free play to forces working within or underneath representation that are not reducible to its logic and that visibly destabilize both the writing and written subject, the author as transcendent unity as well as his fictive creations. However, to insert *The Recognitions* and Gaddis's subsequent novels more fully into the postmodern context, as I now wish to do, it will not be necessary to arm myself with a full-scale or complete definition of postmodernism, especially since this would require a rather detailed account of the term's ongoing evolution since its first appearance.[1] Rather, the importance of postmodernism here is that it urges us to go beyond such features as "loss of self," black humor, widespread parody, and self-reflexivity, which would all be important in situating *The Recognitions* in its historical context, toward an attempt to define the putatively more fundamental reconfiguration of which they would be the visible herald or surface manifestation. Since these features signal a hemorrhaging of credibility with regard to traditional literary representation and the kind of centered subjectivity it entails, they may also mark the site where heretofore "unpresentable" differences might be seen to emerge. If postmodernism does indeed constitute a rupture with the modernist episteme and its foundations in "analytico-referential" discourse, these are the signs by which we might expect to recognize its appearance in contemporary fiction.[2]

THE BREAK WITH MIMESIS IN AMERICAN FICTION

Though stylistically varied, much of the writing of the 1950s and 1960s bears testimony to and sometimes even accepts the instability or fragmentation of what was usually called the "self." The first literary critic to explore this tendency in detail was Wylie Sypher, in a study called *Loss of Self in Modern Literature and Art* published in 1962. Sypher employs the word "modern" rather than "postmodern," but his examples (Beckett, the Beats, the *nouveau roman*) and his general frame of reference (Heidegger, modern science and art, non-Aristotelian logic) indicate that he is primarily concerned with works that no longer fit within the modernist paradigm. Nowhere is this clearer than in his last chapter, bearing the symptomatic title, "The Anonymous Self. A Defensive Humanism." Surveying the nihilism, despair, and meaningless absurdity of 1950s art as exemplified in the work of Beckett, Ionesco, and Dubuffet, Sypher nevertheless clings stubbornly to an admittedly no longer vital humanist perspective within which the "self," having been stripped of its creative powers in the new totalitarian, technological era, is reduced to a fragile subjectivity now only capable of acknowledging its complete alienation. In this tenuous affirmation, moreover, Sypher was only following the pattern evident in American writers of his own generation, writers like Saul Bellow, J. D. Salinger, Norman Mailer, Bernard Malamud (especially in *The Assistant*), and Lionel Trilling, who all found in "neo-realistic" narrative forms an adequate vehicle for their explorations of an existential crisis of the self in post–World War II America.[3]

Significantly, Sypher found support for his "defensive humanism" in the writings of Sartre and Camus. But if these French philosopher-novelists butted against meaninglessness and absurdity as the limit and condition of individual human experience, their successors, the structuralists, might be said to have found in "nonsense" a creative principle, insofar as structuralism demonstrates that "meaning" does not originate in the individual's intentional act but is always produced out of nonsense and its perpetual displacement in a preexistent and underlying system or structure.[4] Similarly, in the early 1960s, a new generation of American writers led by Heller, Nabokov, Barth, and Pynchon found in absurdity and black humor a new creative principle. By decentering characters in relation to fictional and historical structures within which the individual was a continually displaced position (rather than a substantial, entity), these writers began to move away from the mimetic and humanist assumptions that had governed the traditional novel since its inception. One clear indication of the change is that "character" in their novels most often appears as a mask or persona in a textual theater of repetitions and displacements. In Heller's *Catch-22*, for example, the characters are defined completely in relation to the structure of "paper fictions" generated by the military bureaucracy and have no existence outside it. In this sense, "Sweden" is both a utopian realm of escape and the novel's tenuous reference to an "outside" or unstructured exteriority.

Nabokov's *Lolita* reveals a more complex relational structure in the series of masks composed of John Ray–Humbert Humbert–Clare Quilty–"Nabokov" (this last entry referring to the author's self-referential appearance in the afterword). In relation to this series, Lolita is both the only "real" character (in the older sense) and the most explicit occasion for textual play as the sublimation of erotic desire. In Barth's *The Sot-Weed Factor* and Pynchon's *V.*, this type of serial structure composed of characters-as-masks is carried to even more complex elaborations, since it is articulated onto the fabric of history in a series of narrativized historical fictions. Thus, Burlingame's various "disguises" or Stencil's "impersonations" are not simply parodic mirrorings of the novelist as historian but also draw attention to the way in which every history is a construction embedded in and relying upon the fiction-making process.

The recognizable break with realistic fiction initiated by the Byzantine picaresque plots and obviously fictive personae of the historical parody novel was even more pronounced in the surreal and fragmentary fiction published at this time by Hawkes and Burroughs, where the "reality" of the characters was defined in terms of entropic, disintegrating landscapes constructed out of memory, dream, and hallucination, and language, as much as anything else, was the real subject. Hawkes has gone as far as to say that when he started writing he thought of plot and character as the "enemy"; for Burroughs, it was "the word" itself, approachable only in writing conceived as a recording of mental processes produced through his cut-up, fold-in textual manipulations.[5] In their fractured and nightmarish fictions, not only were mimetic assumptions rejected, but the disordering and irrational forces of primary or unconscious processes began to assume a constitutive role in the generation of the literary text.

Overall, then, the "postmodernist breakthrough"—if indeed we can speak about it as such—seems to have necessitated the complete abandonment of humanism, not so much as a collection of abstract notions about "man" as a specific set of assumptions about what governed the production and structure (and therefore meaning, value, and function) of a literary work. In short, the fictional structures adumbrated in these novels of the late 1950s and early 1960s are no longer intelligible as individual structures of intentional "meaning" articulated within a descriptive representation of social reality; if anything, they embed themselves within the more anonymous structures—or within what has come to be conceived as the endless "text"—of culture, language, and the unconscious.

To be sure, such structures were first revealed in modernist explorations. As Freud showed in his case study of Dora, Dora elaborates her own role and repeats her love for her father only in relation to the roles assumed by those around her (K, Madame K, the governess), and the roles that she herself assumes in relation to these others. Yet Freud can only view this kind of decentered structure negatively, since it becomes visible only in and through the symptomology of hysteria. For modern novelists like Joyce, Woolf, Lawrence, or Mann, this kind of splintering of the ego into diverse roles led toward or was part of the apprehension of a mythic and more integrated self. While it may have been true that character as defined in modernist fiction often tends to dissolve into a "stream of atomized experiences, a kind of novelistic pointillism," as Irving Howe describes it, the modern novelist's intention was always to create a newly complex, centered consciousness, open to new modes of being and perception.[6] Thus, even when the modernists intended to expand notions of individual identity to include larger frames of reference which were mythic or archetypal, they never questioned the idea or desirability of identity itself.

The passage from this modernist conception of an expanded individual identity to the postmodernist one of a decentered structure in which the individual is only a locus of transindividual singularities and intensities would seem therefore to involve an acceptance of fragmentation and dissolution of ego boundaries, or at least a more positive exploration of what were formerly taken to be signs of personality breakdown and even schizophrenia.[7] However, to state the case so baldly implies an illusionary or fictional view of the "self," as if it could be abstracted from the structures which make it possible. But as we saw in Chapter Three, no such subject is conceivable outside a structured system of articulations, and this is certainly the assumption of the novels cited above. Yet, undeniably, among many contemporary novelists there is a noticeable tendency at the level of representation to want to get at least one character out of this system, even at the price of his or her sanity or identity. In this perspective, Wyatt's dissolution and disappearance in *The Recognitions* may be taken as a paradigmatic instance which is repeated in countless other examples of postmodern American fiction.[8]

If we ask ourselves what kind of "world" such a structure supports or gives rise to and from which such characters desire to escape, we begin to see why the term "black humor," though never sharply defined, gained such rapid and widespread appeal in the early 1960s, when reviewers, critics, and novelists alike began describing the new fiction and sensibility. For whether the term was used to denote a specific tonal range or stylistic effect, it always implied a certain state of the world, a world gone awry and arbitrary, somehow out of control and proliferating with absurdities to the point where it no longer seemed susceptible to rational understanding or even manageable within a humanist framework. Thus, it was quickly agreed that black humor was "beyond satire," since the latter assumed or depended upon stable, shared values and at least the possibility of social rectification. Many writers like Bruce Jay Friedman (in the Introduction to his anthology *Black Humor*) emphasized that black humor had something to do with the "fading line between fantasy and reality" in modern life, and it is significant that the most telling examples were drawn from the newspapers and television. Friedman himself goes as far as to assert that *The New York Times* "is the source and fountain and bible of black humor."[9] Similarly, Philip Roth zeroes in on the mass media in his essay "Writing American Fiction," published in 1961. Roth relates how the newspaper reportage of the murder of two girls in Chicago explodes into a three-ring circus of absurdly burgeoning "media events," as the victims' mother, the accused, and his mother all become celebrities in a manner that quickly exceeded the novelist's own standards of verisimilitude. Roth's point is that the novelist's more modest inventions can hardly compete in an age in which everyday American reality constantly surpasses "credibility" and even presidential candidates are "believable" only in literary terms, as caricatures and satirical types.[10] In fact, it is precisely this discrepancy that will push writers to such extremes of Menippean satire as Robert Coover's *The Public Burning*, in which Richard Nixon appears as a delirious narrator and major character.

The need to situate the move toward greater self-referentiality in postmodern fiction within this new historical context of the mass media's power to define "reality" would therefore seem inevitable. For if "experience" in the contemporary world presents itself to the novelist as either "unrepresentable" because always already mediated by too many "fictions" of one sort or another, what could seem more logical than an increased self-referentiality within fiction itself, which would now differ from the world of "real" experience precisely by proclaiming or laying bare its own artifice and "constructed" nature. In fact, self-reflexivity in postmodern fiction almost always functions politically, as a refusal of two kinds of complicity: first, with a certain *image* of society that novelistic representation automatically conveys by not admitting chaos, disorder, fragmentation, and dislocation except within the larger, rationalized frame of novelistic conventions; and second, with an *image* of language as a transparent signifying system adequate to or commensurate with the expression of the needs and desires of unified subjects. In an era that witnessed the complete erosion of credibility and coherence in official discourse and the multiplication of differences within and among subjects, self-reflexivity indeed appeared necessary if the novel was to establish its own credibility and claim of relevance.

If modernist self-referentiality served primarily as a means of defining the artwork through spatial form or a purely formal type of closure (the work as autotelic artifact or "well-wrought urn"), postmodern self-reflexivity operates either negatively, as in Sartre's example of the "anti-novel," or critically, as ironic de-definition or self-deconstruction. Pursuing this line of thinking, some critics have therefore defined postmodernism as a move beyond modernist skepticism to a full-fledged ontological and epistemological doubt about language's capacity to signify the real.[11] For the novelists themselves, however, this doubt has obviously not been a cause for despair but a justification for taking full advantage of the dissolving boundaries between the fictional and the real in a new mode of writing usually designated as "fabulation."[12] Fabulation may be defined as a narrative strategy or means of storytelling that does not anchor itself in a transcription of social reality that would guarantee its "truth," but instead refers to another narrative authority or version of events which in turn refers to yet another source. Thus, in a series of nested narratives or embedded versions of events, a whole set of fictions is put into play, and credibility, probability, and the value of a particular fiction—rather than "truth" itself—define what is at stake. Since it does not rely upon mimesis (and therefore the distinction between the fictional and the real) as its primary end and justification, fabulation quickly became a means by which writers could engage with issues in a context in which "events" as represented by the mass media were automatically phantasmatic, and public space became more and more populated with simulacra which could not be discredited by reference to any widely agreed upon or certifiable notion of "reality."

In this perspective, the widespread and intensive use of parody encountered in the emergent postmodern fiction of the 1950s and early 1960s does not simply concern literary precincts alone, since it prefigures this disturbance in the relation of language to reality as a whole. While local parody operates on a clearly delimited segment of the literary surface (as in Joyce's specific parodies in *Ulysses*), widespread or generalized parody (as in Nabokov's *Lolita* and *Pale Fire*) begins to suggest that every representation is only a highly artificial construction whose relationship to actuality may be *only* parodic, or constitute a kind of linguistic "counterfeit." As both fictional strategy and theme, the counterfeit could thus be said to operate as a hinge between the expanded mimetic impulses of modernist fiction and what will later be called postmodernist "textualization."

As we have seen, *The Recognitions* not only stands at this turning point but enacts this very transformation. In fully working out the tendency of widespread parody to give way to "disguised quotation" and textual counterfeiting at several levels, Gaddis's novel participates in a shift in imaginative mode that we now take to be an essential sign of postmodern fiction. In his study *The Counterfeiters*, Hugh Kenner tried to pinpoint this shift in similar terms: "Nearly fifty years after *Ulysses*, juxtaposition has wholly given way to counterfeiting, in a world of image-duplicators; parody to quotation, in a world of nonfictional fiction; classicizing to eclectic connoisseurship, in a world that has turned into one huge *musée sans murs*."[13] For Kenner, who does not seem to have read Gaddis, Beckett and Warhol have the same signal value for contemporary culture as Pound, Eliot, and Joyce had for the modernist culture of fifty years ago. Kenner deftly demonstrates how our current technological power to construct or synthesize automated processes (the computer as a simulation of the brain) ultimately derives from the culture's obsessive working out of empirical and rational imperatives, which in turn calls out for satirical countermeasures. However, rather than pursue connections between the present highly technological culture and the postmodern artistic strategies of counterfeiting, "phosphorescent quotation," and eclectic connoisseurship, he is distracted by affinities with the English satirists of the eighteenth century (1690–1740) and fails to theorize the mutation from modernism to postmodernism to which he so elegantly draws our attention.

Like many American literary critics writing in the 1960s, Kenner sensed profound cultural changes underway that he could not or did not care to theorize. And although much has been written about postmodernism since then, there is still very little consensus—apart from the general feeling that modernism is now receding into the past—about how it should be defined and analyzed. In this respect, it is significant that while postmodernism as an evolving literary term has been current since the 1960s, as a term designating a larger shift in the arts and Western culture as a whole, it began to be frequently used only after or in conjunction with the discussion of new ideas deriving from structualist and poststructuralist theory in the 1970s and 1980s.[14] This point is important for my contention that it is only from within the current postmodern context that we can really begin to read *The Recognitions*, as well as understand why the novel remained largely unrecognized for over twenty years. While Gaddis's first novel manifests the same configuration of features evident in the 1950s and 1960s fiction briefly remarked upon above, it also turns or tropes upon the counterfeit motif in a way that could only assume full significance retroactively, that is, after postmodernism had become a theoretical template for perceiving cultural change. But the inverse may also be true: *The Recognitions* can direct our attention toward what is or should be of signal importance for any theory of postmodernism.

THE RECOGNITIONS AND POSTMODERN THEORY

Let us begin with the premise that there may be a structural or intrinsic reason for much of the current confusion and disagreement about postmodernism. Lyotard, for example, in the passage cited earlier, calls the postmodern that within the modern that cannot be presented: "Postmodernism thus understood is not modernism at its end but in the nascent state, and this state is constant."[15] In these terms, the relationship between modernism and postmodernism would be neither one of continuity, stable opposition, nor paradigm shift (as would be the case in some kind of period break or historical *coupure*). Perhaps postmodernism may be even better conceived as an instance of *Nachträglichkeit*: it comes after modernism in the sense of a belated supplement that reactivates elements of modernism which, in the institutionalization of the latter, have been excluded, repressed, or marginalized.[16] As both an artistic and critical enterprise, therefore, postmodernism demands a reordering and reassessment of modernism, and especially of the latter's claim "to make it new." The experience of *Nachträglichkeit*, of deferred and retroactive action, entails a very different sense of temporality and precludes the possibility of "originating" an event or even understanding it in the self-contained moment of its occurrence. If modernist art privileges the ecstatic fullness of a visionary moment or frames the present against the mythic time of archetypal recurrence, postmodernist art moves toward the decentered repetitions of an endless temporality, as in Beckett's fiction, or the multiplicity of bifurcating virtual times, as in Borges's story "The Garden of Forking Paths."

Another way to formulate this difference in the postmodern literary configuration is to say that postmodern works must create not only their own precursors, as Borges said of Kafka, but also the conditions to which they are in some way a response. That is, these conditions are no longer simply "given" as part of some new experience the artist seeks to render "firsthand." Rather, what he or she confronts is a preselected set of representations that give rise to problems in and of themselves; in other words, postmodernist works depart from a set of cultural representations which they must assume and critique even as they reframe or (re)produce them. (Hence, the importance of pop art as the first sign of postmodernism in the visual arts.) Of course, every representation does this to some extent: every visual representation restructures the visual field in relation to prior representations; every written text is a rewriting of prior written texts. But in postmodernist works, this operation is explicitly foregrounded or thematized, so that prior representations, rather than "lived experience," become the primary material focus, and the "work" itself consists of this continual process of restructuration. The necessity of *Nachträglichkeit*—of deferred action—thus applies not so much to the new contents of experience as it does to the form(s) in which it occurs.

The Recognitions is an exemplary case in point. As a Janus-faced novel standing at the threshold of the postmodern reconfiguration, it reactivates the Faust myth, but not as a centering archetype of Western experience operating according to the modernist "mythic method"; instead, it functions as a desedimented element in a series of textual decenterings and displacements that allows an unrepresentable "difference" to emerge and resonate with other "differences" in other series.[17] More profoundly, *The Recognitions* points to what can now be postulated as the most important conceptual shift underlying the postmodern reconfiguration: the reversal of the Platonic heritage and the counter assertion of the logic of the simulacrum. As we have seen, this reversal resonates through the novel as a special kind of "event" in the Deleuzian sense, a phantasm-event that completely escapes the logic of representation and liberates "difference" as a pure intensity. And it is precisely in this production of textual singularities that the novel presents the "unpresentable," as Lyotard calls it, and thus articulates the postmodern within the modern.

In these terms, Gaddis's *The Recognitions* can legitimately lay claim to being the first American "postmodern" novel. But perhaps more important, it suggests that "the postmodern condition" may be described more specifically as a situation in which "originals" no longer automatically assume primacy over copies, or a model over its image.[18] In an environment defined more and more by the new information technologies of consumer society, we have become increasingly aware of how difficult it is to separate the meaning and effect of a current "event" from its "reportage" or representation and of how the contemporary world is saturated with "copies" without originals, grafts and replications which cannot be reduced to a point of origin or explained by their source. The "reversal" of the Platonic paradigm begins however when we give up the search for the "truth" beneath appearances or the "real" before its distorting appropriation, transmission, and/or representation, and attempt to think the relationship between original and copy, model and image, in a new way.

One such way follows from the Nietzschean attempt taken up by the French poststructuralist philosophers to complete the overturning of the Platonic heritage based on relations of identity and similitude. Above all, this means thinking through the logic of the simulacrum, since it is precisely the simulacrum—as understood in the anti-Platonic sense—that most directly calls into question the hegemony of representation by reversing the latter's degradation of difference. As Deleuze clearly demonstrates, by giving ontological priority to identity, representation necessarily summits difference to the "quadruple links" of a mediation by which it is effectually repressed and degraded or reduced to contradictory, negative status, as in Hegelian philosophy.[19] Now it is precisely this lost and reduced "difference"—variously conceptualized by Jacques Derrida, Jean Baudrillard, and many feminist writers, in addition to Deleuze himself—that defines what is at stake today in contemporary poststructuralist writing: it is what they all seek to reinstate and affirm in positive terms.[20] However differently they define their theoretical projects, these poststructuralist thinkers all take this anti-Platonic "difference" to be primary, both ontologically and politically. Indeed, its current theorization may very well mark the final overthrow of Platonism initiated by Nietzsche and inaugurate the full conceptualization of the postmodern era.

Taking up the Heideggerian theme of ontological difference, Jacques Derrida has initiated a new theorization of writing itself (*écriture*) as a simulacrum. That is, writing does not represent a speech whose "originating" presence in the thought or consciousness of a speaker would be the guarantee of its transcendent meaning; instead, writing is conceived as a differential structure of traces without origin in which spacing (and therefore deferral and divergence, the two meanings of *différence* in French) is demonstrated to be the condition for the assertion of any meaning whatsoever. Derrida invents the neologism or graphic sign *différance* (distinguishable only on the page from the French word *différence*) to show that meaning is never fully present in a representational system but only results from the constant interplay of differential signifiers. As the difference of difference, "differance" is neither a word nor a concept but a simulacrum-concept. In fact, in order to show how such essentially "undecidable" terms as *pharmakon*, "supplement," or "hymen" operate in the respective texts of Plato, Rousseau, and Mallarmé, Derrida must invent a whole series of such simulacrum-concepts—"trace," "gram," "archi-trace"—which allow him to sketch out "on another scene" (the scene of writing) the movement by which a text comes into being and can never remain identical to itself.[21] Although Derrida's deconstructive method of reading has no doubt had its greatest impact on contemporary literary theory and philosophy, it also corresponds to an important strand of postmodern writing that operates directly at the level of language as a graphic signifying system, as in various fictional works by Walter Abish, Raymond Federman, Ronald Sukenick, Steve Katz, and others.

Jean Baudrillard, on the other hand, pushes much further in the direction taken earlier by Hugh Kenner (both, incidentally, were strongly influenced by Marshall McLuhan). In a postmodern perspective, Baudrillard might be said to have literalized the reversal of Platonism, since for him the "real" is simply what can be constructed in order to guarantee the authenticity of our representations, or rather our "simulations." Baudrillard argues that we have passed from an order based on the production of identical objects according to a model of resemblance to a free-floating order of "simulacra" (copies without originals) in which codes at another level generate structural differences in an indeterminate and aleatory process. What, for example, is the exact relationship of the genetic code in DNA to the life substance it somehow informs? The essence of Baudrillard's theory can be quickly grasped by considering his postulation of four successive stages of the image:

> it is the reflection of a basic reality
> it masks and perverts a basic reality
> it masks the absence of a basic reality
> it bears no relation to any reality (it is a pure simulacrum)[22]

In this last stage, the image (or simulacrum) no longer points back to a referent that would guarantee its intelligibility. Instead, it operates in a system of coded differences that play on an earlier system which now provides a kind of fantom referential domain. For example, in his early work, Baudrillard showed that the value of mass-produced consumer objects had nothing to do with their material reality but derived from a sign system in which referential values (like status) function only as structural differences. And the same is true of theory itself: in current theoretical discourse the Marxist political revolution or the Freudian unconscious provides only a pseudoreferential domain for theories that "float" like currency on the world market and assume value only in relation to other theoretical discourses.

Baudrillard takes Disneyland as a revelation of our current entangled orders of simulation. Its simulacra and phantasms—the Pirates, the Frontier, Future World—no doubt function ideologically, as "a digest of the American way of life, a panegyric to American values, [an] idealized transposition of a contradictory reality" (24). But it also conceals the fact that America itself is the *real* Disneyland, just as modern prisons conceal the fact that the social fabric itself, in its "banal omnipresence," has become carceral: "Disneyland is presented as an imaginary order in order to make us believe that the rest is real, when in fact all of Los Angeles and the America surrounding it are no longer real, but of the order of the hyperreal and of simulation. It is no longer a question of a false representation of reality (ideology), but of concealing the fact that the real is no longer real, and thus of saving the reality principle" (25). This last stage of the image, in which conventional representation is everywhere engulfed by simulation—for Baudrillard, the state of contemporary American culture—operates according to a logic of "hyperreality" which seeks to make everything "more real than the real." Photorealist artwork, in which the painter appears to copy a photograph in order to reproduce some aspect of our objective world with meticulous accuracy, conveys the eery sense of hyperreality that Baudrillard seeks to describe. Although his theory takes off from the same point (the reversal of Platonism) upon which *The Recognitions* turns, it obviously goes far beyond the kind of simulation found in Gaddis's novel. Its primary usefulness in the postmodern literary context lies in the way it illuminates the hyperrealist and neosurrealist fiction of the 1980s represented by such writers as Frederick Barthelme, Steve Erickson, William Gibson, and Ted Mooney.

In the theory of Gilles Deleuze, on the other hand, there can be no neo-Hegelian succession of self-contained stages of the image (or of representation), as Baudrillard proposes; such schemes only serve to perpetuate the illusion of an earlier and less mediated (or fictionalized) social arrangement. In contrast to the sense of "reality loss" that animates Baudrillard's work, Deleuze's recent work argues that the "real" is always construed according to the way in which the flux of "desire" is produced, channeled, and coded in a specific type of social field. More specifically, "desire" is governed by different "semiotic regimes" that operate in conjunction with various material or nondiscursive arrangements—a specifically defined territory, a set of tools or technologies, the possible ways that bodies can interact.[23] For Deleuze, literature therefore is less a representation than a mapping of how desire operates in a specific social configuration. Of greatest interest is writing that is "rhizomatic" and which escapes those structures of desire that only reflect the hierarchical, bipolar organization of repressive social structures. In fact, it is only in the pursuit of the rhizomatic wanderings of desire that the writer is able to invent a verbal assemblage (*agencement*) out of the assemblages which created him or her.[24] In this extension of Bergson's concept of multiplicity to new arrangements between words and things, Deleuze's work provides a philosophic parallel to the large and excessive novels of information overload and rhizomatic proliferation published in the 1970s and which were prefigured in many ways by Gaddis's *The Recognitions*. Not surprisingly, then, this strand of postmodern fiction—exemplified most conspicuously by Thomas Pynchon's *Gravity's Rainbow*, Joseph McElroy's *Lookout Cartridge*, and Don DeLillo's *Ratner's Star*—would also include Gaddis's later novels *JR* and *Carpenter's Gothic*. These last two novels function more explicitly as postmodern fictions than *The Recognitions*, which to a large extent is still constrained by the exigencies of representation. I want to conclude therefore with a more detailed account of the terms in which these later novels must be read.

JR: Deterritorialized Speech and the Flux of Capital

If *The Recognitions* plays out and ultimately subverts the copy/counterfeit opposition in its articulation of the logic of the simulacrum, it is not surprising that Gaddis's second novel *JR*, published in 1975, should seek to discover new fictional terms, terms that are appropriate, as one perceptive reader of Gaddis has put it, to an age of "credit and credibility" rather than of belief.[25] The new terms point not to another "novel as simulacrum" but to the novel as "paper empire." This phrase compactly describes both the novel *JR* and its central subject, which is the meteoric growth and collapse of a financial holding company, the JR Family of Companies, headed by a tenaciously greedy eleven-year-old who simply follows the instructions of his elders after his sixth-grade class visits a Wall Street investment firm. The crucial point of the novel, however, is *not* that the JR Family of Companies is a mere paper empire, or a simulacrum mimicking those sturdier, more serious firms that populate Wall Street and of which Governor Cates's investment firm is both prime example and JR's "model." This kind of opposition no longer holds, in the sense that the difference between JR's company and Cates's is not a generative one for the novel, as is the difference between copy and simulacrum in *The Recognitions*. Rather, what is at stake in *JR* manifests itself first as a formal or even technical problem: how is the chaos and flux produced by the paper empires of contemporary finance to be rendered in a prose fiction novel, which is, of course, both another kind of paper empire and its antithesis?

First of all, in order to portray the dizzying effects of Wall Street machinations and the disorders of a purely commercial culture on the novel's characters, Gaddis completely dispenses with narrative and plunges the reader into a postmodern "novelistic space" composed almost entirely of fragmented conversations, interrupted mutterings and stammerings, delirious harangues and jargoned doublespeak. In fact, since the medium of the novel is almost totally reduced to recorded speech, the result might be more accurately designated as a transcribed acoustic collage. That is, the novel collages the discourses of advertising, big business, politics, and public relations, the slang of school kids and street people, the ruminations of drunken intellectual and failed artists, the bitter reproaches of divorcing couples and lovers in turmoil, thereby making these registered "sounds" barely distinguishable from the general background noise of our multimedia environment.[26]

With broken, fragmented speech serving as the novel's primary compositional element, its de-narrativized structure can strive for an almost seamless montage effect. As one reader has noted, all is flow—money, finance capital, video images, water, conversation, a radio playing, one scene or character impinging on another.[27] But in thus seeking to render the flux and flow of contemporary life, *JR* takes great risks, both in its method and "message(s)." As we are whirled from one node of connection to another—from an old family house in Long Island to a local school, then to the local bank, then to a Wall Street investment firm, and finally to an upper Eastside apartment—it becomes clear that no overriding, stabilizing speech will be heard, indeed could be heard, since no identifiable consciousness could be in control or take it all in. For the novel relentlessly demonstrates that it is not production or intelligible purpose but the ceaseless movement and proliferation of useless information and objects that define our world.

Unlike *The Recognitions*, then, *JR* makes no attempt to maintain even the outward conventions of the traditional novel. To be sure, there are characters caught up in events whose actions and responses we take an interest in and begin to follow. But this is made exceedingly difficult by the novel's manner of presentation. Not only has the ostensible author disappeared, but so have even the minimal authorial functions: speakers are usually not identified except by "tics" and idiosyncrasies of speech; shifts from one scene to another are only indicated briefly in lyrical and oblique ways. Furthermore, both time and sequences of action must always be inferred by the reader, with no chapter breaks to help. As a consequence, *JR* often exceeds even the most difficult and recalcitrant of modernist fiction in its demands on the reader. But while it is true that the reader must learn to identify voices, (re)construct fictional situations and supply some meaningful context simply in order to "read" the novel, he or she soon discovers significant patterns of coherence. But with one "structuralist" qualification: in this elaborately self-coded "open work" that teaches the reader how to read it, form and content, order and disorder, discourse and reality can only be defined in relation to one another.

In an early scene set in a Long Island school, the science teacher Jack Gibbs is lecturing to the kids on the concept of entropy:

> —All right let's have order here, order ... ! he'd reached the [television] set himself and snapped it into darkness.—Put on the lights there now. Before we go any further here, has it ever occurred to any of you that all this is simply one grand misunderstanding? Since you're not here to learn anything, but to be taught so you can pass these tests, knowledge has to be organized so it can be taught, and it has to be reduced to information so it can be organized do you follow that? In other words this leads you to assume that organization is an inherent property of the knowledge itself, and that disorder and chaos are simply irrelevant forces that threaten it from outside. In fact it's exactly the opposite. Order is simply a thin, perilous condition we try to impose on the basic reality of chaos....[28]

These assertions suggest, of course, that the processes of reading and writing—classroom activities usually displaced at this school by "video instruction"—should also be construed as "perilous condition[s] we try to impose on the basic reality of chaos." Gibbs's later references to Norbert Wiener and information theory pick up this central thematic concern, but it is his delirious speech that most effectively emphasizes how human communication itself is the most fragile attempt to impose order:

> read Wiener on communication, more complicated the message more God damned chance for errors, take a few years of marriage such a God damned complex of messages going both ways can't get a God damned thing across, God damned much entropy going on say good morning she's got a God damned headache thinks you don't give a God damn how she feels, ask her how she feels she thinks you just want to get laid, try that she says it's the only God damn thing you take seriously about her puts you out of business and goes running around like the God damned Israelis waving the top half of the double boiler have to tell everybody they're right. God damned Arabs mad as hell sitting

there with the bottom half pretend you take them seriously only thing you want is their God damned oil.... (403)

As in the cocktail party chatter in *The Recognitions*, most of the dialogue in *JR* fails as communication, usually because the speakers talk at cross-purposes and can neither order their thoughts nor complete their sentences. Of course, many characters are simply mouthpieces of some type of professional or bureaucratic dysfunction. For example, the utterances of Mr. Whiteback, who is both the school principal *and* president of the local bank, always stall in jargoned redundancy: "—In terms of tangibilitating the full utilization potential of in-school television ... " (39) is his inept attempt to justify the use of audiovisual equipment. But Whiteback's reliance upon bureaucratic jibberish, a tendency Gibbs will later parody (47), hardly conceals the fact that he and his cronies, which include a local congressional assemblyman, are using the school as a clearing house for "home ec" and other educational equipment for their own profit. In Whiteback's office, the telephones for both school and bank business "rant" incessantly, and usually there are three and four conversations going on simultaneously. To complicate matters further, exchanges between characters on the telephone are always literally one-sided, in the sense that only half of the conversation is reported. In this way, the reader is made intensely aware of the extent to which he or she is being forced to "fill-in" and make sense out of information that is partial, confused, and often highly redundant.

Reducing the authorial function to a recording apparatus also enables Gaddis to foreground the importance of the "communication model" in relation to novelistic forms. In the perspective of information theory, traditional novelistic conventions appear as forms of organization that only seem "inherent" to life (or to knowledge, as in Gibbs's assertion above). This naturalistic attitude appears not only naive but inadequate for the contemporary novelist who senses that the "information" in our own environment does not fit into and cannot be conveyed by these forms. A basic premise of information theory is that the more complex the message, the greater its improbability and the more work the receiver must do to decipher it. *JR* actualizes this assumption through its very manner of presentation, leaving it to the reader to discover meaning and significance within what is apparently only noise and redundancy. Consequently, as one critic has shown, reading the novel amounts to acting against "the entropy of the text, [by] tying together speech acts that, in terms of their direction and manner of presentation, tend to disperse, wander, dissipate, dwindle, disappear."[29]

This postmodern shift of the burden of textual coherence to the reader may require some justification. Even the sympathetic reader wants to know if there really is "a story" here that needs to be told in this manner and what will finally make the novel worth the time invested. Of course, this second question contains an implicit irony, since the novel itself is so directly concerned with the worth or value of information. In these terms, moreover, the black-humor vision *JR* projects is as much the inevitable result of reducing empirical realities—both human and otherwise—to "information that must be organized" as it is a matter of any specific content.[30] Nevertheless, one might begin to answer these questions by remarking that *JR* contains a multiplicity of *little* stories, some sad, some incredibly funny, some downright crazy. For the most part, these little stories have to do with the failure and wreckage of human lives, in obvious contrast to the amazing success of JR's financial enterprise. There are stories of lovers separating, families disintegrating, children being neglected, an artist driven to suicide. Not unexpectedly, venality and greed, madness and obsession define the characters, and their enterprisings are enlivened by a dark, satirical humor and air of desperate absurdity. One corporate executive is preoccupied with stocking American parks with game from Africa; another mismanages a sale of toy pistols, which are sent by mistake to an African tribe, with disastrous results. But inconspicuously set off against these stories are the activities of two serious characters, Jack Gibbs and Edward Bast, who elicit both interest and sympathy.

Gibbs, cynical and destitute after wasting most of his life, will snatch a few days of happiness in a lyrically brief love affair with Amy Joubert, a fellow part-time schoolteacher who is being coldly manipulated by her husband for custody of their son and by her uncle, Governor Cates, for her share in the family-owned investment firm. When Gibbs and Amy are pulled apart by forces beyond their control, Gibbs will try to give meaning to his life by completing a study begun sixteen years before of "mechanization and the arts, the destructive element." Unfortunately, he falls victim to the very same loss of energy and organization that he is attempting to analyze. Edward Bast, the novel's naive and romantic artist figure, provides a study in contrast. He is sentimentally obsessed with and thus easily duped by his cousin Stella, who though married, is willing to go to bed with him as part of her scheme to gain control of his shares in their family company. Penniless and unable to say no, Bast is subsequently sucked into the morass of "JR Corp" as JR's "Business Representative." In a chaos-ridden apartment on East 96th Street, Bast finally manages to finish the piece of music he is composing, only to see it become the unlikely and degraded score for a pornographic film.

Such ironies, both comic and catastrophic, inevitably raise the question of how we are to view the novel's achievement of a victory it denies its most serious characters. In a perceptive early review, George Stade, having characterized *JR* as a "chaos of disconnection, a blizzard of noise" and sketched several of its "epicenters of disorder," among them the East 96th Street apartment, has this to say:

> But if you stand back from the wild and whirling words to where you can see the novel as a structure, as a system of relations among its parts rather than as an assemblage of referents to what is outside it, you see something other than the centrifugal forces of disruption at work. You see the equal if opposite centripetal forces of recurrence, reflection and analogy, of interlocking motifs and linked images, of buried puns and covert allusions, connecting the fragments. The esthetic order within the work is experienced as a compensation of sorts for the disorder without to which it refers.[31]

Stade's assertion that the chaos of *JR*'s fragmented surface is held in check and compensated for by an equal assertion of meaningful pattern amounts essentially to reading the novel in modernist terms. No doubt *JR* will often support such a reading: the introduction of Wagner's *Ring of the Nibelungen* as intertexual analogy and motif early in the novel would be one important instance of this aesthetic order. But a postmodern reading might want to question this opposition, insofar as it predisposes us to grasp aesthetic order as existing only in the novel, as something imposed from without, rather than as a means of presentation elicited and even discovered within the material itself. Following Bakhtin's argument (in "Discourse in the Novel") that a tension between centripetal and centrifugal forces always exists within language itself, we might want to ask what forces are acting on the language in JR.[32] The answer lies not in the novel's artistry, which may even deflect our attention from the problem toward a modernist "aesthetic" solution; if anywhere, we must look more closely at the source of the chaos.

JR opens with a conversation in which the elderly Bast sisters, Julia and Anne, recall their first experience of paper money:

—Money ... ? in a voice that rustled.
—Paper, yes.
—And we'd never seen it. Paper money.
—We never saw paper money till we came east.

—It looked so strange the first time we saw it. Lifeless.
—You couldn't believe it was worth a thing.
—Not after Father jingling his change.
—Those were silver dollars. (1)

In a certain sense, this moment stands "outside" the chaos which the novel will soon register, not as a privileged origin or state of youthful, prelapsarian happiness, but simply as the "time before" of another mode of representation, both in the culture generally and for this novel in particular. Yet even in this initial scene, we are not yet fully immersed in the novel's present, for what is crucial is not the change from metal to paper currency but rather the change from cash currency to the even more abstract exchanges enabled by the extention of credit and the whole credit system.

The growth of JR's financial empire parodically illustrates what this evolutionary change makes possible. JR begins by scouring the mail order catalogues, collecting free samples and the penny stock his class invests in a Wall Street firm in a demonstration visit. His "break" comes when, working from a phone booth and disguising his adolescent voice with a "snot rag," he buys a large quantity of surplus picnic forks from the U.S. Navy on credit and then unloads them on the Army for a huge profit. He then acquires an assortment of bankrupt companies and near-worthless vested interests which include an upstate New England mill and brewery, a publishing house, a shipping line (its only vessel capsized), a chain of nursing homes and funeral parlors, pork bellies, sheep-gut condoms, plastic flowers—all of which, through tax write-offs and wheeling and dealing, he consolidates into a corporate "family of companies" that perilously threatens the stability of the stock market.

Though it does not really strain credibility, there is an unmistakably fabulous and parable-like quality to JR's story.[33] But what engages our interest is not so much *how* it all comes about as how well the novel conveys what one critic, adopting a term applied from information theory, calls a "runaway system."[34] Such a system extracts more and more from its environment without any equitable return ("the more you have, the more you get"); thus, in all likelihood, social or economic systems that are runaway finally result in social revolution or self-extinction. In this respect, the "runaway" system depicted in *JR* is strikingly similar to the technological and bureaucratic world order that Thomas Pynchon depicts in *Gravity's Rainbow*, which is also centrally concerned with the reduction of human reality to cybernetically codable "information." What is remarkable about *JR* is that it doesn't so much represent such a system in action as render it vividly present in the speech of its characters. Here is a sample of JR directing operations in a telephone call to Bast:

> Bast? Listen I ... no I know but ... no I know but I was just coming to that where I was telling you where this here General Haight can help us out see this here Ray-X company it's getting screwed on all these dumb fixed-price contracts see where what we want is these here cost-plus ones where you get to ... no I know it but ... no but listen hey ... No but look just let me tell you how it works okay? See you get this here contract to supply something to the government like and then you ... how do I know, I mean just something they want to buy off you like that's where this here General can help us out see so what's neat about these cost-plus ones is you get to add this here percent of how much it costs you to fill this here contract so I mean the more you spend the more you get, see? I mean that's the whole ... no well sure but ... No I know I was always yelling about low-cost operations see but ... no but listen a second hey I mean how do you think the telephone company works where they're always yelling how they have to spend all this here money so they need to raise the rates I mean the more money they can think of how to spend it someplace they get to take this here percent where they keep raising the rates till they're almost bigger than the gover ... no but wait, see the ... No I know you don't I mean I'm just coming to that hey ... no I know I said that but I mean it won't take much longer see we just ... no well I just mean we like we the company, like not really anybody see so ... No but see that's the whole thing Bast see it's not money anyway it's just exchanging this here stock around in like this merging it with this here X-L subsiderary which it's worth like twenty times as much as, you know? See we just give these here Ray-X stockholders one share of X-L's preferred for their share of Ray-X only this here X-L's common stock capitalization is real low see so we have this here tremendous leverage see and ... no well I don't exactly either but that's what this Mister Wiles said see he ... No but ... no I know but.... (465–466)

The "conversation" from which the above is excerpted—and it is not at all untypical—runs on for almost five pages. Such passages make several things clear at once. First, that there can be no adequate human response: no dialogue is possible simply because this is not a human being talking, but money itself. And second, it is not just the language of money but the speech of money, the flux of capital as it enters into and becomes part of verbal communication. Significantly, Bast will soon find himself speaking in a similar manner, as he becomes more and more deliriously enmeshed in JR's schemes. In this way we see human speech itself taken up and thoroughly "deterritorialized"—to borrow Gilles Deleuze and Félix Guattari's useful term—as part of the capitalist exchange process.[35]

Like the speech which attempts to order and control it, finance capital has a "life" of its own that exceeds all attempts to organize it for a meaningful purpose: both speech and capital thus become part of the same runaway system. For Governor Cates, at the helm of a "legitimate" financial empire which is also threatening to go out of control, it's all a game without rules in which you do what you can get away with. The point is emphasized as several of his statements are picked up and then repeated by JR: "—You can't just play to play because the rules are only for if you're playing to win which that's the only rules there are" (301). And later: "—Okay so with these here futures I'm not telling you to do something illegal see I'm telling you what I'm doing and you find out how to do it that's all" (470). To a certain extent, these "players" are as victimized by the system as are the less rich and powerful. Indeed, the cumulative evidence of the novel is that the profit motive has now attained such a hypertrophied state, feeding and being fed by the runaway and entropic system, that human love and goodness are literally no longer able to hold people together.

The victory the novel attains may now be described in somewhat different terms. What Gaddis has done is to take information theory and the communication model as the means by which the flux and disorder of finance capital can be made to pass into and take palpable form within a work of fiction. (In Deleuzian terms, he has created a novelistic assemblage.) Since the reduction of human reality in all its manifold complexity to the organization of information in communication theory is itself already a symptom of the furthest abstraction and deterritorialization of a language or sign system, such a strategy enables Gaddis to depict the destabilizing and entropic effects of capitalism at *its* point of greatest deterritorialization. The most extensive surface of contact between these two systems is, of course, human speech. Thus, by simply recording the speech acts of the characters in all their fluidity and flux, noise and redundancy, the novel has no difficulty showing that capitalism as an informational and communicational system has ceased to be either "economic" or "social" in the basic sense of these words. From this perspective, *JR* intends neither compensation nor redemption; it is simply a demonstration, in the most rigorous terms imaginable, of one aspect of the "postmodern condition" in which we now live.

CARPENTER'S GOTHIC: GADDIS'S HOUSE OF FICTION(S)

At first glance, Gaddis's third and most recent novel, *Carpenter's Gothic*, which appeared in 1984, looks like a highly wrought fragment of *JR*, a coda to its maelstrom, as it were—as if Gaddis had decided to treat in lingering detail one of the many domestic tragedies we only catch a glimpse of in *JR*, by focusing his attention on only one "epicenter of disorder" instead of several at once. Moreover, at least one of the central characters and several of the minor ones could easily have walked off the pages of *JR*. And, as in *JR*, the fractured surface of broken and delirious speech provides the novel's primary medium of presentation, although in *Carpenter's Gothic* the authorial "connecting passages" are more extended and less neutrally descriptive. Finally, questions raised about the futility and waste of contemporary life, about what is really "worth doing" provide thematic links with the previous novels. Yet, for all these similarities, the net effect of the novel is entirely different. In its maintenance of temporal and spatial unities, in its careful elaboration of poetic resonances relatively free of satiric deflation, in its manner of unraveling the patterns of expectation it so deftly articulates, *Carpenter's Gothic* projects a somber, tragic intensity.

The main outlines of the narrative situation are easily recounted. A couple, Paul and Elizabeth Booth, both about thirty-five, have rented an imitation Gothic-styled house above New York along the Hudson River. The husband is an energetic Vietnam veteran now trying desperately to make it as a publicity agent and media consultant for a Reverend Ude, a southern evangelist preacher who first attracted public attention when he accidentally drowned one of his parishioners during baptism, and who is now attempting to inaugurate a crusade against "evil powers" infiltrating the country. Paul's wife Elizabeth, a rather passive, red-haired beauty, is heiress to a trust set up, but also effectively tied up, by corporate interests after her father, owner of Vorakers Consolidated Reserve, a large mining company, committed suicide. Visitors to the house are few but crucial for what unfolds there. Most important are Elizabeth's brother Billy, whose unexpected and usually brief visits are indicative of his nomadic, hippie lifestyle, and Mr. McCandless, the mysterious owner of the house who becomes sexually involved with Elizabeth during one of Paul's frequent absences. It turns out that both Ude and Vorakers Consolidated Reserve are interested in the Great Rift Valley area in Africa: the one wants to build a mission for "harvesting souls," the other seeks a possibly rich mineral deposit; it also turns out that this particular stretch of land has been extensively surveyed by McCandless, a former geologist who knows its geopolitical history in exact and profuse detail.

But while such a sketch may begin to suggest how what happens at the house, which is where the author as recording apparatus stations the reader, is always intricated with events in the world "outside," it hardly conveys the extent to which they must be pieced together from bits of detail conveyed within the exchanges between characters, mostly in Paul's futile attempt to "see how all the God damn pieces fit together" or McCandless's fulminations against the exploitative collusions and conspiracies of government and big business. In fact, the further we penetrate into the novel, the more we learn about the characters and their situations, but the less we understand of the plots—both in the sense of connected events and conspiracies—that are wheeling just beyond our grasp. At the same time, an inner logic of events seems to be developing that, as in a traditional novel, will finally yield some meaningful pattern predicated on the self-determined efforts of the characters to initiate change in their lives.

The problem with the Booth's marriage is signaled early on. From the minute Paul walks in the door, Liz (which is what he calls her) must contend with the obvious fact that what he needs and what she is not is a secretary:

> —Liz it was an hour, one solid God damn hour I couldn't reach you nobody could, that whole list I gave you? These calls I've been waiting for? State Department calling about this spade with his prisons and chicken factories did they call? And these pigs? Drug company bringing in these nutritionists for a look at these pigs did they call? [...] You're on the phone for an hour with Edie, somebody calls they get a busy ... Liz I'm trying to get something going here, line up these clients tell them to check with my home office and you're talking to Edie.36

Paul also involves her in a scam to defraud an insurance company by claiming that, as a result of an airplane crash, she is unable to perform her "conjugal duties"; he continually harasses her about her brother and misses no opportunity to intervene in family affairs in an attempt to obtain access to the trust fund. Though callous and sometimes brutal, Paul is less a monster, however, than a victim of the same world depicted in *JR*.

Elizabeth's relationship with her husband is partly illuminated when her brother Billy (he calls her Bibbs) accuses her of having always gone with "these real inferior types" (90) in order to protect "a secret self":

> —Man like wait Bibbs, I mean wait! That's not what I, I mean it's like you've got this real secret self hidden someplace you don't

want anybody to get near it, you don't even want them to know about it like you're afraid if some superior person shows up he'll like wipe you out so you protect it by these inferior types they're the only ones you'll let near you because they don't even know it's there. I mean they think they've taken over they never even like suspect you've always got the upper hand because that's your strength Bibbs, that's like how you survive [...] (193–194)

However, when McCandless—clearly a "superior person"—shows up (the rental agreement allows him access to a small room in the house where he stores old books and papers), Elizabeth is drawn immediately into a love affair with him that recalls the lyrical interlude Gibbs and Amy Joubert pass together in *JR*.

McCandless is older, worldly, knowledgeable about many things, and an ex-novelist. Many reviewers have taken him to be an author-surrogate, and with some reason. When an ominous intelligence agent named Lester comes seeking the survey data of the area in Africa mentioned above, the two fall into conversation about McCandless's first and only novel:

—You looked better then, didn't you [Lester says]. Like this Frank Kinkead [the hero of the novel], that's what he's supposed to look like isn't it, this cool unwavering glance where he says from now on he's going to live deliberately? (139)

Here Gaddis the novelist may be subtly engaged in self-parody, since the words "to live deliberately" which Lester cites echo *verbatim* Wyatt's last words in *The Recognitions*. In the exchange that follows, however, McCandless's remarks appear to reflect more seriously upon the novel we are reading:

—You saw how it ends.
—I know how it ends. It doesn't end it just falls to pieces, it's mean and empty like everybody in it is that why you wrote it?
—I told you why I wrote it, it's just an afterthought why are you so damned put out by it. This novel's just a footnote, a postscript, look for happy endings I come out mixed up with people like you and Klinger. (139)

Many other examples of this kind of self-reflexivity can be found, most notably in McCandless's conversations with Elizabeth (who is secretly writing a romantic novel).[37] The most apparently significant instance occurs when McCandless's remarks upon the construction of the house:

> —Oh the house yes, the house. It was built that way, yes, it was built to be seen from the outside it was, that was the style, he came on, abruptly rescued from uncertainty, raised to the surface—yes, they had style books, these country architects and the carpenters it was all derivative wasn't it, those grand Victorian mansions with their rooms and rooms and towering heights and cupolas and the marvelous intricate ironwork. The whole inspiration of medieval Gothic but these poor fellows didn't have it, the stonework and the wrought iron. All they had were the simple dependable old materials, the wood and their hammers and saws and their own clumsy ingenuity bringing those grandiose visions the old masters had left behind down to a human scale with their own little inventions, those vertical darts coming down from the eaves? and that row of bull's eyes underneath? He was kicking leaves aside, gesturing, both arms raised embracing—a patchwork of conceits, borrowings, deceptions, the inside's a hodgepodge of good intentions like one last ridiculous effort at something worth doing even on this small a scale, because it's stood here, hasn't it, foolish inventions and all it's stood here for ninety years.... (227–228)

Again, the temptation to read these remarks as reflections on the novel we are reading and on the difficulties that afflict the postmodern novelist is nearly irresistible. Taken in this self-reflexive sense, they hint at a convergence between the problems confronting the writer and the problems the characters themselves must somehow resolve. Indeed, it is the recurrent problem in all of Gaddis's novels, the problem posed by despair itself: what is meaningfully worth doing in a world hell-bent on the destruction of all human values? In Elizabeth's final confrontation with McCandless, however, we hear a voice seeking to resist this despair; furthermore, in the complications which this confrontation entails for the novel, we witness something like the reemergence of a dialogic.

After spending an idyllic day and a half with Elizabeth, McCandless had left rather abruptly with Billy who once again passes unexpectanly on his way to New York. A week later, having heard nothing from him in the interval, Elizabeth returns from a morning in New York to discover McCandless there waiting for her in the house which has just, been burglarized. McCandless soon reveals that he has come back to take her away "for good." But it has been a calamitous week and Elizabeth's feelings are no longer certain. One night, Paul had returned home with a serious knife wound inflicted by a mugger (or an assassin). In self-defense, Paul had killed the young black man, in what seems to have been a flashback in Paul's mind to an experience in Vietnam. Furthermore, it has become apparent that Paul's plans are falling apart as an already complicated situation grows out of his reach and understanding. It turns out that Ude is using him, or rather that Ude is being used by Grimes, the corporate head of Vorakers Consolidated Reserve, in a complicated scheme to force U.S. government intervention in Africa. What's more, when Senator Teakell, seemingly in collusion with Grimes—although his real interest is to sell Africans food and farm products, not mine their mineral resources—departs on a "fact-finding" mission to Africa, his plane is shot down. Though it is by no means clear who is responsible, the incident threatens to blow up into an international confrontation as the United States prepares for a full-scale military intervention off the African coast. But the most devastating event for Elizabeth is that her brother Billy was aboard the senator's plane.

It is against this complex background of events that the final confrontation between Elizabeth and McCandless unfolds. Elizabeth blames McCandless for Billy's death, since it was his impassioned account of Western exploitation and wickedness in Africa that had set Billy in his determination to go there in order to find out what was going on. McCandless's motive, she says, was "to give him [Billy] some dumb kind of strength that wasn't real to try to destroy Paul" (242). Earlier, they had quarreled over the extent to which Paul had been set up and used. In the course of what becomes a complex, multitracked dialogue, Elizabeth begins to cast doubt on McCandless's previously convincing grasp of the situation. To McCandless's accusation that her husband is a killer, she retorts: "All your grand words about the truth and what really happened that don't mean anything because it was one of his own men that's the truth, that's what really happened. He was fragged. Do you know what that means?" To this new knowledge that Paul was not wounded in combat but the victim of an assassination attempt by one of his own men, McCandless can only respond: "It's madness then isn't it, it's just madness ... " (240).

In her own faltering way, Elizabeth persistently argues for a more human meaning to events, or one which makes them more amenable to human responsibility. The most significant example occurs when she discovers that The Great Rift Valley in Africa—the area for which various interests are contending—may even be worthless, and that McCandless, who surveyed it earlier, knows this and refuses to do anything about it. His defense, he keeps repeating, is that no one will listen: "I told you, try to prove anything to them the clearer the proof and the harder they'll fight it, they ... " (246). McCandless now simply wants to abandon the situation, with "madness coming one way and stupidity the other" (233), and take Elizabeth with him to South America. But in a further turn, Elizabeth detects another motive behind this refusal to intervene:

> —And it's why you've done nothing ... She put down the glass,—to see them all go up like that smoke in the furnace all the stupid, ignorant, blown up in the clouds and there's nobody there, there's no rapture no anything just to see them wiped away for good it's really you, isn't it. That you're the one who wants apocalypse, Armageddon all the sun going out and the sea turned to blood you can't wait no, you're the one who can't wait! The brimstone and fire and your Rift like the day it really happened because they, because you despise their, not their stupidity no, their hopes because you haven't any, because you haven't any left. (244)

For this reason, Elizabeth seems to have decided to stay with Paul, who, for whatever his faults, has not succumbed to this kind of despair. Yet we are not at all certain what she will finally decide, since McCandless suddenly agrees to do what he can to stop a possible war over the worthless strip of land in Africa, and hurries off to New York. But here, the drama ends abruptly, in an anguishing denial of any final resolution, for that very night Elizabeth is murdered, apparently struck by a burglar. The novel concludes in a blackly ironic denouement, as Paul, now in control of the family fortune, drives off with Elizabeth's childhood friend Edie.

As I have tried to show, in her confrontations with McCandless Elizabeth intimates that there is another logic to human events in addition to the public and historical one and, specifically, that McCandless's conspiratorial view of history is as much motivated by his own personal despair as it is by an apprehension of the way things really are. Without denying the calamitous nature of historical reality, she argues for a perspectival view, a view of the world that must include the participants. An unexpected visit from McCandless's wife, Elizabeth's last visitor before she is murdered, adds another twist to this view. When Mrs. McCandless alludes to a period when McCandless spent time in a hospital, possibly a mental hospital, and to his son Jack and to his experiences as a teacher, Elizabeth (and the reader) is suddenly forced to consider another facet of McCandless's identity. Surprisingly, Mrs. McCandless even hints that the version of McCandless's experiences in Africa and his earlier life that we have taken to be a factual account may be merely "stories" he made up. McCandless's credibility is not thereby destroyed, however, for his version of events in the novel (and the history with which it is imbricated) not only makes sense but would seem to compel at least a qualified assent; furthermore, his conversation with Lester, although centering on his own literal fictionalizing (and certain mysterious papers), would seem to bestow some authenticity on the account he provides of his earlier life.

Carpenter's Gothic thus concludes with a series of reversals and incongruent perspectives which do not cancel each other out but instead suggest a complex, dialogic interplay between different orders of fictional sense-making. In fact, the theme that much of life is a tissue of fictions is insistently present throughout the novel. We are often reminded that the newspapers and other media distort and misrepresent events and, even worse, "take a picture and make a story out of it." Moreover, the characters themselves are all guilty of making up at least a part of their lives. Paul maintains the fiction that his roots are genteel Southern stock when, in fact, he is an adopted Jew. Even Elizabeth lies to McCandless about her father's death. When he catches her out—he has seen the movie on which her lie is patterned—her simple response is that "when people stop lying you know they've stopped caring" (226). Looking back through the novel, we cannot help but be struck by the number and diversity of fictions interwoven into its texture. Elizabeth and Paul converse by means of little fictions—a telescope on a star that will allow you to look back at your past, the story that children choose their parents just so they can be born, the belief of the African Masai that all the cattle in the world belong to them—"a good serviceable fiction," (121) McCandless remarks. Bible stories, the adventure stories Elizabeth's father read her and which she later realizes are all about himself, novels by Faulkner and Conrad, in fact everything in their conversation turns on one "fiction" or another. Added to which McCandless fulminates deliriously against the "cheap entertainment, anything to fill the emptiness any invention to make them part of some grand design anything, the more absurd the better" (144), while also acknowledging the human necessity of "any lunatic fiction to get through the night and the more far-fetched the better, any evasion of the one thing that's inevitable" (157). But what upsets him most are "the desperate fictions like the immortal soul" (157). Evangelists like the Reverend Ude "talk about their religious convictions and that's what they are, they're convicts locked up in some shabby fiction doing life without parole and they want everybody else in prison with them" (186).

And then there are the "paranoid-sentimental fictions" about the South (224), not to mention the various scams, plots, and conspiracies in motion throughout the novel. As McCandless remarks:

> Paul thinks he's been using Ude but Ude's been using him and Lester's been using them both because he wrote the scenario, set up that site get a few missionaries killed and then that plane gets shot down, Cruikshank pulls out the scenario dusts it off and we're back in the sixteenth century copper, gold, slavery sanitized in what they call the homelands and the cross of Jesus going before. (236)

Yet the one thing *Carpenter's Gothic* asserts unmistakeably, as it unravels our expectations and refuses answers to even basic plot questions, is that these various fictions will not be and could not be set against some absolute and ultimate truth. But by the same token, the novel also refuses the antithetical extreme of a totally relativistic universe where all fictions are equally valid and, hence, equally worthless. To be sure, as a manipulator of various kinds and levels of fiction, Gaddis takes pains to display them for us in all their detailed incongruity and variety of consequence. But finally, if his house of fiction is indeed carpenter gothic in style—a "patchwork of conceits, borrowings, [and] deceptions" (227)—it does not differ significantly in this respect from the fabric of much of contemporary American life. As we see these fictions resonating through the characters' lives, fictions played off and against one another, we are enjoined to take the measure of each one in relation to those lives, to what it makes possible and to what it inhibits. In this most Nietzschean of novels, then, the sense and value of a fiction provide its only measure; the truth itself is "unpresentable."

Counterfeit, copy, simulacrum, paper fiction, "a good serviceable fiction" as opposed to a desperate one—the terms suggest that, from *The Recognitions* to *JR* and *Carpenter's Gothic*, Gaddis's novels undergo less a progression or evolution than a constant redefinition. What gets redefined are the terms by which the novels can compellingly assert their pertinence to contemporary experience. For Gaddis this entails redefining the very form of the novel, which, as Bakhtin reminds us, is a form without fixed rules or categories by which it can be judged, except in relation to its own contemporaneity.

How is art's contemporaneity in turn to be determined? For the last two hundred years, it has been conceived in relation to a theory of modernity. Lyotard's theory of postmodernism now suggests a new turn in this history. The modern work, he states, "allows the unpresentable to be put forward only as the missing contents; but the form, because of its recognizable consistency, continues to offer to the reader or the viewer matter for solace or pleasure."[38] In a postmodern work, on the other hand, the form does not allow this solace or pleasure, but seeks "to impart a stronger sense of the unpresentable." In Kantian terms, it maintains the breach between the concept and the sensible. For Lyotard, therefore, postmodern form is like the Kantian sublime, with its intrinsic combination of pleasure and pain: "the pleasure that reason should exceed all presentation, the pain that imagination or sensibility should not be equal to the concept." For Deleuze, who approaches this Kantian theme with the limits of representation in view, it is in this breach between the concept and the sensible that recognition and common sense are shattered, as the self dissolves and singularities are released like spores. For what is unthinkable and unimaginable ("unpresentable") in the Kantian sublime is the phantasm itself.[39] From this (Deleuzian) perspective, a postmodern form would be one in which the work of art's disjunctive parts communicate in and through the logic of the phantasm.

While readers may disagree about how exactly these terms apply to *The Recognitions*, *JR*, and *Carpenter's Gothic*, it is undeniable that these novels offer neither the solace of good form nor a shareable nostalgia for what is no longer presentable. Unlike the great modernist novels, armed with what George Stade calls their compensatory aesthetic, they provide no refuge in art but counter this impulse with unremitting black humor and satire. For in Gaddis's novels "form" is as much a specific "expression of content" with its own phantasmatic logic of proliferation as it is a means of containing and shaping experience—of making it recognizable. In allowing themselves no other ground to sustain them than a need to mark out and multiply differences within the fictions that both order and disorder our lives, Gaddis's novels not only demonstrate why traditional forms can no longer provide critical access to contemporary experience, they also render the "new contents" of that experience. In this sense, perhaps, they can indeed be said to present the "unpresentable."

Notes

1. For a useful history of the term, see Hans Bertens, "The Postmodern *Weltanschauung* and Its Relation with Modernism," in *Approaching Postmodernism*, ed. by Douwe Fokkema and Hans Bertens (Amsterdam and Philadelphia: John Benjamins Publishing Company, 1986), pp. 9–51.

2. The last chapter of Michel Foucault's *The Order of Things*, originally published in 1966, would seem to support just such a claim. Another detailed account of the modernist epistēmē is provided by Timothy Reiss in *The Discourse of Modernism* (Ithaca: Cornell University Press, 1982). Reiss, in the wake of Foucault, renames the modernist epistēmē "analytico-referential discourse"; it involves

> such notions as those of truth and valid experiment (in science), of referential language and representation (in all types of discourse), of possessive individualism (in political and economic theory), of contract (in sociopolitical and legal history), of taste (in aesthetic theory), of commonsense and the corresponding notion of concept (in philosophy), all of which are hypostatizations of a particular discursive system. (pp. 13–14)

3. In a recent survey of the period, Malcolm Bradbury makes a strong case for the term "neo-realism," having quite correctly pointed out that this fiction does not simply return (after the period of high modernist experimentation) to any nineteenth- or early twentieth-century kind of realism. The problem with the term is that one could make an analogous argument for the "realism" that reappears in American fiction in the 1980s. See Bradbury, "Neo-realist Fiction," in *The Columbia Literary History of the United States*, ed. by Emory Elliott (New York: Columbia University Press, 1988).

4. Cf. Michel Foucault's statements on the (French) reorientation of philosophical thought since the 1950s:

> We have experienced Sartre's generation as a generation certainly courageous and generous, which had a passion for life, politics, existence .... But we, we have discovered something else, another passion: the passion for concepts and for what I will call 'system.' ... By system it is necessary to understand an ensemble of relations which maintain themselves and transform themselves independently of the things they connect ... an anonymous system without subjects .... The "I" has exploded (look at modern literature).

In "Entretien: Michel Foucault" by Madeleine Chapsal, *La Quinzaine littéraire*, 5 (May 15, 1966), pp. 15–16.

5. For Hawkes's statement on character and plot, see "John Hawkes: An Interview," *Wisconsin Studies in Contemporary Literature* (summer 1964), p. 146. Burroughs expresses his belief in the impossibility of direct representation in a passage in *Naked Lunch* (New York: Grove Press, 1966, orig. pub. 1955): "The word cannot be expressed direct .... It can perhaps be indicated by mosaic of juxtaposition like articles abandoned in a hotel drawer, defined by negatives and absence ... " (p. 116).

6. Ricardo J. Quinones convincingly argues this point in *Mapping Literary Modernism* (Princeton: Princeton University Press, 1985). Irving Howe's description

is taken from his introduction to *The Idea of the Modern*, ed. by Irving Howe (New York: Horizon Press, 1967), p. 34.

7. For a discussion of this problematic in the theoretical context of postmodernism, see my article, "Ideology, Representation, Schizophrenia: Toward a Theory of the Postmodern Subject," in *Postmodernism*, ed. by Gary Shapiro (New York: SUNY Press, 1989).

8. In *City of Words: American Fiction 1950–1970*, Tony Tanner emphasizes the recurrent American fear of systems, structures, and organizations, but without establishing any systematic connection between this fear and the subject in contemporary fiction as fluid, mobile, partial, or deliberately schizoid (as opposed to the fragmented or alienated self).

9. Bruce Jay Friedman, "Introduction," *Black Humor* (New York: Bantam Books, 1965), p. x.

10. Philip Roth, "Writing American Fiction," reprinted in *The Novel Today*, ed. by Malcolm Bradbury (Glasgow: Fontana Paperbacks, 1977). Roth states: "The American writer in the middle of the twentieth century has his hands full in trying to understand, describe, and then make *credible* much of American reality. It stupifies, it sickens, it infuriates, and finally it is even a kind of embarrassment to one's own meagre imagination. The actuality is continually outdoing our talents, and the culture tosses up figures almost daily that are the envy of any novelist" (p. 34, emphasis in original).

11. See Hans Bertens, "The Postmodern *Weltanschauung* and Its Relation with Modernism" for a discussion of this point.

12. Robert Scholes, in *The Fabulators* (New York: Oxford University Press, 1967), is to be credited for introducing this term into literary criticism. In the enlarged edition, *Fabulation and Metafiction* (Urbana: University of Illinois Press, 1979), Scholes moves toward a flexible, inclusive definition through discussions of romance (Durrell and Fowles), allegory (Murdock and Barth), metafiction (Barth, Barthelme, Coover, Gass, *et al.*), black humor (Vonnegut, Hawkes, Southern), and historical fabulation (Pynchon, García Márquez, Coover, *et al.*).

13. Hugh Kenner, *The Counterfeiters* (New York: Doubleday Anchor Book, 1973), p. xiii.

14. I would take issue therefore with Andreas Huyssen's statement in *After the Great Divide: Modernism, Mass Culture, Postmodernism* (Bloomington: Indiana University Press, 1986) that "French [poststructuralist] theory provides us primarily with an *archeology of modernity*, a theory of modernism at its state of exhaustion" rather than a "*theory of postmodernity*" (p. 209, emphasis in original). First, because there is not as great a distance between these two projects as Huyssen indicates. Second, while it is true that, with the exception of Lyotard, French poststructuralism does not expressly provide a theory of postmodernity; it has been of enormous influence in the recent formulation of such theories. I might also point out that the term "archeology," while clearly applicable to such modernist works as Joyce's *Ulysses* and Eliot's *The Waste Land*, is used by Huyssen himself in a postmodern sense, since it explicitly assumes a critical and historical distance from modernism.

15. Jean-François Lyotard, "What Is Postmodernism," in *The Postmodern Condition*, trans. by Geoff Bennington and Brian Massumi (Minneapolis: University of Minnesota Press, 1984, orig. pub. 1979), p. 79.

16. This use of the German term *Nachträglichkeit*, meaning "deferred action," derives from Freud, who employed it repeatedly in connection with his view of psychical temporality and causality. For a useful discussion of the term, see the entry under "Deferred Action" in J. Laplanche and J.-B. Pontalis's *The Language of Psychoanalysis* (New York: W. W. Norton, 1973).

17. Of course, Gaddis was not the only writer of the period to refuse the modernist use of myth. Richard Wasson, in "Notes on a New Sensibility" (*Partisan Review*, Vol. 36, No. 3, 1969), shows that contemporary novelists like Robbe-Grillet, Murdock, Barth, and Pynchon all rejected the "mythical method" as a way of integrating self and history into a timeless order.

18. In an essay entitled "Periodizing the 60s" in *The 60s Without Apology* (Minneapolis: University of Minnesota Press, 1984), Fredric Jameson has referred to postmodernism as a "culture of the simulacrum (an idea developed out of Plato by Deleuze and Baudrillard to convey some specificity of a reproducible object world, not of copies or reproductions marked as such, but a proliferation of trompe-l'oeil copies *without originals*)" (p. 195, author's emphasis). Unfortunately, Jameson does not develop the idea any further.

19. By the four aspects of representation (its "quadruple links"), Deleuze means identity in the concept, opposition in the predicate, analogy in judgment, and resemblance in perception. See *Différence et répétition*, especially pp. 44ff.

20. See Alice A. Jardin's *Gynesis: Configurations of Woman and Modernity* (Ithaca: Cornell University Press, 1985) for an attempt to link the concern with "difference" evident in both poststructuralism and feminism.

21. See in particular Derrida's essay "Differance" in *Margins*, trans. by Alan Bass (Chicago: University of Chicago Press, 1982, orig. pub. 1972).

22. See Jean Baudrillard, *Simulations* (New York: Foreign Agents Series, 1983). Page numbers to further references to this book, which is comprised of sections extracted from *L'échange symbolic et la mort* and *Simulacres et simulation*, will be inserted in the text.

23. See, in particular, Gilles Deleuze and Félix Guattari, *A Thousand Plateaus*, trans. by Brian Massumi (Minneapolis: University of Minnesota Press, 1987, orig. pub. 1982), pp. 111–148 and 208–231, as well as my article "Ideology, Representation, Schizophrenia: Toward a Theory of the Postmodern Subject."

24. For a specific illustration of the theory, see Deleuze and Guattari's study *Kafka: Toward a Minor Literature*, trans. by Dana Polan (Minneapolis: University of Minnesota Press, 1986, orig. pub. 1975).

25. Joel Dana Black, "The Paper Empires and Empirical Fictions of William Gaddis," p. 24.

26. In this respect *JR* bears certain affinities with what Fredric Jameson calls the satire-collage, which is "the form taken by artificial epic in the degraded world of commodity production and of the mass media: it is artificial epic whose raw materials have become spurious and inauthentic, monumental gesture now replaced by the cultural junk of industrial capitalism." See *Fables of Aggression*, p. 80.

27. Frederick R. Karl, *American Fictions 1940–1980* (New York: Harper and Row, 1983) p. 190. Karl is to be greatly commended for giving Gaddis pride of place in his detailed but overarching survey of contemporary American fiction.

28. William Gaddis, *JR* (New York: Knopf, 1975), p. 20. Page numbers for all subsequent quotations will be inserted in the text.

29. Carl D. Malgren, "William Gaddis's *JR*: The Novel of Babel," *The Review of Contemporary Fiction*, Vol. II, No. 2 (summer 1982), p. 10.

30. In this subversion of an overarching narrative structure amidst a fragmentation of speech, *JR* illustrates Lyotard's contention in *The Postmodern Condition* that today "the narrative function ... is being dispersed in clouds of narrative language elements—narrative, but also denotative, prescriptive, descriptive, and so on. Conveyed within each cloud are pragmatic valencies specific to its kind. Each of us lives at the intersection of many of these. However, we do not necessarily establish stable language combinations, and the properties of the ones we do establish are not necessarily communicable" (p. xxiv). While it would be going too far to see the disintegration of speech forms in *JR* exclusively in these terms, the relevance of the passage to the novel should be obvious.

31. George Stade, "JR," *New York Times Book Review*, November 9, 1975, P. 50.

32. The centripetal and centrifugal forces within language are discussed by Mikhail Bakhtin to "Discourse in the Novel," pp. 270f.

33. Insofar as its recorded speech acts all refer only to other speech acts, *JR* corresponds in its structure to the definition of fabulation offered earlier. In most postmodern fiction, however, fabulation is achieved through embedded or nested acts of narration or alternative sources of information.

34. Thomas LeClair, "William Gaddis, *JR* and the Art of Excess" in *Modern Fiction Studies*, Vol. 27, No. 4 (winter 1981–1982), pp. 592–593. The term was coined by Gregory Bateson in *Steps to an Ecology of Mind* and developed by Anthony Wilden in *System and Structure*.

35. "Deterritorialization" is a term developed by Deleuze and Guattari in *Anti-Oedipus* (New York: Viking Press, 1977) to describe the inevitable dismantling or destruction of all traditional codes in the growth and expansion of capitalism into all aspects of life. Greatly simplified, their theory proposes that the primordial flux of desire is produced and coded (given meaning and significance) by means of and in relation to a semiotic regime and a territory. In primitive regimes, this primary coding is inscribed on the body, in dance, ritual, and myth in multiple and nonhierarchical forms, and takes as its ultimate referential territory the body of the earth itself. In barbaric regimes, signs undergo a paranoid reorganization and are overcoded, through constant (re)interpretation by a priest class, as certain signifiers are centered and become privileged over others, and the ultimate territory becomes the body of the despot or monarch himself. In civilized or capitalist society, these traditional and archaic codings are progressively undone or decoded, in a process of release and abstraction in which everything of value is such only because of its relation to capital. Compared to the previous regimes, capitalism is both more cynical (or nihilistic) and more productive. First of all, capitalism decodes and deterritorializes all previous traditional value systems, since it recognizes only those values that can be made equivalent to its own (re)production, as Marx has shown in great detail. Thus, in the capitalist regime, there is no longer any corresponding territory except for the deterritorialized body of capital itself. However, in axiomatizing all values in the exchange process—in reducing all human values to the cash nexus—capitalism also releases a tremendous amount of energy and expands

productive capacity beyond all former limits. In order to control and regulate this release of energy and productive potential, Deleuze and Guattari argue, capitalism must defer and displace its own limits and reinscribe (or re-territorialize) them in repressive channels, structures, and inhibitions. In short, by its very nature, capitalism breaks down older social structures and identities which it then must artificially shore up in order to continue to operate.

36. William Gaddis, *Carpenter's Gothic* (New York: Viking, 1984), p. 39. Page numbers to all subsequent quotations will be inserted in the text.

37. For two examples in *Carpenter's Gothic* which refer to *JR*, see the quoted passage on p. 150 containing the phrase "my vision of a disorder which it was beyond any one man to put right" and Elizabeth's summary of Adolph's statement that Paul knows "as much about finance as some snot nosed sixth grader" on p. 209.

38. Lyotard, *The Postmodern Condition*, p. 81.

39. For Deleuze on the Kantian sublime, see *Différence et répétition*, pp. 187ff.

JONATHAN RABAN

At Home in Babel

Every William Gaddis novel tells its story in such a cryptic and allusive way that it can become a cerebral torture, like a crossword puzzle whose setter is named after a famous inquisitor—Torquemada, Ximenes. Reviewing *JR* in the *New Yorker* in 1975, George Steiner called it an "unreadable book"—a remark that got him into hot water with the professional Gaddisites, a solemn crew themselves given to sentences like "Read from this perspective, *The Recognitions* demonstrates the essential alterity of the world, the meta-ethical virtue of agapistic ethics" [Gregory Comnes, in his 1994 *The Ethics of Indeterminacy in the Novels of William Gaddis*]. Certainly Gaddis tries one's readerly patience to breaking point, strewing the foreground of his fiction with obstacles designed to trip one up, slow one down, and generally bring one face to face with the (as it were) essential alterity of the novel as a willful tissue of words. Scaling *The Recognitions* and *JR*, one keeps coming on the remains of earlier readers who lost their footing and perished in the ascent.

Yet on most of the important counts, Gaddis is an engagingly old-fashioned writer. The Victorian spaciousness of his books is in keeping with their big Victorian subjects—forgery and authenticity, wills and legacies, the circulation of money, the workings of the law. His best characters, though never directly described, have a powerful fleshly presence on the page. The

---

From *The New York Review of Books*, Vol. XLI, No. 4, (February 17, 1994). © 1994 by Jonathan Raban.

loutish pathos of JR, the boy capitalist, Liz and Paul Booth's burned-out marriage in *Carpenter's Gothic*, are examples of solidly credible realistic portraiture of the kind one feels that Trollope would have recognized and admired. More than any other writer I can think of, Gaddis really listens to the way we speak now. The talk in his novels is brilliantly rendered, with a wicked fidelity to its flimsy grammar, its elisions and hiatuses, its rush-and-stumble rhythms. When Gaddis's characters open their mouths, they're apt to give voice to sentences like car pileups in fog, with each new thought smashing into the rear of the one ahead and colliding with the oncoming traffic of another speaker's words.

If readers of Gaddis are often hard put to it to follow the novelist's drift, their difficulties are precisely mirrored by those of the characters inside the novel, as when Liz Booth sacks her Martinican cleaning woman in fractured Franglais:

> —Le mardi prochain Madame?
> —Next Tuesday yes will, well no. No I mean that's what I wanted to speak to you about, I mean qu'il ne serait pas nécessaire que, that it's maybe it's better to just wait and I call you again when I, que je vous téléphoner ...
> —Vous ne voulez pas que je revienne.
> —Yes well I mean but not next Tuesday, I mean I'll telephone you again I hope you understand Madame Socrate it's just that I, que votre travail est très bon everything looks lovely but ...
> —J'comprends Madame ... the door came open,
> —et la clef.
> —Oh the key yes, yes thank you merci I hope you, oh but wait, wait could you, est-ce que vous pouvez trouver le, les cartes ... with a stabbing gesture at the mailbox,—là, dans le, des cartes ... ?

Madame Socrate is not so named for nothing. Like a good reader, she understands that the static interference in which the message appears to be shrouded is in fact the message itself. As for the mysterious appearance of Descartes in the morning's mail, it is one of those suggestive coincidences with which Gaddis likes to tease, and sometimes torment, his readers.

He can be very funny, in a way that pointedly recalls the exasperated laughter of Evelyn Waugh, for whom Gaddis has often expressed his admiration in articles and interviews. Waugh's favorite cloak—that of the last surviving patrician in a fallen world of thugs and philistines—has been taken over by Gaddis and trimmed to a (slightly) more democratic American pattern. Like Waugh, Gaddis is funniest when he's gunning for the barbarians at the gate—for the culture of the game show, the shopping mall, the tabloid newspaper, the matchbook cover. Waugh saw the fall of Christendom in the rise of the commercial lower orders. Gaddis sees entropy: the world is not so much going to hell as suffering from the inevitable degradation of energy in a closed system, its language wearing out from overuse. So where Waugh invoked Ecclesiastes and the Book of Lamentations, Gaddis calls in Willard Gibbs and Norbert Wiener (which might in itself be seen as a kind of entropic diminishment). His eccentric personal version of thermodynamics chimes very closely with Waugh's eccentric personal theology, suggesting, perhaps, that gods, physicists, and novelists may share a common black humor as they contemplate the experiments in chaos over which they separately preside.

A Frolic of His Own, Gaddis's fourth novel in nearly forty years, is a country-house comedy, faster in pace and lighter in texture than anything he's done before. It reassembles themes, images, and a large number of characters from the earlier books. There's fresh news of Dr. Kissinger, the globe-trotting proctologist and cosmetic surgeon, of the Rev. Elton Ude, his son Bobby Joe, and of Wayne Fickert, the boy who was drowned by the Rev. Ude at a baptism in the Pee Dee River. The huge postmodernist sculpture, *Cyclone Seven*, last seen in *JR*, in the Long Island town where a child was trapped inside it, has here been moved to Tatamount, Virginia. Its steel jaws now imprison a dog named Spot. Oscar Crease, the gentleman-amateur playwright at the center of the story, is a reworked version of the character of Edward Bast in *JR*; his half-sister Christina and her friend Trish were schoolmates of Liz Booth and her friend Edie Grimes, the "Heiress Slain In Swank Suburb" of *Carpenter's Gothic*. Oscar Crease's play, *Once at Antietam*, had its first performance, in brief quotation, in *JR*, where it was the work of Thomas Eigen (and was dismissed by Jack Gibbs as "undigested Plato").

The Long Island house in which nearly all the action of the book takes place is (like the Bast family mansion in *JR*) an incongruous genteel survivor from another age. Its roof leaks, its verandah sags, and—as a visiting realtor observes—it is in desperate need of the attentions of "old Mister Paintbrush to brighten things up." Its chief asset—worth several millions in "wetlands setbacks"—is a fine view from the drawing room of American literature's most famous pond, which has been trucked in from Massachusetts for the occasion of the book. Like Walden itself, the Crease place is ringed by suburbia: the chainsaws, whose "unanesthetized aerial surgery" began in *JR*, are within earshot of the house, and the driveway now leads straight to the debased language of Chic's Auto Body, Fred's Foto, and the R Dan Snively Memorial Parking Lot.

The hideous red-taloned woman who sells real estate (she envisions the house torn down and replaced by a new one, to be built by "this famous postmodern architect who's doing the place on the corner right down to the carpets and picture frames it will be quite a showplace") bears a strong resemblance to Mrs. Beaver and her plans for Hatton in *A Handful of Dust* (" ... supposing we covered the walls with white chromium plating and had natural sheepskin carpet ... "). There may be another nod in Evelyn Waugh's direction in Gaddis's choice of the name of Crease. The only Crease I know of in the public domain is the Francis Crease who earned half a chapter to himself in Waugh's autobiography, *A Little Learning*—a neurotic calligrapher and dilettante of independent means who might be Oscar's twin.

Oscar Crease is the childish last scion of a distinguished legal family. His grandfather sat on the Supreme Court with Justice Holmes; his ninety-seven-year-old father is a judge in Virginia; in his fifty-odd years, Oscar has managed to write one unproduced play, based on what he believes to have been his grandfather's experience in the Civil War. In a late and ill-advised bid for recognition, he sues the Hollywood producer of a Civil War epic called *The Blood in the Red White and Blue* for plagiarizing *Once at Antietam* and robbing him of his family history.

Broadly—very broadly—speaking, almost everyone in the novel is suing almost everyone else in sight for damages. Some are suing themselves—Oscar is both plaintiff and defendant in a personal injury suit involving his car, which ran over him when the ignition failed and he hot-wired it. People travel through these pages with their attorneys in tow much as people once used to travel with their maids. In the foreground are Oscar's chickenfeed pieces of litigation; in the background are the great cases of the day, like the $700 million suit, known in the tabloids as "Pop and Glow," brought by the Episcopal Church against Pepsi-Cola on the grounds that the church's good name has been stolen by means of an underhand anagram. For every suit there is a countersuit, for every judgment an appeal. Gaddis peoples the book with a throng of injured egos whose only means of asserting that they exist is to go to court. As Christina reasonably observes in the first page, "It's not simply the money ... the money's just a yardstick isn't it. It's the only common reference people have for making other people take them as seriously as they take themselves."

Gaddis likes to set himself technical exercises. In *JR* he had to tell the story in dialogue; in *Carpenter's Gothic* he obeyed the classical unities of time, place, and action. *A Frolic of His Own* is in part an immensely skillful exercise in the mechanics of farce. It is a wonder that the ailing verandah of the house doesn't collapse under the weight of the stream of surprise exits and entrances of lawyers and litigants that it has to bear. Like all good farces, after the sound of laughter has subsided it turns out to have been in deadly earnest.

Gaddis is a mimic of genius and he runs the gamut of stylistic imitation from undetectable forgery to ribald satire. Oscar's play, for instance, of which the reader gets to see about seventy pages, is, unlike the usual text-within-a-text, a real play whose very unevenness convinces one of its authenticity. Brilliant passages, mostly in soliloquy, lead into long stilted debates, which themselves suddenly catch fire and come alive for a few minutes, then go dead again. Unlike the author of the novel, the playwright doesn't know how to move his characters on and off stage nearly fast enough. Yet the central confrontation, between Thomas, the southern heir to northern property, and Bagby, his agent, a commercial "new man" and an early example of the Barbarian genus, is engrossing enough to transcend the play's wonky stagecraft. *Once at Antietam*'s debts to Plato, first exposed in *JR*, are teased out here in detail by a smart Indian attorney, Madhar Pai, in a legal deposition taken during Crease's case against the Hollywood producer; but the play's more immediate debts are to the thoughtful, talkative middlebrow theater of the 1950s, to plays like Anouilh's *Antigone* and Bolt's *A Man for All Seasons* in which large moral questions were acted out by people in period costume, and it has a lot of their dusty charm.

The same goes for the legal documents that are interleaved throughout the book. The cases on which they touch may be farcical, but the attention paid to them by Gaddis's crew of lawyers and judges is of a quality for which one might reasonably pay Mr. Madhar Pai his fantastic hourly rate. This is not *Bleak House*. In *A Frolic of His Own* the language of the law is treated with affection and respect, and the lawyers themselves are honored as the last surviving instruments (even though some of them are very imperfect ones) of order in this disorderly world. The cleverest, most likable character in the novel is old Judge Crease, who appears in written opinions that combine a waspish common-sensicality with bouts of unexpected mental acrobatics. From Crease on *Szyrk* [the creator of the huge piece of sculpture *Cyclone Seven*] v. *Village of Tatamount et al.*:

> We have in other words plaintiff claiming to act as an instrument of higher authority, namely "art," wherewith we may first cite its dictionary definition as "(1) Human effort to imitate, supplement, alter or counteract the work of nature." Notwithstanding that

Cyclone Seven clearly answers this description especially in its last emphasis, there remain certain fine distinctions posing some little difficulty for the average lay observer persuaded from habit and even education to regard sculptural art as beauty synonymous with truth in expressing harmony as visibly incarnate in the lineaments of Donatello's *David*, or as the very essence of the sublime manifest in the *Milos Aphrodite*, leaving him in the present instance quite unprepared to discriminate between sharp steel teeth as sharp steel teeth, and sharp steel teeth as artistic expressions of sharp steel teeth, obliging us for the purpose of this proceeding to confront the theory that in having become self referential art is in itself theory without which it has no more substance than Sir Arthur Eddington's famous step "on a swarm of flies," here present in further exhibits by plaintiff drawn from prestigious art publications and highly esteemed critics in the lay press, where they make their livings, recommending his sculptural creation in terms of slope, tangent, acceleration, force, energy and similar abstract extravagancies serving only a corresponding self referential confrontation of language with language and thereby, in reducing language itself to theory, rendering it a mere plaything, which exhibits the court finds frivolous.

This might be William Empson in a wig and gown. It is a fierce and well-grounded attack on trivial postmodernist pursuits and, in itself, a vindication of Gaddis's own way of writing novels.

True, all his books entail a "confrontation of language with language," but the confrontation is not "self-referential" and never reduces language to theory. In Gaddis's work, language is where we live and what we are. It's all we have. So the play *Once at Antietam* has its own power: it may not be a very good play, but it is, we are made to feel, the best play, the best reckoning with the paradox of his own history, that its author (call him Gaddis, or Eigen, or Oscar Crease) could make under the circumstances. So, too, Judge Crease's own legal opinion, laboring as it does to say something eloquent and true within the constricting conventional frame of the legal opinion, is the best that can be done under the circumstances, which in Gaddis are always adverse. *A Frolic of His Own* is not another novel about narratology: its sharp teeth are genuine sharp steel teeth.

In the most realistic way possible, Gaddis's characters have to struggle to stay afloat on the flux of late-century daily life. The Crease house is under permanent siege—its verandah stormed by callers, its phone ringing off the hook, newspapers piling up in the kitchen far faster than they can be read, and the television in the drawing room pouring out a continuous unlovely medley of bomb-blast pictures interspersed with *Jeopardy*-style questions ("Name three African countries beginning with C .... What breed of African antelope is named after an American car?") and commercials for laxatives and hemorrhoid creams. Oscar is addicted to nature programs, filmed to prove that animal life is as red in tooth and claw as the human variety. On the screen are exhibited pictures of such familiar domestic situations as: "two acorn woodpeckers sharing a nest where one laid an egg and the other ate it"; "the Australian red-back spider jumping into the female's jaws in the midst of mating which he continued undismayed as she chewed at his abdomen"; a "battle among the notorious burying beetles over the corpse of a mouse nicely scraped and embalmed by the victorious couple for their young to eat and then eating the young when they hatched to ensure the survivors of enough food for a stalwart new generation to start the whole thing over again." The TV set is kept switched on throughout the book: it is both a loud source of colored chaos and a faithful mirror of the Crease family in action. In the refrigerator, another chaos, a cole-slaw carton holds the "jelly implants" removed from the breasts of Oscar's infantile and dippy girlfriend, Lily.

Gaddis is at his most Waugh-like in the formal grace with which he manages the wild disorder of the plot. The faster the whirlygig spins, the more one admires its ingenious workmanship. As in Waugh, the proprietor of the machine appears to be standing at some distance from it, his face perfectly impassive, while the riders scream.

Chaos is a state where the whole system of cause-and-effect appears to have given way, where everything happens by accident. In Gaddis's highly controlled version of chaos, the chance properties of the language itself, the puns, anagrams, and coincidental allusions, serve as vital connectors. So we get EPISCOPAL/PEPSICOLA—or the two brands of Japanese car that figure in this legal fiction, the Isuyu and the Sosumi—or the name, Jonathan Livingston Siegal, of the producer of *The Blood in the Red White and Blue*—or the way in which a negotiation over the forthcoming lunch break is recorded in a legal deposition as "Break, break, break on thy cold grey stones, O ... " In a TV commercial for a diarrhea cure, a man is seen running for an airport bathroom; several hundred pages later in the novel, at an airport, an identical running figure is wrongfully accused of stealing a pocketbook belonging to Christina's friend Trish. In another chance collision, the infectious meter of Longfellow's *Hiawatha*, Oscar's favorite childhood poem, insidiously works its way into the later, hurrying scenes of the book, giving Longfellow the opportunity to write a description of Oscar's fishtank (where rapacious nature is again contained by glass):

> neither rose Ugudwash, the sunfish, nor the yellow perch the Sahwa like a sunbeam in the water banished here, with wind and wave, day and night and time itself from the domain of the discus by the daily halide lamp, silent pump and power filter, temperature and pH balance and the system of aeration, fed on silverside and flake food, vitamins and krill and beef heart in a patent spinach mixture to restore their pep and lustre spitting black worms from the feeder when a crew of new arrivals (live delivery guaranteed, air freight collect at thirty dollars) brought a Chinese algae eater, khuli loach and male beta, two black mollies and four neons and a pair of black skirt tetra cruising through the new laid fronds of the Madagascar lace plant.

The book is full of riffs and games like this, each one designed to forge some sort of punning link between one part of the battle and another. Taken together, they have the effect of falling into a pattern that grows more and more intricate the longer you look at it, like the sequence of enlargements in a Mandelbrot set.

Readers—and reviewers especially—ought to feel a disquieting pang of recognition as the climax of the book approaches and Oscar, armed with ice cream and Pinot Grigio, settles in front of the TV set to view the screening of *The Blood in the Red White and Blue*, the catchpenny epic, whose plot somewhat resembles that of his own play. The titles have barely started to roll before Oscar is off, reading into the images on the screen meanings that cannot possibly be there. By the time the Battle of Antietam starts, he has fallen into the language of a demented football commentator:

> —there! a man's shoulder blown off—look out! too late, the boy in butternut hit full in the open mouth, mere boys, mere boys in homespun and blue in a screaming frenzy of bayonets and shellfire—unbelievable, it's unbelievable look at that! Half the regiment wiped out at thirty feet we're taking the cornfield there's Meade, there's Meade in the midst of it there's Meade look at the flags, battle flags the Sixth Wisconsin, Pennsylvania regiments and three hundred of the Twelfth Massachusetts with two hundred casualties now! We're almost there, the Dunker

church Georgia boys trying to get over the fence pffft! shot like laundry hung on a line listen! The Rebel yell listen to it, Hood's division counterattack makes your blood run cold they're coming through! Driving us back they're driving us back, A P Hill coming in from the East Wood I mean D H, D H Hill's division right into the, ooph! Battery B, six old brass cannon it's Battery B charging straight into it look at that! Double rounds of canister hitting them at fifty feet the whole Rebel column's blown to pieces blood everyplace, blood everyplace that's Mansfield, wild white beard's got to be General Mansfield Hooker sending him in with his XII Corps riding down the line waving his hat hear them cheering he's, yes he's hit, horse is down and Mansfield's hit in the stomach God, get him off the field!

No critic with a bee in his bonnet could be more capriciously inventive than Oscar as he deconstructs the blockbuster on the TV screen and reassembles it into a Super Bowl version of the Civil War. What Oscar sees here is neither the movie nor Antietam itself, but his and Gaddis's chief source of information on the battle, Bruce Catton's 1951 book, *Mr. Lincoln's Army*. Oscar's passionate explication of *The Blood in the Red White and Blue* turns out to be Gaddis's devastating parody of Catton's blow-by-blow, newspaperman's prose. (It's strange to turn to Catton's book after reading Gaddis: *Mr. Lincoln's Army* reads exactly like an overexcited football commentary ...)

So it is with the silent pond beyond the window, whose prospect haunts the book. Again and again Christina (who is most nearly the reader's representative in the story) turns to it: while people fight in the drawing room, and animals dine off one another's carcasses on TV, and fish chase fish around the fishtank, life on the pond is orderly and serene. Things there happen in their seasons. The passage of time in the book, as autumn deepens into winter, is marked by the noiseless flight of wild duck, geese, and swans over the water. Each time the pond is sighted, it provokes a burst of beautiful, descriptive prose:

> And where they looked next morning the frozen pond was gone in an unblemished expanse of white under a leaden sky undisturbed by the flight of a single bird in the gelid stillness that had descended to seize every detail of reed and branch as though time itself were frozen out there threatening the clatter of teacups and silver and the siege of telephoning that had already begun with—well when, just tell me when I can talk to him, will you ...

—beautiful, but anachronistic. To write like a contemporary of Thoreau (even a commaless contemporary of Thoreau) is something that can be managed only for a few clauses at a time, before the words are drowned out by the noisy desperation of the present moment. We're separated from the tranquility of the pond by a panel of glass and roughly 150 years.

Gaddis builds around the reader a magnificently ornate and intricate house of words. Every room is furnished in a different style, and one quickly loses count of the competing dialects and idiolects, archaic and modern, literary, legal, vernacular, that are represented here. Christina snaps at her husband: "I mean you talk about language how everything's language it seems that all language does is drive us apart" (which, of course, does exactly what it says). That Gaddis's tall building is Babel, where the Lord did confound the language of all the earth, hardly needs to be spelled out. What makes the novel so enjoyable is how very homely and familiar Babel is made to feel. There's a bed for us all in this oppressively realistic, beautifully designed Long Island madhouse.

CHRISTOPHER J. KNIGHT

A Frolic of His Own:
Whose Law? Whose Justice?

> Now then, Glaucon, is the time for us like huntsmen to surround the covert and keep close watch that justice may not slip through and get away from us and vanish from our sight. It plainly must be somewhere hereabout.
> —Plato's Socrates, *The Republic*, IV

> If I ... speak at length about ghosts, inheritance, and generations, generations of ghosts, which is to say about certain *others* who are not present, nor presently living, either to us, or outside us, it is in the name of *justice*. Of justice where it is not yet, not yet *there*, where it is no longer, let us understand where it is no longer *present*, and where it will never be, no more than the law, reducible to laws or rights.
> —Jacques Derrida, *Specters of Marx*

"There may be something in the notion," Gaddis once mused, "that every writer writes only one book and writes it over and over and over again" (Grove, B 10). Gaddis's fiction certainly seems cut from the same cloth, as he returns again and again to themes (e.g., that which is worth doing; the struggles of the artist in a noisy world indifferent to the effort; and the hurts inflicted by a cash-nexus ethos) that fixate him. Justice is one of these themes, and if I have not addressed it directly as yet, it is because other

---

From *Hints and Guesses: William Gaddis's Fiction of Longing*, (1997). © 1997 by The Board of Regents of the University of Wisconsin System.

matters got in the way. With *A Frolic of His Own*, however, the subject can no longer be put off, for the novel is, first and foremost, a meditation on justice.

Like Plato's Socrates, who believed that "it is no ordinary matter that we are discussing, but the right conduct of life" (603), Gaddis conceives the question of justice as crucial to our lives, even if it promises no easy answer. Yet, if Socrates thought it possible to postulate a theory of justice that should hold sway regardless of time and place, Gaddis, living in the twentieth century, must, whatever his longings, take history more into account. Certainly, the tragic dimension of history (with all its manifest injustices) has been on display in this century's two world wars, the Holocaust, the Gulag, the Cold War, the Vietnam War, the Cambodian genocide, the African famines, Rwanda, and Bosnia. Seldom, if ever, has the world been witness to such wide-scale brutality, misery, and murder, so much so that the *New York Times* has claimed that "At its worst, this has been Satan's century."[1] Thus while it may be true, as Socrates felt, that people in the main are well-meaning and predisposed to the good, this century's atrocities have forced us to take a more skeptical stance toward this truism and, more seriously, to rethink the question of justice itself. It is one reason why the meditation on justice has become one of the epoch's major intellectual forms. Think, for instance, of the impressive work (artistic, legal, political, philosophical, sociological, and theological) that has assumed this form, from such intellectuals as Hannah Arendt, Ronald Dworkin, Michel Foucault, Jürgen Habermas, Vaclav Havel, Agnes Heller, Martin Luther King, Jr., Emmanuel Levinas, Adam Michnik, John Rawls, Alexander Solzhenitsyn, and Charles Taylor, among others. Witness to this century's tragedies, these men and women have not pretended that they could undo or even offset all that has already transpired. Still, they have thought it imperative to reject the politics of fear and hatred, and to move in another direction, commencing with the conviction that justice is misnamed if it does not extend beyond the realm of the privileged few.

A Frolic of His Own, like its author, belongs to this tradition. It is a masterpiece that offers us less a blueprint for justice than a powerful meditation on where it might and might not be found. Its opening line—"Justice?—You get justice in the next world, in this world you have the law" (11)—makes clear just how difficult this search will be, even as the narrative's main East End Long Island locale appears almost walled off from the world's more devastating woes. And yet not only does news of the world's miseries seep—via newspapers, radio, and television—into this semiprotected bower, but it is also the case that this well-to-do exurban community cannot truly isolate itself from the larger national landscape. And here, in the United

States, everything is clearly not okay, especially as the country has resorted more and more to resolving its genuine societal tensions through the means of an adversarial winner-takes-all practice. That is, a nation that has increasingly projected itself (notably during the Reagan, Bush, and, now, Clinton presidencies) in terms that are less cultural or political than economic (i.e., in terms of competition and free markets), has grown accustomed, Gaddis's novel would suggest, to a parallel adversarial practice in its courts and in its more encompassing sense of a judicial ethos. "This free enterprise society is an adversarial society," Gaddis told a *Washington Post* reporter, "so the law emerges from that adversarial attitude. So here we are, all adversaries" (Schwartz, C 2). Justice, if it exists, is more available to those with "deep pockets" than to the citizen of ordinary or less than ordinary means. In *A Frolic of His Own*, justice carries a very expensive price tag, and ends up looking much more like injustice.

To say this, however, implies another standard of justice. To make this standard clearer, we need to examine the novel, for it presents a range of possible understandings, sometimes allied and sometimes in conflict. Specifically, I wish to examine five such understandings: Oscar's sense of justice as something akin to natural law, albeit personally applied; Judge Crease's justice as common law; Harry's justice as legal right; Christina's justice of the heart; and, last, justice as an aspect of the otherworldly, something that makes its presence known in the space of the novel even as it resists specific formulation.

Oscar's Version of Natural Law

More than most, Oscar thinks of justice—eternal, transcendent justice—as something owed him. Others might think of it as an ideal, as something about which we might hope to gain an approximate cognition. That is, most people share Socrates' sense that "perhaps there is a pattern of it laid up in heaven" (Plato, 819), but that it is not likely to be discovered unblemished here on earth. Oscar, however, is something of an innocent, a manchild, unmindful of how even such a sincere wish as his "I only want justice after all" (28), said to the insurance adjuster, must find itself frustrated. His desire for justice is at the heart of his play, *Once at Antietam*, and of his two lawsuits, the first seeking damages for the injuries suffered when run over by his own car, and the second for a film company's alleged theft of his play. As for the play, not only is justice its theme (Oscar: "that's what it's about, my play that's exactly what it's about justice" [54]), but its composition is also thought of as an exercise in justice. That is, Oscar writes the play out of a sense of obligation, first to his grandfather and then to his father. *Once at Antietam*'s protagonist, Thomas (a Southerner and diplomat's son, who, after fighting in the Civil War, takes over his deceased uncle's Pennsylvania mine), is modeled after Oscar's grandfather, Thomas Crease, whose similar history ended with an illustrious career as a Supreme Court justice. As with Learned Hand, who once, parting from Oliver Wendell Holmes, exhorted him to "'Do justice, sir, do justice!,'" only to have Holmes reply, "'That is not my job [...]. It is my job to apply the law'" (285),[2] Justice Crease's reputation was of one obedient to a transcendent justice, an obedience that often put him at odds with the more pragmatic Holmes. Oscar's play, then, is a homage to his grandfather, even as it represents an earnest attempt, in the present, to win recognition from his father, a cold, judgmental, and selfish man, brilliant though he may be. Oscar, whose mother died when he was a child, has been clearly scarred by his father's ill treatment of him. He has never truly grown up, and while he thinks of himself as "the last civilized man" (386), the truth is quite different. Virtually friendless, he lacks social skills and sees the world largely through the lens of his own interest and self-pity. Even when tragedy strikes those near, as it does when Lily's breast implants rupture or, more seriously, when Christina's husband suddenly dies, he cannot imagine that the two women might have more on their minds than the status of his lawsuits. He is a sad, pathetic figure, and had his growing up not been so hard or had his stepsister not shown us another way to view him, he would be rather difficult to like. Still, as his lawyer Basie says, "Always have to like a man that's at the end of his rope" (125), and most readers will take this view. Oscar is the quintessential dangling man, and if he is largely responsible for his adversity, it is also true that an additional share of adversity, in the form of modern civilization, simply comes knocking at his door.

One of the most surprising things connected to Oscar is the quality of his play. It is quite an interesting play, and if, as Jonathan Raban has observed, its "more immediate debts are to the thoughtful, talkative middlebrow theater of the 1950s, to plays like Anouilh's *Antigone* and Bolt's *A Man for All Seasons* in which large moral questions were acted out by people in period costume," it still "has a lot of their dusty charm" (4).[3] The success of the play has much to do with its borrowings: whole dialogues are borrowed, if not lifted, from *The Republic* and *The Crito*; and there are further debts to Rousseau and Camus. Given such antecedents, it is not surprising that the play should seem wiser than its author. Nor is it so surprising that Oscar should be such a poor interpreter of his own play, for his identification with the character Thomas, whose obsession with justice is more innocent than thoughtful, leads him to miss the more encompassing suggestion of the play: that justice is best imagined as an ideal to guide and judge action. But Thomas seeks out justice as if it were reducible to a piece of property; and like Oscar, with his identification of his teacher's salary with injustice ("That salary! that miserable salary month after month just to remind me what injustice really was" [418]), he conflates justice with material success:

> It was an insult, that pension, coming year after year to remind us what injustice was, in case we'd forgotten. In case I'd been able to forget all the plans that he had for me, for a great career in public life, bringing me up to read Rousseau, believing the "natural goodness of man ... " (71)

Thomas is speaking here of his father, the diplomat, but the lines originate in Oscar's own experience with his grandfather, who also urged the boy to read Rousseau and to imagine a life dedicated to the fostering of justice. Both Thomas and Oscar, however, have rather myopic conceptions of justice. They want justice for themselves, particularly economic justice, yet they seem oddly indifferent to the wants of others this way. Thomas, for instance, is an unrepentant slaveowner, who takes the escape of his slave, John Israel (a "black Epictetus" [101]), as a personal affront, much in the way that, later, Oscar reacts to the departure of Basie (a black ex-con now in flight from the authorities) only in terms of how it relates to himself: "What about me[?]" (307). Meanwhile, with respect to Thomas's inheritance, the Pennsylvania mine (a nineteenth-century Plato's Cave), its new owner is less interested in the workers and their conditions than in the fact that his patrimony restores him to some rightful place in the world's hierarchy. Thomas becomes a walking illustration of George Fitzhugh's 1856 polemic *Cannibals All!* which compared Northern industrial practices unfavorably with those of Southern slavery: "You, with the command over labor which your capital gives you are a slave owner—a master, without the obligations of a master!" (Fitzhugh, 17). Likewise, Oscar, when it seems that he will, as a consequence of his suit, be the recipient of tens of millions of dollars from the Hollywood producers of *The Blood in the Red White and Blue*, appears completely indifferent to the labor that went into the film, convinced that this massive transference of capital from many pockets to one represents justice. Were the behavior of Thomas and Oscar reduced to a principle, it would be: what is good for me must be thought good for everyone. Needless to say, it is not a very satisfying equation.

There are, of course, smarter heads in Oscar's play. Thomas's mother, who lives by the wisdom of Matthew 6.19—"Do not lay up for yourselves treasures on earth, where moth and rust consume and where thieves break in and steal, but lay up for treasures in heaven"—is one; and Kane, modeled on Socrates, is another. Unlike Thomas, Kane sees an injustice both in the owning of slaves and in the exploitation of so-called free labor. He speaks of the "terrible silence of slavery" (167) and speaks up for Thomas's unnamed attacker, not because he thinks what he did is right, but because he knows that when a system parcels out its wealth inequitably, justice itself suffers, and it becomes harder to tell right from wrong. Like Socrates, who felt that "when wealth is honored in a state, and the wealthy, virtue and the good are less honored" (Plato, 779), Kane proposes a system of justice that would require Thomas to shed the bulk of his possessions, something that he is not prepared to do. With his "mind stuffed with ambition and the Social Contract in" his pocket, yearning for "a great career in public life" (90), Thomas exhibits the familiar signs of the man of social conscience, but they are trappings only. His proper place is among the "'arms-bearing aristocracy'" (102), and from him, as from Oscar with all his conventional prejudices, we can expect little real contribution toward the righting of present injustices. Rather, we would do better to look to the Kanes or perhaps the John Israels for such contributions, though their fates in the play—with the first sentenced to death on a trumped-up charge of spying, and the second free only until someone captures him or shoots him down—make this hope seem wistful.

In the meantime, Oscar pursues his lawsuits. The first of these, the liability claim consequent upon his accident with the car (the Japanese-made "Sosumi"), can be dealt with more summarily than the second suit. The reason is that this is a classic "pain and suffering" liability suit that, despite Oscar's claim otherwise, has very little to do with justice. Generally, in an accident of this sort, the victim is covered by a no-fault provision, whereby he or she is spared the trouble of proving blame, so that an adequate recompense (e.g., for hospital bills and vehicle damage) can be more quickly disbursed. In a country suffering from a litigation explosion, no-fault has been a godsend in those states, such as Oscar's own New York, where automobile insurance claims once often took months, if not years, to settle. Obviously, there is something—i.e., profits—in this for the insurance companies, but mostly the system has worked well. Regardless, Oscar cannot help seeing in all this civilization's decline: "this No Fault idea it's not even an idea, it's a jerrybuilt evasion of reality of course someone's at fault. Someone's always at fault. It's all a cheap dodge chewing away at the basic fabric of civilization to replace it with a criminal mind's utopia where no one's responsible for the consequences of his actions, isn't that what the social contract is all about?" (251)[4] Convinced that he is mounting the barricades, Oscar employs Lily's lawyer, Kevin, to press a $1.5 million liability claim to make him, once again, whole.

In this first suit, Oscar's lawyers (Kevin is, in time, replaced by Preswig) are classic ambulance chasers, though this appellation speaks of a group whose work, following the relaxation of the professional code, is no longer thought so peripheral to what lawyers do. That is, there was a time when lawyers were forbidden to "stir up litigation." It was against the law to advertise or to seek business, for it was felt that the society would be more at peace with itself if only those disputes that were heartfelt and otherwise irresolvable found their way to court. It was the specter of lawyers drumming up business, bringing neighbor against neighbor, that led even New York City, as recently as 1954, to break "up a circle of eighteen lawyers and nine accomplices operating with 'all the efficiency of a supermarket'" (Olson, 17). Still, over the decades, the prohibitions began to give way, and then, in 1977, following the Supreme Court's extension to lawyers, in the *Bates* decision, of the right to advertise, things began to accelerate in an opposing direction. In 1985, in the *Zauderer* case, the Court ruled that lawyers could solicit parties against particular sorts of defendants, giving encouragement thereby to what used to be known as "bill of peace" cases but what are now more familiarly known as class action suits. A consequence of such climatic changes was that not only did a state such as New York see, in the course of a generation, a three hundredfold rise in the "payouts in suits against doctors and hospitals" (Olson, 5), but there also grew the sense that the rules themselves had been turned upside down. Walter Olson writes:

> On the matter of promotion, the American legal profession did not just relax its old ethical strictures, which would be a common enough sort of thing, but stood them on their head. Down through the mid-1960s the A.B.A.'s ethical canon number 28, against "stirring up litigation," was still very much intact. Within a few years many had come to see stirring up litigation as an inspiring public service, in fact morally obligatory. By 1975 one of the most quoted of the newer legal ethicists, Monroe Freedman, could write provocatively but in all seriousness of a "professional responsibility to chase ambulances." (31)

Along with the turnabout in the rules of promotion, the legal profession also witnessed something like a reversal in its attitude toward contingency fee suits. Traditionally, contingency fee suits were thought an unpleasant necessity. Not everyone could afford a lawyer, yet everyone deserved his or her day in court. Lawyers were, of course, under an obligation to take *pro bono publico* cases, but the obligation was more moral than legal. This being the case, it seemed preferable to allow contingency fee suits, wherein the plaintiff's attorney worked for a percentage of the hoped-for award, rather than to let clients with good cases but weak resources go begging. Over time, all the states moved to legalize such suits, Maine being the last state to do so, sometime in the early 1960s. Still, the contingency fee suit has its downside. The real problem, says Olson, "derives not so much from the conflicts it creates between the interests of lawyer and client as from the even more dangerous identity it creates between their interests as against everyone else's" (44). That is, the contingency suit promotes claims against, and the zealous pursuit of, "deep pockets." It may make overnight millionaires of some, but it has not been a positive experience for justice in general. Rather, as Olson nicely puts it, "Suing people for a share of the proceeds has become, like one or two famous television ministries, a venture in hellfire preaching and unctuous handwringing that enables the practitioners to live in the luxury of Babylon" (46). So attractive have contingency fee suits become that a recent Federal Trade Commission report "showed that 97 percent of lawyers took injury cases only on contingency, refusing to consider hourly rates, however generous" (Olson, 47).

Oscar's own injury suit is less about justice than about money or greed. Kevin, Lily's lawyer, jumps on Oscar's claim, and though the two never meet, he is able, via Lily, to convince him that the $50,000 no-fault coverage is a travesty of justice. So while Oscar's employer continues to pay him and while he suffers no long-term injury beyond an almost undetectable facial scar, he files, on a contingency fee basis, a major suit against his insurance company. Or as he explains to Harry and Christina, "Because she [Lily] says Kevin said I'm probably already well past the threshold limit on all these medical bills so what we're talking about is all this pain and suffering and lost income because of this permanent disfigurement" (57). It is all nonsense, of course, and what makes it even more nonsensical is that, through Kevin's ineptness, Oscar's legal complaint has him, in effect, suing himself (283). There is probably some justice in that, for Oscar would do well to face his own responsibility for both the accident and the nuisance suit. But the long and short of the matter is that Oscar is exploited by a lawyer who views him as an avenue toward riches. Or as Christina rightly tells him: "It's not your constitutional rights this socalled lawyer is asserting, can't you see? He's asserting his own right to exploit your misery for every dollar he can, it's not his pain and suffering is it? his brilliant lecturing career that's in jeopardy? Is he going to pay your hospital bills when you lose? doctor bills? lab bills? this therapist? By the time you get into a courtroom that scar will look like you fell off your tricycle when you were five" (183). Eventually, Oscar sees things this way, agreeing to the insurance company's offer, but not before he, disgruntled with Kevin, seeks out the assistance of another firm, Mohlenhoff Shransky, brought to his attention through its matchbook advertisements. And with the assistance of the firm's Jack Preswig, things threaten to become truly Dickensian, for it is in the nature of product liability suits that not only do the makers of products find themselves sued but so do a whole line of subcontractors, all on the speculation, writes Olson, "that one of them will turn out to be vulnerable" (105). Or as the Ace Worldwide Fidelity agent, Frank Gribble, explains the matter to Oscar:

> —Because liability attaches to anyone who sells the product going back to its manufacturer including the makers of parts supplied by others since it is marketed under the manufacturer's name, if you follow me? Our legal department sought out the person you bought it from who had joined the Navy and so proceeded against the dealer from whom he'd purchased it new and the dealer then sued the wholesaler who has brought suit against the manufacturer who in turn is suing the assembler of the defective component parts whose makers are as you observed in your summons as a witness in the suit being brought against them by the assembler all over the globe [...]. (547)

When it becomes evident to Oscar that he is in tow to a "global car chase" (547), he gives up the suit, wisely if belatedly. Besides, by this point he has already learned something, via his Erebus pictures suit, about the fictiveness of pots of gold lying at the end of litigation rainbows. But I do not wish to equate the two suits too much, for they are different; and if the "pain and suffering" suit is virtually without merit, the latter suit seems otherwise. Whatever the Erebus suit's merits, however, it too starts off as something like a nuisance suit. That is, Oscar, noting the narrative similarities between *The Blood in the Red White and Blue* and his own shelved play, *Once at Antietam*, begins an infringement suit against the Hollywood company even though his most important evidence seems like hearsay. By this, I mean that he starts the suit in motion before he has even seen the film. In fact, the suit travels through two courts and is resolved before he does so. Of course, his convalescent state prevents his attending a movie house; and he sees the film only when the studio, the injunction against its showing lifted, decides to revive the public's interest by showcasing it on television. But the whole early portion of Oscar's legal action has about it the nature of a fishing expedition.

Oscar's legal counsel, Lepidus & Shea's associate Harold Basie, tells him as much. Unlike Kevin or Preswig, Basie is a fine attorney, and ethical to boot. Or as ethical as one who has done time "for something that would curl your hair" (278), and who later lies his way into the profession, can be. Hence, when Oscar tells him that he wishes to press a suit on what looks to be solely coincidental similarities, Basie comes right to the point, telling him that given what he has heard added to the fact that the one tangible piece of incriminating evidence, the purported 1977 rejection letter from Kiester to Oscar, has yet to be located (it never is), he (unlike Szyrk, the creator of "Cyclone Seven") has no case:

> He's got a way better case than you do here. He could shit on a shingle and call it a protected statement under the First Amendment, you can't find that letter rejecting your play you don't even know who you sent it to. You go and serve a complaint on this Kiester they'll respond with an answer and motion to dismiss and they'll probably get it. If they don't and you have to subpoena their records they come after yours too and that means that letter and all that doesn't even come till the discovery process, depositions, documents, interrogatories all the rest of it, motions for summary judgment if that's denied you get ready for pretrial conference maybe get a settlement. If you don't you go to trial, you lose there and you go to appeal spending your money every step, every step you take, disbursements, stenographers, transcripts, all that plus your legal fee I'd just hate to see it, case like this where it looks like you've hardly got one [...]. (114–15)

At first, it does seem as if Oscar has no case. What changes the matter, however, is that Basie, captured by Oscar's evident desperation, begins to take a personal interest in the matter. On his own time, he goes to see the film and becomes more intrigued by the narrative coincidences. Then there is also the matter of a parallel suit, lodged by a film student against Kiester and pertaining to the earlier film *Uruburu*. This suit gives further reason for thinking Kiester neither a careful nor an honest businessman. Together, these factors incline Basie to pursue the case further. It is a considered judgment, mindful of the fact that if he, in the name of his white-shoe firm, should pursue suits without merit, the firm will be the loser in the long run. Or as he tells Christina:

> —Just let's make sure we have one thing real clear Mrs Lutz, see we're not out looking for business, not ambulance chasers. Sam put me on this like kind of a favour to look into it, if I go and get us into some drawn out tangled up case just because the client's got money where I know we'll probably never win it I'm out on the street tomorrow. Maybe we've got something here, maybe worth a try, have to admit it all kind of intrigues me. And now Oscar here, see I've come to like Oscar. (125)

Basie gives an honest assessment of the situation. Still, at this point in the case, it must be thought of as something of a fishing expedition. Basie says as much: "Fish in these waters here a little today and see if we come up with enough to file this complaint he's hell bent on" (124). It is not an unethical strategy, given present legal practices, but it does give evidence, once again, of how much the standards—in this instance, of claimant's notice—have changed over time. That is, in the old law, prior to the 1938 adoption of the Federal Rules of Civil Procedure, "pleadings, among their other functions, served as an immensely important filter in keeping many kinds of litigation out of court entirely" (Olson, 94). It was expected that the claimant's lawyer had already exhaustively investigated and formulated the case, and that the pleading would deal in specific accusations. If it did not, it would be thrown out. Even when the claimant was granted trial, the subsequent proceedings would be framed only within the context of the alleged injustices. There was little room for reconceiving the case in mid-process. Thus while the old system was not without problems, most noticeably when a good case might be thrown out of court because of a failure, in pleading, to foresee the full nature of the injustice at hand, there was also good reason for maintaining a certain strictness in the pleading, or notice, requirements. Olson, summing up the objections of O. L. McCaskill, a prominent mid-century legal scholar, to the proposed changes in the rules of notice, writes:

> Justice was better served, McCaskill maintained, when lawyers did their best to investigate claims carefully before turning them into lawsuits. Once they were allowed to get away with it, however, many would follow the path of least resistance by filing the suit first and then checking out its merits at leisure. Even

when they did know the facts and theory on which they planned to proceed, they would succumb to their natural incentive not to reveal more of their cases than necessary. The minimum commitment to detail needed to get their clients into court would soon become the norm. (99–100)

This is a fair description of what happens with Oscar's suit. Basie has a strong inkling that *The Blood in the Red White and Blue* is, in fact, an infringement upon Oscar's play, but he has no concrete evidence. He knows that he will not have to prove his claim until the trial, so he is willing to take certain chances at this point. Hence, he tells Oscar, with regard to Kiester's rejection letter, "Don't have to produce it right this second Oscar, state in complaint they had this access and face the problem of proof when we have to, taking a little chance on these reasons they gave for rejecting it when we try to claim breach of implied contract as a cause of action" (128). Under the old law, he would have been prevented from going further, but an important element of the 1938 Federal Rules of Civil Procedure was to allow the claimant to state the causes of action in general terms. "Pleadings," writes Olson, "would serve only to put the parties on notice that they were being sued, and briefly state the general subject matter of the dispute" (99). The problem with the new rules of notice is that they often, in the words of Fleming James and Geoffrey Hazard, allow a lawyer into the courtroom even though this person has stated "his claim in very general terms, so that it cannot clearly be discerned what he thinks the facts might be" (Olson, 99). Basie is a better lawyer than this, and though it is true that he proceeds with a case before he knows whether he has one, he does make an effort to specify the nature of the charges. He even warns Oscar, who wishes to charge Erebus with a potpourri of grievances: "Thing is Oscar this is an action for infringement. You get privacy and things like that in there you just confuse things, run a good chance they throw the whole thing out, just stay right with your play there" (164). Accordingly, Basie states four causes of action, all pertaining to Erebus's alleged infringement of Oscar's play. In addition to the allegation of infringement, the complaint alleges "fraudulent conduct" on the part of the several defendants (executives, director, screenwriters, et al.), conduct that has subjected Oscar "to extreme mental and physical distress," so that he should be entitled not only to damages but "to a constructive trust benefit on all profits and gross revenues from 'The Blood in the Red White and Blue'" (178).

Because of the nature of the suit (an infringement action)[5] and because of the fact that Erebus's general counsel has an office in New York, Oscar's complaint is filed in the United States District Court for the Southern District of New York. The choice of venue turns out to be important. Basie has the choice of filing in the defendant's home district—i.e., the Central District of California—or the district wherein the defendant's agent resides. Largely for the reason that Oscar is still convalescing, Basie files the complaint in New York, but this leads them into what is spoken of as "the trap" (299) laid by the Swyne & Dour associate Madhar Pai, counsel for Erebus, Kiester, et al. Pai prefers the New York jurisdiction because his defense strategy, assuming that the court should not grant a dismissal, is to represent Oscar's suit as one about property rather than copyright. And since compared with the laws in other states, California's laws have been unusually liberal in "giving property protection to ideas" (Goldstein, 41), Pai knows that he has a stronger case in New York. This helps to explain the logic of his questions during Oscar's deposition. Here, he knows that, the 1976 Copyright Act, while granting protection to the expression of an idea, does not grant protection to the idea itself, and that, as Paul Goldstein writes, "[i]dea submitters rarely succeed on a property theory .... When courts invoke property doctrine in idea cases it is usually as a gentle way of telling the submitter that he will not recover his action" (41). In addition, when what is being contested, as in the present case, is an implied rather than an expressed contract, courts have tended to give more weight to the question of novelty (Goldstein, 44). Pai's defense very much relies on the decision handed down in 1972 by the New York Court of Appeals, in the *Downey v General Foods Corp.* case (407). There, Chief Judge Fulk wrote, "The critical issue in this case turns on whether the idea suggested by the plaintiff was original or novel. An idea may be a property right. But, when one submits an idea to another, no promise to pay for its use may be implied, and no asserted agreement enforced, if the elements of novelty and originality are absent, since the property right in an idea is based upon these two elements" (Goldstein, 40).

In his deposition questioning, Pai seeks, without of course announcing his strategy, to turn Oscar's case into one that hinges on the protection of an idea:

> Q And the idea, the idea that a man of split allegiances might find himself in a situation obliging him to send up a substitute in his place in each of the opposing armies, while it was hardly an everyday occurrence, was certainly within the realm of possibility wasn't it?
> A Yes, it ...

Q And that the two might even meet in battle?
A Yes, yes that's ...
Q In fact there was at least one such documented instance, was there not?
A That's what my ...
Q Where both were, in fact, slain? In other words, a sort of quirk of history, the kind Shakespeare drew on freely when he needed a plot or a character? He could have pointed to Holinshed and advertised King Lear as based on a true story couldn't he?
A If he, I suppose so, yes.
Q So that in this action you're not claiming protection for an idea. What you claim has been infringed here then is not the idea which occurred to you over a period of time. (203)

Pai's performance at this stage of things is brilliant. He moves Oscar into making protective claims for an idea—"I claim protection for the idea too yes, if the ... " (204)—and, at the same time, makes much of the fact that a good many of the ideas are borrowed from Plato, Camus, and Rousseau: "Plato attributes the idea and the words to Aeschylus whom he names, whereas you have simply lifted them from Plato without ascribing them to anyone the way you've done elsewhere I might add, Camus and Rousseau and I don't know who else" (224). It is largely on the basis of this deposition that the district court judge grants a summary judgment in favor of Erebus pictures. According to the Federal Rules of Civil Procedure (rule 56), a court can hand down such a judgment when there appear to be no triable issues of fact, and when what is at issue is simply the law's application. Here, the judge feels, in the words of Circuit Judge Bone, that the

> story idea central to the play was not sufficiently novel to create "property interest" entitled to protection under New York law in action against the motion picture makers for unfair competition and unlawful use, misappropriation and conversion; that notwithstanding the author's alleged submission of his play to defendant there was no evidence of any intent to contract with regard to the said play by defendant and thus its alleged unlawful use could form neither any basis for action for breach of implied contract, nor any basis for plaintiff's unjust enrichment action, nor for fraud action in that the defendants could not have enriched themselves at the author's expense on the ground that

"plaintiff's alleged submissions lack the requisite novelty under the applicable law" and so falling into the public domain where he could not be defrauded of property he did not own. (405)

As fine as Pai's strategy appears, it is difficult to feel confident about an infringement defense that is so dependent on the issue of novelty. Granted, there have been occasional rulings that concur with the district judge's decision. In a fairly recent decision, for instance, involving the playwright Christopher Durang (*See v. Durang*, 1983), the United States Court of Appeals, Ninth Circuit, supported the lower court's summary judgment decision ("Summary judgment is proper if reasonable minds could not differ as to the presence or absence of substantial similarity of expression"), holding that "the court properly applied the doctrine ['*scènes à faire*'] to hold unprotectable forms of expression that were either stock scenes or scenes that flowed necessarily from common unprotectable ideas. 'Common' in this context means common to the works at issue, not necessarily, as plaintiff suggests, commonly found in other artistic works" (Goldstein, 728). Still, if the well-known United States Appeals Court decision involving Cole Porter (*Arnstein v. Porter*, 1946) seems to have overstated the case—"The principal question on this appeal is whether the lower court, under Rule 56, properly deprived plaintiff of a trial of his copyright infringement action. The answer depends on whether 'there is the slightest doubt as to the facts'" (Goldstein, 726)—there remains a handsome body of precedents suggesting that novelty, as it pertains to artistic properties, is a less than relevant concern. Key cases include *Sheldon v Metro-Goldwyn Pictures Corp.* (1936) and *Alfred Bell & Co. v Catalda Fine Arts, Inc.* (1951), both cited by Circuit Judge Bone. In the first case, Judge Learned Hand famously wrote:

> We are to remember that it makes no difference how far the play was anticipated by works in the public demesne which the plaintiffs did not use. The defendants appear not to recognize this, for they have filled the record with earlier instances of the same dramatic incidents and devices, as though, like a patent, a copyrighted work must be not only original, but new. That is not however the law as is obvious in the case of maps or compendia, where later works will necessarily be anticipated. At times, in discussing how much of the substance of a play the copyright protects, courts have indeed used language which seems to give countenance to the notion that, if a plot were old, it could not be copyrighted. But we understand by this no more than that in its

broader outline a plot is ever copyrightable, for it is plain beyond peradventure that anticipation as such cannot invalidate a copyright. Borrowed the work must indeed not be, for a plagiarist is not himself pro tanto an "author"; but if by some magic a man who has never known it were to compose anew Keats's Ode on a Grecian Urn, he would be an "author," and, if he copyrighted it, others might not copy that poem, though they might of course copy Keats's. (Goldstein, 573)

Here, Hand sounds a little bit like Borges (in "Pierre Menard, Author of the Quixote"), but what he most authoritatively did in this case and elsewhere (see also *Nichols v Universal Pictures Corp.* [1930]) was to make the dependence of artistic originality on novelty seem almost nonsensical.[6] Goldstein writes that "[i]t is some measure of the originality test that Learned Hand propounded in *Sheldon* that, in a long career deciding copyright cases, Judge Hand never once found that a work was insufficiently original to qualify for copyright protection" (578). Art is different from trademarks and patents, and Pai's attempt to conflate them, to argue that Oscar's case should be understood as one of unfair competition rather than copyright infringement, is a clever yet suspect defense. And even if he can get Oscar to state that he wishes to protect the novelty of the play's idea, there are all the other instances when Oscar accents the inseparableness of idea and expression: "When the idea is used in the context of the expression, combined with the expression, then the idea becomes part of the abuse I'm referring to" (204). A judge has only to treat the case as one of copyright infringement for Pai's line of defense to crumble. The reason is, as Goldstein explains, "Copyright law possesses none of the search mechanisms for determining novelty that have developed around patent law's novelty and nonobviousness requirements. The few recorded and largely vain efforts at introducing prior art on the issue of copyright novelty only dramatize copyright law's incapacity to measure novelty systematically" (580).

Oscar, then, wins his case on appeal. By this time, Basie has fled from the scene, the facts of his past having come to the attention of the authorities. That Oscar does win has everything to do with his father's intervention, an intervention carried forward unbeknownst to Oscar. That is, Judge Crease, reading the district court judge's opinion, and seeing that she has let herself be led by Pai's argument, perhaps for the reason that, new to the bench, she is hesitant to preempt state law, takes it upon himself to write the appeals brief; and then sends a young lawyer up to file it. The Judge acts, it seems, less as a father than as a husband of the law. Or as his law clerk later tells

Oscar, "When he got his hands on that decision he was mad as hell. He acted like the closest person in his life had been raped, like he'd come on the body of the law lying there torn up and violated by a crowd of barbarians, what was the matter with you? What in hell was wrong with your lawyers not following it up, letting a wide open trap that was laid for you slip by them for this new judge to fall into" (559). Whatever his motives, his appeal goes to the heart of the matter by making clear that not only are there triable issues of fact to be sorted through but that in an infringement case such as Oscar's, federal copyright law should be thought more applicable than New York's unfair competition law. It is, in fact, a little surprising to see an unfair competition law applied to the relation between a play and a film, for it is the nature of such law that it serves to regulate the relation between commercial ideas and products. Understanding it as an ally of trademark law, Goldstein writes, "Unfair competition embraces a broad continuum of competitive conduct likely to confuse consumers as to the source of goods and services—from the appropriation of relatively nondistributive names and symbols accompanied by acts passing off, to the appropriation of distinctive symbols" (55). Judge Bone himself is receptive to the appeal argument that state law should give way to federal copyright law, summarizing the argument as follows:

> The courts have frequently debated whether laws of unfair competition are similar enough to copyright jurisdiction in its aims to be preempted by Federal copyright law, to which defendant argues that preemption is not absolute in the area of intellectual property. However under the doctrine of pendent jurisdiction a Federal court may take jurisdiction over a State law if, as established by the Supreme Court in United Mine Workers v. Gibb, that State law claim rises out of a 'common nucleus of operative fact' with the Federal claim, and here plaintiff argues for such a common nucleus residing in all his claims rising from defendant's use of his playscript. (406)

In the federal court, Oscar is the recipient of justice—not the ideal justice that he sought, but an apportioned justice, following from the fact that subsequent to the appeals court decision, no legal representative showed up to contest the award's apportioning. In any event, by the nature of the evidence, it would seem that the appeals court decision is, more or less, a sound one. That is, there is every reason to think that *The Blood in the Red White and Blue* makes use of copyrighted materials without permission. The question, however, is who stole the materials and precisely which materials did this person steal? Was it Kiester, the designated recipient of Oscar's play thirteen years before, who, as Oscar has maintained all along, stole the play? Or was it someone else, stealing perhaps something else (e.g., not the copy but the original)? Kiester himself denies, under oath, any remembrance of the play. And it does seem unlikely that besieged as he should have been (while working for network television) with unsolicited scripts, he should remember it, even if he rather than an assistant had been the script's reader and respondee. It is not impossible, but unlikely.[7]

Yet if not Kiester, who? The answer, I think, is John Knize, the Holmes Court scholar, "Civil War 'buff,'" schoolmate of Kiester, and, of course, screenwriter for *The Blood in the Red White and Blue*. Knize himself first comes to our attention not in connection with the film but through his letter to Oscar, asking whether the latter might be willing to share his reminiscences respecting his grandfather, Justice Thomas Crease. "Professor Crease," he writes,

> Perhaps my earlier letter did not reach you. I am researching material for a book on the Holmes Court, of which I understand your grandfather, Justice Thomas Crease, was a colourful member, well known for his conflicts with his associate Justice Holmes though it was said they were warm friends through their shared youthful experience in the Civil War, both having suffered wounds, I understand, at Ball's Bluff and Antietam. (23)

The point is, Knize knows the whole Thomas Crease story. He has read all the archival material, if, as I believe, he is "the outsider" the historical society's "old biddies" let "in to read them" (501). He did not need Oscar's play to write the screenplay for *The Blood in the Red White and Blue*. And according to sworn testimony, Knize and the other writers have never seen or read Oscar's play. Bone: "All these five were examined by deposition; all denied that they had ever encountered, known of, read or used the play in any way whatever; all agreed that they had based the picture on material in the public domain provided by Knize" (405). Judge Crease knows this. That is why in his Seventh Cause of Action, "which is against Kiester and his head writer Knize only" (412), he "claims misrepresentation, deceit and fraudulent conduct in the misappropriation and conversion of copyrighted material on deposit at certain public institutions" (412). It is also why he "read them [the biddies] the riot act" when he discovered that Knize had been allowed to see his father's papers. It might even partly explain his own decision to have his law clerk burn all of his private papers upon his death.

If Knize rather than Kiester is the main culprit, we still have a case of the misappropriation of copyrighted materials. Not of Oscar's own materials but of his grandfather's—the ownership of which belongs to Judge Crease and then, only after his death, to Oscar. Justice has been done, sort of, yet again we find evidence that there was too little investigation before Basie filed Oscar's claim. In fact, if the defendants are judged strictly in terms of the original claim, they should be found innocent and Pai's argument the right one. But they are not judged so, for the accusation changes its form on appeal. Hence, we have a case that the changes in the rules of notice have allowed to go through the courts before its import was properly understood even by its claimant.

Judge Crease and the Common Law

No one can accuse Judge Crease of not understanding the law. While Oscar's notion of justice would leap over legal particulars, Judge Crease's entire understanding of justice is rooted in these particulars, in those Hamletian "Words, words, words" (181) that leave Oscar so baffled, yet which, as Harry tries to explain, are for his father the law's heart and soul. Law and language, language and the law—they have the Judge's entire attention. As a craftsman, he knows that language is slippery, that laws are never perfect; but he also knows that some things—language and law included—are better than others, not better per se, but better in the world in which men and women live. After his death, his clerk speaks of "this love he had for the law and the language," but also of how he would "diddle them both sometimes because when you come down to it the law's only the language" (559). Crease's faith finally rested on the law as expressed in language, a faith that, the clerk says, served him well enough: "what better loves could a man have than those to get him through the night" (560). This is why Harry, mindful of the Judge's fidelity here, earlier speaks of him as one who is "[t]rying to rescue the language" (285).

This sense of the man is evident in the three extensive examples we have of his work: the two decisions pertaining to the Szyrk case and the instructions to the jury in the Fickert case. Like his spiritual father, Justice Holmes, Judge Crease is a strict constructionist, sharing the former's view that a judge's "first business is to see that the game is played according to the rules whether" he likes them or not (Holmes, 394). The judge may be a representative of authority, but authority itself lies elsewhere, in the laws that the legislative and executive branches, both state and federal, have hammered out. These laws all have a specific aspect about them, reflecting the needs and demands of their communities. There is no universal law, no Mount Sinai-like commandments that can be said to supersede ordinary common law. It is because Judge Crease believes this that he holds Holmes's dissenting opinion in the "Black and White Taxi Co." (1928) case in such high regard (46). There, Holmes wrote:

> Books written about any branch of the common law treat it as a unit, cite cases from this Court, from the Circuit Court of Appeals, from the State Courts, from England and the Colonies of England indiscriminately, and criticize them as right or wrong according to the writer's notions of a single theory. It is very hard to resist the impression that there is one august corpus, to understand which clearly is the only task of any court concerned. If there were such a transcendental body of law outside of any particular State but obligatory within it unless and until changed by statute, the Courts of the United States might be right in using their independent judgment as to what it was. But there is no such body of law. The fallacy and illusion that I think exist consist in supposing that there is this outside thing to be found. Law is a word used with different meanings, but law in the sense in which courts speak of it today does not exist without some definite authority behind it. The common law so far as it is enforced in a State, whether called common law or not, is not the common law generally but the law of that State existing by the authority of that State without regard to what it may have been in England or anywhere else. (199)

The Holmes dissent does, in fact, go to the heart of Crease's understanding of the law. For him, laws have a strict purview. He is quick to dismiss the appeal, by Szyrk's counsel, to early English common law "as ornamental" and demonstrating "no clear parallel in the laws of this Commonwealth" (32). He takes little notice of a similar appeal made in defendant James B's crossclaim (35). And later, in the Fickert case, he instructs the jury to disregard the Reverend Bobby Joe's testimony attributing the boy's death to Satan, reminding it of one Pennsylvania case wherein a complaint against Satan had to be "dismissed for its failure to discover Satan's residence within the judicial district" (430). For Judge Crease, people make laws so as to designate what is, and is not, acceptable behavior within a given community. These laws may conceivably embody a greater, more divine justice, but that is no reason to invoke such justice in the courtroom. As far as he is concerned, "God has no place" in his courtroom (293).

Crease himself may, or may not, believe in the Deity. It is impossible for us to say, though he clearly has no allegiance to any organized religion, and goes so far as to stipulate in his will that his grave not be "marked by a cross or any other such barbaric instrument of human torture" (444). It is true that, like Holmes, he does not entirely refrain from appeals to some sort of universal justice. His understanding of art, as reflected in the Szyrk case, certainly appears dependent on some undefined notion of transcendental truth: "there remain certain fine distinctions [respecting the argument that 'Cyclone Seven' is art] posing some little difficulty for the average lay observer persuaded from habit and even education to regard sculptural art as beauty synonymous with truth in expressing harmony as visibly incarnate in the lineaments of Donatello's David, or as the very essence of the sublime manifest in the Milos Aphrodite, leaving him in the present instance quite unprepared to discriminate between sharp steel teeth as sharp steel teeth, and sharp steel teeth as artistic expressions of sharp steel teeth" (34). Like Holmes who once ruled that "[i]t would be a dangerous undertaking for persons trained only to the law to constitute themselves" as art critics (Goldstein, 576), Crease refrains from letting his own poor opinion of Szyrk's work interfere with the plaintiff's claim for justice or blunt him to the fact that there are many others who think the work important. Still, Judge Crease clearly has another standard of art in mind, and this cannot be thought a complete irrelevancy.

But the point remains that Crease's philosophy of justice is a version of Occam's razor, the principle reminding us that "[w]hat can be done with fewer [assumptions] is done in vain with more." Law, which has no theory, never having worked one out,[8] does best in this view when it refrains from making appeals to ancient precedents, or other forms of justification otherwise distant. This explains why Crease, in the James B decision, quotes Holmes's famous cat's clavicle remark (from *The Common Law*): "But just as the clavicle in the cat only tells us of the existence of some earlier creature to which a collarbone was useful, precedents survive in the law long after the use they once served is at an end and the reason for them has been forgotten. The result of following them must often be a failure and confusion from the merely logical point of view" (292). Precedents themselves are highly valued—they are the law's basis—but not those precedents that have lost their relevancy.

In this view, law is less about logic—though logic continues to be central—than about experience. That is, if "[t]he official theory is that each new decision follows syllogistically from existing precedents" (Holmes, 54), going back to some original law or constitution, the truth is that "[t]he felt necessities of the time, the prevalent moral or political theories, intuitions of public policy, avowed or unconscious, even the prejudices which judges share with their fellow-men, have had a good deal more to do than the syllogism in determining the rules by which men should be governed" (Holmes, 51). The courts are legislative, no matter how much its officers disavow such intentions. The fact is that each generation rewrites the laws according to its own axiology, so that, says Holmes, "[w]e could reconstruct the corpus from them [the newly written decisions] if all that went before were burned" (73). Perhaps, but the rewritten rules are not identical with their predecessors. Some rules are maintained over time, yet even when they are it is, as Holmes states, because present-day interpreters have found a way to make them correspond with current values: "as the law is administered by able and experienced men, who know too much to sacrifice good sense to a syllogism, it will be found that, when ancient rules maintain themselves ... new reasons more fitted to the time have been found for them, and that they gradually receive a new content, and at last a new form, from the grounds to which they have been transplanted" (55). It is a situation that, as Sanford Levinson has more recently put it, "highlight[s] one of the central mysteries of ... constitutional faith: the process by which 'best constitutional analysis' is subtly transformed in the passage of time so that A becomes not-A, without amendment ever being deemed necessary" (302).

Here, while law refuses to seek mooring in a universal, it does not pretend to be unmoored. It recognizes legal precedents as well as the opinions of the time, though Holmes and Crease, as strict constructionists, give more weight to the former than to the latter. All in all, the law is understood as a tacit thing, something that exists whether we will it or not, and something that has existed for as long as anyone can remember. This does not transform it into a universal, but it does suggest that the law has a gravity and a continuity about it which should be respected. Certainly, Holmes and Crease feel this way about the law, for they revere it; and they know their way about as if they were born to it. In a sense, they exemplify Stanley Fish's contention that "[t]o be a judge or a basketball player is not to be able to consult the rules (or, alternatively, to be able to disregard them) but to have become an extension of the 'know-how' that gives the rules ... and the meaning they will immediately and obviously have" (258). Never quite a complete body of knowledge, the law is always reaching out to that point when it shall perfectly realize itself. Were this to happen, however, it would be a dead thing, for transformation and growth are as crucial to the law as to any other living body. Thus Holmes writes, "The truth is, that the law is always approaching, and never reaching, consistency. It is forever adopting new principles from life at one end, and it always retains old ones from history at the other, which have not yet been absorbed or sloughed off. It will becomes entirely consistent only when it ceases to grow" (55).

Holmes and Crease are both sensitive to the fact that law is as much the consequence of a community's values as their molder. This does not prevent them from wishing to free the law from the realm of individual circumstances. Crease, in the Fickert case, supports this view with a Holmes quotation: "The law ... takes no account of the infinite varieties of temperament, intellect, and education which make the internal character of a given act so different in different men. It does not attempt to see men as God sees them, for more than one sufficient reason" (429). Here, the law is best thought of as indifferent to a person's particular fortunes: it judges the homeless person no differently than the corporate executive. And it tries to escape not only all forms of sentiment—as when Judge Crease instructs the Fickert jury to evaluate the testimony "unclouded by either prejudice or sentiment" (426)—but also all moralizing. True, a community's morality and its law often share the same field, yet they are different things, and both Holmes and Crease would almost prefer that the law were able to strip itself of morality's terminology. As Holmes wrote: "For my own part, I often doubt whether it would not be a gain if every word of moral significance could be banished from the law altogether, and other words adopted which should convey legal ideas uncolored by anything outside the law. We should lose the fossil records of a good deal of history and the majesty got from ethical associations, but by ridding ourselves of an unnecessary confusion we should gain very much in the clearness of our thought" (78). And, no doubt, lose something quite valuable in the process.

My point is that Holmes and Crease, while brilliant, seem short on compassion and empathy, making them less complete justices than, say, Learned Hand. In fact, Hand himself spoke of Holmes's limitations this way, writing that "He slipped, if slip he did, only because his imagination was too narrow. Man was more richly endowed than he supposed" (47). It is a fair judgment of a man who, in the end, let his war experience too fully color his understanding of life in general. For Holmes, life was always interpreted as a Darwinian struggle, always "red in tooth and claw." Here, human beings are likened to "a predatory animal," "the sacredness of which "is a purely municipal idea of no validity outside the jurisdiction," it being clear "that force ... is the *ultimate ratio*" (Aichele, 144). Was Holmes simply being honest? Perhaps, but I also find a hardness of heart, of the sort that made his description of African Americans as an "impulsive people with little intelligence or foresight" and his still hurtful words in the *Buck v. Bell* sterilization case ("it is better for all the world if instead of waiting to execute degenerate offspring for crime, or to let them starve for their imbecility, society can prevent those who are manifestly unfit from continuing their kind"; "three generations of imbeciles is enough") seem of a piece (Aichele, 148; 149).

Crease shares this same gravelish temperament. He would, says Christina, "give Jesus thirty days [in jail for contempt] if he could" (433), and one believes it. Determined to execute the law without regard for the more ordinary emotions that people attach to their affairs, Judge Crease comes across as insensitive and even cruel. His allusion, in the Fickert case, to Catholicism as one of "those widespread cults of mainly foreign origin" (428) is an example of plain bigotry, and his dealings with Southerners (the court's chief petitioners) are likewise seldom free of bigotry and condescension. No wonder Christina describes him as "one of the most selfish men who ever lived," and as one whose only interest in people was as "pawns" before the law (487). He thinks of himself, as do those near to him, as something like the Old Testament God ("for I the Lord your God am a jealous God, visiting the iniquity of the fathers upon the children to the third and fourth generation of those who hate me," Exodus 20.4), and is almost always spoken of as "Father." Christina says that he never "forgives and forgets" (326); and Oscar, while granting Christina's suggestion that his father is familiar with the Bible, comes back with "all right then maybe the Old Testament" (432). Certainly, his relation with his son has this cast to it, for he is always the stern judge and never the loving father. Here, the story that Christina tells Harry about Oscar as boy, building his canoe, is quite poignant and explains much about the older Oscar's relation—so inimically desperate—to his father:

> Harry don't tell, don't get Oscar's hopes up, I mean this whole brittle shell he's put together for who he thinks he is now but suddenly I look through that mangy beard and cigar smoke and see the face of the little boy down there by the pond that day with the little canoe he'd made, he'd spent days at it stripping the bark off a beautiful white birch that stood there and Father, Father looking at it without a word like some terrible open wound, looking at the canoe sunk in the mud and he had the poor tree cut down the next day without a word, gone without a trace he never mentioned it again but he never let Oscar forget it, just with a look, it was all too heartbreaking [...]. (397)

There is, then, good reason for thinking justice a more complicated and richer thing than even Judge Crease imagines.

HARRY AND THE JUSTICE OF WHAT IS RIGHT

Harry is a fitting recipient for Christina's story, for he, like Oscar, had a troubled relation with his father, a Chicagoan who made a fortune in textiles. The father was especially troubled by Harry's early ambition to be a writer. Thinking it "an unprofitable vocation for 'sissies'" (526), he forced the son into permanent exile. The son, however, did not become a writer, though it was as a consequence of his reading, particularly of Dickens, that he turned to law. Initially, Harry's motives were that of the idealist; he saw "the law as an instrument of justice" (527) and wanted to help right the world. His youthful enthusiasm moved him to work for "a number of small public interest law firms" (527) before disillusionment set in. We are not specifically told why he became disillusioned. However, it is suggested that as with his prior experience in divinity school, where he found his instructors and classmates responding to difficult questions with easy answers (527), he turned away from public interest law for the reason that his object—justice—seemed too removed. In short, he was naive; and in reaction he turned to corporate law, a practice with no pretensions about justice, but extraordinarily remunerative. In a moment of pique, Harry tells Christina that he went in to corporate law because it was about money and nothing else: "Why I went into corporate law in the first place where it's greed plain and simple. It's money from the start to finish, it's I want what you've got, nobody out there with these grievances they expect you to share" (44). But the explanation is not entirely true. Harry capitulated to the values not only of his father but of the society, but he also knows that he has given in to something that he does not believe in. Thus, if he does not altogether like the person whom he has become, he is still capable of admiration for those, like Oscar, who struggle against the odds to make something worth doing work (e.g., Oscar's play), as opposed to seeking an easier success in something that was not worth doing in the first place. Or as Christina, after Harry's death, tells Oscar: "I think he admired you, that he really admired what you'd tried to do because he'd tried it himself that's what he used to say, about failing at something worth doing because there was nothing worse for a man than failing at something that wasn't worth doing in the first place simply because that's where the money was, it was always the money ... " (529).

Harry sells out. In a society where corporate lawyers earn ten to twenty times the average citizen's wage, corporate law is a privileged demesne, whose lords appear indifferent, if not hostile, to the reformer's desire for greater economic and social justice. More than once Christina refers to Harry's firm, Swyne & Dour, as "William Peyton [the] third and his four hundred thieves" (395), and this seems an apt description. Certainly, the firm's major case, defending Pepisco against a suit by the Episcopal Church over trademark infringement (Pepsi-Cola is an Episcopal anagram), is about nothing so much as money, and to devote to it years of one's life, as Harry does, can make sense only if money is a paramount value. Money is not Harry's paramount value, but it has become something like a necessity. Driving back from the Hamptons in their Jaguar, Harry turns to Christina and asks her whether she could really "live in a place like Massapequa [a middle-class Long Island town, where Gaddis himself was raised] and drive around in a broken down Japanese" car (308). The matter comes up in response to Christina's complaint that Swyne & Dour is overwhelmingly white and male: "Out of two, three hundred lawyers you've got there every one of them white? male? and you need a black face or two in the window before some antidiscrimination law wakes up and hands out a good stiff fine in the only language they speak up there, money?" (308). Harry grants the truth of the charge, but, thinking more about survival than justice, defends the practice:

> —Look Christina, a place like Swyne & Dour you're not even proposed as a lateral partner unless you're bringing along a million and a half or two in billings with you, I've told you that. You think Basie or any of them's got that kind of client base? Never been a black partner the whole time I've been there, never even more than two black associates at once and they didn't last long either, did I ever say it wasn't about money? (308)

Despite Harry's corporate values, he retains a strong vestigial sense of why he first went into law. He has turned away from thinking of the law "as an instrument of justice" and toward thinking of it as "a vehicle for imposing order on the unruly universe" (527), but he still feels an obligation toward what is "right." The word or concept occurs repeatedly in reference to him, as in Christina's "It's simply what's right that's what Harry always [said]" (531), or as in his own critique of Pai's work: "but you get a feeling that he's got the answer ready before he hears the question, takes short cuts, doesn't look back, sets up the game himself as if he's the only player. He'd rather win than be right" (388).

What does it mean to "be right" in this context? We know that Harry has become disillusioned with the concept of an ideal justice. He seems not to use "right" as a synonym for it, though the term clearly retains a strong ethical aspect. It also retains, without evincing the strictness of the law, a legal aspect, as if to say that the right can, in its best evocations, combine what is good with what is required. In fact, right might be thought of as a circumscribed justice, as that which declares itself true within the domain of historical, political, and social circumstances. Here, where true justice is thought out of reach and where the law often vindicates the crook and the fool (399), right appears like a quasi-ideal. It is the sort of compromise that gets articulated in the idea of the social contract, be it Rousseau's eighteenth-century version or, for us today, John Rawls's "justice as fairness." People are understood to have both rights and obligations, not one without the other but both together. People live in a state of interdependency, and if they wish to be the recipients of social justice, they need to do all in their power to extend such justice to others, even those about whom—for reasons of economic, ethnic, regional, religious, or gender difference—they might feel indifferent or worse. Rawls writes, "Political liberalism assumes that, for political purposes, a plurality of reasonable yet incompatible comprehensive doctrines is the normal result of the exercise of human reason within the framework of the free institutions of a constitutional democratic regime" (xvi).

Harry himself subscribes to this form of political liberalism. He wants a system that protects him from other people's systems and orders. When Christina mentions that all Oscar wants "is some kind of order," Harry quickly follows with an allusion to European fascism:

> —Make the trains run on time, that was the ...
> —I'm not talking about trains, Harry.
> —I'm talking about fascism, that's where this compulsion for order ends up. The rest of it's opera. (11)

But even if political liberalism is what it purports to be—i.e., measured, moderate, tolerant—it still is a system in its own right, one that, when in place, displaces other systems. Rawls appears hesitant to acknowledge this—i.e., hesitant to acknowledge that as a system, political liberalism does not simply referee conflicts among society's groups but also influences the direction of resolution, and thereby assumes a more than passive role. Rawls would like to think that political liberalism is categorically different from other systems, that it is less like an epistemology and more like a place holder, facilitating people's interactions without also determining them. To this end, he proposes a theoretical model that sharply distinguishes between "background culture," which is social (e.g., "religious, philosophical, and moral"), and "justice as fairness," a political operating system that, again, impartially mediates conflicts (14). The background culture is said to be made up of numerous "comprehensive doctrines," doctrines that, individually, entail beliefs that place their members at odds with those professing different allegiances. Such doctrines are, Rawls suggests, inherently oppressive, and would, were it not for political liberalism's intervention, battle for state power so as to ensure their own hegemony: "a continuing shared understanding on one comprehensive religious, philosophical, or moral doctrine can be maintained only by the *oppressive* use of state force. If we think of political society as a community united in affirming one and the same comprehensive doctrine, then the *oppressive* use of state power is necessary for political community" (37; italics added).

Rawls's use of the word *oppressive* here, like his pairing of religious belief with gestures of intolerance, is not without significance. It is true that communal systems are, by nature, coercive. They predicate themselves on some real or imagined authority, and they expect their members to acknowledge this and to display a certain ascesis, itself part of a more general sacrificing of individual wants before societal needs. Coercion, however, is not oppression, and communities that predicate their togetherness on moral, philosophical, or religious grounds need not, ipso facto, be thought more oppressive than the community that predicates itself on the ground of political liberalism. In particular instances, much will depend on where persons stand in relation to the community's doctrinal ground, a situation that Rousseau acknowledged could prove oppressive, even in a liberal state, to the individual opposed to such ground: "In order, then, that the social pact may not be a vain formulary, it tacitly includes the engagement, which can alone give force to the others—that whoever refuses to obey the general will shall be constrained to do so by the whole body; which means nothing else than that he shall be forced to be free" (22). Here, coercion is ratcheted up a notch or two, to a point where it begins to look exactly like that which the liberal state seeks to oppose: oppression. Yet this state's own freedoms can to some, especially those lacking the resources to use them to advantage, appear oppressive. And even when the liberal state is in place, there is no guarantee that acts of intolerance will be banished.

A Frolic of His Own offers plenty of evidence to suggest that even those people—Harry, Christina, Oscar, Judge Crease, Pai, Trish, et al.—philosophically opposed to intolerance may, in their blindness, act in ways that smack of bigotry. For instance, Basie has disparaging things to say about "those Jews in Hollywood" (99); Oscar tries to honor Basie's race by telling a story of "the sheer artistry, smooth[ness], [and] unhurried[ness]" of the black men who pickpocketed his money on the Fifth Avenue bus (106); Pai believes that "blacks lack a counting gene" (364) and further believes that religion as practiced by "Sikhs, Iraqis, Afghanis," among others, testifies to the fact that "they're all raving maniacs" (375); Trish sees in her mother's long devoted servant "a thousand years of Irish Catholic ignorance" (359); Harry speaks of Pai, whom he calls "Mudpye," as the firm's "token ethnic," a "real red brick university product" (241); Christina, meanwhile, when she is not offering fine discriminations between wealth and riches ("you don't become wealthy building parking garages you simply get rich there's quite a difference" [503]) or consigning Catholics to slums ("these millions of Catholics jamming every slum you can think of" [269]), works on perfecting her Stinking Creek accent:

> Just a good thing they had a fine man like the Judge to hold this trial [the Fickert trial], had it down there at Wink County Court with some jury from Tatamount and Stinking Creek where everybody knowed how Billy Fickert shacked up with that fertilizer salesman before she married Hoddy Coops after Earl took off for Mississippi when they run him out for throwing lye down Hoddy's well a jury like that would have give the whole store away, can you tell me how Father could have put up with that for thirty years? can you? (498)

Actually, it is not so clear that the Judge's tenure on the federal bench for the Southern District of Virginia has been "a good thing." This is not to deny the incommensurableness of his legal mind. It is to wonder, however, whether a man of his opinions, so emphatically at odds with those of the local community, can actually weigh the concerns of his court's constituents fairly. I do not say "justly," for that, once again, invokes standards of a larger order. But can he rule fairly? That is, do the people of his jurisdiction believe that when they enter his courtroom their own concerns and values will be respected, or do they believe that Federal Judge Crease is, as Thomas Jefferson once wrote, part of that "corps of sappers and miners, steadily working to undermine the independent rights of the States, and to consolidate all power in the heads of that government in which they have so important a freehold estate" (Levinson, 295)? They clearly believe the latter; hence the wide-scale approval that meets Senator Bilk's call for his impeachment following the Judge's overturning of the jury verdict in the James B case. Before a large outdoor crowd, the Senator stirringly reminds them of:

> where this government interference with our sacred state's rights so many died for is leading us, sending in these Federal judges that take our great American language and twist the words around to mean whatever they want, calls God no better than a cat's shinbone, calls this beautiful land of ours a botched Creation and throws God right out of the courtroom, you heard him, do whatever they please because they're appointed for life. Well we have an answer for that, call it impeachment right there in the Constitution and that's the message I'm taking back up to Washington. They pay him with your good U.S. tax dollars and I'm going to tell them to take a look at one, take a good look at a U.S. dollar bill where it says In God We Trust and that U.S. dollar's gospel enough for me. (295)

It is not necessary to like or agree with this Jesse Helms incarnation to wonder whether federalism, with its adherence to the principles of political liberalism, is not experienced as something like an encroachment by a significant minority of communities and even states. At one point, Pai, taking note of the fractiousness of American life, comments to Oscar: "It's not a country it's a continent, eight or ten million Italians, Swedes, Poles, fifteen or twenty million Irish, thirty million English descent, twenty five million Germans and the same for blacks, six million Jews, Mexicans, Hungarians, Norwegians and this horde of Hispanics pouring in it's a melting pot where nothing's melted" (373–74). It is true enough to make one pause, and to wonder whether such diversity can ever be reconciled under a single rule of law, federalism, and under a single political principle, liberalism. To wonder whether *E Pluribus Unum* is not itself a contradiction in terms. And to wonder whether we (political liberalists) should even think such a situation desirable.

To repeat my point, liberalism may not only be coercive, it may, to use Rawls's word, be "oppressive." There is plenty of evidence in *A Frolic of His Own* to suggest that what we have in the United States is something like an undeclared civil war, wherein things are held in check, to the extent that they are, by a federalism that, in its less attractive moments, appears to stifle rather than to mediate differences. Here, I would like to quote a critic of political liberalism, Bhikhu Parekh, who, in his essay "Superior People: The

Narrowness of Liberalism from Mill to Rawls," points out that, despite liberalism's claim of inclusion, it has always had an oppositional, and thereby excluding, dimension:

> Since the Millian liberal developed liberalism against the background of colonialism and since he presented it as the major source of difference between the Europeans and the non-Europeans, he was led to define it in contrastive terms. Liberalism was seen as the opposite, the antithesis, of the allegedly tradition-bound non-European ways of life. Not surprisingly, it became obsessively anti-tradition, anti-prejudice, anti-custom, anti-conformity, anti-community, and both defined extremely narrowly and exaggerated the importance of such values as autonomy, choice, individuality, liberty, rationality and progress. Since the Millian liberal needed sharply to separate himself from non-European ways of life, he also redefined *himself* in the light of the way he had defined them. Liberalism thus became the other of its other and gave itself an impoverished identity. (12)

Parekh is particularly attentive to Millian liberalism and its semblance to colonial politics. But he also sees present-day liberalism (i.e., Rawlsian) as part of the same continuum, and as opposed to many of the same values (e.g., tradition, custom, community, and religion). The opposition tends, of course, to be less explicit than implicit. Liberalism does not so much oppose local traditions and customs so much as try, through the federal government's offices, to coerce recalcitrant state and local communities into submitting to "enlightened" behavior. The point is, whether this behavior be enlightened or not, the long-term effect has, good consequences notwithstanding, also fostered an often banal, and sometimes deleterious, cultural homogeneity, parts of which are on display in inner-city blight, suburban tract housing, and mall culture. Here, I am not arguing one side or the other, so much as suggesting that political liberalism has tended to focus more on those things it would eradicate (e.g., local prejudice, illiteracy, and poverty) and less on the consequences of its actions, which, constructed as the anti-image of the other (e.g., local patterns and behaviors), have not always been pretty. The long and short of the matter is, as Thomas Nagel writes, that "[w]hen we try to discover reasonable moral standards for the conduct of individuals and then try to integrate them with fair standards for the assessment of social and political institutions, there seems no satisfactory way of fitting the two together. They respond to opposing pressures which cause them to break apart" (*Equality and Partiality*, 4–5).

In *A Frolic of His Own*, Nagel's insight is played out even in the federal courtroom, the space most identified with a disinterested respect for rights. That is, the court experiences pressures from all directions, and in the end it is not always clear that an impartial justice is the result. But before pursuing this point, I should point out once more that there is also a strong reformist edge to Gaddis's satire. His critiques are the consequence of outrage, the outrage of one who (in the tradition of a Swift or Twain) witnesses something good turned on its head and who would like to see things righted. Gaddis offers an indictment less of the entire legal profession than of that segment—e.g., "pain and suffering" specialists and corporate lawyers—that has made self-enrichment its true object. For other segments, and especially for the judiciary, he seems to have great respect. Or as Jonathan Raban notes in his review, "This is not *Bleak House*. In *A Frolic of His Own* the language of the law is treated with affection and respect, and the lawyers themselves are honored as the last surviving instruments (even though some of them are very imperfect ones) of order in this disorderly world" (4). I would qualify the Raban statement somewhat. For again, while it is true that Gaddis shows respect for the skills of a Pai or a Basie, and for both the skills and the integrity of a Harry, it is also clear that he sees litigators as knuckling under to greed. "It's always about money" (58), in fact, becomes a refrain here. Still, for the writings of a Learned Hand or an Oliver Wendell Holmes, Jr., Gaddis has nothing but respect. As he told one interviewer, "I would much rather read legal opinions than most fiction .... I'm fascinated by legal language. I think it is stunning—it's always trying to anticipate contingencies" (D. Smith, 38). A byproduct of this respect and fascination is that we get characters like Judges Crease and Bone, learned elders who chose the law, long ago, because it was a place where a love not for money but for justice and language could be entertained.

However, to return to my argument, even with the best-intentioned jurists, the law has a way of being partial. For one, the expense of litigation makes it difficult for anyone without impressive means to bring suit. The bill for Oscar's own suit against Erebus is well over a hundred thousand dollars. In cases such as Oscar's, those parties with "deep pockets" can, by drawing the process out, via discovery, petitions, and counterclaims, often force the other party to settle for less than its claim or even to drop the suit for lack of means. Oscar himself is offered a two-hundred-thousand-dollar settlement by Erebus, and only his foolhardiness makes him turn it down.

Meantime, even when the legal process aims, in Harry's words, to arrive at the right answers "within the framework of the law"—"what the whole of the law's all about, questions that do have answers, sift through all the evidence till you come up with the right ones" (454)—the process is still filtered through the interests and biases of the participants. I have already mentioned Judge Crease's bias against Southerners, but there are others to take note of as well. For instance, the various biases of all the people involved play a crucial part in Oscar's case. For one, Oscar is referred to Lepidus & Shea because he wants to be represented by a Jewish lawyer. When Basie, a black man, is assigned to his case, his hopes decline. It does not matter that Basie is a fine attorney. Oscar will judge him as prejudice, not evidence, dictates. Thus when Christina tells him that Harry thinks the man "brilliant," Oscar responds: "Brilliant! I had to do all the work myself Christina, lead him along step by step pointing things out trying to get a straight answer from him, trying to get him to take the whole thing seriously while he rambled on about his acting career in some thimble theatre sitting there blowing smoke rings as though we were having a chat about baseball" (121). None of this is true, but Oscar has a hard time seeing beyond his prejudices. So, of course, does Pai, who similarly underestimates Basie's skill owing to his skin color, and who, in the deposition meeting, treats the latter with noticeable condescension. Later, he tells Oscar, "I spotted that black they palmed off on you for a fraud the minute we got into your deposition" (363), a remark that goes unsupported by evidence. Meanwhile, Basie seems to know the lay of the land. He is aware of the fact that the appeals court for the Second Circuit has a history of reversing the district court's decisions, and he knows that this is likely to occur in their own case, overseen as it is by a woman new to the bench. In such a case, he reasons it might be better to lose the first decision and then win on appeal. Or as he tells Christina:

> See they've assigned this case to this brand new district court judge, no track record you can't tell which way she'll go [...]. Say she finds for the defendant and throws it out, then what. Maybe that's good Mrs Lutz. You take how many cases lose in the district court and win on appeal because that's where this Second Circuit appeals court's got a real appetite for cutting down the court below so maybe you play to that. Maybe that's how we play it. (264–65)

In fact, it is not a bad strategy, though Harry is aghast when Christina relays it: "But that's not, you go in to win you don't plan to lose so you can win on appeal" (300). Still, as the facts stand, it turns out not to be a bad plan, for the appeals court is presided over by Judge Bone, who possesses, as someone said of Holmes, a streak of "the mean Yankee" (E. Wilson, 756). Or as Harry puts it:

> sitting on the Second Circuit bench as long as anyone can remember, cut from the same cloth as old Judge Crease, he doesn't suffer fools gladly I've seen him take a young woman prosecutor right off at the knees, got himself a name over the years for being a sort of misogynist so this wild card Oscar drew on the bench better have had her act together [...]. Little bit of the old puritan xenophobe too, get Mudpye up there with his secondhand red brick arrogance trying to deliver his oral argument and you can't tell. (396–97)

Like Crease, Bone is a first-rate jurist, yet when justice is filtered through his misogyny and his xenophobia, it starts to seem less and less like justice. And then, as happens here, when Bone recognizes the appeals brief as the work of his own colleague, Judge Crease, whatever chance Pai had successfully to defend the appeal goes out the window. Pai cries "conspiracy," as well he might, for as stated above, strictly understood, there is good reason for thinking his the better legal argument. Here, however, "justice as fairness" turns out to be not quite so "neutral" as Rawls imagines. Thus, while the Gaddis novel honors jurists like Crease and Bone, it does so knowing that the system's dedication to right will always be skewed in the direction of this or that interest or bias.

CHRISTINA AND THE JUSTICE OF THE HEART

Christina offers yet another take on this question of justice. She has not Oscar's Platonic sense of justice, nor does she demonstrate much interest in the more legal and political ascriptions of her stepfather and husband. Her sense of justice tends to be more intuitive, more from the heart. For her, Oscar's suit, like so many others, has nothing to do with justice. Rather, it is about his need to be taken seriously, for people to listen to him, even if he has to threaten them in the only language most people understand: money. Or as she tells Harry:

> Trains? fascism? Because this isn't about any of that, or even the "opulence of plush velvet seats, brilliant spectacle and glorious singing" unless that's just their way of trying to be taken seriously

too—because the money's just a yardstick isn't it. It's the only common reference people have for making other people take them as seriously as they take themselves, I mean that's all they're asking for isn't it? (11)

I am tempted to describe Christina's sense of justice in the context of Carol Gilligan's category of "the ethic of responsibility." Gilligan, author of *In a Different Voice*, opposes this ethic, predicated "on the concept of equity, the recognition of differences in need" (164), to that of rights, which itself "is predicated on equality and centered on the understanding of fairness" (164). Beyond this, Gilligan, now famously, identified each of these ethics with one of the sexes. For her, the ethic of rights, with its attempt to balance "the claims of other and self" (164-65), is identified with men; the ethic of responsibility, with its fostering of "compassion and care" (165), is identified with women. The thesis has been both highly praised and scorned. In the first instance, many were happy to find that women had a unique contribution to make to the discussion of justice. In the second instance, many were also upset to find the differences between men and women essentialized this way. The fear was that the old head-and-heart distinction was being refashioned but not rethought. If this were the case, Gilligan's book would not be of much long-term help to those women wishing to break free of traditional stereotypes.

There has, in fact, always been something quite traditional about Gaddis's women characters. One recent reviewer has spoken of the "sexism, even misogyny" of the earlier novels (Feeley, 87). While that charge needs proving if it is to be taken seriously,[9] it is clear that the novels' ethical arguments are closely identified with female characters, e.g., Esme in *The Recognitions*, Amy in *JR*, and Elizabeth in *Carpenter's Gothic*. This is also true in *A Frolic of His Own*. Raban himself goes so far as to call Christina "the reader's representative in the novel" (5), though this overlooks how dialogic this novel, like its predecessors, is. Still, Christina is an attractive character, often endeavoring to hold everything together when most others are on frolics of their own. In the opening scene, she furnishes Harry with a present (ginger preserves) for the hospital patient, Oscar, and gently admonishes him for what he intended to give Oscar (Judge Crease's opinion in the Szyrk case): "That was very thoughtful Harry, it was just the wrong thought" (12). She has a way of responding to others' needs as if they were her own. This is something that none of the others appear capable of, though if the commandment to "love thy neighbor as thyself" is to be taken seriously—and not as, in Pai's words, "a plain oxymoron" (376)—behavior of this sort appears requisite. The fact is, it is the aptly named Christina who is there for Oscar during his convalescence; for Harry when the stresses of his job become intolerable; for Trish when she needs someone to take her situation seriously; and for Lily when she needs to have an operation. She is also the person to whom Basie is truly able to talk about Oscar's case, and perhaps the reason why he stays with it despite Oscar's obduracy.

In short, Christina practices an ethic of love. While events sometimes make her seem peremptory and shrill, to the point that she begins not to like what she sees in the mirror—"and I look at myself and see somebody I don't like because I can't stand what it's [the overworking of her husband] doing to me either" (396)—her deep attachments to both Oscar and Harry, as well as her concern about Basie, attest to her singularity and importance. In a novel in which people's declarations of affection almost always have an ulterior motive—Oscar likes Lily for her youth and beauty; Lily likes Oscar as her sugar daddy; Trish likes her boyfriend for his youth; he likes her for her money; Trish likes Bunker for his money, and Bunker likes her for her comparative youth; Trish likes Pai for his success, and Pai likes Trish for her money—Christina appears different. She affects no fake emotions. If she does not like one, one knows it:

—Just, I just wish you liked me.
—So do I Lily. (24)

Her attachments appear sincere, even for Oscar, who is not an easy person to like. Christina has known and lived with him since they were children and knows the causes of his disquiet, knows that his bluster hides all kinds of hurt. She feels for him, even as she is put in the unhappy role of having to mother him. Her affection for Harry, meantime, is for an equal, a person of intelligence, maturity, and kindness. What she resents here, however, is that she has a rival, Swyne & Dour, that demands from him every waking hour. Repeatedly, she must remind Harry that she is his wife, that she has reason for expecting him home, and so on. Harry's attempts to explain his situation often only make things worse. Christina tells him, "I mean you talk about language how everything's language it seems all that language does is drive us apart" (386). Still, despite the friction, the relationship is a loving one. Christina can, in fact, be quite eloquent as to why this is so:

—I mean I love you Harry, I love your hands and your stubborn fighting yourself that drives me crazy when you won't take the shortcut like the rest of them and I love your hands on me and what they do and the stiff stubborn hairy Ainu that's like all the rest of you when I look around us at the pieces of my absurd pointless life before we met all strung out in front of us worried about Father, about the house and poor Oscar out there with his whole life in the lap of the gods and your smile, shaking your head it's such a patient, sad smile looking for what's right, what you said once, not what is just but what is right? (396)

Perhaps it is Christina's liking for Basie that best reveals her depth. The two get along together right from the start. Basie has previously met Harry, and this gives them a common handle, leading to Christina's story about the hairy Ainu. Liking Christina, Basie later clips out a newspaper story on the Ainu, which he presents to her. It is a simple but telling gesture. It also allows the making of a connection between the plights of the Japanese Ainu and the American black. The long despised Ainu turn out, it seems, to be the ancestors of the Samurai, "this fancy top elite warrior class way up there in the nobility" (265–66), and the suggestion is that a similar reversal—from being denigrated to being respected—might follow for African Americans. The possibility, of course, depends on the receptivity of the community's majority to minority members' contributions. It is a simple matter of justice, but rights, if not justice, can be blinkered. The paltry gestures of Swyne & Dour, with its two or three minority associates, testify to what sort of attention the mainstream community is prepared to bestow. While sensitive to such realities, Christina does not patronize Basie. There are even times when she gets quite upset with him, believing, for instance, that his trip to Hollywood for depositions might have been carried out less expensively. Still, she attends to what he has to say in a way that Oscar, for instance, cannot. She comes, then, to see that Basie's involvement in Oscar's case gave evidence that "[h]e wasn't just a smart lawyer and a sweet natured man a real man, he was our friend!" (565). Or as she tries to explain to Oscar:

> —I mean can't you see what happened, Oscar? that it was really Basie who laid the trap? Sitting here with the clock running and he kept saying we'll take them on appeal, that the Second Circuit likes reversing district judges to keep them on their toes didn't he say that? and that Harry said Judge Bone on the appeals court was a crusty old misogynist he'd seen him take a smart young woman judge right off at the knees once like this new woman judge just to teach her a lesson, don't you think Basie knew it too? (564)

Christina goes on to argue, to a deaf Oscar, that Basie knew the district court judge was mistaken on a point of law—i.e., the question of whether federal copyright or New York State's unfair competition law was most applicable—and that "he let it pass, he let their error pass on purpose so he could base the appeal on it that was the real trap!" (564). Basie did an impressive job with Oscar's case, though there were a few things, particularly during discovery, that he might have done better. Still, much of what Christina says in defense of Basie's handling of the case strikes me as true, and what seems even more true is her conclusion—reached via the heart rather than the syllogism—that Basie was their friend. This may seem a sentimentalism, particularly when placed alongside Judge Crease's more astringent notions of justice. However, I personally prefer Christina's notions of justice to those hitherto examined. Unlike Oscar's notion, with its myopic failure to take into account others' needs, or his father's notion, with its failure to weigh the heart's concerns, Christina's notion of justice seems more empathic and intuitively sound. And this last point is not irrelevant. Thomas Nagel has argued, in *Equality and Partiality*, that in any theory of justice

> the use of moral intuition is inevitable, and should not be regretted. To trust our intuitions, particularly those that tell us something is wrong even though we don't know exactly what would be right, we need only believe that our moral understanding extends farther than our capacity to spell out the principles which underlie it. Intuition can be corrupted by custom, self-interest, or commitment to a theory, but it need not be, and often a person's intuitions will provide him with evidence that his own moral theory is missing something, or just that the arrangements he has been brought up to find natural are really unjust. Intuitive dissatisfaction is an essential resource in political theory. (7)

Among *A Frolic*'s characters, Christina is the most intuitive, the person whom one most trusts to do the right thing, even if her solutions lack Oscar's urgency, Judge Crease's dispassion and her husband's pragmatism. Of course, there is no one right path here, not even Christina's, for they all must be considered and weighed against one another, and even then justice will often be "found and lost again and again." This said, I would like to examine one more place where justice appears to lurk: the domain of nature.

The Pond as Evocative of a More Encompassing Justice

I like what Nagel has to say regarding the relation of intuition and justice, and I think it applicable not only to Christina's notion of justice but also to something larger. That is, if it would be helpful or wise to seek out one person or location wherein justice—albeit so constitutionally dialogical—is most fully present in this novel, I would point to the pond. A living thing, the pond is not, however, a thinking thing, and it offers us no theory of justice per se. Still, it appears to exemplify justice, particularly in its moments of virtual timelessness, when it is so at odds with the ethic of billable hours. Repeatedly in *A Frolic of His Own*, there are descriptions of the pond and its visitors that make Oscar's freneticism and its variants seem almost meaningless, as if Christina were onto something when she tells her stepbrother that "if you'd had a fatal heart attack it wouldn't have mattered whether you had tenure or not would it?" (20). The point is not that life's small victories do not matter or that things are meaningless. Rather, it is that things need, in one form or another, to be understood sub specie aeternitatis. That is, much like the night in the "Time Passes" section of Woolf's *To the Lighthouse* or the snow in Joyce's "The Dead," the pond seems to wrap, or threaten to wrap, everything "in a chill mantle of silence":

> Down the bare hall the outside doors clattered again, the obstinate whine of a car's starter, the cough of the engine, the wrath of crows down there on the lower lawn where she looked out over the brown grasses stirring along the edge of the pond's surface teeming with cold which seemed to rise right up here into the room to wrap them each in a chill mantle of silence pillaged by the clatter of all that had gone before the more intense in this helpless retrospect of isolation where their words collided, rebounded, caromed off those lost boundaries of confusion echoing the honking tumult of Canada geese in skeins blown ragged against the uncharted grey of the sky out over the pond, each thread in the struggle strung to its own blind logic from some proximate cause blinded to consequence and the whole skein itself torn by the winds of negligence urging their hapless course [...]. (317)

It is a scene that is both enigmatic and beautiful. "[B]ut my God, it is beautiful isn't it," Christina says, making us wonder whether it might not be the artist rather than the jurist who is best able to speak to its justice, its truth. Kant writes that "[a]n *aesthetic idea* cannot become a cognition, because it is an *intuition* (of the imagination) for which an adequate concept can never be found" (I.210). The definition accords with Christina's own conception of the artist as one who, unlike the jurist, seeks to escape the containment of laws: "where it's all laws, and laws, and everything's laws and he's done something nobody's told him to, nobody hired him to and gone off on a frolic of his own I mean think about it Harry. Isn't that really what the artist is finally all about?" (399). The answer seems to be yes, but to the extent that the artist is, like the Conrad quoted by Pai ("You remember Conrad describing his task, to make you feel, above all to make you see? and then he adds perhaps also that glimpse of truth for which you have forgotten to ask?" [363]), possessed of exceptional vision, it might make more sense to identify this artistry not with Oscar, the playwright, but with Christina. Granted, Oscar writes a fine play, but the play, as mentioned, earlier, is wiser than he. Ordinarily, he is quite myopic, and the entire motif having to do with his glasses, sometimes dirtied, sometimes lost, adds to this. But Christina, as Raban points out (5), seems more than anyone else drawn to the pond, to this spot which (like similar scenes in the earlier Gaddis novels, e.g., the El Greco sky in *The Recognitions*, the evening sky in *JR*) represents something like a test of vision, so shiftily do things move in and out of focus. The motif is an important one. At one point, after a discussion about Ilse's sister, who "can hardly see" because of her cataracts, Christina calls Oscar's attention to the squirrel, "[o]ne of Hiawatha's mangy little refugees," outside on the upper lawn: "look. Look, can you see him out there? [...]—did you see him? You think maybe he was trying to tell you something?" (322–23). Oscar refuses to look, and turns instead to his book. Meantime, the television offers a documentary on a Scottish loch, with the narrator telling of the way that the lake changed in appearance, "often dramatically," each time he looked back at it. Here, the narrator's attention is almost philosophical: *"At times there is a clarity of detail at great distances when, for example, each branch of a thorn tree on the far bank is minutely sharp to the eye. Instantly it will become a dull strip of grey, and without a cloud in the sky to account for the change. This can produce mild hallucinations as the middle distance advances and recedes"* (324). The description also has a haunting follow-up, with the narrator saying, *"and you can soon begin to feel oppressed by the strange gloom, of this lake, with its isolated houses and its wide lawns that slip into the water as if the lake were slowly flooding"* (324).

The passage is, in fact, borrowed from James Fox's *White Mischief*, and has clear thematic importance. It is picked up again, somewhat later, with Oscar gazing out over the pond where each branch on the leafless trees standing out sharply on the opposite bank blurred into a dull strip of grey without a cloud in the sky, putting down the pages to steady himself as the whole middle distance seemed to come closer and fall away, abruptly seizing up some pages he'd left on the sill there and bracing himself as though facing an audience intent for the facts not the words, not the sound of the language but its straightforward artless function,—Grant's army ascending the Tennessee River to disembark at Pittsburg Landing where Buell's divisions were to join it, the Confederate army deployed in battle lines near the Shiloh church barely two miles away in the gloom that had descended out there over the pond where the few isolated houses and the wide lawn below seemed to slip into the water as though the pond were flooding [...]. (346)

Here, faced with a mystery, Oscar turns to "fact," to language sheared of its aesthetic force. It is a betrayal of sorts, for the pond, in its inexpressible beauty, requires an imaginative response, an effort to reconcile its aporetic power with more quotidian existence. (Cf. Thoreau's "A lake is the landscape's most beautiful and expressive feature. It is earth's eye; looking into which the beholder measures the depth of his own nature.") It even might be said to require musings of a metaphysical sort, the sort that should require a person to seek some kind of reconciliation between one's life and its own most apparent aporia, death.

This is, of course, a novel saturated in death. There are twenty thousand plus ghosts from the battle at Shiloh and a like number from that at Antietam, in addition to other, more approximately identified personages who have crossed the border into death either sometime before or during the course of the narrative. These include Oscar's great-grandmother, Justice Thomas Crease, Winfred Riding, Mrs. Mabel, Elizabeth Booth, Judge Crease, Trish's mother, Harry, Lily's brother Bobbie, Wayne Fickert, and, of course, Spot. It is a veritable ghost story, reminding us of Nietzsche's remark, in *The Gay Science*, that "[t]he living being is only a species of the dead, and a very rare species." This ghost story, meanwhile, begins with Christina referring to the hospitalized Oscar as dressed in "this shroud" and "laid out like a corpse" (19), a description, that puts him in a flutter, and recalls the black-suited man seeking out those willing to take "messages to the other side" (20). Throughout there are numerous mentions of things such as "last rites" (349), "sitting [...] on the other side" (421), "[l]aying up treasures in heaven" (432), funeral home conversations that search for "some affirmation to deny and obliterate the reality that had brought them together" (461), movies that threaten to snatch "everybody up to meet the Lord in the clouds" (462), Oscar looking "like a schoolboy on his way to a funeral" (486), the law clerk as both "memento mori" and "messenger [...] to the other side" (504, 517), the house as "cold as a tomb" (515), suing "from the other side" (551), and chain saws loud "enough to wake the dead" (575). In addition, there are repeated references to the authored work—be it a brief, an opinion, a play—that seeks immortality. Justice Crease's papers, write the historical society women, "properly belonged to the ages" (339); Judge Crease's opinions are also written to be read long past his death (443–44); and Harry's brief in the "Pop and Glow" case is said to be "enough in itself to immortalize him in the annals of First Amendment law" (578). Meanwhile, Oscar's bid for immortality hangs on *Once at Antietam*. When Christina jokingly brings up the possibility that he might have died in the hospital, Oscar has a sudden fright about his play's mortality: "Because my work, it would exist wouldn't it, its only claim to existence would be in this fraudulent counterfeit this, this vulgar distorted forgery and the thing itself, the original immortal thing itself would never be ... " (421). Rebuked by Christina for discussing his play in terms (i.e., of immortality) that he refuses to use with regard to ordinary people, Oscar goes further in his explanation:

> —That's it yes! Sunday mass nailing down their immortality one day a week so they can waste the rest of it on trash, or the ones who squander it piling up money like a barrier against death while the artist is working on his immortality every minute, everything he creates, that's what his work is, his immortality and that's why having it stolen and corrupted and turned into some profane worthless counterfeit is the most, why it's sacrilege, that's what sacrilege really is isn't it? Isn't that really why I got into all this? (422)

It is a sad confession. This man who has no real friends to speak of (his stepsister aside), and who has rightly surmised that there is "nobody around who seems to care whether I live or I [die]" (254), nevertheless puts all his hopes in a play that he himself will, in time, judge to be "all sort of stiff and old fashioned" (489). Later, his third act will be used, by Lily, as kindling, like Judge Crease's and Harry's papers. This fate seems to cast a gloomy shadow over the hoped-for immortality of the writer, be it that of the jurist, lawyer, or playwright. Certainly, there is an innocence in thinking that one's work will create the possibility of immortality. In fact, we might think that possibility an impossibility no matter what one does. And yet the impossible always entails an element of the possible, a truth that Derrida explores in his own meditation on death and dying, *Aporias*: "Is this [death] an aporia? Where do we situate it? In the impossibility or in the possibility of an impossibility (which is not necessarily the same thing)? What can the possibility of an impossibility be? How can we *think* that? How can we *say* it while respecting logic and meaning? How can we approach that, live, or *exist* it? How does one *testify* to it?" (68)

Gaddis does not answer these questions, either in *A Frolic of His Own* or in the earlier novels. He seems desirous of keeping the questions open. This certainly appears to be the case in *A Frolic of His Own*. I have spoken of the novel as a meditation on justice, and I think it is this. But it is, I believe, a meditation that, like Plato's *Republic*, conceives the question as intertwined with that of our mortality. That is, just as the *Republic* begins its search for justice with the "apprehensions and concern" expressed by the aged Cephalus about how he has lived his life and what might be the consequences in the hereafter (Plato, 579; this passage is also quoted in Oscar's play, 214), the Gaddis novel also begins by linking justice and death: "Justice?—You get justice in the next world, in this world you have the law" (11). This formulation helps us only so much. It does not answer our questions so much as postpone them, and gives credence to the sense that our understanding can take us only so far, and that there is a limit—a border—beyond which things are shrouded in a fundamental mystery. Socrates himself said as much. So it is, perhaps, no surprise that at novel's end there is one final allusion to Socrates, this time to *The Crito*, that same text that formed the subtext of *Once at Antietam*'s third act. This last allusion is somewhat veiled, as it needs to be, for it involves an identification of Harry, with his drink and pills, with Socrates and the hemlock (Gaddis uses the word *hemlock* on page 585). If the comparison were to be made too explicit, it would seem ludicrous, but Gaddis offers it in terms of the mildest of hints, and it seems perfectly right. Of course, *The Crito* is about the need to live honorably and rightly within the context of the laws in place. This is what Harry, like Socrates, chooses to do, even when those same laws finally appear too circumscriptive. He dies loyal to the firm, the same firm that has treated him so shabbily and, in short, unjustly.

The novel does not end with Harry's death, however, for there is one more scene, following Lily's burning of Harry's papers. This takes place under the sway of the pond, the pond as it was earlier described with its waters almost flooding, threatening to drown all, and "the far bank gone abruptly in a dull strip of grey" (585). Here, not only does "the middle distance" seem "to advance and recede" (585), but time itself seems to take on a mythic aspect, as the story of Hiawatha once again, as it has throughout the novel whenever attention turned to the pond, intersects with the present moment. That story was addressed to those "Who believe, that in all ages / Every human heart is human, / That in every savage bosom / There are longings, yearning, strivings / for the good they comprehend not, / That the feeble hands and helpless, Groping blindly in the darkness, / Touch God's right hand in that darkness / And are lifted up and strengthened" (Longfellow, 4–5). The Gaddis story is addressed to a rather different, much less sentimentally inclined audience. This explains why Gaddis's allusions to the poem appear both serious and comic. Still, the novel does not appear to renounce those "longings" spoken of by Longfellow. How could it, for they are so basic? Instead, these longings appear, as they often appear in Gaddis's work, almost masked, reflective of the author's own deliberate apophaticism. No matter, for the last scene gives, in its way, a clear indication of the intersection of the palpable with the impalpable, with "the whole pond" appearing "to heave as it ebbed from the foot of the lawn in a rising swell toward the other side like some grand seiche coming over it rocked by a catastrophe in the underworld" (585), invoking a world no less magical and mysterious than Hiawatha's own. It is, again, as if we are not so much in a world eclipsed by tragedy as in a ghost story, much like Joyce's "The Dead" to which Gaddis's last line—"Lily! Lily come here quickly I can't, Lily help me!" (586)—seems to make specific allusion. Whatever the case, Christina's girlish laughter, brought on by the boyish tickler (see also 13, 23), concludes the novel in a way that should make the pessimists among Gaddis's critics hesitate.

Notes

1. "Remembering Auschwitz," *New York Times* editorial, 26 January 1995, A 16 (national ed.). In *The Death of Satan*, Andrew Delbanco, though he agrees that "We live in the most brutal century in human history," is also struck by the fact that while "the work of the devil is everywhere, ... no one knows where to find him[,]" for "instead of stepping forward to take the credit, he has rendered himself invisible" (9). In short, he writes, "[a] gulf has opened up in our culture between the visibility of evil and the intellectual resources available for coping with it" (3).

2. I quote here from the Gaddis text, but the story is authenticated in several sources, including Francis Biddle's *Justice Holmes, Natural Law, and the Supreme Court* (71) and Gary J. Aichele's *Oliver Wendell Holmes, Jr.: Soldier, Scholar, Judge* (140).

3. Steven Moore tells me that *Once an Antietam* is, in fact, Gaddis's own shelved play, written in the late 1950s. Oscar's play, however, is said to have been

written in the mid 1970s (1777). Moore's statement is also confirmed in the Gregory Feeley interview (87). See also Gaddis's mention of the play in a 1962 letter (a novel begun, rebuilt into an impossibly long play [very rear guard, Socrates in the US Civil War]) quoted by Kuehl and Moore (*In Recognition*, 12). Finally, in the 1984 Logan and Mirkowicz interview, Gaddis says, "But I did write along play which is perfectly terrible. I take it down and look at it once a while, and I know there is a play in there, if I could just pull it out. Or a novel, but it doesn't interest me that much, so I put it back and someday it may interest me again."

4. Of course, there is something of Gaddis in all this. Responsibility, or its opposite, is a crucial concern in his work. Asked a question, by Malcom Bradbury, about the matter of responsibility, he offered a long answer, the upshot of which is that things in general seem too much out of control, with no one willing to take responsibility: "I find very much the world we live in as one that is practically out of control, and especially where we're living now—the present administration, and the Pentagon, and what have you—that no one is responsible. It's the party where all the kids are and the parents have left home ... " (*Writers in Conversation*).

5. "Section 1338 of the Judicial Code defines the jurisdiction of federal district courts over federal intellectual property actions and over certain state claims connected to federal intellectual property actions" (Goldstein, 195).

6. Not to everyone, however. Supreme Court Justice William Douglas, in a 1971 dissenting opinion, wrote that the standard that would apply "novelty" concerns to patent but not copyright cases was a misstatement of justice: "no reason can be offered why we should depart from the plain import of this grant of congressional power and apply more lenient constitutional standards to copyrights than to patents.... To create a monopoly under the copyright power which would not be available under the patent power would be to betray the common birthright of all men at the altar of hollow formalisms" (Goldstein, 580).

7. Goldstein writes:

Of the three national TV networks, one, NBC, currently is receiving 30,000 to 40,000 suggestions of all types every year. These figures include everything from letter outlines to pilot films. One department alone received from 7,000 to 10,000 "approaches" a year. From 2,000 to 3,000 get some serious study. Ten thousand story submissions of all types are offered. The effect of this tremendous influx is obvious. At the present time, the idea-submission lawsuits confronting the networks probably accounts for sixty-five percent of all suits against them in the area of copyright, defamation, right of privacy, and unfair competition. (26-27)

8. This is a rephrasing of Holmes's "The law did not begin with a theory. It has never worked one out" (64).

9. See Steven Weisenburger, *Fables of Subversion* (236-37), for a discussion of misogyny's connectedness to satire, both traditionally and in Gaddis.

PETER WOLFE

The Importance of Being Negligible

"Gaddis remains one of the least read of major American writers" (1989, 1), says Steven Moore at the start of his book, *William Gaddis*. Not only has Moore judged well; he has also raised an issue that needs raising at the start of any full-length study of his man: Gaddis *has* found only a small audience, as would any novelist who relies so heavily upon literary allusions, mirror images, and suggestive repetitions. Continuing to reason with acumen, Moore explains this neglect. He says *JR*, Gaddis's 1975 novel, "makes extraordinary demands upon the reader" (64), a view seconded by another important Gaddis critic, John Johnston: "*JR* often exceeds even the most difficult and recalcitrant of modernist fiction in its demands on the reader" (1990, 198). Nor is *JR* an anomaly in the Gaddis canon. In the first book inspired by Gaddis (1922–), a Ph.D. dissertation written at NYU, Peter William Koenig calls *The Recognitions* "extraordinarily complex" (1970, 14).

Gaddis's abundance of sources, his syntactic complexity, and his page-long paragraphs do tax the reader. He slights narrative tempo, preferring images and counterimages to a fast-moving plot. His prose is thick and dense. He rarely helps us find our way into the lives of his people. These lives, once they reveal themselves to us, look flaccid. Gaddis does not use them to describe or promote virtue, suggest models of morality, or punish the evil that men have always done. What is more, the victims of this evil

---

From *A Vision of His Own: The Mind and Art of William Gaddis* (1997). © 1997 by Associated University Presses, Inc.

often deserve better than they get from him. With apparent indifference, he describes good people, like Elizabeth Booth of *Carpenter's Gothic* (1985) or Harry Lutz of *A Frolic of His Own* (1994) as discounted, maybe even scorned and exploited, by those they have helped.

Yet along with this injustice, Gaddis portrays the comedy and wonder of social reality. Few writers are as difficult to define or label. Though dauntingly magisterial, he can also be wickedly funny. Moore also reports his saying that he considers his work as "more traditional than his critics do" (1989, 11), and Louis Auchincloss, while deeming him "one of the great innovative novelists of the age" (1987, 38), also calls him "something of an antimodernist" (38). He does rail against the stagnation and sleaze that the morally exhausted souls of Samuel Beckett both accept and try to make the most of. Behind the elaborate research, the esoterica, and the carefully hewn prose, his books have healthy vital signs. To Gaddis, wisdom inheres not in philosophy, psychoanalytic knowledge, or intellectual achievement, but in a sense of things that grow from a lived life—what he calls in *Recognitions* "living it through" (896, 898). The first words of *JR* foreshadow the difference between those flat, lifeless membranes known as paper money and real wealth, i.e., intangible assets. Then Gaddis, careful not to take himself too seriously, uses this difference to distinguish storytelling from the rich vibrancy of firsthand experience. He also knows the healing power of human touch. Elizabeth Booth has no ears for the words of her lover after learning that her husband has been shot and her brother killed. "Just hold me" (246), she tells McCandless twice, disregarding the elaborate rescue plot he is rehearsing for her.

Her words recall those spoken by Lucy Feverel after a long absence from her husband in *The Ordeal of Richard Feverel* by George Meredith, a Victorian novelist who probably puzzled and put off readers of that period as much as Gaddis has those of today. Like Meredith, Gaddis both recognizes and respects narrative tradition. Elements of *Gothic*, of romance, and of apocalyptic fiction pervade his books, along with those of the *Bildungsroman*, the hero of which will gain self-awareness along with a keener insight into the world at large. And if the progress made by Wyatt in *Recognitions* and Edward Bast in *JR* looks trivial, so does that of Fielding's hero in *Tom Jones* and Dickens's Pip in *Great Expectations*. Gaddis neither makes weighty demands on his protagonists nor does he scathe them for failing to meet his standards of excellence. These protagonists are more likely to scathe themselves. Like Richard Feverel or Paul Morel in Lawrence's *Sons and Lovers*, Wyatt, Bast, and Oscar Crease of *Frolic* all suffer for love, for the loss of love, and from the fear of dying before they reach self-fulfillment. Like

Carlyle, Dostoyevsky, and Kafka, these men evoke the nineteenth-century idea of the suffering genius—the isolate struggling toward an artistic ideal while yearning for the commonplace pleasures enjoyed by ordinary, well-adjusted mortals.

In ways, Gaddis stands closer to these earlier writers than he does to his contemporaries. He has always communicated with the reader on his own terms. At the outset, he toyed briefly with the innovations of others, but soon invented his own vehicles of vision. These vehicles are impressive. Thanks to his devouringly kinetic imagination, he captures essences as well as externals. Yet his gift for mordantly sardonic comedy, his grasp of the sensory overload of urban life, and his intuitive feel for the surreal aspects of America have created for him his own legend, one that cuts free from literary schools. The actuality of his art has become subsumed under a strange marriage of admiration and neglect. He even resembles the vividly portrayed outcasts he writes about.

Despite the extraordinary powers of observation and reflection he displayed in *Recognitions*, he earned so few royalties and friends with his first novel that he had to stop writing fiction in favor of working in industry to support his family. The decades between 1955 and 1975 relegated him to neglect. But not total neglect; the acclaim of a few major critics brightened the obscurity. This brightness has burned steadily if not intensely. Though he remains little read, he won National Book Awards in 1976 and 1994, together with several other important honors. These have secured his status as an outstandingly gifted writer who addresses a very small audience; Gaddis is a largely ignored major novelist.

Forty years brewing, this anomaly is justified. During much of this time, he had no books in print. And the odd copies of his work found in libraries and used-book stores made it clear from the outset that the patience, time, and goodwill of aspiring readers would be sternly tested. Besides being daunted by Gaddis's abundance and complexity, these readers soon found that they couldn't rely on many of the guidelines and strictures they had used in the past to make sense of other novels, including those of the most mandarin stripe. "Don't bring a God damned thing to it can't take a God damned thing from it" (605), grumps a character in *JR* about the reluctance of readers to make an effort comparable to that of the writer. But Gaddis can discourage the most diligent. Where, for instance, does one collect one's thoughts or catch one's breath? Sentences of two hundred words or more, besides containing several arcane references, can appear in a paragraph spreading over two pages. Next, Gaddis resists being deconstructed, historicized, or destabilized. Vying with a modernist urge in his work to totalize order is a delight in life's oddities and incongruities. He can no more stay within rational or aesthetic categories than he is able to ignore them. Wyatt of *Recognitions* and the title figure of Gaddis's next novel drop from view for more than two hundred pages at a stretch. Furthermore, Wyatt, *JR*'s Edward Bast, and Oscar Crease of *Frolic*, all of whom qualify as protagonists, may be mad when they take their leave of us; Liz Booth, their counterpart in *Carpenter's Gothic* is dead.

This strategy shows Gaddis discrediting the idea of character in fiction. He invites a further inference. If the stable, centered human subject no longer exists in fiction, then the actions of fictional characters stand free of the laws of cause and effect. Coherence and psychological motivation lose out to incoherence and entropy. But the loss cannot be easily assessed. Here is no celebration of disorder as in Nathanael West or John Hawkes. The satire of Gaddis affirms the basic conditions of both life and art as it denies them. That *Recognitions* collapses artistically in its last-chapter description of the collapse of the western Christian state creates a mirroring relationship that tempers the devastation. Like the phrase from the book's next-to-last sentence, "soared in atonement" (956), the word *recognition*, Gaddis's term for a theophany, joins with the many coincidences in the three later novels to imply the redeemability of the everyday. The prevalence of mirrors in the Gaddis canon also robs death of its finality. To reduce death to a counterimage is to drain much of its force and dread. Like Wyatt, we can set aside our anxieties and "live deliberately" (900).

Tom Le Clair's *Art of Excess* provides important insight into Gaddis's attempt to do justice to the world's richness and complexity. Gaddis's "profoundly informed, inventively crafted, and cunningly rhetorical" (1989, 2) king-size books, said Le Clair, give the impression of mastery over the power systems regulating modern life. A network of overt and covert messages, *JR* presents big business as a collage of noise, scraps of cultural data, and assumptions about the interplay of commerce, politics, and the family. Gaddis is a collector, and we are processors. We have to "see, sort, and judge" (28) the text for ourselves. Le Clair's concept of the reader as someone who unscrambles and then resites a text from the level of stasis to that of process also applies to *Frolic*, which came out after *The Art of Excess*. Details in *Frolic* pertaining to the law, to food preparation, and to real estate form a "power system" that, thanks to Gaddis's synthesizing vision, enlarges the collaborative reader's capacity to sort out life's apparent messiness and intransigence.

John Kuehl's *Alternative Worlds* finds in writers like Gaddis, Joseph McElroy, and Alexander Theroux patterns like reflexivity, entropy, and the impulse to play (often in the form of slapstick or the pun) probing a reality beneath appearances (1989, 293). The theater provides Robert Coover a matrix for the interaction of President Richard Nixon and Ethel Rosenberg in *The Public Burning* (Kuehl 1989, 226). The alternate reality that shapes both character and event occurs in Gaddis, too, as in the many changes rung on the motif of forgery in *Recognitions* and the mounting importance of cannibalism in *Frolic*. Tropes like Brigadier General Pudding's eating of the freshly passed turds of the dominatrix Domina Nocturna in Thomas Pynchon's *Gravity's Rainbow* and Nixon's sodomizing by Uncle Sam in *The Public Burning* describe a culture both displaced and degraded. Like Coover and Pynchon, Gaddis mixes humor and horror, preferring parody, carnival, and the grotesque over realism to depict a world encroaching upon violence. Yet he takes a friendlier attitude toward the formalism and humanism associated with traditional satire. A genius both free-floating and tightly disciplined, he knows that, whereas fantasy divides people, myth joins them. Thus the references to alchemy in *Recognitions* and to Richard Wagner in *JR* invoke a lost unity, but one perhaps within close enough reach of the margins of life today to guide us, thanks to its built-in faith in the therapeutic, the normative, and the corrective. As Steven Weisenburger shows in *Fables of Subversion*, Gaddis is much less abrasive and degenerative in his satire (1995, 101, 145) than Flannery O'Connor and James Purdy.

A descriptive term that captures the impulse behind Gaddis's imaginative intent is that of actualism. Introduced in Susan Strehle's *Fiction in the Quantum Universe*, actualism stems from Werner Heisenberg's belief in reality's dynamism. This "human interpretation of a nonhuman reality" (Strehle 1992, 7) accounts for the throb and surge of experience. Surprises can flare out at any time. Thus accident replaces causality in *JR*, says Strehle, noting, as well, the wealth of characters and events in the book irrelevant to the book's central action (118–19). This randomness not only clears a path to meaning but also constitutes meaning. Gaddis's belief in the folly of relying too heavily upon reason in our random world takes the form of an acute attentiveness to items like news headlines and an advertisement on a bag of potato chips, and lastly the link between speech—with all of its slippages, repetitions, and trailings off—and personality. Life's solid surface in Gaddis is always threatened by the irrational currents lurking underneath. To convey this drama, he may show center and circumference changing places. Tropes may combine or collide; a TV cartoon in *Frolic* mirrors in childish, but disturbingly accurate, form the devastation wrought in both the law and the bulldozed property adjoining the Long Island home near which most of the book's action takes place.

Amid this storm of mirror images lies the impulse to simplify. All artists should study Titian, claims Wyatt, because, like El Greco (*R* 872), they can profit from his economy of means. Wyatt's last appearance before he goes off "to live deliberately" (900) prefigures Jack Gibbs's advice about paring down any system to the fewest possible units: "more complicated the message, more God damned chance for error" (403). Elusive enough on its own, this economy sorts ill with a world that resists reason, justice, and order. Gaddis sets his fiction amid chaos. In phase with an answering universe, his plots meander and fragment in places where tightening is expected. Events that have started to cohere as a pattern will suddenly disallow unity and clarity. Analogously, bonding hardly exists in the canon; most of Gaddis's important characters stand apart from society, from a moral code or a job that will give them self-validation, and, finally, from themselves.

Gaddis treads the same dangerous path. His defiance of authority includes a career-long tendency to shake his fist at narrative conventions. And at the reader, too? Time and again, this former president of the *Harvard Lampoon* misleads us and then makes us feel foolish for having fallen into his trap. A villain like Recktall Brown of *Recognitions* can be sympathetic, even pathetic. A dove, symbolizing peace and innocence, is killed by some innocent children at the start of *Carpenter's Gothic*. The heroes of both *JR* and *Frolic* are weak. The abundance of separations and divorces in the canon shows love ending in indifference or hatred. Doubt and even impiety mar the faith of the pilgrims who go to Rome in *Recognitions* to witness the canonization of a saint. Though *Recognitions* also insists on the priestly dedication of both a minister and his artist-son, it describes these men as maladjusted and full of pain.

This piercing description clashes with Gaddis's Arnoldian belief that art and religion are our last stays against anarchy. But there is also the joy Gaddis takes in the free existence of things, that is, their apartness from the mind that perceives them. Enhancing this paradox is the lack of both artistic growth and deepening of vision he demonstrates. Though he refines his technique, he directs it to different aesthetic and moral challenges in each of his books. His artistry seems to have been in place from the start. So thoroughly is he in charge of his materials that he gives the impression of having been born whole as a writer.

Another of his defining marks comes in his resistance to critical formulas. Much of the discussion of him since 1989, though illuminating, misses his central creative nerve. His antirealism, for instance, is usually exaggerated. Though *Recognitions* lumped him in with the antirealists, his other books are doggedly realistic, more so than the works of writers usually called realists, like

Bellow and Updike. He does wrench time; things move ahead more quickly in his books than they would in the everyday world. Nonetheless, Gaddis is a new realist or hyperrealist because of the vigor with which he conveys the molecular reality of things. Perhaps he belongs in a category that has no name. But, as Kipling liked to say, that's another story. Let's shelve the question of categories in favor of looking at some of the ways he has combined erudition, intuition, and rhetorical genius to create a body of work all his own.

I

Our everyday world has Gaddis's attention. To borrow Isaiah Berlin's famous definition of Tolstoy, Gaddis is both hedgehog and fox, a pluralist and a possessor of unitary vision. Though driven by a strong innate sense of order, he accepts mystery, meaninglessness, and contradiction. His artistic self also responds vividly to life's abundance. Like Whitman, he takes joy both in naming things into existence and in seeing his descriptive flair bring them to comic life; he revels, too, in the richness of social transactions. At other times, an extended image will reveal the menace that grows with each novel:

> The sound of thunder approached from the street's corner, a Department of Sanitation truck stopping every ten or twelve yards to open the huge maw at its back and masticate the immense portions left out to appease it with gnashings of reckless proportions, glass smashed and wood splintered between its bloodless gums. (*R* 316)

His belief in oneness declares itself in his Joycean love of dialectic, coincidence, and parallel at many levels. For all his variety, his work has a basic simplicity. Abstractions abound, together with a running contrast between substance, "the imperceptible underlying reality" (94), and accident, the data we perceive. And though the multiform data called forth by his exuberance fail to slot into place, they do graze patterns of order suggestive of the Joycean motif of "almosting it." This grazing he calls a recognition, that is, an act of heightened attention or a moving into the light. It occurs but rarely; maybe seven times in a lifetime, says Wyatt (*R* 92), can we foresee what is to come or savor its full meaning. The rest of the time finds us stubbing along by trial and error.

Gaddis's vigorous rendering of things we can touch, feel, and smell recalls Joyce, too, along with Joyce's love of small talk. But this sensory abundance also imparts a Victorian flavor. Though Gaddis lacks the warmth and the steady, unhurried pace of Dickens, the sharply hewn clarity distinguishing the gallery of grotesques and caricatures in *Recognitions* gives a Dickensian sense of urban plenty. Gaddis can make you laugh, break your heart, or send shudders through you in his portrayals of our indifference to underdogs. He hasn't put these unfortunates in a world friendlier than the harsh, pitiless one their real-life counterparts face daily. Instead, he imbues his world with a vibrant strangeness by showing it as a series of jump cuts, conversational fragments, and near misses. The rhythms it creates evoke the jagged pulse of jazz. Gaddis raises caricature to the level of hallucinatory realism, catching people in flashes of heightened introspection close to hysteria.

These people are both individuals and modern types. They stand too near the edge to be outgoing and friendly, to try to enjoy themselves, or to make friends. Nerve-racked, they contradict the belief that the world is a nice place, after all. Whether they learn from or even survive their ordeals remains unclear. Like Dickens and Dostoyevsky, Gaddis is interested in the way we influence one another, the images we print on one another's mind, and the gravitational pull exerted between us, despite our protests. But rather than defining this dynamic, he immerses us in it, conveying its force by a barrage of images nightmarish and mundane.

A Gaddis novel will barrage us for pages with such images. But it will also angle them from oblique perspectives. Rather than inviting our participation, they will place us under a strain, sometimes repelling our attempts to enter the action they refer to. Writing about *Recognitions*, Minkoff points out ambiguous pronoun references (23) along with "a bewildering distribution of tense changes, halting or jerking punctuation marks, and stubborn immobile words" (1976, 26). This recalcitrance coats everything. Gender confusion frets several of the people in *Recognitions*, a novel that questions identity itself. Certain characters are known only by their first names (Janet, Stanley, and Benny); some by their last (Mr. Pivner and Fuller); the identity of one (the Town Carpenter) is expressed by one of his jobs; a would-be playwright assumes the name of one of his characters; and the book's main figure (Wyatt) undergoes two name changes near the end. In similar fashion, Elizabeth Booth answers to different names when addressed by the three most important living men in her life—her brother, her lover, and her husband. The defining marks that lend life stability and cohesion are just as blurred in *JR*. Nothing can fight off change in that book. A hedge and a house disappear; another house is ransacked; a street changes its name; and many of the traditional guidelines of the student–teacher relationship reverse—all within six weeks or so. Conveying the larger meaning of this inconstancy are both the fragments of TV shows that lace the action and, particularly, the frequent misquotations of major poets like Keats, Tennyson, and Kipling. Hitting in from different angles and using different vocal registers, the book describes a society so far out of control that it has unknowingly severed many of its cultural roots.

But these snapped ties can also rejoin; Gaddis's jagged atonalities sometimes resolve themselves in melody and harmony. The resolution can occur quickly. Straightforward narrative asserts itself as early as the fourth paragraph of *Recognitions*, which reads, "This is what had happened" (3). Depending upon his intent, Gaddis may disrupt disruption with the simple and the straightforward. Jack Gibbs's conversation with Marian Eigen in *JR* about her marital problems with Tom displays Gaddis's skills as a domestic realist. Instead of taking sides or casting blame, Gaddis recounts Marian's woes in her own voice. If her litany of grievances combines resentment and guilt, Gibbs's replies also contain a realistic mix of compassion and gall, since he knows that his friend Tom's career is at stake together with his marriage.

Gibbs tests Gaddis's gift as a domestic realist again when he and Amy Joubert spend two days alone together. As Lawrence does in his description of Will and Anna Brangwen's honeymoon in *The Rainbow*, Gaddis conveys with stunning psychological accuracy both the defensiveness and the indifference that punctuate his lovers' passionate exchanges. The mood swings, the painful self-disclosures, and the moments of lyrical surrender jostling one another in the two days of intimacy convey the breadth of Gaddis's sensibility. The care with which he watches and listens to people discloses an ability to suppress himself; no exhibitionist, he. If he is, as Moore claims, "the greatest writer of dialogue in the history of the novel" (1982, 6), his ability to withdraw from the page helps justify the honor. A self-absorbed writer could not capture the style, spirit, and rhythm of his people's voices, particularly when those voices are raw or burdened with care. But passages like the romantic interlude of Amy Joubert and Jack Gibbs in *JR*, while giving delight, serve an important warning: Gaddis writes so well about so many things that he discourages critical attacks. If we're bored, confused, or fatigued by his work, we're tempted to blame ourselves; we haven't invested enough of ourselves in the work. This nagging feeling of inadequacy will persist—even diverting our attention from the texts. The beauty or the wit of a passage we do grasp, rather than lending comfort, will make us wonder about the number of gems we have overlooked en route.

The most popular disclaimer invited by Gaddis, after the one directed to his alleged obscurity, refers to his bitterness; "nowhere in this whole disgusting book is there a trace of kindness or sincerity or simple decency," carped a reviewer of *Recognitions* (Kuehl and Moore 1984, 18 n. 28). Brian Stonehill confronted this issue when he wrote, "Gaddis's theme is the way we live and what is wrong with it" (1988, 114). Taking our cue from Stonehill, we can agree that Gaddis often plays the scold. *Frolic* includes one of Dickens's angriest attacks on English industry. The one-time novelist McCandless in *Carpenter's Gothic* says that fiction stems from outrage (158), a statement Gaddis repeated in a videocassette interview (Bradbury 1986b). Perhaps the statement has an unintended irony. A sentence of over two hundred words in *Carpenter's Gothic* (216–17), heavy with smoky, convoluted syntax, makes us wonder if some inner demon is driving Gaddis to vex his readers with the difficulty of his prose. At more sober moments, we ponder Elizabeth's comment: "I mean I think people write because things didn't come out the way they're supposed to be" (158)—together with McCandless's reply, "Or because we didn't" (158).

The failure to which McCandless and Elizabeth refer can be a prod. Whereas success brings contentment, failure spurs activity. First, it asks that we shake off both self-pity and the temptation to blame others. Next, it has us probe the sources of our failure. Which of our mistakes brought us down? And what can we do to avoid repeating them? There's also a bright side to explore. Which new options can we test? And which new skills can we develop to improve our chances for success? Finally, how can we live with ourselves if we fail to reach our goals? One answer comes from E. M. Forster's *A Passage to India*, which Gaddis liked well enough to quote in *JR* (486). The festival crowning the third and last section of Forster's 1924 novel shows that, because all of us have at least one important failure in our pasts, only a God who excuses failure can be divine. An answer closer to home comes in Gaddis's April 1981 essay in *Harper's*, "The Rush for Second Place." As Jack Gibbs says in *JR*, "Order is simply the thin, perilous condition we try to impose on the basic reality of chaos" (20). The organized, the stable, and the neat all oppose nature. Yet this opposition causes problems noted in the *Harper's* essay: "The more complex the message, the greater the chance for error. Entropy rears as a central preoccupation of the time" (1981, 35).

Ockham's razor has cut a path into the twentieth century. Whereas simple answers or messages trivialize, complex ones admit error. Where can we turn? A book like Dale Carnegie's *How to Win Friends and Influence People*, which Gaddis satirizes in *Recognitions*, helps illuminate the problem. Carnegie's 1940 book sidesteps both the risk and hard work of searching for answers within ourselves and evolving our own value systems. In a class he used to teach at Bard College, Gaddis would try to "raise questions for which there are no distinct answers" (*Bard College Bulletin*, November 1984). He found the inexplicable a source of energy. It stimulated thought and discussion. The ready-made answer, like the political ideology or the religious dogma, on the other hand, blocks thought and thus robbed his students of a chance to test their wits.

Gaddis's fiction chimes with his classroom technique. He has forsaken the balanced and integrated for the episodic novel because, for him, the latter reflects more accurately both the private moral self and the ultimate meaning of life. We pass through a series of interludes which we ourselves unify. To find that evolving principle of unity is to gain vital self-knowledge. The public self's concern with image, status, and civil or political issues makes up but a small part of the drama. And this part must be *kept* small. Gaddis's highly developed and refined art looks askance at American middle-class values; it portrays no cozy homes where simple family joys are celebrated and sustained. But it also charts the restiveness and upheaval caused by cultural collapse. Here is no abdication of social conscience. Though Gaddis deplores his countrymen's struggles for cash, goods, and status, his questions about their souls arrow to the inner realities structuring their lives. *Recognitions* uses Puritan notions of virtue and rightness to disclose the darkness of our hearts. Religion in the book is an instrument used by the powerful to extend their power. Rather than caving in to cynicism, elitism, and moral disdain, the book shows lonely, badgered people trying to halt the downflow of their lives by reaching out to one another, albeit on their own terms. *JR* extends the pattern. Besides showing characters both courting and resisting love, the book forecasts the decline of the United States a decade later into a society very much like those of the third world, where the rich and the privileged are sharply divided from the poor and the defenseless. The book also explains this coming polarization. The upward distribution of wealth in the 1980s concentrated too much power in too few hands.

Here is how the sad split took place. The Reagan years reduced welfare appropriations, deregulated businesses, raised interest rates, and encouraged heavy borrowing against budget deficits. These policies helped turn the U.S. from being a creditor into being a debtor nation. The proliferation of mergers in the 1980s caused factory closings, farm foreclosures, and joblessness. But the woes kept spreading, as Gaddis foresaw. The contempt for environmental controls shown by the bosses of Typhon International, the large New York brokerage that controls so many lives in *JR* (one boss speaks of "this environmental nonsense on this gas line consortium" [696]), prefigures many of the decade's crises: the extinction of species, the drowning of humanity in its own toxic wastes, and the universal threat caused by the greenhouse effect. Eleven-year-old J. R. Vansant becomes a one-person multiconglomerate by adopting policies he overhears being discussed in the executive men's room of Typhon. These policies cohere as both a simple truth and a formula for corporate success. (*Recognitions* contains the phrase, "philosophy in the public latrine" [305].) Now the public condones all kinds of compromise and betrayal if they stem from the executive suite—or toilet. One of Typhon's chiefs has the honorific title of Governor, and he's called a great American by one of his employees. Another chief must clear his desk of all paperwork that will link him to an inside trading scam before he goes to Washington to serve on a congressional cabinet. This stonewalling of any investigation of his misconduct presages by more than a decade the doings of real-life Wall Street felons like Ivan Boesky and Michael Milken.

Carpenter's Gothic also describes the U.S. as the victim of its supposed protectors. What has damaged us, Gaddis believes, is a reverse imperialism. Junk-bond empires built with taxpayers' money have made us an economic colony, dominated by foreign products, foreign investments, and the foreign politics we have paid to put into place. *Gothic* is a guidebook to the age's corruption of the American Dream. It claims that we are all living on borrowed time. American foreign policy in the 1980s ignored democratic ideals, loyalty to one's friends, and improving the living conditions of third-world people. Greed infected all. The infection entered our bloodstream like this. In order to help large American firms with strong ties in Washington, our country would back an up-and-coming separatist movement abroad and set up in the movement's name a sovereign state under an obedient leader who looked respectable. The next steps included getting UN recognition and then instituting tax-shelter laws and a dollar-linked currency. Speeding the process in *Gothic* is the groundswell of fundamentalism that shook the 1980s. This groundswell reinstated the laissez-faire economics favored by Washington, a system controlled by men whose lofty moral principles clashed with their casual business practices. While the Reverend Elton Ude claims to be fighting Marxism in Africa with his Christian Recovery Mission, he is secretly helping a big-time politician slide into place a large agribusiness based on cheap native labor. More than business, politics, and religion are involved, too. The speed with which ideas, phrases, and characters both reappear and interact in far-flung places describe the inevitability with which the public and the private collide.

Gaddis's microcosm for the United States has always been New York City, where he was born and in and around which he has lived most of his life. "Well if this is the cultural center of the world you can give it right back to the Indians" (636), says a minor character in *Recognitions* about Manhattan

Island. The decades have validated his words. *Recognitions* forecasts the violence that would later erupt in Central Park, Crown Heights, Bensonhurst, and Howard Beach. Civilization in our country's capital of finance, communication, and the arts is imploding. A "bustling stream of anonymity, moving forth in an urgency of its own" (559), the New York of *Recognitions* is arrogant and frenetic. Policemen, cabdrivers, and office workers pass before us together with pretenders and hangers-on from the *haute monde* of arts and letters. Nearly all of them are jittery. Many of them are seen during the Christmas season. Chaotic and disjointed, New York awaits a charge of vitality, which is most needed to shake the winter doldrums. So forlorn is this city of dreadful night that when the charge occurs, in the form of pregnancy, it's scorned and terminated. Then, a party guest gives his maid a hysterectomy for Christmas. As Otto walks through the "concentric ice-ridden chaos" (695) of midtown Manhattan, he overhears the following scrap of conversation:

—Look, Leroy ...
—Dis city ...
—Leroy ...
—Dis (696)

Gaddis's invocation of hell's capital city (Moore 1982, 255) captures the chaos gripping New York: a house burns, an innocent man is arrested, and a suicide occurs. At chapter's end, Otto is alone and numb, "surrounded by ice, among the frozen giants of buildings" (699). Redemption seems ages away from this granite nightmare.

JR redirects most of Gaddis's criticism of New York to Long Island, where "the remnants of pavement, the rusted length of a car's muffler and the sodden heaps of a mattress" (663) marring a residential street depict suburban blight. This eyesore also reflects an inner malaise. Greater New York suffers from both physical and moral incoherence. Signs of renewal, like a new cultural center and housing development, coexist with sagging fences, the rusting hulks of cars, and derelict washing machines. The small Long Island town where much of the action of *JR* unfolds has become a monster, exhibiting at the same time different aspects of growth and collapse. While new shopping malls and highway extensions are bringing the nameless town into the urban network, apparitions like weed-choked yards and mud slides show it being reclaimed by nature. The genteel suburbs can even be as dangerous as the urban inferno. During the course of the action, a house is robbed, a car is stolen, and a student is killed in the parking lot of a school.

The educational system has aggravated this crisis. Administrators use their power to promote their business interests rather than curbing the formation of teenage drug and sex clubs. Expensive high-tech teaching aids they bought in past years have gone unused and are being replaced with new ones. Programs like adult education, prenatal care, and Great Books are giving way to hobby shows. Books and, with them, literacy itself get the shortest shrift. Not only do school budgets allocate more money to blacktopping the parking lot than to books, but the first revenue source the district superintendent and a school principal tap in times of fiscal constraint is the book budget.

Nor does this scorn for the written word give signs of easing. During the course of the book, a preadolescent student gives birth in the school nurse's office, a teacher is jailed for child molesting, and nearly every talented faculty member gets fired. That other supposed safeguard of civilized values, tradition, also suffers a setback. By renaming Burgoyne Street Summer Street, the town councillors have replaced the colorful with the flat and the bland-sounding. Still worse, they have denied their heritage. General John Burgoyne (1722–92) was a hero of the American Revolution; ignorant of tradition, those responsible for the renaming blunder must have felt that the name, Burgoyne, sounded too French. Spending a minute or two with an encyclopedia would have told them that their locally honored winner of the battle of Saratoga was English.

The New York City of Gaddis's next book, *Carpenter's Gothic* (1985), is still uglier and more self-defeating, even though none of the recorded action occurs there. In fact, the Hudson River Valley town where the book takes place probably stands farther from the city than does the Long Island suburb of *JR*. Noisy, dirty, and overcrowded, the Manhattan of *Carpenter's Gothic* repels us as much as Musil's Vienna or Vargas Llosa's Lima. The backup of cars from Westchester County to the George Washington Bridge leaves commuters testy and short-tempered. The "fruitless torment of a wild cherry tree" (36) near the house where the action unfolds shows that the exhaust spewed out by the idling engines of these immobilized cars has killed some of the local fauna. The fauna-killing pollution can uncoil from the city itself. The asthmatic Elizabeth Booth cannot live there because the air is so foul. Her rare visits to the city wring her. When she goes to the ladies' room at Saks, a thief reaches over the top of her locked stall and lifts her purse from the hook where it was hung. But the thief is not through plaguing her. Using a false name, one of the thief's friends telephones Elizabeth, impersonates a store executive, and claims that he has recovered her purse and wants to return it to her. Then, having lured her back to the store, the caller ransacks her unattended house.

Her husband fares still worse, since he adds to the violence that wrings Elizabeth. Mugged in "broad daylight" (200) in midtown Manhattan, Paul turns on his attacker and kills him. The speed with which he strikes back discloses the stress, anger, and frustration caused by coping with New York. And he is not even a New Yorker. What he is is trapped by the coils of the city. If urban malaise nearly kills him and then turns him into a killer, it also, ironically, provides his livelihood as Reverend Ude's media consultant. Gaddis's decision to have Paul kill his mugger in Manhattan is artistically apt, since Ude's peace crusade has adopted many warlike practices, like teaching its aspiring missionaries both weapons use and hand-to-hand combat. This militarism can only step up the pressure of surviving in upbeat, arrogant New York, the place, incidentally, where Elizabeth's brother Billy decides to board the plane to Africa in which he will soon die.

Cities have always worried Gaddis. He wasn't being cute or clever when he said of Paris in *Recognitions*, "age had not withered her, nor custom staled her infinite, vulgarity" (63). The home of Picasso, Stravinsky, and James Joyce in the 1930s, when Wyatt also lived there, Paris prided itself in being the West's center of artistic experiment. But it spawned venality, too. Gaddis goes to perhaps excessive lengths to spoof the American tourists whose gaffes—perpetrated in the name of sophistication—spoiled what little of the town's charm had survived the local lust for cash. "Paris had withdrawn from any legitimate connection with works of art" (73) in favor of greed ("everything was for sale" [73]). One spoiler, the Parisian art critic, Crémer, writes for the journal, *La Macule*, i.e., the stain, blot, or blemish (Moore 1982, 103). Crémer offers to praise Wyatt's paintings in exchange for 10 percent of whatever the paintings earn. Crémer, significantly, will turn up in New York City fifteen or twenty years after Wyatt rejects his offer, authenticating an old master that Wyatt had painted himself. The blemish has spread. Perhaps its poison has spread, too. Gaddis claims that in interwar France four million Frenchmen had venereal disease (73), and one of the most riveting impressions of Wyatt's Paris days is the sight of a cancer-ridden prostitute. The words of another guest at a New York reception run the cancer through a five hundred-year shaft of time: "Oh, this pious cult of the Middle Ages," rails Basil Valentine. "Is there a moment of faith in any of their work, in one centimeter of canvas? Or is it vanity and fear, the same decadence that surrounds us now?" (690).

Gaddis has posited both the Middle Ages and the Paris of the Lost Generation and the long weekend as counterfeit ideals. His purpose? To voice his belief that the golden age never existed. All ages have been corrupt. The cultural and spiritual crises infecting our century stem from long-standing malaise. As Crémer's presence in New York implies, this malaise has sapped new-world energy. Late in *Carpenter's Gothic* it comes out that the founder of the financial dynasty that controls so many of the characters shot himself when he was about to be indicted for bribery. The nineteenth-century house where his daughter Elizabeth lives, built in the style called Carpenter Gothic, disregards the comfort and convenience of its inhabitants. The house's owner and the book's oldest character, McCandless, embodies the dregs of an exhausted, besmirched tradition. All that's left of this wearer of frayed, faded clothes, besides his sex drive, is talk, along with the tobacco and booze his death wish drives him to consume.

The many references to the Church in *Recognitions* suggest values beyond the reach of today's urban-industrial state, where all is disposable, replaceable, or for sale. The recurrence of Christmas imparts a mood of hope, which is enhanced by the abundance of religious materials permeating the action. But Faust sold his soul to the devil centuries ago, and American Puritanism survives only as a sin-obsessed New England spinster and her mad alcoholic minister-brother, who later defects to Mithraism. The seventh chapter of part 2, the book's longest at 78 pages, ends in a series of one-liners spoken by strangers who have wandered into the frantic, numbing action. These one-liners imply that humanity has lost its substance and vitality, subsisting only as a straggle of disembodied voices:

—It finally stopped snowing? Well I'll be damned.
—Merry Christmas.
—And it finally stopped snowing.
—Happy Yom Kipper.
—Well I'll be damned. (646)

In view of what follows it, the chapter's epigraph, from Darwin's *Origin of Species*, "We will now discuss the struggle for existence" (*R* 568), implies that this eternal clash yields no winners. It never did. Before we adapt to reality, we have to know what it is. How to gain this knowledge? Gaddis wants us to ask. Alchemy lost out to the more exacting demonstrations of chemistry, having been "turned out like a drunken parent, to stagger away, babbling phantasies to fewer and fewer ears" (132). The repudiation of alchemy was overdue. The philosopher's stone had eluded all its would-be discoverers, and no base metal ever soared to gold during alchemy's ten-centuries-long heyday. That "lonely and problematic read" (Comnes 1994, 89), *JR* substitutes a reverse form of magic. Nothing in the book is stable. Some Wall Street tycoons watch a nun dissecting a cat in a program made for closed-circuit educational TV; a report on Alaska (misspelled "Alsaka") written by JR as a class assignment circulates among the same tycoons. One Mr. Grynszpan, credited by some insiders for being "the Eminence grise behind the [JR] company's meteoric expansion" (711), never appears. He cannot, since he doesn't exist. By transacting nearly all of his business by telephone, a dirty handkerchief stuffed into the mouthpiece to disguise his voice, JR has already confirmed facelessness as a corollary of financial success. Nonexistence is but a step away.

II

How much of this drift to nonbeing has its roots in the past cannot be said. As an eleven-year-old, JR carries very little of the past with him. Gaddis's books shuttle between fantasy, realism, and modernism, challenging and even dismantling their meanings. Minkoff's reference to Gaddis's "aggressive appetite for suggestive but unresolved inclusion" (1976, 16) sheds useful light on his presentation of value judgments. So engrossed is Gaddis in the telling of his stories that questions of morality fade inside his representation of reality. The laws of discourse can part company with the laws of physical nature; the universe we inhabit resists language and concepts. But he shouldn't be indicted for violating comic distance. Yes, there is something unresolved, outsize, and even oppressive about his writing. But he can also make us laugh. And his treatment of alchemy in *Recognitions* shows that, rather than blurring his focus, he wants to impart the dynamism of cultural experience. Language and culture do shape our understanding of reality; our efforts always glean some reward. The critic Theodore Ziolkowski said of Hermann Broch, whose novel *The Sleepwalkers* (1932) Jack Gibbs reads in *JR* (724), "Broch longed for totality and simultaneity. [...] He wanted to encompass all of life—and all at once" (3).

He could have been describing Gaddis. Whereas the discrediting of alchemy by chemistry made scientific method more accurate and systematic, it also leached away some of its wonder and excitement. Gaddis's romantic self prefers it over chemistry. Alchemy was an art as well as a science, and some of its laws had the charm and resonance capable of forestalling the menace of entropy. With its belief that life glows with magical properties, alchemy affirms spiritual hope; from the dross of earthly sludge can be distilled some universal principle. The very transformation of base metal into gold through the application of this principle implies the redemption of mankind. Housing spirit, the commonest materials presume a metaphysical continuum. To experiment with them is to perform an act of faith and of worship. To write about them, as Gaddis does, is to imply our perfectibility. The alchemical strain in his work defies the postmodernist belief that life cannot be known or improved. However misguided or outmoded, alchemy denies both our helplessness and insignificance. Like the running motif in *Recognitions* of The Self Who Can Do More (253, 385), it endorses progress, morality, and a belief in life's underlying order. It also prefigures Heisenberg's belief that an observed system will interact with its observer. The prospective redeemer can hope for redemption himself, an idea Gaddis underscores in his novel (605) by referring to Tolstoy's *Redemption* and by repeating in both Latin and English the proposition, *Semper aliquid haeret*, or, something always sticks (*R* 336, 470, 491, 836).

A work as sensitive to redemption as *Recognitions* can't be called nihilist or perverse. But these terms persist. When told that his book-in-progress sounds difficult, Jack Gibbs answers, "Difficult as I can make it" (*JR* 244). He might have been speaking for his author. If Gaddis rejects the moral bleakness of postmodernism, he accepts much of the school's aesthetic. His work enacts the subject matter it deals with, evoking life's deeper disjunctions by splintering traditional storytelling modes. He risks tiring, boring, and irritating the reader for a good reason: he wants to depict the underlying strangeness of the world. This strangeness comes across in different ways. Wyatt's puritanical Aunt May refers to "evil spirits who deceive good people by keeping the path to Paradise littered with filth" (*R* 39). Dostoyevsky found merit in this idea. Otherwise his Alyosha Karamazov would not have suffered so deeply when the fresh corpse of his mentor, the holy Father Zosima, began to stink (*Brothers Karamazov* supplies the epigraphs for part 1, chapter 6 and part 2, chapter 4 of *Recognitions*).

The idea occurs in *Recognitions* in many ways, nearly all of which defy causality and common sense as we know them. Pilgrims en route to Rome to witness the canonization of a saint read anti-Catholic books like Margaret Shepherd's *My Life in a Convent* and Rebecca Reed's *Six Months in a Convent*. Many of the book's dislocations of logic refer to religion, reminding us that God uses witches both to test the faithful and to punish the wicked, a point argued in the *Malleus Maleficarum* (1488), a work very much on Gaddis's mind during the writing of *Recognitions* (Moore 1982, 86). Sometimes, Gaddis will distract us with verbal clutter, as in this overwritten passage:

> The room was filled with the strident ring of a telephone bell. It shivered the metal sails on the man o' war, brought forth an undisciplined tinkle of broken glass, and a frantic shade of

movement concerted in seizure: breathing the hoarse aspirate initial of greeting, waiting, listening, everything stopped. (*R* 502)

He will also misdirect our attention with false clues or mingle the coarse with the refined. He may introduce a line of reason, only to snap it and discard it to avoid telling or showing all. But he also implies the benefits to be gained by this rejection of follow-through. In part 1, chapter 1, Gwyon tells his artist-son Wyatt that so long as he leaves the portrait of his dead mother, Camilla, unfinished, he will be haunted by her. The dramatic encounter that ends before resolving itself stays in our minds, inviting us to supply resolution and meaning ourselves. But Gaddis can surprise us by supplying a useful summary or insight himself. He will usually do it, though, in a throwaway fashion, putting his revelation in the mouth of an unlikely character or hiding it in a swarm of irrelevancies, where it may go unnoticed. Sometimes, an important disclosure can be buried in a series of press reports either on the radio or in a newspaper. The value of a disclosure may also be challenged as soon as the disclosure is made. Tom Eigen, who makes some of the most trenchant insights in *JR*, is suddenly called "some fucking graverobber" (616) by the young woman he's trying to seduce, the quondam lover of his recently dead friend. Such passages refocus our attention; we become more active, alert, and observant, like Brecht's ideal theatergoer. Shaken out of our passive groove, we grow more receptive to stimuli.

A scene may rouse our activity by containing its own intercheck. In *JR*, a man who is getting an enema complains about an economic system that has failed him. The torrent of words ending his impassioned speech coincides with an explosive discharge of the shit his enema helps dislodge. Some time later, Edward Bast, the man's hospital roommate, unburdens *himself*, only to find that he has been addressing a corpse. Such disruptions of continuity and closure throw us off stride, diverting our attention and blocking narrative drive. *Recognitions* has many passages that stop just short of reaching a dramatic climax at odds with the book's narrative intent. A scene in part 2, chapter 2 that threatens to invite the charge of intellectual aloofness shows the rich art dealer Recktall Brown and his unlettered black servant, Fuller (whom Brown later calls a "dumb nigger" [357]). Displaying more wit than dullness, Fuller baffles his paymaster by questioning the moral legitimacy of adopting evil means to fight evil. Then he discusses a crisis of faith a minister friend is undergoing because he has started to doubt whether he is the man Jesus died for. Fuller's heady talk with Brown introduces one more challenge to the spirit—that of accepting the existence of mermen as counterparts of mermaids. But the spark ignited by these challenges loses some of its brightness, and the white gloves on Fuller's hands give his talk with Brown the look of a minstrel act.

This intercheck qualifies, without negating, the import both of Fuller's questions and Brown's failure to answer them. Conveying Gaddis's comic sense, it also shows that he is not introducing problems to vex the reader. Entering his fictional universe gives glimpses of both larger truths and the opposition these truths face as they try to merge with the historical process. Perhaps Gaddis is an epistemological novelist (Comnes 1994, 6,147). Exploring what has happened to us and what we do to resist the flow of circumstances, he discloses hidden sources of response. Everything is weird, yet at the same time recognizable. His characters are lonely, but not abandoned. Events graze them, press against them, and jostle them. Living without safety or comfort, they look in vain for reliable guidelines. Few are happy in their jobs, their homes, or their lives. Like exiles, they wander a great deal. But they lack the patience, the goodwill, and the self-esteem to profit from their travels. Culture has become something to ransack, and the love of a good woman that would end their wanderings, like that of Peer Gynt's Solveig or the Flying Dutchman's Senta, gets either overlooked or scorned. Man has lost control of his existence; he cannot recognize his best chances, let alone act on them. By sidestepping love and by reducing the treasures of the past to their market value, he denies the healing power of nature, of the unconscious, and of tradition. He has chosen death over life.

Love remains the biggest stumbling block for Gaddis's people. Gaddis describes love: the way people fight it, run from it, and, sometimes, costively accept it. This resistance is validated. Love is always difficult, disruptive, and painful, even for those who need it the most, like Oscar Crease of *Frolic*. The needy do perceive the importance of investing their hearts. Gaddis will often put them in a family setting because this is where they feel their apartness most keenly. Ties smudged or snapped in childhood, in their families of origin, can cloud the future for them. Wyatt learns that growing up cannot heal the wounds inflicted upon him as a boy. He lost his mother at age four, after which his father avoided him, particularly when Wyatt was most needy—during a near-fatal boyhood illness and the trying, questioning years of adolescence. As a man in his thirties, Wyatt calls a "departing back" his father's "most prominently distinguishing feature" (*R* 398).

The family that provides more grief than warmth is a staple of *JR*, a book where infidelities abound, marriages crack, and child visitation rights are either breached or disregarded. The absence of a child who does not return home after a field trip goes ignored, or at least unmentioned by his parents to the school authorities in charge of the trip. Either the parents overlooked the absence or don't care about it. The family continues to raise deep questions. The discovery near the end of *Carpenter's Gothic* that McCandless has a son makes us wonder why he had told Elizabeth that he has no children. For the background to an answer, we can mention the earrings Gwyon had given to Camilla as a wedding present. Symbolizing unity and wholeness, these large golden hoops draw blood from two women who wear them thirty-five years apart. The suspicion that love opens veins persuades Esme, a poet, a mother, an artist's model, and the second wearer of the earrings, to speak home truths to a sleeping Wyatt. Love's inherent dangers frighten people. Gaddis quotes some lines from Sir John Suckling's poem "Love's Offence" that speak to this issue: "Love is the fart of every heart; It pains a man when 'Tis kept close; And others doth offend, when 'tis let loose" (*R* 629). But he defines love more broadly than does Suckling's poem. Thus Frank Sinisterra's wife turns off her hearing aid when Frank begins talking about his favorite subject, his skill as a forger. Soon, he will put eserine in his eyes, an effect of which is that he cannot, or does not have to, see her. Then he will smash her hearing aid. Intimate talk foils intimacy. In *Carpenter's Gothic*, Elizabeth never speaks as tenderly either *to* or *about* her brother Billy until she learns of his death.

Conversation of any kind deepens the fear of confronting love and hence the loneliness of Gaddis's people. Characters in Gaddis talk to themselves. They rarely listen to one another, and they will interrupt their interlocutors just as they are about to be given information they have asked for. It is almost as if they are afraid of facing the demands that this information will create. They resist being helped. Talk in Gaddis, as in Harold Pinter, can be a form of silence or a mask. Speech walls in Gaddis's people, substituting a self that the speakers feel safe showing others. But this verbal smoke screen can drift out of control. McCandless equates talk with death in his description of his last conversation with Elizabeth's brother, Billy. This is where Billy resolves to fly to Africa on what proves to be his death plane: "I couldn't get a word in, that's what he talked about he couldn't stop talking about it" (*CG* 233). And why shouldn't nonstop talk lead to death? As a denial of the reality of both speaker and hearer, it already is deathly.

But if Gaddis portrays characters undoing themselves, he also shows ways of self-enhancement. Most of his people are humanized by an occasional flash of sweetness or the wish to improve their lives. The motif of The Self Who Can Do More (*R* 253, 385; *JR* 389) implies a better self we all harbor, glimmers of which light our humdrum, or even sordid, daily acts. This self calls to mind the beautiful statue Praxiteles found inside the marble block surrounding it (*R* 57, 124). All of us parody a better self within; we can all do more. But even though we ignore this self, and even insult it, we cannot suppress it. Soon after a man in *JR* beats his wife, he displays a gentle, wondering side, reminiscing about how, as a boy, he and his father used to watch the circus come to town and set up its tents and fairway stands. A flustered Paul Booth contradicts himself amid a cloud of whiskey fumes because he has to promote the policies of the charlatan Reverend Ude in order to draw a salary. Nearly every drinking glass in the house and, presumably, some of the cups have their rims chipped by the desperation with which he pours his drinks.

The Self Who Can Do More that these jagged chips call forth rarely escapes into the open. Yet at times it seems to be preparing for such a leap. Redemption is always possible. But nobody has a clear title to it. Some characters who impress us favorably will let us (and themselves) down. As Gaddis's comments about him show, Thomas Eigen of *JR* (who, like his author at the time, had published one big but neglected novel) fits this category:

> I started him out as being, sort of getting my own back, as it were. He starts out being quite a good fellow who has had bad luck, but as it went on he became very unpleasant, and finally by the end of the novel, he was thoroughly unpleasant, thoroughly, because this is the way he developed in the novel. (Bradbury 1986)

Eigen's moral plunge reflects Gaddis's belief in the opacity of the human self. People cannot claim to know either themselves or others; they can even overturn their author's intentions for them. But if identity is stubborn and slippery, it is also renewable. We can improve our lives. Sometimes, a new name can aid self-renewal. By calling Frank Sinisterra Mr. Yak and Wyatt both Stephan and Stephen, Gaddis endorses their new identities; Wyatt even answers to his new name. His Thoreauvian resolve, the last time we see him, "to live deliberately" (*R* 900), is to be taken seriously, as is Edward Bast's parting resolve to fail, if he must, in his own way rather than "at other people's things" (*JR* 718).

That the resolve comes from Bast while a hospital patient commands attention. Most of Gaddis's people suffer from loneliness and loss. They brood a good deal, sometimes to the verge of breakdown. As in Thomas Mann, breakdown threatens artists (like the musicians Edward and James Bast, the painters Wyatt and Schepperman, and the writers Eigen, Gibbs, and Oscar Crease) more than it does the rest of us. As an artist's vision refines, it weakens the artist's tie to the everyday; the artist becomes disoriented, even deranged, by living in the light of divine creation. His conversation includes elisions and repetitions, indicative of a wavering of attention, and he neglects his health. Gaddis accepts the modernist notion of the artist as outsider. Schepperman, James Bast, his student Reuben, and the sculptor Szyrk of *Frolic* are all so alienated they never appear. The road to artistic expression contains so many dangers that it wrecks the artist's chance for a full life. Childless and divorced, Wyatt lives alone in a cold-water hovel far from his circle of social and business acquaintances (he has already forsaken marriage and friendship). His mother died on a ship bound for Spain, and his father is lost to him. The pursuit of salvation through art deepens his woes. Besides ruining his marriage and landing him in a slum, it undermines his well-being.

The artist must be ready for such upheavals. But to what end? Gaddis invites us to ask. The practice of art is grinding, merciless work with few rewards. The numerous references to the personal trials of Mozart and van Gogh in *JR* and to Puccini's tragic diva Tosca in *Recognitions* evoke the pain dogging the artist. The pain flares outward. Writers rarely finish their books in Gaddis, and the books that do go to press tumble into a void, regardless of their merits. Artistic merit is a side issue. Stanley's organ mass in *Recognitions* is noted "with high regard, though seldom played" (956), a fate that foretells that of Thomas Bast's opera, *Philoctetes*. Schepperman's paintings have been confiscated; Szyrk's twenty-four-ton sculpture comes close to being destroyed. Perhaps Jack Gibbs and Elizabeth Booth judged wisely by leaving unfinished their books-in-progress.

But perhaps they didn't act by design. Judgments are a caution in Gaddis, mostly because human nature as he portrays it is so tricky and multilayered. *Recognitions* accepts the instability and fragmentation of selfhood, creating a world in which identity defies verification. Life's many demands undercut the stability of being just one person at a time. "Wyatt has no proper identity," says Johnston; "he can only be defined in relation to a shifting series of differences, which in turn refer to other differences" (1990, 135). Any insights into people that can be coaxed out of this shifting series come gradually and have only tentative value. As Thomas Eigen proved in *JR*, Gaddis will invite judgments he later overturns. The more time we spend with his people, the more clearly we see the pitfalls of judging them. Many of them resist judgment. Sensitive, intelligent Amy Joubert has only visited her brother once in the ten years he has spent in a mental home.

But the unsympathetic can also touch our hearts. One of Amy's father's more ambitious junior executives, Davidoff, claims that he once wrote a novel. Even the most arrant opportunist may have a redeeming sensitivity and flair Gaddis finds worth calling to our attention. By narrowing the gulf between his sympathetic and scurvy characters, he improves his fiction, making it more believable and dramatic. One of his favorite devices for revealing character comes with the piecemeal exposition. (*Recognitions* refers to the doctrine of progressive revelation, "which finds man incapable of receiving truth all of a lump" [132].) The key insight into character that is withheld, while stopping the action from peaking too early, helps create an even flow and texture. It also gives Gaddis the chance to get into his people's lives. He reworks narrative conventions in order to focus on what his people are rather than what they do. By freeing them from the riggings of a plot, he lets them create the plot.

As Johnston notes, the reader must stay alert to give shape and meaning to Gaddis's character portraits: "It is always possible that a seemingly isolated or random item, no matter how small or insignificant, forms an element in some series, or series within a series" (1990, 40). Because Gaddis sometimes approaches his subjects and themes obliquely, rather than frontally, an apparent trifle may become important, even crucial. For instance, Jack Gibbs owns five shares of a family firm in Astoria that could either create a deadlock or swing the balance of power in any attempted takeover of the firm. Accordingly, a woman in *Recognitions* says that one of Katherine Mansfield's loveliest passages appears in a book review that nobody will see (125; also *JR* 486). Merit and value must be sought out. The banished Philoctetes, the title figure of Thomas Bast's opera, becomes vital to his country's welfare because of his skill in archery; the same leaders who exiled him later need his help in the Trojan War. Thus they fetch him from the island of Lemnos, where they had banned him, and take him, along with his bow and arrows, to Troy, where he kills Helen's abductor, Paris.

Gaddis's practice of seeing something important out of the corner of his eye tallies with a sensibility dark and absurdist in the Eastern European vein. Like people, words and things resist expectation, Gaddis wrenching both fictional and linguistic conventions to suggest the thinness of the stays undergirding civilization. Not only do apparent trifles take on a hidden importance and words assume dark, private meanings; Gaddis's ability to invest data with a life of their own also gives everything the potential for shock and violence. Even nonsense threatens to crush us, as in the party scenes in *Recognitions*, where the guests act like trapped mad children. Their wildness can be explained. They have substituted the secular attainments of money, fame, and foreign travel for the more difficult work of love. The book turns the self-reflexive world it describes into a hall of mirrors in which every distorted image both hides and carries the truth. A good example is the recurring symbol of the mirror itself. To avoid the mirror is to deny self-confrontation, including one's capacity for spiritual self-transcendence, as the *cruz con espejos* (cross with mirrors) in Gwyon's parsonage shows. Yet the mirror can be looked into for too long. Absorption in one's image both fosters egotism and distracts us from the rich variety of the world external to us.

In this dance of reflected images, elements of good and bad flash across one another, blot each other out, and fade away. Transcendence and descendence interlock; a walking away can be a walking toward; the banished Philoctetes can be sought out and then courted. Savagery and spirituality fuse in a story used in *Recognitions*, Robert Louis Stevenson's "Olalla" (1885). The fusion is indicated in a poem, allegedly translated from Spanish, that the story quotes:

> Pleasure approached with pain and shame
> Grief with a wreath of lilies came.
>
> (Stevenson 1923, 341)

The character associated with Stevenson's story, Reverend Gwyon's kitchen girl Janet (Stevenson wrote another story called "Thrawn Janet") conveys another vital aspect of Gaddis—his belief that people with subtle, complicated minds can be tricked by simplicity. Janet is retarded and perhaps mad. At one point, she invites a neighbor's bull to mount her, following the example of King Minos's wife, Pasiphae, mother of the Minotaur. But this creature of animal frenzy will also provide one of the book's most tender moments: when she kisses Wyatt on his wounded cheek, she defines damnation as life without love, and she assures him that "no love is lost" (*R* 442). Janet is spanning classical and Christian myth. Just as Jesus thanked God for hiding "these things [important truths] from the wise and prudent" in favor of revealing them "unto babes" (Matt. 11:25), so can childish characters like Janet and Fuller speak wisdom.

Another reversal of expectation that brings some unsettling fun comes in the way characters have of sabotaging themselves. Just when Davidoff is about to be given the answer to a nagging problem, he changes the subject (*JR* 520). Later, a funeral director whose mortuary is about to merge with the multiconglomerate JR Family of Companies asks to meet JR. When the meeting does take place, Brisboy is too self-absorbed to notice what is going on. In *Gothic*, Paul Booth keeps interrupting his wife Elizabeth or changing the subject when she starts to answer a question or give him an important phone message. Telephones defeat him. Twice, help he desperately needs comes in a collect phone call. But each time he refuses to accept charges. He spurns this help because he lacks the imagination, the patience, and the kindness of heart to make room in his life for anyone else's needs. His caller is Elizabeth's best friend, Edie Grimes, the daughter of a business tycoon. Paul's narrowness has defeated him. Whereas he denies the well-connected Edie, he spends $265 on a floral bouquet for another girlhood friend of his wife who cannot help him at all.

As often happens in Gaddis, this truth emerges by steps. The steps can be hidden. Bypassing exposition, Gaddis will cut to the middle of an ongoing action and leave us to find our own way in. Characters may speak so excitedly or drunkenly that they bypass logical connections. An important passage may appear in a foreign language that Gaddis won't translate. Other key data may come to us in sentence fragments, shorthand ("Chs fmds lk clths" [*R* 351]), or in bold italics (*F* 470). Sometimes, Gaddis will run an obscure reference before us, daring us not to look it up, as if he expects it to mean as much to us as to him. This practice can be overdone, as in the scene in *Recognitions* where he invites us to disparage Otto for calling the little-known German philosopher Hans Vaihinger (1852–1933) "Vainiger" (120). Sometimes, he will report only part of a scene. He has Elizabeth tell her brother, "I wish you wouldn't smoke" (*CG* 3) without first describing Billy either taking out or lighting a cigarette. By eliminating the acts that prompted Elizabeth's rebuke, he's not only practicing good narrative selection and economy; he's hinting, too, at the richness of experience by indicating that he is only showing a part of it.

This part may assert its force glancingly, by chance references. It may also surprise us. Jack Gibbs says, "[I]f I wrote a novel it would end where most novels begin" (*JR* 248). He adds later, "[T]hat's what any book worth reading's about, problem solving" (499), a point that Gaddis repeated in his 1986 TV interview with Malcolm Bradbury. Perhaps the two ideas mesh. The notion that fictional endings introduce new tensions rather than easing existing ones can cause problems—for the reader, certainly, since it violates the contract which posterity has put in place, joining reader to writer. Eleventh-hour discoveries like Paul Booth's Jewishness and the existence of McCandless's son Jack show Gaddis introducing surprises to the end and, thus, refocusing the reader's attention. The same tactic appears in *JR*. A flurry of plotting in the book's last one hundred pages calls up repressed emotions, but without confronting them. A character has been shot and is expected to die. The shooting has been blamed on his wife. But Gaddis scuttles the dramatic potential of a criminal investigation. The plot tightens only briefly. Instead of developing the strife in Norman and Stella Angel's marriage that could have led to violence, Gaddis cuts to another room in the hospital where Norman is being treated. He shows a different patient, perhaps near death himself, discussing details of investment banking and stock sales. Why? Does the juxtaposition of scenes imply a link between the world of finance and Norman's gunshot wound (which turns out to have been self-inflicted)?

The question matters because it fuels the belief that truth in fiction can be reached by means other than continuity and closure. Rebelling against the liberal humanism, the coherence, and the stability of fictional tradition, fragmentation in Gaddis challenges usual notions of meaning. A bizarre cluster of images or a baffling juxtaposition of scenes may not unearth an answer. But it can suggest new ways in which answers may be approached. *JR* introduces some pornographic snapshots, the main subject of which looks like Norman Angel's secretary. Though the subject's identity is never confirmed, speculations about it stir the loins of several characters. Perhaps this psychodrama supersedes factual verification, since it heats so much blood. (It might have even prompted Norman Angel to shoot himself.) In *Recognitions*, mirror images leach reality away from the subjects being reflected, Gaddis's nonintegrative technique redefining boundaries between shadow and substance.

III

Johnston claims that "knowledge and the quest for truth and authenticity in *The Recognitions* are often subverted by madness, hallucination, and delirium" (1990, 161). This reading only applies to a few specific scenes. The shocking, the fantastic, and the unresolved all improve, rather than subvert, the chances for fulfillment. The welter of dismembered limbs in the novel imply the splintered, fragmented nature of reality. And reality must be taken on its disconnected terms to be understood. This disconnection makes its greatest impact on the inner planes of perception: Gaddis's leaning on the title of Henry James's *Turn of the Screw* (1898) for the only two chapters *The Recognitions* bestows titles upon conveys his belief in the shortcomings of reason. Just as James's governess killed her young charge Miles by tightening the screws of Puritanism on him, so does the relentless application of reason to impulse and intuition cause grief. The good tight fit gained by a screw whose head lies flush with the length of wood it has penetrated will cause splitting and splintering if forced below the surface; the length of wood will be ruined. The warning that it is unreasonable to rely too heavily on reason finds voice in Marie-Louise von Franz's *Alchemy: An Introduction to the Symbolism and the Psychology*. If the conscious mind craves clarity and precision, von Franz said, the unconscious traffics in paradox and mystery (1980, 156). Alchemy fascinates Gaddis because it probed levels of deep interaction where reason was secondary. The production of the philosopher's stone subsumed but also transcended reason. The redemption of matter was a psychological as well as a scientific procedure, the psyche projecting itself into the physical realm. Even the stars could influence the success of a procedure.

Because that procedure was not strictly mental nor material, it could only be conducted by means of a symbolism both confusing and arcane. Thus Gaddis, particularly in *Recognitions*, favors a narrative texture that is thick and messy with a good deal of spillover. Such a texture squares with his ontology. Jung has discussed the folly of arbitrarily imposing clean, consecutive discourse upon the kind of reality Gaddis is reaching towards— one that isn't only a show of externals but also a scumbling of depths, shadows, and puzzling alternatives:

> Oddly enough, the paradox is one of our most valuable spiritual possessions, while uniformity of meaning is a sign of weakness. [...] Only the paradox comes anywhere near to comprehending the fullness of life. Non-ambiguity and non-contradiction are one-sided and thus unsuited to express the incomprehensible. (Jung 1968, 16–17)

Perhaps Gaddis's clearest description of reality as a network of submerged activities that cling together, provided that they are looked at correctly, comes in Otto's story of a forged painting:

> It was a forged Titian that somebody had painted over another old painting, when they scraped the forged Titian away they found some worthless old painting underneath it, the forger had used it because it was an old canvas. But then there was something underneath that worthless painting, and they scraped it off and underneath that they found a Titian, a real Titian that had been there all the time. It was as though when the forger was working, and he didn't know the original was underneath, I mean he didn't know he knew it, but it knew, I mean something knew. (*R* 450–51)

The counterfeit can hide authenticity, and shreds of information can form patterns of knowledge. Probing in the right places will help us unearth the substance underlying accident, i.e., "the properties inherent in the substance which are perceived by the senses" (94). But probing isn't always necessary. A recognition can come unbidden. Wyatt talks about having spent a month in Switzerland in order to look at the Jungfrau. Yet the mountain remained hidden by clouds. Only as he stood on the railway platform waiting for his Paris-bound train did the mountain emerge from the clouds, "as though it had come from nowhere" (93). This emergence constitutes a recognition as valid as that created by the discovery of the Titian underlying two forgeries. Like the wisdom that can grace the simple and the ignorant more easily than it does the sophisticated, the shared world of ordinary experience offers miracles.

The knowledge that surfaces are not to be despised or ignored has led Gaddis to combine layered and compressed writing with straightforward discourse. Central to the outlook that governs his style is Otto's statement about the discovery of the Titian. Here is the heart of it: "I mean he [viz., the forger] didn't know he knew it, but it knew, *I mean something knew*" (emphasis added). Far from being a blind, sludgelike mass, the universe has acquired both consciousness and purpose. Material reality in Gaddis has a will of its own, proof of which is the way inanimate objects push into life. These objects are not passive, but kinetic, "forming their own network of intensities" (1982, 45), as Stephen-Paul Martin says. "The landscape is threatening because it insists on being itself" (47), Martin adds. We dismiss landscapes because we lack the mind-set to see that the objects on them contain features that bristle and drive out.

Our failure matters. While we're busy setting apart appearance from reality and also accident from substance, we have come under scrutiny ourselves. The threat Martin refers to is real. Subject and object have traded places. Wyatt's epiphany, or recognition, "I don't live, I'm ... I am lived" (*R* 262), shows perception as an act of creation rather than as one of merely passive recording. The paradox this view of perception entails no doubt pleased Gaddis: Wyatt grows by accepting his littleness; the world pulsates with new meanings as soon as he denies his centrality in it. Gaddis keeps before us the idea that our world consists of independent centers of significance. Some of them, he believes, have metaphysical properties. Speaking of the eccentric American author of *The Book of the Damned* (1919), Wyatt tells his wife, Esther, "Charles Fort says maybe we're fished for, by supercelestial beings" (*R* 87).[1] The notion of the fisherman being fished for goes well with Gaddis's description of the universe as a hall of mirrors in which shadow and substance can reverse and the searcher turn into that which is being sought. Our efforts both to know and save ourselves have been perhaps foiled by designs long entrenched.

To convey this irony, Gaddis mentions Izaak Walton's *Compleat Angler* (*R* 298); he quotes the statement, "Life as [*sic*] what happens to us while we are busy making other plans" (*JR* 486); he presents the following line of verse in *Carpenter's Gothic*: "While we wait for the napkin, the soup gets cold" (31). Rather than shaping events, Gaddis's people find themselves caught by forces beyond their control and sometimes their comprehension. They haven't fit themselves to reality. Gaddis dramatizes their plight in different ways. By keeping the chronology of his books vague and even elusive, he enacts some of the pressure of living amid guidelines and controls that cannot be seen or felt, let alone made sense of. The paradigms we use to interpret reality mirror each other more than they do a transcendent autonomy. At best, they serve as palimpsests for the God-quest that sends a McCandless all over the Southern Hemisphere. The following passage conveys so well the centricity of the unfathomable in life that Gaddis allegedly stopped the production of *Recognitions* after the book had gone to press in order to include it: "[N]o one has even begun to explain what happened at the dirt track in Langhorne, Pennsylvania about twenty-five years ago, when Jimmy Concannon's car threw a wheel, and in a crowd of eleven thousand it killed his mother" (566).

The occurrence of such a wildly improbable event suggests the working of large mystical and magical forces in the universe. Trying to capture this heaving, omniform world drama is like wrestling an invisible opponent without limbs. Wyatt claims that "every solution becomes an evasion" (96), and Jack Gibbs seconds this view by calling order "a thin, perilous condition we try to impose on the basic reality of chaos" (*JR* 20). The more we organize experience, the more we flatten it and drain its color. Any code is reductive. Messy, matted, and thickly textured, reality laughs at logic. Yet the artist is *supposed* to create patterns that make sense of the chaos within and without. As Basil Valentine says in *Recognitions*, "[T]he priest is the guardian of mysteries. The artist is driven to expose them" (261). Gaddis creates patterns of order by describing life as a Joycean "chaosmos," a system that both invites and resists meaning (Johnston 1990, 40, 130). Otto's statement, "somehow you get used to living among palimpsests" (*R* 599), helps explain the idea. The surface of life is pitted and scarred, impastoed and overlaid. Most of our lives is also lived in layers, with the projects, plans, and even selves by which we define ourselves in different states of readiness. But many of our projects and plans do get finished, even though the results do not always please us. Perhaps they needn't. Things that do not work out for the best will work out for the second best, and we are mostly content. The onion in Ibsen's *Peer Gynt*, a play referred to eight times in *Recognitions* (Moore 1982, 330), has no discernible core, but it's still tasty. *The Flying Dutchman*, mentioned six times in the book (Moore 1982, 337), may never reach home port, but it is still seaworthy. Appearances offer rewards, perhaps even to those searching for the substance underlying them; appearance interacts with substance.

The argument carries forward. Living contentedly among palimpsests recalls Keats's concept of negative capability. It is a taking on trust. What looks from our finite standpoint like incoherence and ambiguity teaches us that life defies explanations. Yet it runs fairly smoothly for the most part. Unfortunates like Jimmy Concannon's mother remind us that the horror is there, waiting all the time. A palimpsest is a monumental brass that has been reengraved on the reverse side. It is also a paper written on twice or more, the original script having been carelessly erased, so that some of it remains, forming an overlay design. The design is partly visible, just as our "chaosmos" will sometimes hint at its unity. Gaddis often uses parody to tease out this unity. Early in *Recognitions*, for instance, Gwyon's Aunt May dies soon after the destruction of her cherished hawthorn bush. Her death invokes Hawthorne's Beatrice Rappacinni, another woman identified with flora. But the invocation is ironical; Beatrice was young and beautiful, whereas Aunt May has dried into old age. Her pale, wasted looks, which recall Beatrice's scientist-father, will recur in her grandnephew, Wyatt, who is nearly as victimized by her as Beatrice was by her father Giacomo. This recurrence is richly suggestive. Wyatt's pinched pallor (Gaddis refers to his "knotted-up face" [866]), along with Aunt May's destructive innocence and the destroyer of her hawthorn bush, a pet ape, flood Hawthorne's 1844 story with wild new gleams. They also lend exciting depths to Gaddis's ideas about the drives infusing the artist's vision.

Elsewhere, the indirect revelation, perhaps grazed in a subordinate clause, outweighs realistic storytelling in Gaddis. Though the boundary between body and mind remains unfixed, it yields some answers. Wisdom can also be scratched along the edges of the palimpsest or buried inside life's bloat. The genius with which Gaddis has recovered hidden sources of vitality recalls that of the alchemist. Steven Weisenburger may be speaking home when he calls Gaddis "in many respects [...] the most disciplined writer of this generation" (1982, 13). It takes outstanding control to cope with intransigence, rarely, if ever, straining and often making us laugh. It's the rare novelist who sets himself such difficult work. The stubbornness of Gaddis's narrative materials could make him today's bravest writer, too.

Irradiating both his courage and his sense of humor is a healthy moral balance. All four of his novels open late in the year, imparting an autumnal awareness of missed chances and a waning of energy that winter's onset always brings. Yet entropy has not claimed all. Autumn provides splendors of her own, and, in another Keatsian parallel, they move us all the more for being savored in decline. The aura they impart remains. Koenig is right to say that *Recognitions* condemns "the entire modern world" (1975, 61). But the book, angry as it is, will relent in its condemnation. Just when it seems that Gaddis's venom will never let up, he strikes in with a touching, delicate insight. Though angry, he is not hostile. He can write with tenderness and lucidity about the human heart under stress. Basically, he shows good, decent people who sometimes go wrong when faced with the rigors of staying good and decent.

Their problems are aggravated by the disruption and abandonment careening through the novels. The first scene of *Recognitions*, in which displacement is a major trope, shows Gwyon and Camilla far from home. Suddenly, Camilla dies, leaving Gwyon a widower and Wyatt a motherless three-year-old. Most of the characters are also out of the country at book's end, perhaps inviting a catastrophe beyond that shown in the last paragraph, the death of a composer playing his own music in a cathedral that collapses on him. The homelessness motif recurs in *Carpenter's Gothic*, a novel whose people also spend a good deal of time abroad. Near the end, Billy Vorakers dies in a plane that is shot down over Africa. And as if his death has caused a virus of disaster within his family, his sister, Elizabeth, dies within a few days. This pattern also governs *JR*, with the absence of the Bast family head, James. James's absence robs his circle of its cohesiveness and stability. His two sisters leave Long Island, where they have lived for twenty years. A nervous breakdown sends James's son Edward to a hospital. Other woes ray out from family strife. JR lives with a mother who's rarely home (presumably because she's a nurse); her nonappearance in the book underscores his aloneness. Amy Joubert, Jack Gibbs, and later, Tom Eigen, all either separated or divorced, live away from *their* children. Nobody in the novel leads a happy, fulfilled life. Perhaps such a boon would not be recognized. Perhaps it would be sabotaged if it were. When Marion Eigen says that she wants a man "who's happy with what he's doing," she is told, "You're not asking much are you?" (*JR* 269). Both this retort and the upheaval surrounding it refer to Gaddis's childhood, which included seeing his parents divorce at age three and being sent to boarding school as a five-year-old (Moore 1989, ix).

The canon includes more shock waves of this trauma. Otto of *Recognitions*, Jack Gibbs and Freddie Moncrieff of *JR*, and Billy Vorakers,

Paul Booth, and Jack McCandless of *Gothic* all were sent to boarding school. The anxieties of childhood have stayed with Gaddis, just as they did with Dickens, Kipling, and Graham Greene. But if they darkened his outlook, they didn't twist it. He is self-referential without being self-absorbed. To find the past and work out its meaning, he has looked outward as well as in. And his vision takes strength from his extraordinary powers of observation and reflection. His oeuvre, which is both a survey and a critique of modern culture, stems from unremitting, ferocious work as well as vision. Products of excavation, cultivation, and careful tending, his books embody values that have been pondered and weighed. Though he condemns what has happened in our cities and suburbs, he shows little enthusiasm for the pagan, the primitive, and the raw. Neither does he put violence at the heart of things, extol blind faith over reason, or claim that only the mysterious can survive. He enjoys being on a level with life. Passages like the following express his delight in surfaces:

> The red glare in the alcove windows spread through the cold living room setting the walls ablaze with the sun's rise red on the river below, gleaming in the empty bottle and glass beside the wing chair. (*CG* 254)

He also appreciates both the heft and the pressure of things. This appreciation helps build a solid world, one that challenges our perceptions and makes us wonder which values to believe in. Resisting the conventions of plot, the world as he shows it conveys a mystery beyond art that he can only describe or explain in part. His people grope; they're at odds with both themselves and others; their most important relationships can crack without warning; a husband and three parents of leading characters all die during the six or eight weeks it takes *Frolic* to unfold. But something links Gaddis's people subtly and invisibly. Despite their fractiousness, their lives knit: Otto of *Recognitions* plans to dine with a father he has never met; Amy Joubert marries her father's junior partner in *JR*; in *Gothic* Mrs. McCandless drops in on an ex-husband she has not seen for two years; Oscar Crease of *Frolic* writes a play to mend fences between himself and a father he has not spoken to for years. Gaddis is keenly attentive to the complexities of motives, especially those governing the shaky peace between people living together like the di Cephalises in *JR* or the Booths in *Gothic*.

An important feature of Gaddis's vision consists of its ability to turn in on itself, a motif suggested by the self-consuming winged serpent, the ouroboros, which appears on the title page of *Recognitions*. Gaddis is one of today's most self-reflexive writers. His corpus makes up a four-volume *Song of Myself*, commenting, by turns affectingly and hilariously, on both itself and its author. His America, like Whitman's, is burgeoning. But it is also collapsing, most notably the Long Island suburb of *JR* that is being reabsorbed by nature at the same time it is joining the urban network. The novel's many images of disintegration and breakdown imply that this shuttling rhythm will end in rest and silence. At other times, it seems that Whitman's original energy, embodied by JR's boundless animal enthusiasm for money, will sustain and perhaps even redeem society. Recalling Flaubert's paradox that any author must be present everywhere but nowhere to be seen, the authorial self suffuses the Gaddis canon. And why not? Taking his lead from Whitman, Gaddis portrays America by portraying himself, an American like many of his readers and characters but more so, because of his zest for life, his creative vision, and his rhetorical genius. A microcosm within a macrocosm, he vibrates to the same rhythms that drive his countrymen. America already lies inside him, waiting to be encountered.

The process governing the encounter has already been outlined. John Kuehl and Steven Moore cite resemblances linking Gaddis to Gibbs, Gall, and Eigen, writers all, whom financial need drew to the worlds of business and media in *JR* (1–19). Along with the musicians Bast, these men enact the plight of the artist in postwar North America. Each must set aside his art to earn money until he wins a grant that frees him to do his creative work without distraction. (Edward Bast does win a grant but gets bilked out of the money that goes with it.)

Gaddis knows freedom. But having won a National Institute of Arts and Letters award (1963), two NEAs (1963 and 1974), a MacArthur Foundation Fellowship (1982), and a $50,000 Lannan Foundation lifetime achievement award (1993) has not quieted his anxiety. A character based on him called Willie appears briefly several times in *Recognitions*. The book Willie is writing about salvation replicates the one he appears in. Basil Valentine, after learning that it is based on both the Clementine *Recognitions* from the third century and Goethe's *Faust*, forecasts "a rather small audience" (373) for it. His phrase recurs at a party, where Willie, one of the guests, hears that he is either drunk or "writing for a very small audience" (478). *JR* also uses the phrase. Discussing the "important book" (417) that took him seven years to write and appeared in print, like *Recognitions*, without a dust-jacket photo, Tom Eigen cites "a very small audience" (417) as the reason the book is out of print. The wounds opened by the real-life decision this fictional event was based on have been slow healing. Using anagrams like *I Chose Rotten Gin*, *Ten Echoes Rioting*, and *The Tiger on Sonic*, *JR* reprints excerpts from some of the hostile reviews that helped sink *Recognitions* commercially, together with thinly veiled versions of the reviewers' names, viz., Glandvil Hix (Granville Hicks) and M. Axswill Gummer (Maxwell Geismar) (*JR* 515–16; Kuehl and Moore 1984, 18 n. 28).

Sarah Gaddis's novel *Swallow Hard* (1991) revives her father's phrase, "a small audience," along with some of the biographical trimmings surrounding it. Both of Lad Thompkins's long, difficult books lacked dust jacket photos and dedications; the dust jackets of both were printed in red, black, and gold. Winner of a Guggenheim grant and a National Book Award, the heavy-smoking Thompkins wrote speeches to support his family because his first book sold poorly and his second took twenty years to write. Then Thompkins describes one of his critics, a tracer of sources for his first book (based on Moore 1982), as "a man bent on having at least as small an audience as I do" (307). (For the origin of the title of *Swallow Hard*, see *JR* 650; also *F* 299, 454).

The opposition to serious writing that curtails the readership of a William Gaddis keeps stabbing out of *JR*: publicists try to smuggle advertising material into literary works without authors' permission; the publishing executives they work for resent the meager royalties they pay to authors; a Long Island school spends ten times as much money on paper towels than on books ("Books you don't know what you're getting into" [25]). By the time Gaddis wrote *Gothic*, his self-referentiality had lost some of its sting. Much of what remains of it is voiced through McCandless, a character (like Tom Eigen) with whom Gaddis first identifies and then withdraws from. Both McCandless and Gaddis are divorced fathers of about the same age; both are writers and polymaths who have lived abroad and know foreign languages; both share an interest in the past and have done some teaching (Gaddis at Bard College and the University of Connecticut). Did Gaddis use McCandless and Oscar Crease, who's teaching at a Long Island community college during the present-tense action of *Frolic*, to ask whether his artistic calling entitled him to freedoms forbidden to the rest of us?

An answer perhaps lies in the figure of Richard Wagner. Gaddis warmed to Wagner's self-concept as the great visionary artist whose revolutionary music dramas captured the soul of modern man. His own books, at once critiques of modern culture, treatises on fiction, and self-explorations, have a Wagnerian scope and resonance. Wagner's life may have touched Gaddis as vitally as his art. Both men appear to have undergone crises with women (as did McCandless); Gaddis divorced twice, and Wagner impregnated two women while they were married to other men. Both men worried about money and Wagner frequently slinked out of houses and even countries to escape creditors. His career is echoed in *JR* in James Bast's marriage to his brother's ex-wife (whom he may have impregnated while she was still wed to Thomas), in Bast's later jail term, and in the disheveled, ill-fitting clothes, financial woes, and cruelty of the writers Eigen and Gibbs.

Another thing: Wagner was short. Peter Burbage said of him, "In height he was diminutive, a trifle over five feet" (1979, 16). Though a full eight or nine inches taller, Gaddis identifies with this shortness; Dinitia Smith, who interviewed him in 1993, called him "small" (1994, 40). He appears in *Recognitions* both as "Willie," a diminutive term, and as Wyatt, whose initials he shares and whose littleness he highlights by contrasting it with the bulk of Wyatt's father, Reverend Gwyon. The motif resurfaces in *JR*, whose eponym may not have been short, even though, as an eleven-year-old, he stands much lower than the adults he deals with most of the way. Gaddis may have felt the same kinship with him that he felt with Wyatt; the victim always feels small and weak alongside his large, powerful persecutors. But his disadvantages have taught him how to cope, as they did Wagner's Alberich. Whereas the adults in *JR* get easily distracted, JR focuses his attention. But he builds most of his dynasty while out of view. The acquisition of managerial skills has hamstrung Gaddis as well as him. Both his powers of concentration and the solitude he needs to transact the deals that earn him millions make him a poor novelistic subject. JR's frequent presence would clash with Gaddis's social criticism, since he's antisocial. In his single-mindedness, he forfeits those activities that help promote normal, healthy growth in youngsters his age. Self-denial as a function of worldly success is also a theme running through Wyatt's life. Both in Paris and New York, Wyatt avoids other artists and their hangouts in order to learn how to paint. And learn he does, as does JR, who, with each succeeding appearance, speaks more persuasively about high-level finance. So well does he do his job that he nearly becomes one with it. Discussing his polymorphic JR Family of Companies with him, someone says, "[T]here isn't any inside," adding, "[T]he only inside's the one inside your head" (644). Ironically, JR the runny-nosed latchkey child acquires a multiconglomerate because he lacks the warmth of friends and family. Like Alberich, who steals the Rheingold in Wagner and whose role he plays in a school production, he settles for gold; he'd have preferred love. And Alberich is, advisedly, a dwarf.

Perhaps Gaddis's long, difficult books also represent a second choice; writing and then publishing a big book could compensate for being, or feeling, small. He broke into print between boards as a novelist, not a short story writer, and he did so with a 956-page tome. Only after winning several literary prizes and being inducted into the American Institute of Arts and Letters did he write a novel of average (262 pages) length. The two earlier books whose great size fueled his demand to be noticed and appreciated invoke Alfred Adler's doctrine of masculine protest. Just as Napoleon used imperial conquest to compensate for his littleness, so did Gaddis's need to prove himself lead him to write books of outstanding length and difficulty. But he also saw the benefits of littleness. By making extraordinary demands on himself, he could confirm his pawn status as a wellspring of creativity.

This psychological reading of Gaddis gains force from his daughter Sarah's *Swallow Hard*. Lad Thompkins is "not tall or imposing" (26), and both of his names evoke smallness and immaturity. What's more, he seems to view himself as small. He claims twice (17, 54) that another man wears lifts, or platform heels. This claim is revealing. Only a man who would like to be taller than he is would notice, let alone comment on, another's attempts to add inches to his height.

Inches of another kind enrich the picture. On the desk of a Wall Street executive's office in *JR* lies a copy of Ernest Hemingway's *A Moveable Feast* (205). The book is cracked open to page 190, the place where Hemingway, after having Scott Fitzgerald drop his shorts, tells him that his penis isn't small, as his wife Zelda had claimed. Gaddis alluded to the dropped-shorts episode to puncture arrogance. The copy of Hemingway's book that Edward Bast glances at belongs to Crawley, a racist and a macho-talking killer of animals. Despite his posturing, Crawley, who calls Africa "nothing but a lot of niggers driving around in hats and neckties" (*JR* 204), might be harboring painful self-doubts—like Hemingway himself, the target of some ridicule in *Recognitions*. But Gaddis isn't through with penises. A young woman who is handling the uncircumcised Edward Bast's in a bubble bath mentions "this little wart under here" (*JR* 550).

Carpenter's Gothic contains a similar moment. While making love to McCandless, Elizabeth asks, "What's [...] this little place, it's like there was a little scab" (162). Gaddis's attentiveness to penises is intriguing. Do his readers symbolize for him the adult world of his parents that stowed him in a boarding school at age five, patronized him during the long years when *Recognitions* remained unfinished and unpublished, and then ignored the book? If we do, then his revenge is apt. He has tricked us into looking at his prick. Like McCandless and Bast, he has taken the controlling masculine role, forcing us into the more passive female one. In view of the homophobic undercurrent in *Recognitions*, the implications of this show of power is clear. But they are also smudged. Gaddis is too honest to enjoy his schoolboy prank. McCandless's jittery answer to Elizabeth, "Good God, I don't know what it is, it's a battle scar, laid out here like one of your grasshoppers pinned on a board" (*CG* 162), shows an anxiety Gaddis may share. Having just enjoyed intercourse with Elizabeth, McCandless should feel mellow. But his allusion to Eliot's Prufrock both jades his mellowness and blunts the cutting edge of Gaddis's revenge. Perhaps it shatters revenge altogether. If a harmless question makes McCandless see himself as an insect wriggling on a pin, then revenge has moved out of reach. We can never redress childhood wrongs.

NOTE

1. For further information on Fort, see Moore 1982, 111.

Chronology

1922	William Gaddis is born on December 29 in Manhattan.
1925	Parents divorce and he lives with his mother.
1941	Begins studying at Harvard University.
1943	Joins staff of the *Lampoon*.
1944	Becomes president of the *Lampoon* staff.
1945	Leaves Harvard without a degree.
1945	Works at the *New Yorker* as a fact checker.
1947	Spends the next five years traveling throughout Latin America, Europe and North Africa, and begins work on *The Recognitions*.
1955	Publishes his first novel, *The Recognitions*. Marries Pat Black.
1957	Works in several fields, including public relations and corporate speech writing, and begins work on *JR*.
1962	*The Recognitions* published in England.
1963	Receives National Institute of Arts and Letters grant.
1967	Teaches a class in Creative Writing at the University of Connecticut. He and Pat Black are divorced. Marries Judith Thompson. Receives National Endowment for the Arts grant.
1974	Receives second National Endowment for the Arts grant.
1975	*JR* published.
1976	Wins the National Book Award. *JR* published in England.

1977	Distinguished visiting Professor at Bard College.
1981	Receives a Guggenheim fellowship.
1982	Receives a MacArthur Foundation Fellowship.
1984	Inducted into the American Academy and Institute of Arts and Letters.
1985	*Carpenter's Gothic* published along with reissues of his first two novels. Earns nomination for PEN/Faulkner Award for *Carpenter's Gothic*.
1986	*Carpenter's Gothic* published in England.
1994	Publishes *A Frolic of His Own*. Receives the National Book Award.
1995	Receives the National Book Critics' Circle Award for *A Frolic of His Own*.
1998	Dies December 16 of prostate cancer.
2002	*Agape, Agape* published.

Contributors

HAROLD BLOOM is Sterling Professor of the Humanities at Yale University and Henry W. and Albert A. Berg Professor of English at the New York University Graduate School. He is the author of over 20 books, including *Shelley's Mythmaking* (1959), *The Visionary Company* (1961), *Blake's Apocalypse* (1963), *Yeats* (1970), *A Map of Misreading* (1975), *Kabbalah and Criticism* (1975), *Agon: Toward a Theory of Revisionism* (1982), *The American Religion* (1992), *The Western Canon* (1994), and *Omens of Millennium: The Gnosis of Angels, Dreams, and Resurrection* (1996). *The Anxiety of Influence* (1973) sets forth Professor Bloom's provocative theory of the literary relationships between the great writers and their predecessors. His most recent books include *Shakespeare: The Invention of the Human* (1998), a 1998 National Book Award finalist, *How to Read and Why* (2000), and *Genius: A Mosaic of One Hundred Exemplary Creative Minds* (2002). In 1999, Professor Bloom received the prestigious American Academy of Arts and Letters Gold Medal for Criticism, and in 2002 he received the Catalonia International Prize.

JOSEPH S. SALEMI teaches humanities at New York University, and classics at Hunter College and Brooklyn College, CUNY. He has translated the works of the fifteenth-century French mystic Jean Gerson, and his poetry has appeared in different anthologies including *Studies in Poetry*.

SUSAN STREHLE KLEMTNER is Professor of English at the State University of New York at Binghamton. She has published articles on Gaddis, Barth, Heller, Gardner, Nabokov and Pynchon in such journals as *Critique, Modern Fiction Studies* and *Contemporary Literature*.

JOHN Z. GUZLOWSKI is Professor of English at Eastern Illinois University and an established poet. His writing has appeared in such journals as *Markham Review*, *Journal of Evolutionary Psychology*, and *Critique*.

MIRIAM FUCHS is Associate Professor of English at the University of Hawai'i at Mānoa. Her writing on Modern Literature includes articles on Hart Crane, Djuna Barnes, and Coleman Dowell in such journals as *The Hollins Critic* and *The Review of Contemporary Fiction*.

STEPHEN H. MATANLE is Associate Professor of English at the University of Baltimore. His study of Gaddis' novel *JR* was included in the anthology *In Recognition of William Gaddis*, and his poetry and fiction have appeared in *The Georgia Review* and *Poetry*.

ELAINE B. SAFER is Professor of English at the University of Delaware. Her literary focus has been on the American comic novel and the works of John Milton, and her essays have appeared in *Studies in the Novel*, *Critique*, *Milton Studies*, and *Milton Quarterly*.

STEVEN MOORE has been an associate editor of the *Review of Contemporary Fiction*. His essays have appeared in *Critique*, *Pynchon Notes*, and *The Review of Contemporary Fiction*, and he is the author of *A Reader's Guide to William Gaddis's "The Recognitions"* and *William Gaddis*.

JOHN JOHNSTON is Professor of English at Emory University and has been an essayist and scholar of contemporary American literature. He is the author of *Carnival of Repetition: Gaddis's* The Recognitions *and Postmodern Theory*.

JONATHAN RABAN is a British writer living in the United States. His most recent books are *Bad Land* (1996), *Passage to Juneau* (1999), and the novel *Waxwings* (2003).

CHRISTOPHER J. KNIGHT is Professor of American Literature at the University of Montana. He is the author of *The Patient Particulars: American Modernism and the Technique of Originality*, as well as articles on Gertrude Stein, Woody Allen, and Ernest Hemingway.

PETER WOLFE is a member of the English faculty at the University of Missouri-St. Louis. He is the author of *Dreamers Who Live Their Dreams: The World of Ross Macdonald's Novels*, and *Something More Than Night: The Case of Raymond Chandler*.

Bibliography

Aldridge, John W. *The American Novel and the Way We Live Now*. New York: Oxford University Press (1983): 46–52.

Auchincloss, Louis. "Recognizing Gaddis." *New York Times Magazine*. 15 November: 36, 38, 41, 54, 58.

Bakker, J. "The End of Individualism." *Dutch Quarterly Review of Anglo–American Letters* 7 (1977): 286–304.

Balazy, Teresa. "A Recognition of *The Recognitions*." *Traditions in the Twentieth Century American Literature*. Ed. Marta Sienicka. Poznan, Poland: Adam Mickiewicz University Press (1981): 23–33.

Banning, Charles Leslie. "William Gaddis' *JR:* The Organization of Chaos and the Chaos of Organization." *Paunch* 42/43 (1975): 153–65.

Benstock, Bernard. "On William Gaddis; In Recognition of James Joyce." *Wisconsin Studies in Contemporary Literature* 6 (Summer 1965): 177–89.

Berkley, Miriam. "PW Interviews William Gaddis." *Publisher's Weekly*, (July 12, 1985): 56–57.

Black, Joel Dana. "The Paper Empires and Empirical Fictions of William Gaddis." *Review of Contemporary Fiction* 2 (Summer): 22–31.

Comnes, Gregory. *The Ethics of Indeterminacy in the Novels of William Gaddis*. Gainesville: University Press of Florida, 1994.

Durand, Regis. "On Conversing: In/On Writing." *Su-Stance*, no. 27 (1980). 47–51.

Eckley, Grace. "Exorcising the Demon Forgery, or the Forging of Pure Gold in Gaddis's *Recognitions*." *Literature and the Occult: Essays in Comparative*

Literature, ed. Luanne France. Arlington: University of Texas Press, 1977.

Gregson, David E. "*The Recognitions.*" *Survey of Contemporary Literature*, ed. Frank N. Magill. Englewood Cliffs: Salem Press, 1977.

Grove, Lloyd. "Harnessing the Power of Babble: The Rich, Comic, Talkative Novels of William Gaddis." *Washington Post.* (August 23, 1985): B1, B10.

Johnston, John. *Carnival of Repetition: Gaddis's* The Recognitions *and Postmodern Theory*. Philadelphia: University of Pennsylvania Press, 1990.

Karl, Frederick. "Gaddis: A Tribune of the Fifties." *In Recognition of William Gaddis*, eds. John Kuehl and Steven Moore. Syracuse: Syracuse University Press, 1984.

Kermode, Frank. *The Sense of an Ending: Studies in the Theory of Fiction*. London: Oxford University Press, 1967.

Lathrop, Kathleen L. "Comic-Ironic Parallels in William Gaddis's *The Recognitions.*" *Review of Contemporary Fiction* 2 (Summer, 1982): 32–40.

Lawrence, D.H. *Studies in Classic American Literature*. New York: Viking Press, 1964.

LeClair, Tom. *The Art of Excess: Mastery in Contemporary Fiction*. Urbana: University of Illinois Press, 1989.

Madden, David. "On William Gaddis's *The Recognitions.*" *Rediscoveries*, ed. David Madden. New York: Crown Press, 1971.

Moore, Steven. "Chronological Difficulties in the Novels of William Gaddis." *Critique* 22 (1980): 79–91.

——— "'Parallel, Not Series': Thomas Pynchon and William Gaddis." *Pynchon Notes* 11 (February 1983): 6–26.

Ozick, Cynthia. "William Gaddis and the Scion of Darkness." *Metaphor and Memory*. New York: Knopf Press, 1989: 16–22.

Reed, John. *Prelude to Chemistry: An Outline of Alchemy*. Cambridge: MIT Press, 1966.

Safer, Elaine B. *The Contemporary American Comic Epic: The Novels of Barth, Pynchon, Gaddis, and Kesey*. Detroit: Wayne State University Press, 1988.

Sawyer, Tom. "False Gold to Forge: The Forger Behind Wyatt Gwyon." *Review of Contemporary Fiction* 2 (Summer, 1982): 50–54.

——— "*JR:* The Narrative of Entropy." *International Fiction Review 10*, No. 2 (Summer, 1983): 117–22.

Schaber, Steven C. "*JR.*" *Masterplots 1976 Annual.* Ed. Frank N. Magill. Englewood Cliffs: Salem Press, 1977: 151–53.

Stark, John. "William Gaddis, Just Recognition." *The Hollin's Critic* 14, No. 2 (April 1977): 1–12.

Stathis, James J. "William Gaddis: *The Recognitions.*" *Critique* 5 (Winter 1962–63): 91–94.

Stonehill, Brian. *The Self-Conscious Novel: Artifice in Fiction from Joyce to Pynchon.* Philadelphia: University of Pennsylvania Press, 1988.

Strehle, Susan. *Fiction in the Quantum Universe.* Chapel Hill: University of North Carolina Press, 1992.

Tabbi, Joseph. "The Compositional Self in William Gaddis's *JR.*" *Modern Fiction Studies* 35 (Winter 1989): 655–70.

Tanner, Tony. *City of Words: American Fiction 1950–1970.* New York: Harper & Row, 1971: 393–400.

Thielemans, Johan. "Gaddis and the Novel of Entropy." *TREMA* 2 (1977). 97–107.

Towers, Robert. "No Justice, Only Law." *New York Times Book Review* 9 (January 1994): 1, 22.

Waite, Arthur Edward. *The Secret Tradition of Alchemy.* London: Stuart and Watkins Press, 1969.

Weisenburger, Steven. "Contra Naturam? Usury in William Gaddis's *JR.*" *Money Talks: Language and Lucre in American Fiction*, ed. Roy R. Male. Norman: University of Oklahoma Press, 1981: 93–110.

Wertheim, Larry M. "Law as Frolic: Law and Literature in *A Frolic of His Own.*" *William Mitchell Law Review* 21 (1995): 424–56.

Werner, Craig Hansen. *Paradoxical Resolutions: American Fiction Since James Joyce.* Urbana: University of Illinois Press, 1982: 165–81.

Acknowledgments

"To Soar in Atonement: Art as Expiation in Gaddis' *The Recognitions*" by Joseph S. Salemi. From *Novel: A Forum On Fiction* 10, no. 2, (Winter 1977): 127–136. © 1977 by *Novel: A Forum On Fiction*. Reprinted by permission.

"'For a Very Small Audience': The Fiction of William Gaddis" by Susan Strehle Klemtner. From *Critique: Studies in Modern Fiction* XIX, no. 3, (1978): 61–73. Reprinted with permission of the Helen Dwight Reid Educational Foundation. Published by Heldref Publications, 1319 Eighteenth St., NW, Washington, DC 20036-1802. Copyright © 1978.

"No More Sea Changes: Hawkes, Pynchon, Gaddis, and Barth" by John Z. Guzlowski. From *Critique: Studies in Modern Fiction* XXIII, no. 2, (Winter 1981–82): 48–60. Reprinted with permission of the Helen Dwight Reid Educational Foundation. Published by Heldref Publications, 1319 Eighteenth St., NW, Washington, DC 20036-1802. Copyright © 1981.

"'*il miglior fabbro*': Gaddis' Debt to T.S. Eliot" by Miriam Fuchs. From *In Recognition of William Gaddis*, eds. John Kuehl and Steven Moore (1984): 92–105. © 1984 by Syracuse University Press. Reprinted by permission.

"Love and Strife in William Gaddis' *JR*" by Stephen Matanle. From *In Recognition of William Gaddis*, eds. John Kuehl and Steven Moore (1984): 106–118. © 1984 by Syracuse University Press. Reprinted by permission.

"Ironic Allusiveness and Satire in William Gaddis's *The Recognitions*" by Elaine B. Safer. From *The Contemporary American Comic Epic: The Novels of Barth, Pynchon, Gaddis, and Kesey* (1989): 11–137. © 1989 by Wayne State University Press. Reprinted by permission.

"*Carpenter's Gothic*; or, The Ambiguities" by Steven Moore. From *William Gaddis* (1989): 112–135, © 1989 by Twayne Publishers. Reprinted by permission of The Gale Group.

"Toward Postmodern Fiction" by John Johnston. From *Carnival of Repetition: Gaddis's* The Recognitions *and Postmodern Theory*, (1990): 183–214. © 1990 by University of Pennsylvania Press. Reprinted by permission of the University of Pennsylvania Press.

"At Home in Babel" by Jonathan Raban. From *The New York Review of Books* XLI, no. 4, (February 17, 1994): 3–4, 6. © 1994 by Jonathan Raban. Reprinted by permission of the author.

"*A Frolic of His Own:* Whose Law? Whose Justice?" by Christopher J. Knight. From *Hints and Guesses: William Gaddis's Fiction of Longing*, (1997): 201–239. © 1997 by The Board of Regents of the University of Wisconsin System. Reprinted by permission of the University of Wisconsin Press.

"The Importance of Being Negligible" by Peter Wolfe. From *A Vision of His Own: The Mind and Art of William Gaddis*, (1997): 15–51, © 1997 by Associated University Presses, Inc. Reprinted by permission.

Index

Abish, Walter, 1
Accidents, 25–26, 166, 223
Ace Worldwide Fidelity Insurance, 181
Actualism, 223
Adler, Alfred, 255
African episodes, 114
After the Great Divine: Modernism, Mass Culture, Postmodernism (Huyssen), 134, 159
Agnes Deigh *(The Four Quartets)*, 54–55, 72
Aichele, Gary J., 176, 216
The Ainu. *see* Harry Lutz *(A Frolic of His Own)*
Alchemy
   alchemical laboratories, 98
   allusions to, 83–87, 223
   as cultural experience, 235–236
   levels of deep interaction, 246
   pursuit of gold, 83–84
   repudiation of, 234
Alchemy: An Introduction to the Symbolism and the Psychology (Franz), 246
Alchemy (Burckhardt), 85, 98
"Alchemy" (Shumaker), 85, 98
Alfred Bell & Co. v. Catalda Fine Arts, Inc., 187
Allert *(Death, Sleep & the Traveler)*, 31–34
Alternative Worlds (Kuehl), 222–223
Ambiguity, 104, 117, 121–122
American Fictions 1940–1980 (Karl), 74, 96, 141, 160

Amy Joubert *(JR)*
   Edward Bast and, 62
   Elizabeth Booth compared to, 116
   Esme compared to, 65
   ethics of, 207
   Jack Gibbs and, 58, 144, 227
   JR and, 26, 68
   reference theory of language, 64–65
   sack of coins, 25
   teaches to be worthwhile, 27
Ancilla to the Pre-Socratic Philosophers (Empedocles), 60, 69
Ann diCephalis *(JR)*, 61
Anne Bast *(JR)*, 27, 64, 145–146
"The Anonymous Self: A Defensive Humanism" (Sypher), 129
Anouilh, Jean, 167
Antigone (Anouilh), 167, 176
Anti-Oedipus (Deleuze and Guattari), 148, 161–162
Apocalypse genre, 109–110
Aporias (Derrida), 215
Approaching Postmodernism (Fokkema and Bertens, eds.), 128, 158
Arendt, Hannah, 174
Arnie Munk *(The Recognitions)*, 116–117
Arnold, Matthew, 224
Arnstein v. Porter, 187
Art and artists
   affirming and denying conditions of, 222
   artists seek to escape laws, 212

as connection with inner self, 37–38
as expiation, 3–14
Flemish, 18, 76, 86, 99
Judge Crease and, 193
metaphysical significance of, 19, 247, 248
originality and novelty of, 188
in postwar North America, 129, 252
reality and, 4, 6–7, 96, 241
Titian, 224
upheavals from, 240–241
as worthy activity, 21, 27–28, 85
"At Home in Babel" (Raban), 163–172, 204
At Swim-Two-Birds (O'Brien), 117
Atkins, Stuart, 100
Auden, W. H., 31, 41
Augustine, St., 1
Aunt May *(The Recognitions)*, 236, 249
Autobiographical writing, 119

Babel, story of, 65
Bagby *(A Frolic of His Own)*, 167
Bakhtin, Mikhail, 145, 156, 161
Barth, John, 32, 39–40, 130
"Bartleby the Scrivener" (Melville), 115
Basie. *see* Harold Basie *(A Frolic of His Own)*
Basil Valentine *(The Recognitions)*
  on artists and mysteries, 248
  on *Clementine Recognitions*, 77–78
  forecasts small audience, 252
  on pious cult, 233
  Recktall Brown and, 84–85
  Valentinus as basis for, 76, 84–85
  Wyatt and, 10–11, 13
Bast, Anne *(JR)*, 27, 64, 145–146
Baudrillard, Jean, 138–139, 160
Bazin, Germain, 5, 15
Beckett, Samuel, 135, 220
Benny *(The Recognitions)*, 95
Benstock, Bernard, 17, 29, 80, 98
Bergson, Henri, 81, 98

Berlin, Isaiah, 225
Bertens, Hans, 128, 133, 158, 159
Bibbs. *see* Elizabeth Booth *(Carpenter's Gothic)*
Bible, 110, 112, 113, 155, 165, 178, 196
Biddle, Francis, 176, 216
Bigotry, 177, 200–201
Billy Vorakers *(Carpenter's Gothic)*
  on Bibbs' secret self, 150–151
  death of, 103, 239, 250
  Elizabeth Booth and, 102, 103, 114, 149, 239
Black, Joel Dana, 140, 160
Black and White Taxi Co. case, 192
Black humor
  accidents portrayed with, 25
  Brown and Fuller, 90
  despair portrayed with, 21–23
  in failures of recognition, 19–20
  from frustrated desire, 99
  Gaddis' vision of, 18
  Gibbs and Bast, 144
  of Gogol, 72–73
  killing and canonization of little girl, 80–81, 82
  mummy scene, 82–83
  name Stephen Asche as, 80
  new creative principle found in, 129
  overview, 131–132
  from reducing empirical realities, 144
  suicide or death argument, 75
  water separating father and son, 79
  Wyatt and Brown's contract, 89–90
Black poodle, 90–91
Bleak House (Dickens), 114
"A Bleak Vision of Gothic America" (Busch), 114, 124
Bloom, Harold, 1–2, 259
Boarding school, 250–251
Bolt, Robert, 167
Book of Revelation, 110, 112, 113
The Book of the Damned (Fort), 247
Book Review Digest, 96
Booth *(Carpenter's Gothic)*. *see* Elizabeth Booth; Paul Booth

Borges, Jorge Luis, 135
Bosch, Hieronymus, 10, 13, 91, 94
Bouts, Dirc, 76
Bradbury, Malcolm, 71, 95, 129, 158, 228, 244
Brisboy *(JR)*, 243
Broch, Hermann, 235
Brothers Karamazov (Dostoyevsky), 236
Buell, Lawrence, 97
Bunker *(A Frolic of His Own)*, 208
Burbage, Peter, 254
Burckhardt, Titus, 85, 98
Burgoyne, John, 232
"Burnt Norton" (Eliot), 51, 53
Burroughs, William Seward, 130, 158
Busch, Frederick, 114, 124

Camilla Gwyon *(The Recognitions)*
   canonization of, 80, 82, 95
   death of, 46, 80, 97, 250
   earrings of, 50–51, 239
   procession in San Zwingli, 88
   reincarnation of, 48
   spirit unifies living and dead, 50–52
   Wyatt and, 79, 80, 97
Camus, Albert, 79, 86, 97, 129, 176, 186
Cannibals All! (Fitzhugh), 177
Cantos (Pound), 8
Capitalism, 161–162, 175
Carlyle, Thomas, 221
Carnegie, Dale, 95, 101
Carpenter's Gothic
   African episodes, 114
   ambiguous times, 101–102
   anachronism in, 106, 124
   apocalypse, hopeful and despairing, 109–110
   Aristotelian unities, 106
   author as recording apparatus, 149, 150
   "cloistral" fiction, 106, 115
   corruption of American dream, 230
   fundamentalists, 108, 110, 121
   as Greek drama, 114–115
   as Harlequin romance, 111–112, 151–152
   homeless motif, 250
   the house, 105–106, 152
   JR compared to, 116–117, 149
   lies in, 155
   as metafiction, 117–124
   minor fictions in, 155–156
   nature and production of fictions, 117
   NYC as ugly and self-defeating, 232
   objective vs. subjective writing, 118–119
   philosophic conflict in, 104
   postmodernism of, 149–156
   Pythian Mining, 117
   questions without answers, 101–102
   reader's responsibilities, 228
   realistic portraiture of characters, 164
   The Recognitions compared to, 116–117
   satire of social structure, 71–72
   suicide in, 234
   symmetry of, 106–107
   synopsis, 102–104, 106, 149
   titles for, alternate, 111, 119
   Vietnam War, 115–116
Carpenter's Gothic characters. *see also* Billy Vorakers; Elizabeth Booth; McCandless; Paul Booth
   Chigger, 115
   Edie Grimes, 165
   F R Vorakers, 102
   Frank Kinkead, 117
   Lester, 104, 117, 120, 122–123
   Madame Socrate, 164
   McCandless' son, 239
   Reverend Elton Ude, 102, 104, 109–110, 149
   Senator Teakell, 103, 153
"*Carpenter's Gothic*; or, The Ambiguities" (Moore), 101–124
"Carpenter's Gothic" (Toney), 122, 125
"Carpenter's Gothic" (Warren), 119, 125

Catalda Fine Arts, Inc., Alfred Bell & Co. v., 187
Catch-22 (Heller), 129
Catholicism, 196, 201, 236
Catton, Bruce, 171
Chaby Sinisterra *(The Recognitions)*, 81
Chaos
   controlled, 169–170
   as reality of *JR*, 20, 22–26, 57–69, 141, 144–145, 248
   in *The Recognitions*, 19, 94–95, 118
   verbal clutter, 236–237
Chapsal, Madeleine, 129, 158
Characters. *see also specific characters by first name*
   as body parts, 62–63
   forces beyond their control, 248
   hallucinatory realism of, 226
   idea of in fiction, 222
   include writers writing, 118, 123, 241
   injured egos go to court, 166
   lack dignity, 8, 95
   levels of identification of, 226
   lives knit in spite of differences, 251
   make up parts of their lives, 155
   metaphysical and earthly, 13–14
   names of, 226–227
   powerful, fleshy presence, 163–164
   resist help, talk to themselves, 239
   sabotage themselves, 243–244
   scathing to themselves, 220–221
   self-enhancement of, 239–242
   separation from selves and others, 57, 61, 66–69
   severed from their origins, 45, 48, 241
   timeless knowledge of, 54–55
   weak heroes, 224
Chigger *(Carpenter's Gothic)*, 115
Christianity, 108, 110, 243
Christina Crease *(A Frolic of His Own)*
   conception of the artist, 212
   death of husband, 176
   ethic of love, 208–209
   Harold Basie and, 208–210
   on Judge Crease, 196
   justice of the heart, 206–210
   Oscar and, 209–210, 211, 214
   on Oscar's childhood, 196
   as proponent of ethics, 207
   Walden Pond and, 171–172, 212
City of Words: American Fiction, 1950–1970 (Tanner), 42, 48, 56, 87, 96, 99
Clair, Tom Le, 222
Clementine of Rome, Saint, 97
Clementine Recognitions, 76–83
   predecessor of *The Recognitions*, 1, 74
   synopsis, 77–78
   title of *The Recognitions* from, 76
"Cloistral" fiction, 106, 115
Coach Vogel *(JR)*, 25
Coen *(JR)*, 64
Coercion vs. oppression, 200
Collected Poems 1909-1962 (Eliot), 43, 56
The Columbia Literary History of the United States (Elliott, ed.), 129, 158
Comedy, 19–20, 95, 165, 221
Comic Terror: The Novels of John Hawkes (Greiner), 32, 33, 41, 42
"Comic-Ironic Parallels in William Gaddis's *The Recognitions*" (Lathrop), 75, 97
The Common Law (Holmes), 193
Communal systems, 200
Communication, 163–172
   conversational fragments, 63–66, 172, 226
   in *The Crying of Lot 49* (Pynchon), 34
   deepens fear of love, 239
   language, tension within, 145, 226
   loss of, 23–24, 78, 143, 161
   money speaking, 147–148
   reality as, 148
   in relationships, 208–209
   speech and personality, 223
   by telephone, 66–67, 147, 235, 243–244
Comnes, Gregory, 163, 234, 238

Compassion vs. money, 26, 207
Compleat Angler (Walton), 248
The Complete Works of Nathanael West, 110, 124
The Confidence Man (Melville), 109, 110
Congressman Pecci *(JR)*, 26
Conrad, Joseph, 114, 123
Consciousness, 251–252. *see also* unconscious
Conversations of Goethe with Eckermann and Soret, 89, 99
Coover, Robert, 132
Copyright law, 185–191
The Corrections (Franzen), 2
The Counterfeiters (Kenner), 134, 159
Counterfeiting, 81, 95
Counterfeits vs. values, 96, 233
Crawley *(JR)*, 255
Crease. *see* Christina Crease; Oscar Crease *(A Frolic of His Own)*
Creationist trial in Smackover, 108
The Crito (Plato), 176, 215
Cruden's *Concordance*, 117
The Crying of Lot 49 (Pynchon), 2, 31, 34–36
Cyclone Seven sculpture, 165, 167–168

"Dad" diCephalis *(JR)*, 61
Dan diCephalis *(JR)*, 25, 61, 66
Darconville's Cat (Theroux), 107, 124
Darwin, Charles, 234
Davidoff *(JR)*, 241–242, 243
The Day of Doom (Wigglesworth), 109
The Day of the Locust (West), 110, 124
"The Dead" (Joyce), 211, 216
"*Dead Souls:* The Mirror and the Road" (Fanger), 73, 96
Dead Souls (Gogol), 71, 72, 95
Death. *see also* Camilla Gwyon
  alive or dead equated, 96
  character's responses to, 22, 44
  Elizabethan meaning of, 113–114
  in *A Frolic of His Own*, 213–216
  Hawkes' coma/rebirth scene, 32
  talk equated with, 239
Death, Sleep & the Traveler (Hawkes), 31–34, 41
Death of a Salesman (Miller), 73
The Death of Satan (Delbanco), 174, 216
Delbanco, Andrew, 174, 216
Deleuze, Giles, 136, 137, 139–140, 148, 157, 160, 161–162
Derrida, Jacques, 173, 215
Deterritorialization, 148, 161–162
Diary of a Mad Housewife (Kaufman), 101
Dickens, Charles, 114, 220, 226, 228
"Differance" (Derrida), 137–138, 160
Différence et répétition (Deleuze), 137, 157, 160, 162
Discourse, 19, 235
"Discourse in the Novel" (Bakhtin), 145, 156, 161
The Discourse of Modernism (Reiss), 128, 158
Dispatches (Herr), 116, 124
Donaldson, James, 76, 78, 97
Dostoyevsky, Fyodor, 221, 226, 236
Douglas, William, 217
Doves, 114, 224
Downey v. General Foods Corp., 185
Dr. Weisgall, 54–55
Draws on earlier writings, 74
"The Dry Salvages" (Eliot), 52, 53–54
"Dryad in a Dead Oak Tree: The Incognito in *The Recognitions*" (Seelye), 80, 97
Durang, See v., 187
Dworkin, Ronald, 174

Early Netherlandish Painting (Panofsky), 76, 97
"East Coker" (Eliot), 117
Eckley, Grace, 86, 99
Eco, Umberto, 73, 76, 88, 96, 97
Ed Feasley *(The Recognitions)*, 75

Edie Grimes *(Carpenter's Gothic)*, 165
Edward Bast *(JR)*
   elbows Amy Joubert, 62
   as failed artist, 21, 27
   failure to "see," 68
   JR's use of language and, 64
   naive and romantic artist, 144
   realization about worth, 28
   resolution to fail, 240–241
   suffering for love and fear, 220–221
   sympathetic but powerless, 22–23
   talking to a corpse, 237
   Wyatt compared to, 20
Eliot, T.S., 43–56
   "Burnt Norton," 51, 53
   Collected Poems 1909-1962, 43, 56
   "The Dry Salvages," 52, 53–54
   "East Coker," 117
   The Four Quartets, 43–46, 50–55, 117
   Gaddis and, 2
   "Gerontion," 47
   "Hysteria," 59
   "Little Gidding," 52
   The Love Song of J. Alfred Prufrock, 256
   "Tradition and the Individual Talent," 56, 119, 125
   The Waste Land, 8
   "What the Thunder Said," 53
Eliot in His Time: Essays on the Occasion of the Fiftieth Anniversary of "The Waste Land" (Litz, ed.), 56
Elizabeth Booth *(Carpenter's Gothic)*
   Amy Joubert compared to, 116
   autobiography/diary of, 118, 119, 120
   Billy and, 102, 103, 114, 149, 150–151, 239, 250
   death of, 114, 123, 250
   exploited by those she helps, 220
   fragmentation of, 119
   Harlequin romance of, 111–112, 151–152
   heart attack of, 103
   lies about her father's death, 155
   Lucy Feverel echoed by, 220
   McCandless and, 103, 108–109, 151, 152–154, 220, 255–256
   names, significance of, 226
   overview, 149
   as persecuted maiden, 108
   pretense to culture, 106
   as proponent of ethics, 207
   as schoolmate of Christina, 165
   speaking Franglais, 164
   theft of purse and home, 232
Elliott, Emory, 129, 158
Emerson, Ralph Waldo, 75, 97
Empedocles, 59–62, 69
Empedocles: A Philosophical Investigation (Lambridis), 60, 69
Empedocles' Cosmic Cycle: A Reconstruction From the Fragments and Secondary Sources (O'Brien), 60, 69
The Enchafed Flood or the Romantic Iconography of the Sea (Auden), 31, 41
Encyclopedia Britannica, 117
Enter Mysterious Stranger: American Cloistral Fiction (Male), 106, 115, 124
"Entretien: Michael Foucault" (Chapsal), 129, 158
Entropic process, 23–25, 130, 142–143, 148, 165, 250
Episcopal Church v. Pepsi Cola, 166, 198, 214
Equality and Partiality (Nagel), 203–204, 210–211
Erebus, 184, 186, 204
Eroticism, 63, 245, 255
Esme *(The Recognitions)*
   Amy Joubert compared to, 65
   Camilla's earrings, 50–51, 239
   inexplicable splendour of, 46
   as proponent of ethics, 207
   struggles through chaos, 19, 118
Esther Gwyon *(The Recognitions)*, 7, 10, 12

The Ethics of Indeterminacy in the Novels of William Gaddis (Comnes), 163
Eucharist, 79–80, 80
"Exorcising the Demon Forgery, or the Forging of Pure Gold in Gaddis's *Recognitions*" (Eckley), 86, 99

F R Vorakers *(Carpenter's Gothic)*, 102
Fables of Aggression (Jameson), 141, 160
Fables of Subversion (Weisenburger), 207, 217, 223
Fabulation, 133, 146, 161
Fabulation and Metafiction (Scholes), 133, 159
The Fabulators (Scholes), 133, 159
Failure, 228, 240–241, 247
"Fakery and Stony Truths" (Ozick), 71, 95–96
Faust (Goethe), 2, 76, 87–94, 100
Federal Rules of Civil Procedure, 183, 184, 186
Federalism, 202–203
Fickert, Wayne *(A Frolic of His Own)*, 165
Fickert case, 192, 195, 196, 201
Fiction in the Quantum Universe (Strehle), 223
Fiedler, Leslie, 107, 108
Fielding, Henry, 220
Finnegans Wake (Joyce), 17
Fish, Stanley, 194
Fitzhugh, George, 177
Flaubert, Gustave, 252
Flax, Neil M., 100
Flemish art, 18, 76, 86, 99
"Flemish Art and Wyatt's Quest for Redemption in William Gaddis's *The Recognitions*" (Knight), 86, 99
The Floating Opera (Barth), 32, 39–40
The Flying Dutchman, 249
Fokkema, Douwe, 128, 158
""For a Very Small Audience": The Fiction of William Gaddis" (Strehle), 17–28, 39, 42

Forgery
as motif in *The Recognitions*, 223
of Recktall Brown, 84–85, 91
restoring paintings, 85–86, 93–94, 246–247
of Wyatt Gwyon, 8–9, 38, 45–76, 91–92
The Form of Faust (Jantz), 93, 100
Forster, E. M., 228
Fort, Charles, 247
Foucault, Michael, 65, 70, 128–129, 158, 174
The Four Quartets (Eliot), 43–46, 50–55, 117
Fox, James, 212–213
Frank Gribble *(A Frolic of His Own)*, 181
Frank Kinkead *(Carpenter's Gothic)*, 117
Frank Sinisterra *(The Recognitions)*
atonement for Camilla's death, 55
Camilla's death and, 46, 55
as Mr. Yak, 81–83, 240
passport for Wyatt from, 80, 97–98
wife of, 239
Wyatt and, 19, 53, 80, 97–98
Franz, Marie-Louise von, 246
Franzen, Jonathan, 2
Free enterprise, 161–162, 175
Freud, Sigmund, 130–131
Friedman, Bruce Jay, 132, 159
A Frolic of His Own, see also *Once at Antietam*; justice
accidents happen, 166
Ace Worldwide Fidelity Insurance, 181
bigotry in, 177, 200–201, 204, 205
The Blood in the Red White and Blue, 166, 169, 170–171, 177, 189–190
breast implants in the fridge, 169
chaos, controlled, 169–170
communication in, 208–209
a country-house comedy, 165
Cyclone Seven sculpture, 165, 167–168
death in, 213–216
farce as motif, 166–167

fish tank, 170
injured egos go to court, 166
justice in, 175
Long Island house, 165–166, 168–169
as meditation on justice, 173–175
nature, domain of, 165, 169, 171–172, 211–215
no-fault insurance, 178–179
postmodernism, attack on, 168
reader's responsibilities in, 222
synopsis, 165, 172
TV cartoon mirrors devastation, 223
Walden Pond, 165, 171–172, 211–213, 215–216
A Frolic of His Own characters. *see also* Christina Crease; Harold Basie; Oscar Crease
Bagby, 167
Bunker, 208
Dr. Kissinger, 165
Fickert, Wayne, 165
Frank Gribble, 181
Harry Lutz, 191, 197–206, 205, 220
John Israel, 177
John Knize, 190–191
Judge Bone, 186, 187, 189, 190, 205–206
Judge Crease, 188, 190, 191–197, 201
Kane, 178
Kevin, 179
Kiester, 182, 190–191
Lepidus & Shea, 182, 205
Lily, 176
Madhar Pai, 167, 185–188, 191, 201, 202, 205, 206
Mohlenhoff Shranksky, 181
Preswig, 179
Reverend Elton Ude, 165, 230
Senator Bilk, 201–202
Sir Arthur Eddington, 168
Swyne & Dour, 185, 198, 208–209
Szyrk, 165, 169, 182, 193, 241
Thomas Crease, 167, 176–177, 190
Trish, 201, 208

"*A Frolic of His Own*: Whose Law? Whose Justice?" (Knight), 173–216. *see also* justice
Fuchs, Miriam
biographical info, 260
"*"il miglior fabbro"* Gaddis' Debt to T.S. Eliot," 43–56, 93, 100
Fuller *(The Recognitions)*, 90, 237–238
Fundamentalism, 108, 110, 121

"Gaddis: A Tribune of the Fifties" (Karl), 80, 98
Gaddis, Sarah (daughter), 253, 255
Gaddis, William
awards of, 221, 252
biographical info, 1, 101, 221, 252, 255
discipline of, 249–250
Eliot and, 2, 43–56
as epistemological novelist, 238
"fiction stems from outrage," 228
Gogol and, 71–73
golden age and, 233–234
mimic of genius, 167
parodies himself, 151
on personal responsibility, 217
postmodernism and, 1, 128, 134, 236
Pynchon compared to, 2, 23, 73
quest for redemption, 99, 236, 240
sexism or misogyny of, 207
as social crusader, 114
Waugh compared to, 164–165, 166
on writing his play, 217
Gaddis, William, style of. *see also* Black humor; Characters; Metaphors; Parodies; Reader's responsibilities; Symbolism; Themes
ambiguity, intentional, 104, 117
angry and insightful, 250
belief in opacity of human self, 240
blurring of time, 52–55, 76
deceptiveness of simplicity, 243
defamiliarizing present reality, 73–74, 111

discourse, 19, 235
fabulation, 133, 146, 161
irony, 2, 60, 65–66, 71–95
massive novels, 254–255
mordantly sardonic comedy, 221
narrative strategies, 104–115
overview, 157, 219–220, 225, 251–253
paradoxes, 246, 247, 252
self-referential, not self-absorbed, 251–253
straightforward narrative, 227
Gaddis, William, works of, see also *Carpenter's Gothic*; *A Frolic of His Own*; *JR*; *The Recognitions*
"The Rush for Second Place," 71, 73, 95, 116, 124, 228
"Why I Write," 71, 95
"Gaddis Anagnorisis" (Leverence), 83–84, 92, 97, 98, 100
"Gaddis and the Cosmic Babble: Fiction Rich with the Darkly Funny Voices of America" (Grove), 73, 96
Gaddisites, 163
Gall *(JR)*, 21, 59, 252
"The Garden of Forking Paths" (Borges), 135
The Gay Science (Nietzsche), 213
Geismar, Maxwell, 73, 96
General Foods Corp., Downey v., 185
Genuine vs. original, 4–5, 18
"Gerontion" (Eliot), 47
Ghosts, 213–214
Gibbs, Willard, 165
Gilligan, Carol, 207
Goethe, Johann Wolfgang Von, 2, 76, 87–94, 99
Goethe's Faust: A Literary Analysis (Atkins), 100
Gogol, Nikolai, 71, 72, 95, 96
Goldstein, Paul, 185, 187–188, 217
Goodwill, 64
Gothic novels, 107
Governor Cates *(JR)*, 26, 148
"Gravity's Rainbow" (Poirier), 125

Gravity's Rainbow (Pynchon), 140, 146, 223
Great Expectations (Dickens), 220
Greiner, Donald J., 32, 33, 41, 42
Grove, Lloyd, 73, 96
Guattari, Félix, 139, 148, 160, 161–162
Guzlowski, John Z.
biographical info, 260
"No More Sea Changes: Hawkes, Pynchon, Gaddis, and Barth," 31–41
Gwyon. *See* Camilla Gwyon; Wyatt Gwyon *(The Recognitions)*
Gynesis: Configurations of Woman and Modernity (Jardin), 137, 160

Habermas, Jürgen, 174
Hamlet (Shakespeare), 31
Hand, Learned, 176, 187, 195, 216
A Handful of Dust (Waugh), 166
Hannah *(The Recognitions)*, 119
Harlequin romance, 111–112, 151–152
"Harnessing the Power" (Grove), 106, 124
Harold Basie *(A Frolic of His Own)*
Christina and, 208–210
Oscar and, 176, 182–184, 191, 205–206
past of, 188
Harris, Charles B., 39, 42
Harry Lutz *(A Frolic of His Own)*, 191, 197–206, 205, 220
Harvard Lampoon, 224
Havel, Vaclav, 174
Hawkes, John, 31–34, 41, 130, 158, 222
Hawthorne, Nathaniel, 111
Hazard, Geoffrey, 184
Heart of Darkness (Conrad), 114, 123
Heisenberg, Werner, 236
Heller, Agnes, 174
Heller, Joseph, 129
Hemingway, Ernest, 255
The Hermetic Museum (Waite), 76, 84, 97

Herr, Michael, 116, 124
Hiawatha (Longfellow), 169–170, 216
Hicks, Granville, 73, 96
Holmes, Oliver Wendell, 176, 192, 193–196, 216, 217
The House of the Seven Gables (Hawthorne), 111
House of words, ornate, 172
"The House that Gaddis Built" (Bradbury), 71, 95
How to Win Friends and Influence People (Carnegie), 95, 101
Howe, Irving, 131, 158–159
Hugh Selwyn Mauberley (Pound), 7
Humor. *see* Black humor; Comedy
Huyssen, Andreas, 134, 159
"Hysteria" (Eliot), 59

Ibsen, Henrik, 238, 249
"Icebergs, Islands, Ships beneath the Sea" (Busch), 32, 41–42
The Idea of the Modern (Howe), 131, 158–159
"Ideology, Representation, Schizophrenia: Toward a Theory of the Postmodern Subject" (Johnston), 131, 139, 159, 160
"*"Il miglior fabbro"* Gaddis' Debt to T.S. Eliot" (Fuchs), 43–56, 93, 100
Immortality, 214
"The Importance of Being Negligible" (Wolfe), 219–256
In a Different Voice (Gilligan), 207
In Recognition of William Gaddis (Kuehl and Moore, eds.), 74, 80, 97, 98, 216–217, 228, 252
Influence on each other, 226
"Influential couple scrutinize books for Anti-Americanism" (Kleinman), 104, 124
Inner consciousness, 251–252. *see also* Unconscious
"Innovation and Repetition: Between Modern and Post-Modern Aesthetics" (Eco), 73, 76, 88, 96, 97
"Intricacies of Plot: Some Preliminary Remarks to William Gaddis's *Carpenter's Gothic*" (Thielmans, 123, 125
"Introduction to *A Reader's Guide to William Gaddis's The Recognitions*" (Moore), 91, 96, 100
"Introduction" to *Black Humor* (Friedman), 132, 159
"Introduction to *Dead Souls*" (Wellek), 72, 96
"Ironic Allusiveness and Satire in William Gaddis's *The Recognitions*" (Safer), 71–95
Irony, 2, 60, 65–66, 71–95

Jack Gibbs (*JR*)
 Amy Joubert and, 58, 144, 227
 attributes Marx quote to Empedocles, 59–60
 on communication, 23–24
 disarray of limbs, 62
 on entropy, 23, 142–143
 as failed artist, 21
 five shares of family firm, 242
 Gaddis' as, 252
 Marian Eigen and, 227
 preoccupation with order and chaos, 57–59, 144, 248
 spills pail of slop, 25
 struggles of, 118
 on Whiteback's language, 64
James, Fleming, 184
James, Henry, 245
James, William, 101
James Bast (*JR*), 241, 254
Jameson, Fredric, 136, 141, 160
Jane Eyre (Austen), 112
Janet (*The Recognitions*), 243
Jantz, Harold, 93, 100
Jardin, Alice A., 137, 160

Jeffers, Robinson, 113, 120, 123, 124
John Cates *(JR)*, 26, 148
John Crémer *(The Recognitions)*, 85, 94, 98, 233–234
"John Hawkes: An Interview," 130, 158
John Israel *(A Frolic of His Own)*, 177
John Knize *(A Frolic of His Own)*, 190–191
John of the Cross, St., 1
Johnston, John
   biographical info, 260
   "Ideology, Representation, Schizophrenia: Toward a Theory of the Postmodern Subject," 131, 159
   on knowledge and truth, 245
   on reader's responsibilities, 242
   "Toward Postmodern Fiction," 127–157
Jokes, banal, 75
Joubert. *see* Amy Joubert *(JR)*
Joyce, James, 2, 17, 133, 211, 216, 225–226, 248
JR. see also Reality and realism
   age of "credit and credibility," 140
   art fails to redeem, 21
   black humor in, 18, 21–23, 25
   broken, fragmented speech, 141
   Carpenter's Gothic compared to, 116–117, 149
   chaos, 20, 22–26, 57–69, 141, 144–145, 248
   characters as body parts, 62–63
   commerce, politics and the family, 222
   dance in, 62–63
   despair in, 21–23
   deterritorialization, 148, 161–162
   dialogue, 63–65, 141
   education problems, 232
   emotions, repressed, 244–245
   Empedocles' world in, 60–62
   emptiness of business world, 22
   entropic process in, 23–25, 142–143, 148
   evening sky, 212
   eyeglasses, 68–69
   goodwill defined, 64
   injuries and accidents, 25–26, 223
   irony in, 60, 65–66
   Long Island in, 231–232, 252
   modernist vs. postmodernist reading, 145–146
   money, 25–27, 147–148
   Mozart and van Gogh, 241
   multiplicity of little stories, 144
   multiplicity of words, 63–66
   Once at Antietam in, 165
   parody of JR's empire, 146
   postmodernism of, 140–148
   Pythian Mining, 117
   reader's responsibilities, 141–144, 219, 221, 241–242
   The Recognitions compared to, 18–23
   scope of, 20–21
   seamless, about things coming apart, 57, 141
   separation from selves and others, 57, 61, 66–69
   settings of, 26
   spilling, falling, scattering, 24–25, 62
   stabbing at reviewers, 253
   synopsis, 250
   visual perceptions in, 67–69
JR characters. *see also* Amy Joubert; Edward Bast; Jack Gibbs; JR Vansant
   Ann diCephalis, 61
   Anne Bast, 27, 64, 145–146
   Brisboy, 243
   Coach Vogel, 25
   Coen, 64
   Congressman Pecci, 26
   Crawley, 255
   "Dad" diCephalis, 61
   Dan diCephalis, 25, 61, 66
   Davidoff, 241–242, 243
   Gall, 21, 59, 252
   Governor Cates, 26, 148

James Bast, 241, 254
John Cates, 26, 148
Julia Bast, 27, 64, 145–146
Major Hyde, 26
Marian Eigen, 227
Miss Flesch, 25
Mister Duncan, 28
Mr. Beaton, 64
Mr. Grynszpan, 235
Mr. Skinner, 68
Norman Angel, 27, 244–245
Schepperman, 21, 25, 27, 241
Schramm, 21, 27–28
Stella Angel, 144, 244–245
Thomas Eigen, 21, 165, 240, 252
Vern, 65
Whiteback, 64, 65–66, 68, 143
"JR" (Stade), 145, 161
JR Vansant (*JR*)
  Amy Joubert and, 26, 68
  apathetically driven, 20, 21, 26
  arranging his limbs, 62
  as entropic agent, 25, 148
  focuses attention, 254
  intangible objects not perceived by, 68
  as junior to elders, 27
  Paul Booth compared to, 117
  telephone usage of, 66–67, 147, 235
  witness to political deception, 230
Judge Bone (*A Frolic of His Own*), 186, 187, 189, 190, 205–206
Judge Crease (*A Frolic of His Own*), 188, 190, 191–197, 201
Julia Bast (*JR*), 27, 64, 145–146
Justice, 173–216
  as common law, 191–197
  encompassing, 211–215
  A Frolic of His Own as meditation on, 173–175
  of the heart, 206–210
  as legal right, 197–206
  as personal natural law, 175–191
  price of, 175
  suffers from uneven distribution of wealth, 178

Justice Holmes, Natural Law, and the Supreme Court (Biddle), 176, 216

Kafka, Franz, 221
Kafka: Toward a Minor Literature (Deleuze and Guattari), 139, 160
Kane (*A Frolic of His Own*), 178
Kant, Immanuel, 157, 212
Karl, Frederick, 74, 80, 96, 98, 141, 160
Kaufman, Sue, 101
Kazin, Alfred, 17, 29
Keats, John, 249, 250
Kenner, Hugh, 134, 138, 159
Kevin (*A Frolic of His Own*), 179
Kiester (*A Frolic of His Own*), 182, 190–191
King, Martin Luther, Jr., 174
Kipling, Rudyard, 225
Kirkus, 73, 96
Kissinger (*A Frolic of His Own*), 165
Kleinman, Dena, 104, 124
Klemtner, Susan Strehle
  biographical info, 259
  "For a Very Small Audience: The Fiction of William Gaddis," 17–28, 39, 42
Knight, Christopher J. *see also* Justice
  biographical info, 260
  "Flemish Art and Wyatt's Quest for Redemption in William Gaddis's *The Recognitions*," 86, 99
  "A Frolic of His Own: Whose Law? Whose Justice?," 173–216
Koenig, Peter W., 57, 69, 85, 86, 93, 98, 99, 100
  on complexity of *The Recognitions*, 219
  on *The Recognitions*, 250
  "Recognizing Gaddis' *Recognitions*," 57, 69, 86, 99
  "'Splinters from the Yew Tree': A Critical Study of William Gaddis's *The Recognitions*," 85, 98
  "The Writing of *The Recognitions*," 93, 100

Kramer, Heinrich, 236–237
Kuehl, John, 74, 80, 97, 98, 216–217, 222–223, 228, 252

Laing, R. D., 41, 42
Lambridis, Helle, 60, 69
Langbaum, Robert, 49, 56
Language, 64–65, 172. *see also* Communication
The Language of Psychoanalysis (Laplanche and Pontalis), 135, 160
Lannan Foundation lifetime achievement award, 252
Laplanche, J., 135, 160
Lathrop, Kathleen L., 75, 97
"Laughter" (Bergson), 81, 98
Lauzen, Sara E., 117, 125
Lawrence, D. H., 220, 227
LeClair, Thomas, 96, 146, 161
Leg incident, 99
Lepidus & Shea *(A Frolic of His Own)*, 182, 205
Lester *(Carpenter's Gothic)*, 104, 117, 120, 122–123
Leverence, John, 83–84, 92, 97, 98, 100
Levinas, Emmanuel, 174
Levinson, Sanford, 194, 201
A Lexicon of Alchemy (Rulandus), 85, 98
Liberalism, 199–203
Lillo, Don De, 2, 140
Lily *(A Frolic of His Own)*, 176
Literary Transcendentalism: Style and Vision in the American Renaissance, 97
Literature and the Sixth Sense (Rahv), 72, 96
"Little Gidding" (Eliot), 52
A Little Learning (Waugh), 166
Litz, A. Walton, 56
Liz Booth. *see* Elizabeth Booth *(Carpenter's Gothic)*
Lolita (Nabokov), 130, 133
Longfellow, Henry Wadsworth, 169–170, 216

Lookout Cartridge (McElroy), 140
Loss of Self in Modern Literature and Art (Sypher), 129
Love, romantic vs. Gothic, 111
Love and Death in the American Novel (Fiedler), 107, 108
"Love and Strife in William Gaddis' JR" (Matanle), 57–69
"Love Offence" (Suckling), 239
"The Love Song of J. Alfred Prufrock" (Eliot), 256
Lully, Raymond, 83, 85, 99
Lyotard, Jean-François, 127, 135, 157, 159, 161, 162

MacArthur Foundation Fellowship, 252
Madame Socrate *(Carpenter's Gothic)*, 164
Madden, David, 19, 29, 87, 99
Madhar Pai *(A Frolic of His Own)*, 167, 185–188, 191, 201, 202, 205, 206
Major Hyde *(JR)*, 26
Male, Roy R., 106, 115, 124
Malgren, Carl D., 143, 161
Malleus Maleficarum (Kramer and Sprenger), 236–237
A Man for All Seasons (Bolt), 167, 176
"The Man That Corrupted Hadleyburg" (Twain), 115
Mann, Thomas, 240–241
Mapping Literary Modernism (Quinones), 131, 159
Marian Eigen *(JR)*, 227
Martin, Stephen-Paul, 247
Marx, Karl, 60, 161–162
Mason and Dixon (Pynchon), 2
Matanle, Stephen H.
  biographical info, 260
  "Love and Strife in William Gaddis' JR," 57–69
Materialism, 95, 177, 247
Mather, Cotton, 73
McCafferty, Larry, 117, 125

McCandless *(Carpenter's Gothic)*
  about the house, 152
  as antichrist, 110
  conservative values of, 104–105
  credibility destroyed, 155
  diagram of religious and political groups, 122
  Elizabeth Booth and, 103, 108–109, 151, 152–154, 220, 255–256
  fiction of his self, 120
  "fiction stems from outrage," 228
  figuratively batters Elizabeth, 114
  on fundamentalism, 110, 121
  Gaddis' as, 253
  as Gothic hero-villain, 108
  mad or deceptive?, 122
  novel of, 117, 118, 119–120
  overview, 102–103, 149
  quoting Shakespeare, 112–113
  son of, 239, 244
McCaskill, O. L., 183–184
McElroy, Joseph, 140
Melville, Herman, 1–2, 3, 31, 41, 109, 110, 115, 122
Memling (Bazin), 5, 15
Meredith, George, 220
Metafiction, 117–124
Metaphors
  Gwyon father/son relationship, 10, 38, 48
  reality and art, 4, 6–7, 96, 241
  the sea and sea changes, 31–41
  Seven Deadly Sins painting, 10, 13, 91, 94
Metaphysics
  allusions to, 19, 23, 247
  Conconnon's mother, 248, 249
  as possibilities assumed as facts, 120–121
  significance of art and artists, 19, 247
Metro-Goldwyn Pictures Corp., Sheldon v., 187, 188
Michnik, Adam, 174
Miller, Arthur, 73

Milton, John, 73
Miner, Bob, 17, 29
Minkoff, Robert L., 226, 235
Mirroring, 4, 219–223, 242–243, 245, 247–248
Misogyny, 207, 217
Miss Flesch *(JR)*, 25
Mister Duncan *(JR)*, 28
Moby-Dick (Melville), 1–2, 3, 31, 41, 109, 122
Modernism, 130–131, 145–146, 221–222, 235, 241. *see also* Postmodernism
Mohlenhoff Shranksky *(A Frolic of His Own)*, 181
Money
  Bast sisters' discovery of, 27, 145–146
  compassion vs., 26, 207
  corporate law and, 197–198
  Gogol's view of, 73
  justice available for, 175
  ordering power of, 25–27
  speaking with, 147–148
  waste of, in education, 232
  worth of, 27
Moore, Steven
  biographical info, 260
  "*Carpenter's Gothic*; or, The Ambiguities," 101–124
  on Gaddis' play, 216–217
  "Introduction to *A Reader's Guide to William Gaddis's The Recognitions*," 91, 96, 100
  In Recognition of William Gaddis, 74, 80, 97, 98, 216–217, 228, 252
  William Gaddis, 219
Mordantly sardonic comedy, 221
Motifs. *see* Themes
A Moveable Feast (Hemingway), 255
Mozart, 241
Mr. Beaton *(JR)*, 64
Mr. Grynszpan *(JR)*, 235
Mr. Lincoln's Army (Catton), 171
Mr. Skinner *(JR)*, 68

Mulligan Stew (Sorrentino), 117
Mummy, 82–83
My Life in a Convent (Shepherd), 236
The Myth of Siryphus and Other Essays (Camus), 79, 86, 97

Nabokov, Vladimir, 130, 133
Nachträglichkeit, 135–136, 160
Nagel, Thomas, 203–204, 210–211
Naked Lunch (Burroughs), 130, 158
Names,
  Gaddis' treatment of, 226–227
Napoleon, 255
Narrative strategies, 104–115
Narrative texture, 246
National Book Awards, 221
National Institute of Arts and Letters award, 252
Nature, 75, 117, 165, 169, 171–172, 211–215
"Nature" (Emerson), 75, 97
NEA awards, 221, 252
Neo-realism, 129, 158
"Neo-realist Fiction" (Bradbury), 158
New England Gothic tradition, 107
"New Modes of Characterization in *The Waste Land*" (Langbaum), 49, 56
New Republic (magazine), 17, 29
New York City, 230–232
New York Times, 174, 216
The New Yorker, 17, 29
Newsweek (magazine), 17, 29
Nietzsche, 104, 137, 156, 213
Night Fishing at Antibes (Picasso), 55, 74
Nixon presidency, 20, 29
"No More Sea Changes: Hawkes, Pynchon, Gaddis, and Barth" (Guzlowski), 31–41
No-fault insurance, 178–179
Norman Angel *(JR)*, 27, 244–245
"Notes on Metafiction: Every Essay Has a Title" (Lauzen), 117, 125
"Notes on New Sensibility" (Wasson), 136, 160
Novelistic assemblage, 148

Objective vs. subjective writing, 118–119
O'Brien, Denis, 60, 69
O'Brien, Flan, 117
Occam's razor, 193
Odysseus, 93
Oedipa Maas *(The Crying of Lot 49)*, 31, 34–36
"Olalla" (Stephenson), 243
"Old Age" (Emerson), 75, 97
Oliver Crease, 220–221
Oliver Wendell Holmes, Jr.: Soldier, Scholar, Judge (Aichele), 176, 216
Olson, Walter, 179–181, 183
"On the 'Great Lacuna' and the Pact Scene," (Staiger), 89, 99
"On William Gaddis: In Recognition of James Joyce" (Benstock), 17, 29, 80, 98
"On William Gaddis's *The Recognitions*" (Madden), 19, 29, 87, 99
Once at Antietam (A Frolic of His Own)
  desire for justice as heart of, 175–176
  first showing is in *JR*, 165
  as Gaddis' own play, 216–217
  lawsuit: for plagiarizing of, 166, 175, 181–191
  Oscar's bid for immortality, 214–215
  overview, 167
  quality of, 176–177
Oppression vs. coercion, 200
The Ordeal of Richard Feverel (Meredith), 220
The Order of Things (Foucault), 65, 70, 128–129, 158
Organic decay, 113, 124
Origen, 46
Origin of the Species (Darwin), 234
Originality, 4–5, 18, 42, 96, 97, 136–139
Oscar Crease *(A Frolic of His Own)*
  Basie and, 176, 182–184, 191,

205–206
bigotry of, 201, 205
The Blood in the Red White and Blue,
    watching, 170–171
childhood of, 176, 196
Christina and, 209–210, 211, 214
conflates justice with material success,
    177
Edward Bast reworked, 165
justice as personal natural law,
    175–191
lawsuit: for plagiarizing his play, 166,
    175, 181–191
lawsuit: run over by his own car, 166,
    175, 178–181
nature TV programs and, 169, 212
overview, 166
quintessential dangling man, 176
use of, 253
Otto Pivner *(The Recognitions)*
    call to Hans Vaihinger, 244
    echo of masses in *The Waste Land*, 48
    Eliot echoed by, 43, 44
    failure to recognize his father, 19
    forged painting story, 246–247
    interest in rape of little girl, 81
    in NYC, alone and numb, 231
    reading Dale Carnegie, 95
    struggles of, 118
    on suffering, 6
    Wagner *(Faust)* compared to, 90
Ozick, Cynthia, 71, 95–96, 113, 124

Pai. *see* Madhar Pai *(A Frolic of His Own)*
Pale Fire (Nabokov), 133
Palimpsests, 248–249
Panofsky, Erwin, 76, 97
"Paper Currencies: Reading William
    Gaddis" (Weisenburger), 80, 98
"The Paper Empires and Empirical
    Fictions of William Gaddis"
    (Black), 140, 160
Paradoxes, 246, 247, 252

Parekh, Bhikhu, 202–203
Paris, 233
Parodies
    of a better self within, 240, 243
    of Catton's *Mr. Lincoln's Army*,
        170–171
    Gaddis, of himself, 151
    JR's financial empire, 146
    as linguistic "counterfeit," 133
    in postmodernism, 133–134, 146
    The Recognitions, of itself, 4
    teasing out unity with, 249
    of transformation by the sea, 32,
        39–40
A Passage to India (Forster), 228
Pastora (The Recognitions), 92–93
Paul Booth *(Carpenter's Gothic)*
    "fit the piece together," 103–104
    Jewish heritage of, 155, 244
    JR compared to, 117
    kills his attacker, 233
    moral and intellectual bankruptcy of,
        102, 103, 106, 115, 116, 150
    overview, 149
    self-sabotage of, 243–244
    in Vietnam War, 115–116, 153
Pedlar's Progress: The Life of Bronson Alcott
    (Shepard), 75, 97
Peer Gynt (Ibsen), 238, 249
Penises, attention to, 255–256
Pepsi Cola, Episcopal Church v., 166,
    198, 214
"Periodizing the 60s" (Jameson), 136,
    160
Peter, Saint, 78, 81
Picasso, 55, 74
Pilgrim Hymnal, 117
Pintner, Harold, 239
Plagiarism, 21
Platonic heritage, 136–138, 139, 167,
    176, 186, 215
Plato's Socrates, 173, 174, 175
Plots meander and events disintegrate,
    224

Poirier, Richard, 116, 125
Politics, 199–203, 229–230
Politics of Experience (Laing), 41, 42
Pontalis, J.-B., 135, 160
Pop and Glow lawsuit, 166, 214
Porter, Arnstein v., 187
The Postmodern Condition (Lyotard), 157, 162
Postmodern Fiction: A Bio-Bibliographical Guide (McCafferty, ed.), 117, 125
"The Postmodern *Weltanschauung* and Its Relation with Modernism" (Bertens), 128, 133, 158, 159
Postmodernism, 128–157
    anti-Platonic "difference," 136–138, 139
    attack on, 168
    black humor and, 131–132
    characters as masks, 129–130
    "credit and credibility" vs. belief, 140
    Cyclone Seven sculpture, 165, 167–168
    Deleuze's role in developing, 139–140
    Derrida's role in developing, 137–138
    dissolution of ego boundaries, 131
    entropic landscapes, 130, 142–143, 148
    fragmented conversations, stammerings, 141
    Gaddis' approach to, 236
    modernism vs., 130–131
    as *Nachträglichkeit*, 135–136, 160
    overview, 127–128, 156–157
    parody in, 133–134, 146
    reader's responsibilities, 141–144
    The Recognitions and, 134–140
    rejection of mystical method, 136
    self-referentiality and, 132–133
    Sypher and, 128–129
Pound, Ezra, 7, 8, 12
"Practica" (Valentinus), 76, 84, 97
Pragmatism (James), 101
Praxiteles, 239–240
Prelude to Chemistry: An Outline of Alchemy (Read), 84, 98
"The Presence of the Sign in Goethe's Faust" (Flax), 100
Preswig *(A Frolic of His Own)*, 179
Progressive revelation, 242
The Public Burning (Coover), 132, 223
Puccini, 241
Pynchon, Thomas
    Brigadier General Pudding, 223
    Gaddis compared to, 2, 23, 73
    Gravity's Rainbow, 140, 146, 223
    Gravity's Rainbow, review of, 116, 125
    Oedipa's fear of the sea, 31, 34–36
    postmodernism of, 140
    "runaway" system of, 146
    V., 130
Pythian Mining *(JR)* and *(Carpenter's Gothic)*, 117

Quinones, Ricardo J., 131, 159

Raban, Jonathan
    "At Home in Babel," 163–172, 204
    biographical info, 260
    on Christina, 207, 212
    on Gaddis, 1
    on *Once at Antietam*, 176
Radcliffe graduates, 94
Rahv, Philip, 72, 96
The Rainbow (Lawrence), 227
Rational or aesthetic categories, 222
Ratner's Star (Lillo), 140
Rawls, John, 174, 199–200, 203, 206
Read, John, 84, 98
Reader's responsibilities
    follow the real story, 163, 164, 237
    in general, 227–228
    interpret allusions, mirroring, 219, 221, 222
    interpret garble, 244
    making judgments (not), 241–242
    postmodernism and, 141–146
Reality and realism
    antirealism of *The Recognitions*,

224–225
of art, 4, 6–7, 96, 241
black humor from reducing, 144
chaos and, 20, 22–26, 57–69, 141, 144–145, 248–249
as communication, 148
defamiliarizing of, 73–74, 111
dynamism of, 223, 235
encompassed by *The Recognitions*, 3
Gibb's conversation with M. Eigen, 227
magisterial and funny, 220
morality and, 235
neo-realism, 129, 158
as network of submerged activities, 246–247
portraiture of characters, 164
postmodernism and, 130, 132–133, 138–139
Recktall Brown *(The Recognitions)*
allusion to devil-nature of, 87, 89, 91
diamond ring as symbol of, 72
forgery scam with Valentine, 84–85, 91
Fuller and, 90, 237–238
greed of, 9
moral caricature of, 10
sympathetic villain, 224
Wyatt exploited by, 18, 85
Recognition means theophany, 222
The Recognitions
alchemical pursuit of gold, 83–84
alchemy in, 83–87, 223
allusions to alchemy, 83–87, 223
an epic of consciousness, 2
as apocalypse (hopeful), 109
arrogance of suffering, 6, 12
banal jokes, 75
black humor in, 19–20, 75, 99
Carnival Masque scene, 87–88
Carpenter's Gothic compared to, 116–117
cathedral scene, 86–87
chaos in, 19, 94–95, 118

characters
lack dignity, 8, 95
levels of identification of, 226
metaphysical and earthly, 13–14
severed from their origins, 45, 48, 241
timeless knowledge of, 54–55
condemns modern world, 250
contrasts, Flemish to modern art, 76
despair portrayed in, 21–22, 23
development and civilization of, 55–56
displacement as major trope, 250
El Greco sky, 212
exploration of aesthetic recognition, 20
Faust compared to, 2, 76, 87–94, 100
first person/third person voice, 49–50
gender confusion in, 226
Gothic mode in, 107
irony in, 71–95
isolation of conscious and unconscious, 36–39
JR compared to, 18–23
as mimetic aesthetic, 96
mirroring relationships, 222
as modern labyrinthine novel, 95
monastery, 53
Mount Lamentation, 44
mummy scene, 82–83
New York and, 230–231
objectivity vs. subjectivity, 119
obsession, 3–4
omnipresence of inexplicable, 1
Paris, 233
parody of itself, 4
postmodernism of, 128, 134–140
progressive revelation, 242
Puccini's *Tosca*, 241
Puritan notions of virtue, 229
Radcliffe graduates, 94
reader's responsibilities in, 236–237
reality encompassed by, 3
reality of art, 4, 6–7, 96

recognitions, 19–20, 54, 97
religion, exploration of, 2, 19–20, 77, 79–80, 82–83, 94, 95, 234
San Zwingli, 52–53
savagery and spirituality fuse, 243
scope of, 18–19
The Self Who Can Do More, 236, 239–240
self-reflective aspects of, 4
Semper aliquid haeret, 236
Seven Deadly Sins painting, 10, 13, 91, 94
synopsis, 18, 95
verbal clutter in, 237
The Waste Land and, 2, 43–48, 50–55, 74, 108
The Recognitions characters. *see also* Basil Valentine; Camilla Gwyon; Esme; Frank Sinisterra; Otto Pivner; Recktall Brown; Wyatt Gwyon
Arnie Munk, 116–117
Aunt May, 236, 249
Benny, 95
Ed Feasley, 75
Esther Gwyon, 7, 10, 12
Fuller, 90, 237–238
Gwyon father/son relationship, 10, 38, 48, 78–80, 237
Hannah, 119
Janet, 243
John Crémer, 85, 94, 98, 233–234
Pastora, 92–93
Simon Magus, 1
Spanish girl, 80–82
Stanley, 5, 11–12, 86–87, 241
Stanley's mother, 87
Willie the writer, 2, 36, 87, 252, 254
Yák, 81–83, 240
Recognitions of Clement, The Ante-Nicene Fathers (Roberts and Donaldson, eds.), 76, 78, 97
"Recognizing Gaddis' *Recognitions*" (Koenig), 57, 69, 86, 99
Redemption (Tolstoy), 236

Rediscoveries (Madden), 19, 29, 87, 99
Reed, Rebecca, 236
Reiss, Timothy, 128, 158
Religion, exploration of
 aesthetics and, 19–20
 apocalypse and, 109–110
 art as, 21, 27–28, 85
 as assumed facts, 120–121, 155
 Catholicism, 196, 201, 236
 Christianity, 108, 110, 243
 Clementine Recognitions and, 77, 79–80, 82–83
 as conservative values, 104–105
 diagram of religious groups, 122
 God, absence of, 94, 95
 Judge Crease, 193
 pilgrims feel doubt and impiety, 224
 as power, 229
 in *The Recognitions*, 234
 reincarnation, 121, 122
 religious experiences, 2
"Remembering Auschwitz" (*New York Times* editorial), 174, 216
The Republic (Plato), 173, 176, 215
Reverend Elton Ude (*A Frolic of His Own*), 165, 230
Reverend Elton Ude (*Carpenter's Gothic*), 102, 104, 109–110, 149
Ring of the Nibelungen (Wagner), 145
Roberts, Alexander, 76, 78, 97
Roth, Philip, 132, 159
Rousseau, Jean Jacques, 176, 177, 186, 199
Rugoff, Milton, 73, 96
Rulandus, Martinus, 85, 98
"The Rush for Second Place," 71, 73, 95, 116, 124, 228

Safer, Elaine B.
 biographical info, 260
 "Ironic Allusiveness and Satire in William Gaddis's *The Recognitions*," 71–95
Salemi, Joseph S.

biographical info, 259
"To Soar in Atonement: Art as Expiation in Gaddis's *The Recognitions*," 3–14, 19, 29, 86, 99
San Zwingli, Spain, 52–53, 79, 82, 88
Sartre, Jean-Paul, 129, 133
Satire, 7–8, 71–95, 223
Satire of, 7–8, 71–72, 75, 223
Schepperman *(JR)*, 21, 25, 27, 241
Scholes, Robert, 133, 159
Schramm *(JR)*, 21, 27–28
Scientific lore, 19
Sea changes, 31–41
See v. Durang, 187
Seelye, John, 80, 97
The Self Who Can Do More, 236, 239–240
Senator Bilk *(A Frolic of His Own)*, 201–202
Senator Teakell *(Carpenter's Gothic)*, 103, 153
Seven Deadly Sins (Bosch), 10, 13, 91, 94
Sexuality, 63, 245, 255
Shakespeare, William, 31, 49, 112
Sheldon v. Metro-Goldwyn Pictures Corp., 187, 188
Shepard, Odell, 75, 97
Shepherd, Margaret, 236
"Shine, Perishing Republic" (Jeffers), 113, 124
Shumaker, Wayne, 85, 98
Simon Magus *(The Recognitions)* inventor of Gnosticism, 1
Simulations (Baudrillard), 138–139, 160
Sin
    originality as, 42
    Seven Deadly Sins painting, 10, 13, 91, 94
    Wyatt and, 53, 81, 85, 100
Sinisterra. see Frank Sinisterra *(The Recognitions)*
Sir Arthur Eddington *(A Frolic of His Own)*, 168
Six Months in a Convent (Reed), 236

Slavery, 177–178
The Sleepwalkers (Broch), 235
Smith, Cindy, 74, 97
Smith, Dinitia, 254
Socrates, 173, 174, 175, 215
Solzhenitsyn, Alexander, 174
Sonnet seventy-three (Shakespeare), 112–113
Sons and Lovers (Lawrence), 220
Sorrentino, Gilbert, 117
The Sot-Weed Factor (Barth), 130
Southern Gothic tradition, 107
Space, Time and Structure in the Modern Novel (Spencer), 52, 56
Spanish girl *(The Recognitions)*, 80–82
Spatialization, 52
Specters of Marx (Derrida), 173
Spencer, Sharon, 52, 56
"'Splinters from the Yew Tree': A Critical Study of William Gaddis's *The Recognitions*" (Koenig), 85, 98
Sprenger, James, 236–237
Stade, George, 145, 161
Staiger, Emil, 89, 99
Stanley *(The Recognitions)*, 5, 11–12, 86–87, 241
Stanley's mother *(The Recognitions)*, 87
Steiner, George, 17, 29, 163
Stella Angel *(JR)*, 144, 244–245
Stevenson, Robert Louis, 243
Stonehill, Brian, 228
A Streetcar Named Desire (Williams), 111
Strehle, Susan, 223
Subjective vs. objective writing, 118–119
Suckling, Sir John, 239
Summary judgment, 187
"Superior People: The Narrowness of Liberalism from Mill to Rawls" (Bhikhu), 202–203
Supermarket Gothic, 107
Swallow Hard (Sarah Gaddis), 253, 255
Swyne & Dour *(A Frolic of His Own)*, 185, 198, 208–209
Symbolism
    black poodle, 90–91

of Bosch painting, 10, 13, 91, 94
Camilla, of flowering corpse, 46
diamond ring, Mickey Mouse watch, 72
of doves, 114
Sypher, Wylie, 129
Szyrk *(A Frolic of His Own)*, 165, 169, 182, 193, 241
Szyrk vs. Village of Tantamount et al. *(A Frolic of His Own)*, 167–168

Tanner, Tony, 42, 48, 56, 87, 96, 99
Taylor, Charles, 174
Teakell, Senator, 103, 153
Technical exercises, 166–167
Telephones, 66–67, 147, 235, 243–244
The Tempest (Shakespeare), 49
Themes. *see also* Art and artists; Chaos; Communication; Death; Forgery; Metaphysics; Money; Reality and realism; Religion, exploration of; Sin; Time
 ambiguous times, 101–102
 capitalism, 161–162, 175
 comedy, 19–20, 95, 165, 221
 communication, difficulties with, 23–24, 63–67, 78, 143
 counterfeiting, 81, 95
 counterfeits vs. values, 96, 233
 dignity, 8, 28, 95
 emptiness of business world, 22
 end of civilization, 229–230, 242–243
 entropic process, 23–25, 130, 142–143, 148, 165, 250
 exploration of aesthetic recognition, 20
 materialism, 95, 177, 247
 mirroring, 4, 219–223, 242–243, 245, 247–248
 oblique approach to, 242
 obsession, 3–4
 originality, 4–5, 18, 42, 96, 97, 136–139
 recognitions, 19–20, 54, 97
 The Self Who Can Do More, 236, 239–240
 shallowness of others, 8, 72–74
 short people, 254–256
 unconscious, 32–36, 36–39, 41
 unreliability of visual perception, 67–69
Theology vs. thermodynamics, 165
Theroux, Alexander, 107, 124
Thielmans, Johan, 123, 125
Thomas Bast, 241, 242
Thomas Crease *(A Frolic of His Own)*, 167, 176–177, 190
Thomas Eigen *(JR)*, 21, 165, 240, 252
Thompkins, Lad, 253, 255
Thoreau, Henry D., 213
A Thousand Plateaus (Deleuze and Guattari), 139–140, 160
Time
 anachronisms, 106, 124
 blurring of, 52–55, 76
 "there will be time," 44
 timeless knowledge of characters, 54–55
 vague and elusive, 248
Time (magazine), 17, 29
"To Soar in Atonement: Art as Expiation in Gaddis's *The Recognitions*" (Salemi), 3–14, 19, 29, 86, 99
To the Lighthouse (Woolf), 211
"Todd Andrews, Ontological Insecurity, and *The Floating Opera*" (Harris), 39, 42
Todd Andrews *(The Floating Opera)*, 32, 39–40
Tolstoy, Leo, 236
Tom Jones (Fielding), 220
Toney, Richard, 122, 125
Tosca (Puccini), 241
"Toward Postmodern Fiction" (Johnston), 127–157
"Tradition and the Individual Talent" (Eliot), 56, 119, 125

Transcendental Club, 75
Transcendental references, 74–75
Trish *(A Frolic of His Own)*, 201, 208
The Triumphal Chariot of Antinomy (Valentinus), 76, 84, 97, 98
Trollope, Anthony, 164
Truth emerges slowly, 244–245
Trystero, 35
Turn of the Screw (James), 245
TV set, 169
Twain, Mark, 115

Ude. *see* Reverend Elton Ude
Ulysses (Joyce), 2, 17, 133
Unconscious, 32–36, 36–39, 41
Underworld (Lillo), 2
Unfair competition law, 189

V. (Pynchon), 130
Valentinus, Basilius, 76, 84–85, 97, 98
Values vs. counterfeits, 96
VCR *(Carpenter's Gothic)*, 102, 104, 115, 149
Vern *(JR)*, 65
Victorian flavor, 163–164, 226
Vietnam War, 115–116
Village Voice, 17, 29
Vorakers. *see* Billy Vorakers *(Carpenter's Gothic)*
Vorakers Consolidated Reserve, 102, 104, 115, 149

Wagner, Richard, 145, 223, 253–254
Waite, Arthur Edward, 76, 84, 97
Waits, Tom, 123
Walden Pond, 165, 171–172, 211–213, 215–216
Wall Street, 140–141
Walton, Izaak, 248
Warren, James Perrin, 119, 125
Wasson, Richard, 136, 160

The Waste Land (Eliot), 2, 8, 43–48, 50–55, 74, 108
Waugh, Evelyn, 164–165, 166, 169
Webster's New Collegiate Dictionary, 118, 120, 123
Weisenburger, Steven, 80, 98, 207, 217, 223, 249
Wellek, René, 72, 96
West, Nathanael, 2, 110, 124, 222
Weyden, Roger van der, 76
"What is Postmodernism" (Lyotard), 135, 159
"What the Thunder Said" (Eliot), 53
White Mischief (Fox), 212–213
White Noise (Lillo), 2
Whiteback *(JR)*, 64, 65–66, 68, 143
Whitman, Walt, 225, 252
"Why I Write," 71, 95
Wiener, Norbert, 142, 165
Wigglesworth, Michael, 109
"William Gaddis, JR, and the Art of Excess" (LeClair), 96, 146, 161, 222
William Gaddis (Moore), 219
"William Gaddis Rails Against Misrepresentation" (Smith), 74, 97
"William Gaddis's *JR*: The Novel of Babel" (Malgren), 143, 161
"William Gaddis's *The Recognitions*" (Madden), 19, 29, 87, 99
Williams, Tennessee, 111
Willie the writer *(The Recognitions)*, 2, 36, 87, 252, 254
"Wise Men in Their Bad Hours" (Jeffers), 120, 123
Wolfe, Peter
  biographical info, 260
  "The Importance of Being Negligible," 219–256
Women, ethics and, 207, 208
Woolf, Virginia, 211
"Writing American Fiction" (Roth), 132, 159
"The Writing of *The Recognitions*" (Koenig), 93, 100

Wyatt Gwyon *(The Recognitions)*
  alter egos of, 10–12
  arrogant satire, 7–8
  art and, 5–7, 37–38, 85, 224
  awareness, lack of faith, 12–13, 45–46
  bread with father's ashes, 79–80
  Camilla and, 79, 80, 97
  character of, 9–10
  Clement story and, 77, 78–79, 80
  dissolution and disappearance of, 131
  Edward Bast compared to, 20
  Esme and, 85
  Esther and, 7, 10, 12
  father/son relationship, 10, 38, 48, 78–80, 237
  fever and delirium of, 36–37, 47–48
  focal point of debate on art, 4
  forgeries of, 8–9, 38, 45, 76, 91–92
  in France, 233, 247
  Gaddis as, 254
  God's grace, longing for, 77, 85, 88, 91–92
  on grazing, 225
  heroic stature, 18
  his mind is not his own, 2
  identify defined by shifting differences, 241
  learning to paint, 254
  Odysseus compared to, 93
  on originality, 5, 18
  Otto and, 90
  pursuit of salvation, 241
  Recktall Brown's exploitation of, 18, 85
  restoring paintings, 85–86, 93–94, 246–247
  Rev. Gwyon and, 10, 38, 48, 78–80, 94
  seeks the inner sea, 31, 36–39
  sin and, 53, 81, 100
  Stanley compared to, 11–12
  as Stephan/Stephen, 18, 80, 97–98, 240
  suffering for love and fear, 220–221
  surrendering idea of perfection, 52
  survival of, 109

Yák *(The Recognitions)*, 81–83. *see also* Frank Sinisterra

Zauderer case, 179
Ziolkowski, Theodore, 235
Zwingli, Huldreich, 82